A HISTORY
OF CHRISTIANITY
IN JAPAN

Christian World Mission Books

Richard H. Drummond, *A History of Christianity in Japan*

Justo L. Gonzalez, *The Development of Christianity in the Latin Caribbean*

Stephen Neill, *The Story of the Christian Church in India and Pakistan*

Jane M. Sales, *The Planting of the Churches in South Africa*

R. Pierce Beaver, *All Loves Excelling*

Elizabeth Kelsey Kinnear, *She Sat Where They Sat: A Memoir of Anna Young Thompson*

Kenneth Strachan, *The Inescapable Calling*

William J. Danker, *Profit for the Lord*

A. Theodore Eastman, *Chosen and Sent: Calling the Church to Mission*

Donald C. Lord, *Mo Bradley and Thailand*

Paul B. Pedersen, *Batak Blood and Protestant Soul: The Development of National Batak Churches in North Sumatra*

David M. Stowe, *Ecumenicity and Evangelism*

R. Pierce Beaver, *To Advance the Gospel: The Collected Writings of Rufus Anderson*

R. Pierce Beaver, *Pioneers in Mission*

James A. Scherer, *Justinian Welz: Essays by an Early Prophet of Mission*

Max A. C. Warren, *To Apply the Gospel: Selections from the Writings of Henry Venn*

A HISTORY
OF CHRISTIANITY
IN JAPAN

by

RICHARD HENRY DRUMMOND

WILLIAM B. EERDMANS PUBLISHING COMPANY
GRAND RAPIDS, MICHIGAN

*To Pearl
who also loves
the people and the land of Japan*

Grateful acknowledgement is given to Burns and Oates Ltd., London, England, for permission to quote from *Saint Francis Xavier* by James Broderick, S.J.

CONTENTS

TSUGARU

●Takaoka
(Hirosaki)

OSHU
(MUTSU)

Sendai●

●Inawashiro
▲●Wakamatsu

H

U

S

N

OWARI

Yeda▲

●Kiyosu

OMI ●Azuchi Hanamatsu ●Nagoya

Kamakura●

SURUGA Odawara●

ei

●Nara

Fuchu●
(Shizuoka)

ISE

ATO

N

▲ SITE OF CHURCH

EDITORIAL FOREWORD

None of the generalizations usually made about the Christian churches in Asia or about the past experience of overseas mission agencies applies to Japan; Japan as a nation and people defies generalization. The primitive, ancient, medieval, modern, and contemporary all exist in Japan in a marvelous *modus vivendi* with one another that is matched nowhere else. Japan has modernized and industrialized without breaking cultural and religious continuity with its ancient heritage. The arts and individual craftsmanship have not been destroyed by high scientific and technological achievement nor by mass production. The course of the planting and development of the churches has been unique, and determined in large measure by the peculiar social and political events and trends of the times as well as by unchanging aspects of the Japanese character. There are more puzzles and problems about Japanese Christianity than about any other Christian community in Asia or Africa, and these are intimately related to the local situation. This church is predominantly urban, not rural as elsewhere in Asia, and almost confined to a narrow stratum of the middle class. Only now is it beginning to reach out more widely into society. Although a small church, it has tremendous influence in national life, and it may have a nebulous constituency of ten times its actual formal membership. The main Protestant churches from the beginning were under indigenous leadership, and escaped the usual stifling missionary paternalism. It is the bodies created since World War II which have had such an experience. Yet Japanese Christianity looks exceedingly

Western, although some evidence of adaptation is to be found. This is the one younger church which has long had a super-abundance of clergy and has been theologically mature, although perhaps more in a European than a Japanese manner. New life now appears to be emerging.

Illumination on all these and other unique features of Japanese Christianity is brought out by Professor Drummond in this book. He has attempted an outline history of the totality of Christianity in Japan — Roman Catholic, Protestant, and Orthodox — from the sixteenth century to the present, and to have all of this brought to a reader in one volume is a genuine contribution. The author has been forced to deal with each major branch of the church separately since each was hitherto self-contained in its own history and there was little interaction. Fortunately, as the sections on the present period reveal, the churches are now drawing together in ecumenical brotherhood and common action, and the next period of history will be that of the church, rather than the churches, in Japan. Professor Drummond draws on the fruits of Japanese scholarship as well as the works of Western missionaries and scholars, and he brings to the task a personal understanding and competence gained in many years of residence and service in Japan.

A History of Christianity in Japan is a CHRISTIAN WORLD MISSION BOOK, belonging to the series on "Discipling the Nations," which relates to fruits of the mission out of the Western nations in the great era of world mission now ended. The seven series deal with every aspect of the world mission of the church of Christ — history, theory, methods, functional approaches, regional studies, biography, and source materials of exceptional value to students. The authors are recruited from many nations and churches.

R. PIERCE BEAVER
Editor

PREFACE

This book represents, to my knowledge, the first attempt to compose in English a comprehensive history of Christianity in Japan since 1909, when Otis Cary's work was published in two volumes. In Japanese the most recent such work is Hiyane Antei's *Nihon Kirisuto Kyōshi*, of which the last edition was printed in 1949. Many important studies of more limited range, however, have been published in recent years, and it would appear to be in order once again to attempt a survey of the entire Christian movement in Japan, Roman Catholic, Protestant and Orthodox.

Since this work is primarily a survey, I am not generally able to offer new or original interpretations of the many historical problems which intrigue the specialists. The footnotes, however, should indicate ample material for those who wish to pursue further any specific problems. My own personal acquaintance with Japan includes thirteen years of service as a Protestant missionary, and I experienced personally many of the events of the period after the Second World War. I have also striven to employ the results of the research of both Japanese and Western scholars over the entire period of this study. In particular, I have sought to see the whole and its parts with the sympathetic understanding of one looking from within as well as from without.

I should like to draw the attention of the reader at this point to what may be called the persistent issue in the history of Christianity in Japan. This is the confrontation of the transcendental perspectives of Christian faith, particularly the Christian obligation to obey God rather than man, with the traditional tendency of Japanese political leadership to make loyalty to the political and social structures of the land a religious obligation surpassing all others. It will be seen again and again that the crises faced by both missionaries and Japanese Christians issue from one form or another of this confrontation. Awareness of the primary role played by this confrontation is vital to an understanding of the course of the Christian movement in Japan (cf. Robert N. Bellah, *Tokugawa Religion,* pp. 13-17, 31-39, 79-88, 104).

I wish to express my deep thanks to the several persons who have graciously read this book in manuscript and offered helpful suggestions and corrections. They are Professor Hiyane Antei, of Tokyo Union Theological Seminary, Father Joseph Jennes, C.I.C.M., of Oriens Institute for Religious Research, Tokyo, and Bishop Vladimir, presiding bishop of the Orthodox Church in Japan. I must, however, accept full responsibility for all interpretation and any remaining errors of fact.

I wish to thank in a special way my wife who proofread the entire manuscript and with whom I had the experiences and developed the perspectives that made possible the writing of this book. My warm thanks are also due Dr. Calvin Schnucker, dean-emeritus of the Theological Seminary, the University of Dubuque, for his unusual efforts in arranging for the typing of this manuscript. I should like also to cite the name of the man who more than any other was both spiritual mentor and practical guide during my years of service in Japan. He is the Rev. Matsuo Mikizō, long-time pastor of Yukinoshita Church in Kamakura, perceptive preacher and dedicated pastor, scholar, teacher, author of distinction, valiant and creative laborer in manifold works of the Kingdom.

In the writing of Japanese names I follow the common order of the language, the surname first followed by the given name. The chief exception to this rule is the case where a Japanese Christian is cited by giving with his surname a baptismal name of Western origin. I regularly indicate the long vowels of Japanese words with the single exception of Tokyo; both vowels are long, but it is so well known and appears so frequently in the text that it seemed pedantic to mark it with long vowels each time.

RICHARD H. DRUMMOND

The Theological Seminary
The University of Dubuque
Dubuque, Iowa

I

THE BACKGROUND OF LAND
AND PEOPLE

THE BACKGROUND OF LAND AND PEOPLE

1

CONFRONTATION WITH THE JAPANESE PEOPLE AND CULTURE WAS
seen from the beginning to be one of the greatest challenges in
the history of the Christian world mission. In a letter to Goa
in India written less than two months after he had landed in
Japan on August 15, 1549, Francis Xavier expressed views which
neither he nor his companions and successors in the early Roman Catholic mission had reason essentially to change. He
wrote:

> They are the best race yet discovered, and I think that among non-
> Christians their match will not easily be found. Admirable in their
> social relationships, they have an astonishing sense of honor and es-
> teem it above all other things . . . The Japanese are full of courtesy
> in their dealings with one another . . . They are monogamists, and
> they abominate thieving and punish robbers invariably with death.
> Of all the peoples I have seen in my life, Christians included, the
> Japanese are the most rigorously opposed to theft, and there are few
> robbers in the country. They are a well-meaning people and very
> sociable and anxious to learn. They take pleasure in hearing of the
> things of God, especially such as they can understand, and they have
> no idols made in the shape of beasts, but believe in men of ancient
> times who, as far as I can make out, lived as philosophers. Many Jap-
> anese adore the sun and others the moon. They like to be appealed
> to on rational grounds, and are ready to agree that what reason
> vindicates is right.[1]

---

[1] James Broderick, S.J., *Saint Francis Xavier*, pp. 361-362; Georg Schurhammer, S.J. and Joseph Wicki, S.J., *Epistolae S. Francisci Xaverii*, vol. 2,
pp. 186-188.

Xavier's account is at points naive and mistaken, but his overall evaluation of the people and their culture is essentially that of other Jesuits who could base their judgments upon wider experience. Alessandro Valignano, the Italian vicar-general and visitor of the order in the Orient, wrote twenty-five years later:

> The Japanese have rites and customs so different from those of other nations that it looks as if they studied of set purpose to be unlike any other race on earth . . . What I could not get over in all this was that a people so utterly unlike ourselves should yet be so highly civilized . . . The way they eat is equally astonishing, neatly and elegantly, with much composure, and their table service like their clothes is always immaculately clean.[2]

The Jesuit missionaries were aware from the beginning that they were among their cultural equals and comported themselves accordingly.

2

The first account of Japan and its people given to the West is that of Marco Polo, largely fanciful but containing some historical facts such as the attempted invasion of the island by Kublai Khan. Polo's sources of information were, of course, entirely Chinese, and particularly significant is his report that the inhabitants of Zipangu (Japan) have fair complexions, are physically well proportioned and are civilized in their manners.[3]

The origins and early history of the peoples inhabiting the Japanese islands are obscure and still much debated by archaeologists and cultural anthropologists.[4] It is clearly established, however, that the Japanese people after the birth of Christ represent the fusion of several racial groups and cultural strains, including a people of early Caucasian stock, now known as Ainu. There is evidence of ancient peoples who apparently

---

[2] Broderick, op. cit., pp. 363-364.

[3] Milton Rugoff, ed., The Travels of Marco Polo, pp. 230-234.

[4] Nihon no Hajimari, vol. 1 of Nihon no Rekishi, pp. 7-39. Each volume of this series is a joint production in which a dozen or more specialists participated and represents a consensus of contemporary Japanese historical scholarship.

did not have knowledge of the manufacture of pottery, but an abundance of material is extant from the period of neolithic culture. This period is normally differentiated into two types of cultural emphasis, the Jōmon, so designated from the rope pattern which characterized its pottery, and the somewhat later Yayoi type, the name taken from the site near Tokyo University where such pottery was first found.

Both types of pottery have been found in neolithic sites all over Japan, but the prominence of the Jōmon style is more frequent in the North and East; where it is found together with the Yayoi pottery, the Jōmon is generally from a lower level. The Jōmon type is therefore presumed to be somewhat older and representative of a more isolated, though artistically highly developed, neolithic culture. Both of these styles are evidently the result of cultural influences from the northern Asian continent. Linguistic and other evidence, however, points to influences stemming also from southeastern Asia and possibly the islands of Oceania and Indonesia. The cultural level achieved from the resulting amalgam was high; some scholars assert that the technique of the manufacturing of weapons and tools and the originality of design and ornament of pottery mark this as one of the most advanced neolithic cultures in world history. The quality of cultural sophistication was such that it is probably safe to say that "the artistic talent of late Japan was rooted in the prehistoric past."[5]

In spite of authentic originality of Japanese artistic adaptation, major cultural developments were perhaps without exception the consequence of stimuli from the Asian continent, especially from China, through the channel of Korea, which left its own cultural imprint. Artifacts representative of the bronze culture of China, which reached its zenith under the Chou Dynasty, were found in many sites with Yayoi pottery. Under these influences the transition from neolithic culture began in western Japan during the first century B.C. and in the central part of the country perhaps two or three centuries later.

Following the late neolithic period with some overlapping

---

[5] N. G. Munro, in G. B. Sansom, *Japan, A Short Cultural History*, pp. 5-6.

is the age of the sepulchral mounds which made use of both bronze and iron. These tombs of the rulers, called *misasagi,* are very large. That of the emperor Nintoku (died *ca.* 400 A.D.) is approximately twelve hundred feet long and ninety feet high, and together with its moats it covers eighty acres. In the stone chambers of these mounds many jewels, ornaments, weapons and other objects of bronze or iron have been found, along with vases similar but technically superior to Yayoi pottery. Outside but near the mounds were found the famous *Haniwa* figures, which reveal clearly not only much of the cultural life of the period but also the sophisticated artistic level. These relatively abundant finds represent the Japanese adaptation to the influences and energies issuing from the cultural explosion of the Han Dynasty in China (206 B.C. — 220 A.D.).

The Chinese document, The *Wei Chih,* written in the third century A.D., describes the manners and customs of the land of the Wa (the Japanese) in the period of the sepulchral mounds. The men are said to tattoo their faces and decorate their bodies with designs, but the people are skilled in agriculture and the manufacture of silk and linen fabrics. They drink intoxicating liquor and practice divination. In their society they maintain strict distinctions of rank. There are many small kingdoms, but preeminent among them is the state of Yamatai (or Yabadai), which to some degree exercises dominion over the others. The ruler of Yamatai is a woman called Pimiko or Himiko, who is also a diviner or medium.[6]

The Japan that emerged into known history in the seventh century A.D. had thus long received cultural influence of many kinds from the Asian mainland. Very likely the more or less centralized state which had developed, possibly from the end of the fourth century A.D., with its center in the province of Yamato, east of the modern city of Ōsaka, was achieved primarily through the superior equipment and skills developed from the contacts with the civilization of China. Some Chinese language and literature had been known to scholars in Japan increasingly from at least the third century A.D.; record exists,

---

[6] Himeko is an archaic Japanese title meaning sun-daughter, in effect princess or queen.

however, of envoys being sent to China by various principal-
ities in Japan from 57 A.D.[7] The two oldest documents of Japanese origin, the *Kojiki* (Record of Ancient Matters) and the
Nihongi, or *Nihonshoki* (Chronicles of Japan), compiled in
712 and 720 respectively, were both written in the Chinese
script, the latter in the Chinese language.

The emergence of a more or less centralized state in the middle of Japan made contacts with the continent of Asia possible
on a new scale and prepared for an influx of both Chinese and
Korean cultures beyond that of previous centuries. The strength
of this state, which apparently included much of Kyūshū
and exercised some measure of control even as far north and
east as modern Hirosaki, was such that substantial military
expeditions were apparently attempted against the kingdom of
Silla in southern Korea. We may properly stress, therefore,
both the growing politico-military and economic strength of
Japan itself and the greatly accelerating process of cultural
importations and influences from the Asian mainland. It may
be added that immigrants from China and Korea and their descendants were predominant in the new class of artists, specialists in reading and writing, and skilled craftsmen. The result
of these influences upon the native Japanese culture was what
Japanese historians generally designate as the Asuka Period
(*ca.* 500-710 A.D.), the Nara Period (710-781), and the Heian
Period (781-1191).

Through these centuries we note an ascending level of achievement in letters and the arts, sophistication of social life, com-
plexity of governmental institutions and some improvement in
the forms of economic production, especially in the crafts. We
need to remember that during the T'ang Dynasty (618-906
A.D.) China was probably militarily the most powerful, politically the best administered, and culturally the most advanced
country in the world. "It was an age," as G. B. Sansom writes,
"of intellectual ferment, of spiritual fervour, and of artistic
excitement."[8] China was the despair as well as the envy of the

---

[7] L. Carrington Goodrich, ed., *Japan in the Chinese Dynastic Histories,*
tr. by Tsunoda Ryūsaku, pp. 2, 7-16.

[8] Sansom, *op. cit.*, p. 85.

culturally more backward, aristocratically oriented Japanese of
the period, but with the energy characteristic of their people
in almost every age they strove first to imitate, then to assimilate
and finally to create an authentically Japanese culture. Rapid
development was achieved in the arts. In the area of political
and social life, however, changes were slower and generally
superficial. Japan in this period never achieved anything like
the Chinese system of a bureaucracy selected and promoted for
merit. The remarkable cultural achievements and related benefits were largely confined to the imperial court, the nobility and
the Buddhist clergy.[9]

This situation, combined with a growing effeminateness and
moral irresponsibility in the cultural life of the Heian court,
set the stage for the next great period of Japanese history, the
Kamakura (1192-1333). The name is taken from the capital
city of the new government. The forms of the old imperial
government were left largely intact, but the actual government
was almost completely exercised by provincial knights and landlords who emerged to wield real power in place of the effete
aristocracy of Kyōto. This new structure of power was focused
in a military leader called *shōgun* (generalissimo).

After a century and a half of relative order and security the
Kamakura coalition broke down and was replaced by the leadership of the Ashikaga family with the capital restored in
Kyōto. This period is called the Muromachi (1338-1573). The
latter part of this period, from the close of the fifteenth to the
beginning of the last quarter of the sixteenth century, is known
as the *Sengoku Jidai*, the age of the country at war. Even in
the fifteenth century there was continuous warfare in one district or another, but this condition worsened as the power and
authority of the Ashikaga Shogunate weakened. By 1500 the
whole country was at war.

The first appearance of Portuguese traders and Christian
missionaries came therefore toward the end of the longest period
of sustained military strife and general disorder in the known

---

[9] The Chinese chronicles of the Wei Dynasty (220-265 A.D.) record that
in Japan men of the lower class withdraw to the grass at the side of the road
when they meet a man of rank. When they address him, they show their
respect by either squatting or kneeling with both hands on the ground.

history of Japan.[10] The first decades of Christian work coincided with the most strenuous efforts of the first feudal lord (*daimyō*, great name) to succeed once again in stabilizing and unifying the country. This was Oda Nobunaga.[11] He was followed by Toyotomi Hideyoshi; their eras are named respectively the Azuchi and Momoyama, from the central castles of each ruler. Together these eras extended from 1574 to 1600. This was the period of greatest Christian growth in what has been called "the Christian century in Japan." The Edo or Tokugawa period (1600-1867) began with the forces of unification firmly in control and determined to break all opposition, actual or potential. Included in the category of potential opposition was the Roman Catholic Christian movement; its virtual extirpation became a major element in the foreign as well as domestic policy of Japan for the following centuries. We shall consider this and related problems in more detail later.

3

The first stage of Japanese religion of which we have considerable knowledge is termed early Shintō.[12] This word, literally the way of the *Kami* (sacred forces or beings), came to designate the indigenous religious tradition of the Japanese as distinguished from more obvious foreign importations like Buddhism, Confucianism and Christianity. There are, however, numerous indications that early Shintō was much indebted to influences from Korea in the centuries before Christ, especially through the clans of Izumo in western Japan. On the other

[10] In consequence of the strife, farmlands were often abandoned and poor harvests were frequent. Many of the aged and orphans were seen on the roads begging food and even in Kyōto men, women, and children died of starvation before the gates of the great Buddhist temples. In 1461 the bodies of those who thus died and were thrown into the bed of the Kamo River were so numerous as to block the flow of the river; the stench of the decay was unbearable. Cf. Ebisawa Arimichi, *Kindai Nihon Bunka no Tanjō*, p. 5.

[11] In the agglutinative Japanese language the surname is regularly given first, followed by the given name and whatever title may be appropriate.

[12] For earlier periods see Joseph M. Kitagawa, "The Prehistoric Background of Japanese Religion," *History of Religions*, II/2 (Winter 1963), 292-328.

hand, to the Japanese of that period, the cultural associations of Shintō were primarily indigenous. This consciousness has been very important both in preserving Shintō as a vital element in the religious history of Japan and in maintaining the distinctive cultural identity of the Japanese people.

Early Shintō was characterized by a cosmic orientation that ascribed sacred power to natural objects, including men, in so far as they participate in or are endowed with the force which is from "above" (kami). This world view is not identical with pantheism or notions of the sacredness of the whole universe, although such views are found in the history of Japanese religion. Man and nature may be or become sacred; they are not, however, intrinsically sacred, they are sacred only by virtue of the Kami who (or which — there is ambivalence as to the presence of the personal element) work in and through them. The central role of shamans, what we may term spiritualistic mediums, in this tradition is obviously related to this world view. We have noted early references to a queen who was also a medium. This shamanistic tradition, which included a profound reverence for dreams, has remained a vital element in Japanese popular religion to the present.

The primary attitude toward the Kami was positive and grateful, although there was also a strong belief in the existence of malevolent kami who must be warded off or placated. The cult of Shintō particularly emphasized purification ceremonies; the primary concern, it is thought, was not for purification from moral evil but from physical defilement. At least one, however, of the ancient norito (ritual prayers) lists as sins certain sexual violations and cutting living flesh; in the category of "heavenly sins" are listed a number of offenses which we would call anti-social, such as breaking down the ridges between paddies, covering up irrigation ditches, releasing the sluices, setting up stakes, etc.[13] The Japanese sense of sin or evil was, and is, not as inchoate as is sometimes affirmed.

Japanese Shintō constituted, of course, a richer religious complex than this brief notation of primary characteristics indicates. In comparison, however, with the forms of Buddhism

---

[13] Joseph M. Kitagawa, *Religion in Japanese History*, p. 13.

which were introduced from China, it was simple and primitive. Among the earliest books brought from China were the Chinese canonical writings which form the classics of the Confucian tradition. The principles of Confucianism exercised considerable influence upon Japanese life, especially political thinking, during the Nara and later in the Edo period. This was primarily an intellectual phenomenon, however, and limited to the learned classes. Confucianism in Japan never became a source of religious vitality among the populace. Far more profound, widespread and lasting in its effects was the great religio-cultural complex of Chinese-Korean Buddhism.

Buddhism was probably introduced into the western kingdom of South Korea called Paekche in 384 A.D., and some knowledge of it had probably penetrated the eastern kingdom of Silla before the end of the fourth century. Its official adoption in Silla, however, was not until the reign of Pep-Heung (514-539).

Buddhism is said to have been formally introduced into Japan when the king of Paekche presented Buddhist images and scriptures to the Japanese court in either 538 or 552 A.D. with the recommendation that this new religion, though difficult to explain and to comprehend, was the most excellent of all doctrines and effected the realization of all desires. Under the patronage of the powerful Soga clan, Buddhism became solidly established among a considerable segment of the nobility. The primary motives for its adoption were, first, the association of Buddhism, its scriptures, images and elaborate ceremonies, with the enormous prestige of Chinese civilization, and second, because it was believed to convey a unique spiritual power useful to the rulers who adopted it.[14] Generally, it should be added, the adoption of Buddhism did not mean the rejection of Shintō, and throughout the subsequent history of Japan most Japanese have participated in both religious traditions.

We do not have space to discuss in detail the subsequent development of Buddhism in Japan after its vigorous espousal by Prince Shōtoku in the last decade of the sixth century. Suffice it to say that in the Nara and Heian periods, Buddhism

---

[14] Watanabe Shōkō, *Nihon no Bukkyō*, p. 72.

played a central role in the cultural achievements of the time but still largely confined its influence to the nobility and the area in or near Nara and Kyōto. Six schools or sects came to be officially recognized by the court in Nara, but after the removal of the capital to Kyōto, two were founded which had increasing influence during the whole of the Heian period. These have subsequently continued to play a prominent role in Japanese religious, cultural and political life. They were the Tendai School, founded by Saichō (767-822), also known as Dengyō Daishi, with its center on Mt. Hiei near Kyōto, and the Shingon School, founded by Kūkai (774-835), or Kōbō Daishi, on Mt. Kōya in the present Wakayama Prefecture. In the Kamakura period, however, Buddhism developed more indigenous forms and became a part of the common life of the people. During this period, creative Japanese religious figures developed schools more suited to the needs of ordinary men. The most outstanding of these figures were Hōnen (1133-1212), the founder of the Pure Land School, Shinran (1173-1262) of the True Pure Land School, Nichiren (1222-1288) of the Nichiren School, Eisai (1141-1215) of the Rinzai Zen School, and Dōgen (1200-1253) of the Sōtō Zen School.

The role played in Japanese political life by Buddhist temples and monks should not be ignored. By the end of the Nara period the temples had grown greatly in wealth and power, and priests increasingly exerted their influence in politics for personal and partisan advantages. In the Heian period, however, the two new schools of Tendai and Shingon developed into great complexes containing thousands of monks and retainers, many of them armed and trained to use their arms at the request of the monastic leaders. The personal lives of many of these monks were dissolute, but even more disturbing to society were their incursions into Kyōto to burn, loot and destroy in order to preserve their independence and further their interests in the political disorder from the Kamakura period into the period of the wars.

Sociologically, the Pure Land and Nichiren schools represented different bases of power from the older sects, but they too frequently resorted to arms, although perhaps for more socially justifiable reasons. They were in fact among the last enemies to be subdued by Nobunaga and Hideyoshi in their drive to unify Japan.[15] The political role of Buddhist institutions and the consequent resentment and even hatred which they engendered in the emerging political leaders of the second half of the sixteenth century created an atmosphere, at least in certain ruling circles, relatively favorable to the spread of the Christian faith.

Another important point is that the disorder and destruction of the period of warfare preceding 1550 apparently did not entirely disrupt economic life. In fact wealth and productive power increased rather than diminished during this time, and the confusion lessened somewhat the barriers between the classes and in general favored social mobility.[16]

---

[15] *Tenka Tōitsu, Nihon no Rekishi*, vol. 7, pp. 24-30, 35-36, 50.
[16] Sansom, *op. cit.*, pp. 426, 430, 435-436.

II

THE EARLY ROMAN CATHOLIC
MOVEMENT
1549-1859

A. FRANCIS XAVIER AND THE BEGINNINGS OF THE CHRISTIAN MISSION

1

THE FIRST EUROPEANS TO SET FOOT ON JAPANESE soil were three Portuguese who were engaged in contraband trade along the Chinese coast. Their ship, which was a Chinese junk, was blown off its course in a typhoon and landed on the island of Tanegashima, directly south of Kyūshū, in either 1542 or 1543. They were kindly received and able to exchange their merchandise for silver as well as to repair their vessel. The firearms which they carried caused particular excitement among the Japanese; they were evidently able to buy some harquebuses at this time, and local smiths succeeded in making copies within the first year. The firearms constituted one of the strongest reasons for the cordial welcome of Portuguese traders, since most of their merchandise was Chinese. In any case, over the next few years Portuguese ships came regularly to Japanese ports in Kyūshū. Japanese historians regard these events as the waves of world history breaking on the shores of Japan in a totally unprecedented way.[1]

The initial evaluation of the Europeans as human beings is partly revealed in the account, as recorded in the Japanese chronicle *Yaita-ki*, of the Chinese sailor who used Chinese ideographs to interpret for the first party to land on Tanegashima. The Chinese called the Portuguese traders *Seinamban* (Southwest Barbarians) and were doubtful of their system of man-

---

[1] *Tenka Tōitsu, Nihon no Rekishi*, vol. 7, p. 58.

ners and etiquette. They ate with their hands instead of using chopsticks and showed their feelings without self-control. They could not read (Chinese ideographs) and spent their lives roving here and there. They were without fixed abode and made their living by bartering goods, but they appeared nevertheless to be a harmless sort.[2]

Some knowledge of Christian faith and practice was communicated to at least a few Japanese by Portuguese traders before the arrival of any missionaries.[3] But formal Christian instruction begins with the landing on August 15, 1549 in Kagoshima, the capital of Satsuma and the southernmost city of Japan, of a party of three missionaries, three Japanese and two servants. The missionaries were Francis Xavier, Father Cosme de Torres, and Brother Juan Fernandez. The Japanese included the famous Yajirō, the refugee from Kagoshima whom Xavier had first met at Malacca in December of 1547. Xavier's person and achievements were so noteworthy and his presence so significant for the mission in Japan that a brief account of the man and his background is proper.

Francis Xavier, born in Spanish Navarre on April 7, 1506, was the third son of a Basque family of the lesser nobility. He was apparently attracted to the Protestant movement during his eleven years at the University of Paris, but although he was "the lumpiest dough" Ignatius Loyola had ever kneaded, he was eventually won over by his Basque fellow countrymen to become one of the original band of the Society of Jesus. The goal of these men was simply to devote themselves to the service of God and their neighbor by vows of chastity and poverty and to make a pilgrimage to Jerusalem. Their primary aspira-

---

[2] C. R. Boxer, *The Christian Century in Japan*, p. 29.

[3] Okada Akio, *Kirishitan Bateren*, pp. 5-6. There is also speculation that Nestorian Christianity in China had influenced some of the early leaders of Buddhism in Japan, such as Kūkai (Kōbō Daishi), the founder of the Shingon sect in Japan. Cf. Natori Junichi, *Historical Stories of Christianity in Japan*, pp. 9-10. Furthermore, there is mention in the ancient *Shoku Nihongi* of the arrival in Japan in the fall of 736 of three *Keijin*, who may have been Nestorian monks. These men came in the entourage of a high official, Nakatomi Nashiro, on his return from China; they were presented to the emperor, Shōmu. Nothing further, however, is known of their activity or influence. Cf. Hiyane Antei, *Nihon Kirisuto Kyōshi*, pp. 1-4.

tion, "after their personal sanctification," was to work "directly for the salvation of souls." Elsewhere they expressed their aims as "the fulfillment of the divine will in all things and the conservation of our unity."[4]

The five chapters which condensed the rules of their society included the revolutionary one of a special, explicit vow of obedience to the pope. Beyond the obligations of Catholics in general, they were to undertake with prompt good will whatever assignment the pope might give them, no matter how distant or dangerous. The emotive force of this vow is properly understood in the context of the fiery ordeal of the *Spiritual Exercises*, the thirty-day spiritual regimen which created a single-minded, disciplined body of ready Christian workers such as the church had rarely known in its history. Francis Xavier committed himself to this order of service without reservation and was fully ready to obey the command of the pope whom he served in the already vast and growing overseas colonies of Portugal. He sailed for India on April 7, 1541.

Xavier was still medieval in his religious and cultural orientation, and he often identified the glory of God and the glory of Portugal. But to defend or explain some of his views, one must remember that with apparently sincere religious motivation both the Portuguese and Spanish sovereigns aimed in their overseas colonial enterprises at "the increase of our holy Catholic faith."[5] Xavier, however, was not an uncritical supporter of Portuguese colonial policy as it operated on the field; on occasion he expressed his criticisms to both governor and king. Yet he had no qualms about the relationship between *Império* and *Fé;* his first concern was with the spread of the faith, and he pushed on to areas where the Portuguese neither did nor could rule. In his plans to evangelize Japan and China, he clearly did not think to depend upon Portuguese political power or military force.[6] He hoped to win the entire populace of Japan either by converting its rulers or by gaining their favor and permission to preach freely. But this procedure was

---

[4] James Broderick, *Saint Francis Xavier*, pp. 70-71.

[5] *Ibid.*, pp. 74-75.

[6] Ebisawa Arimichi, *Kindai Nihon Bunka no Tanjō,* pp. 9-10.

no substitute for proclaiming the faith and teaching believers of every class.

If Xavier initially had little knowledge or understanding of non-Christians, Loyola had less. Shortly after his conversion Ignatius met a Moor in Spain and considered whether it was not his duty to kill the dog. Xavier's procedure in South India was to encourage small boys whom he had won to a measure of allegiance to seize the small clay idols of the Hindu shrines, "smash them, grind them to dust, spit on them and trample them underfoot."[7] His notion of the spiritual condition of non-Christians was that God, who is most faithful in all his doings, does not dwell with infidels and takes no pleasure in their prayers.[8] The invocations of the gentiles are displeasing to God, for all the gods of the nations are demons (omnes dii gentium demonia).[9] Xavier literally believed that the souls of non-Christians are lost unless Christians come to their rescue with the empirical gospel and sacraments;[10] all those who worship idols go to hell.[11] He believed that the divine life is given to babies through Christian baptism[12] and like Augustine held that unbaptized babies go to hell.[13] With regard to the Chinese captain whose pirate junk carried them to Japan and who later died, a man "good to us," Francis sorrowfully declared that his soul was in hell.[14]

There is reason to believe, however, that Xavier qualified these judgments as a result of his experiences in Japan, even though they evidently constituted a central element of his

---

[7] Georg Schurhammer and Joseph Wicki, Epistolae S. Francisci Xaverii, vol. 1, pp. 164-165, 274.

[8] Ibid., p. 123.

[9] Ibid., p. 148. Xavier qualified this position somewhat, as we have noted, so as to say that in Japan among the objects of faith in both Buddhist and Shintō tradition were "men of old, who were (so far as I understand) persons who lived like philosophers." Yet the land was, so he said, wholly of idolaters and enemies of Christ. Ibid., vol. 2, pp. 187-188, 201.

[10] Broderick, op. cit., p. 256.

[11] Schurhammer and Wicki, op. cit., vol. 1, p. 382.

[12] Ibid., p. 466.

[13] Broderick, op. cit., p. 437.

[14] Ibid., p. 357. Cf. J. López Gay, "Pre-evangelization in the Primitive Mission of Japan," The Japan Missionary Bulletin, XVIII/9 (November, 1964), 587.

motivation to mission. Earnest Japanese were troubled because they could not reconcile the infinite goodness and mercy of God with the fact that he had not revealed himself to them and their ancestors before the Jesuits arrived. And if, as the latter taught, all who did not worship the true God went to hell, then their ancestors must all have gone there. Xavier reported in a letter to Europe that the Lord helped the missionaries to deliver the Japanese from this terrible misgiving. They explained to the inquirers that the moral law and knowledge of God were imprinted on men's hearts from the beginning, that the Creator of all peoples had taught them apart from human mediation.[15] In this way the missionaries tried to affirm the unqualified goodness and justice of God without ascribing any divine significance or value to the non-Christian religions.[16]

This rather savage theology, however, does not comprise the whole of Xavier's personality and life. Besides his breviary and a kind of catechism, his formal intellectual provender in Asia was limited to an anthology containing excerpts from the Scriptures, Jerome, Gregory the Great, Eusebius, Cassian and other church fathers. But his thought was not limited to the ranges of this material. He soon learned that China strongly influenced Japanese culture; this led him to believe that Japan would best be Christianized after the church had been widely planted in China. The last journey of his life therefore was to work toward this, the culmination of what became world-encompassing visions and plans. The vast range of Xavier's thought, however, always included a concern for his own moral and spiritual progress as well as for the physical and spiritual needs of those he met. Although he knew hot anger, he is said never once to have allowed himself to be enraged. With few exceptions he gave the impression of being happy, and the Spanish or Portuguese adjective *alegre*, meaning cheerful or merry, was frequently used of him.[17] His compassionate labors on behalf of the sick and poor on land or sea moved those

---

[15]Schurhammer and Wicki, *op. cit.*, vol. 2, pp. 262-267. Cf. Okada, *op. cit.*, pp. 44-45.

[16] Okada, *op. cit.*, pp. 40-41.

[17] Broderick, *op. cit.*, pp. 61, 105, 427, 472.

who observed him to admiration and emulation. His zealous efforts on behalf of the social, economic and political welfare of the Paravas on the southeastern coast of India were characteristic of his Christian witness; the spirit which they expressed marked from the beginning the mission in Japan. His way was to deal lovingly with men as individuals, even though he once urged the king of Portugal to order the establishment of the Inquisition in India to protect the Christian life of those who had been baptized into the faith.[18]

Many are the accounts of Francis' manner of evangelization in India, how he went up and down the streets and into the squares of Goa and later into the villages of the coastland, ringing a bell and crying out to the children and others to hear him. His method was to teach the faith everywhere in capsular form. He stressed learning by heart the Apostles' Creed, the Ten Commandments, the Lord's Prayer, the Ave Maria, the Salve Regina and the Confiteor in the language of the people. But he was careful to explain the "law of Christ," which, he said, must be observed in order to save one's soul. In other words, he was not bound to a mechanical, *ex opere operato* faith-practice to the extent that he has sometimes been portrayed. He himself reported that in a single month in India he baptized more than ten thousand men, women, and children, but he was scrupulously careful to teach the converts himself, albeit in capsular form, and to make arrangements for continued instruction as well as worship.[19]

One more aspect of Xavier's faith deserves mention in order to understand comparable practices in the later mission and church in Japan. He was medieval enough to carry a relic from the Apostle Thomas' supposed grave in San Thomé to the end of his life. In peril at sea he depended much on the saints in glory. If he commended himself to the Lord God, he did so with appeal to the intercession of his brethren of the Society of Jesus, living and dead. While danger lasted, he committed himself to the protection of the angels, praying to them choir by choir. He took for his protectress the Virgin

---

[18] *Ibid.*, pp. 69, 102-105, 168, 174, 189-190, 239-240.
[19] *Ibid.*, pp. 120, 141-142, 207, 240.

Mary, and finally trusted wholly in the infinite merits of the passion and death of Jesus Christ, his Redeemer and Lord. He believed that typhoons were caused by demons on the prowl and that the invisible presences experienced by Portuguese merchants in an abandoned Japanese house were the work of the devil to keep the Christian missionaries out of Japan. Yet his view was of an orderly universe in which God ruled supreme and good over all, including the devil and his minions.[20]

Francis had the reputation of a miracle-worker among the Portuguese in his own lifetime. There is considerable evidence that he had what we now call the gift of extra-sensory perception.[21] In Japan as elsewhere he was reported to have cured the sick by making the sign of the cross over them or sprinkling them with holy water. To men and women who told him of their or their children's infirmities he gave, as he had done in India, a piece of paper on which he had written some verses from the Gospels and told them to wear it on their breasts in order to be cured. The reports are numerous and incontestible that in fact many cures were effected by these methods. Francis himself attributed the healings to the great mercy of God, who works through the faith of men; for him, therefore, the practice was clearly no magical exercise. It may be assumed, to be sure, that various levels of understanding of such practice existed among the Japanese converts; some may have viewed the objects used as little more than a talisman or fetish. Yet what we may call these elemental religious practices were important in the later spread of the Christian faith in Japan. They were as common among the other fathers and brothers as among Japanese Christians.[22]

2

Francis Xavier on his return from the Moluccas (Indonesia) to Goa in India stopped briefly at Malacca (in Malaysia) in December of 1547. Here he met three young Japanese, a young

[20] *Ibid.*, pp. 301-302, 359, 354.
[21] *Ibid.*, pp. 234, 273, 290, 453, 499.
[22] *Ibid.*, pp. 398-400, 431, 145. Cf. *Tenka Tōitsu*, p. 64.

man of the *samurai* or knightly class, known to us only by the
name of Yajirō, or his baptismal name of Paulo de Santa Fé,
and his two attendants.[23] Yajirō had asked for refuge aboard
a Portuguese trading vessel, as a result of killing a man in his
native city of Satsuma. He was taken aboard and brought to
Malacca where after some further traveling he finally met the
santo padre of whom he had been told so much.

Yajirō was a knowledgeable and sensible man, although by
no means learned — he could read only the native syllabary
or *kana* of his language, not the Chinese ideographs indispensable to all scholarly communication. Xavier learned much
about Japan from him, including some mistaken notions about
the land and the people. His account, however, convinced
Francis that better opportunities to spread the faith existed in
Japan than in India because the people "have an eager desire
for knowledge and instruction." Yajirō even assured Francis
that since the Japanese are guided entirely by reason, the
"king," the nobility and all other people of discretion would
become Christians if Francis would answer their questions
satisfactorily and allow them to observe his conduct for six
months.[24]

Xavier was to learn by bitter experience the irony of these
overly sanguine expectations, but he may possibly have questioned their face value from the beginning. In any case, he
probably reasoned from his recent experience of evangelism in
the Moluccas that Japan would be an easier field because
no Muslim influence was there. He, therefore, sent Yajirō, who
already spoke Portuguese moderately well, to the seminary in
Goa for training, and then, a year and a half later, he and
Yajirō landed in Kagoshima on August 15, 1549.

The small party was warmly received by Yajirō's family,
with whom they lived while in the area. On September 29,

---

[23] There are many variations of the spelling of this name in the original
texts, but Yajirō seems to have the best support. Cf. Ebisawa Arimichi,
Kirishitanshi no Kenkyū, p. 322.

[24] Broderick, *op. cit.*, pp. 296-297. Francis also saw in December of 1547
the report on Japan written by the Portuguese sea captain Jorge Alvares;
this account is translated into German in Hans Haas, *Geschichte des Christentums in Japan*, vol. 1, pp. 269-279.

Xavier was received in kindly fashion by Shimazu Takahisa, the feudal lord of Satsuma, who significantly granted him permission to preach throughout his fief. One of the reasons for this permission, however, was to bring Portuguese trade to a harbor in Takahisa's territory. This trade with Japan, we may note, was exceedingly profitable for the Portuguese. From about 1547 all trading vessels sent were a monopoly of the crown, and one ship was dispatched each year from Goa and another one or two from Macao. The ship from Goa was a large sailing vessel of from 600 to 800 tons, and the round trip took about three years. The profit from one voyage was said to be from 150,000 to 200,000 ducats (*cruzados*).[25] But proportionate if not equal profits were made by the Japanese; since Japanese merchants came from afar to trade with the Portuguese, fortunate indeed was the *daimyō* whose territory held a harbor used for this trade by the Portuguese. Observing the respect shown the missionaries by the European ship captains and crews, Takahisa went so far as to allow his subjects to become Christians.

Xavier and the other missionaries were first regarded by the Japanese, including Buddhist monks, as representatives of another sect of Buddhism.[26] Indeed, Xavier himself was astonished to find many practices and institutions in Buddhism which resembled those in the Catholic Church. The elaborate ritual of Buddhism made use of symbols and instruments surprisingly similar: praying-beads, sacred vestments, bells and chanting, images, incense and holy water. There were monastic institutions for both men and women, the invocation of "saints" was practiced, as was the making of pilgrimages. Francis at first wondered whether Chinese and Japanese Buddhism had not been influenced by the Apostle Thomas or by Nestorian missionaries. This surmise was true concerning the Nestorians,

---

[25]Silk and other products of China sold in Japan at a price from two to four times higher than in Macao. *Tenka Tōitsu*, p. 61. Cf. Boxer, *op. cit.*, p. 109. *Cruzado* is the name given in 1457 to a Portuguese gold coin of the value of 400 *reis*. It remained official tender until 1835, and during the period of our concern it was generally in parity with the more widely used European ducat (*ducado*).

[26] Okada, *op. cit.*, pp. 27-28, 30.

but Francis later decided that in Japan there had been no knowledge of the true God or of Jesus Christ.[27]

Xavier found all the people, laymen as well as priests, very friendly to the missionaries. At first the latter were totally dependent on Yajiro as interpreter; in his long letter to Goa Francis wrote that they were among the Japanese as but mute statues (*entre ellos como unas statuas*).[28] Yajiro had learned considerable Portuguese, but the chief difficulty was his inadequate knowledge and understanding of Japanese Buddhism, both its doctrines and practices. For example, he employed the term *Dainichi* to designate God. This term, however, is Japanese for Mahāvairocana, the Great Sun Buddha of the Shingon School, whose fifty-foot bronze statue was housed in Nara in the largest single wooden building in the world. Yajiro also used the Japanese word for the Buddha, *Hotoke*, as another term for God, *Jōdo* (the Pure Land of Japanese Buddhism) to denote heaven, *Buppō* (the Law of Buddha) for the law of God or religion, and *Sō* (Buddhist monk or priest) for Catholic priest. Yajiro, however, should not be blamed too severely, as the Japanese language at the time lacked terms which could denote with precision many Christian concepts. The problem of finding or inventing suitable terms remained with the church for a long time, and Francis later settled on the Latin word *Deus* as the term for God least likely to cause misunderstanding among the Japanese.

Over the winter of 1549-50 the three missionaries in Kagoshima began to learn the difficult Japanese language without dictionary or grammar but with the important help of their faithful friend Yajiro. Some older biographers of Francis Xavier repeat the hagiographic legends of Francis' miraculous gift of tongues, but the better sources are unanimous in affirming the contrary, that he found Oriental languages particularly difficult and never became proficient in any. Brother Fernandez, barely twenty-three years old, was the most proficient of

[27] Broderick, *op. cit.*, p. 444. Yajiro, however, affirmed the presence in Japan of a veritable monotheistic faith. While his explanation was in part mistaken, this affirmation is a truer statement of the historical fact than Xavier's negative conclusion. Cf. *ibid.*, p. 391; Okada, *op. cit.*, p. 36.

[28] Schurhammer and Wicki, *op. cit.*, vol. 2, p. 201.

the three, but even he could make himself understood only with difficulty after struggling for two years. During the winter Francis prepared a lengthy exposition of Christian doctrine in Portuguese, which together with the Apostles' Creed, the Ten Commandments, the Lord's Prayer and other prayers, Yajirō put into Japanese using the *hiragana* syllabary. These were then transliterated into the Latin script and the shorter items faithfully memorized by the missionaries. Francis, however, was determined to do more than communicate the faith in capsular form in Japan, and he worked hard to prepare the longer exposition. It began with the creation of the world and pre-Christian scriptural history which dwelt disproportionately on the destruction of Sodom and Gomorrah, gave a detailed account of the life of Christ, and finally declared the certainty of the last judgment.

Xavier had many conversations with Buddhist monks through his interpreter.[29] Some of them he respected highly both for learning and nobility of life, especially an elderly abbot named Ninjitsu of the Sōtō Zen monastery of Fukushōji. Like the early Portuguese trader Alvares, however, Francis was horrified by widespread homosexuality among the Buddhist monks and he attacked this practice as well as Buddhist doctrines.[30] The resulting strong opposition increased as the number of Christian converts grew; there were perhaps one hundred by the end of the year's stay in Kagoshima. The next Portuguese trading vessel, moreover, dropped anchor at Hirado, a port in the northwestern part of Kyūshū, belonging to an enemy of the *daimyō* of Satsuma. Disappointed by the loss of his expected monopoly of trade and instigated by the Buddhist

---

[29] The term "bonze" occurs frequently in English books to denote the Buddhist clergy; it is the European approximation to the pronunciation of the Japanese word "bōzu," or more politely, *Obōsan*. These men were properly monastics, but at this period the Pure Land schools permitted their clergy to marry, and many of the monks of other sects had relationships with women which were more or less tacitly permitted by their lay adherents. Especially in the smaller temples in the provinces the term "priest" more accurately designated the man and his function than "monk."

[30] Boxer, *op. cit.*, p. 35; Okada, *op. cit.*, pp. 15-16. The form was especially that of pederasty, practiced with the young boys entrusted to the care of the temples for their education.

monks, Takahisa compelled the missionaries to leave, although he did not molest the Japanese converts.

Xavier and his co-workers left Kagoshima for Hirado in August of 1550. Here the *daimyō*, Matsuura Takanobu, received them very courteously. They started work at once with the permission of Takanobu, and Brother Fernandez began to preach in Japanese without an interpreter. Again their efforts resulted in a considerable number of converts; the prospects for continuing effective work were excellent. Xavier, however, from the beginning of his stay in Japan, had entertained the hope of going to Kyōto and meeting the "king of Japan" in order to obtain permission from him to preach the gospel throughout the kingdom. He thought also that a letter of introduction from the king of Japan would allow him to enter China and gain a hearing there. The missionary methodology of Xavier had never been to win small groups of converts here and there, but to aim at Christianizing whole nations, in accordance with the long tradition of the medieval church in Europe.

Francis as yet knew very little of the political situation of mid-sixteenth-century Japan. The emperors, while retaining considerable spiritual authority and valued for bestowing titles of nobility and other distinctions, had almost no political power. The long-declining power of the imperial court and the nobility of Kyōto had been largely displaced by the camp government (*bakufu*) of Kamakura that from 1192 under the leadership of a *shōgun* had dominated much of the land, especially the central areas of Honshū. The Kamakura Hōjō regime was in turn replaced in 1338 by the Ashikaga family, whose *shōgun* governed again from Kyōto. But by the middle of the sixteenth century, the power of the *shōgun* was little more than a political fiction except in the larger Kyōto area (Gokinai); the great feudal lords governed their own territories with little effective interference beyond their own rivalries.[31] At this time, however, the *daimyō* of Owari (the area about the modern Nagoya), Oda Nobunaga (1534-1582),

[31] Many of these lords were technically provincial constables (*shugo*) of the *shōgun* and received their administrative powers by delegation. In the course of time, however, the *shugo* had become practically autonomous or

had already begun the arduous and bloody process of unifying the country under one central rule. Of all this Francis Xavier was almost totally unaware.

In the fall of 1550 Francis set out for Kyōto accompanied by Brother Fernandez and Bernardo, one of the early converts from Kagoshima and a member of the *samurai* class.[32] Father de Torres remained to care for the small flock of perhaps one hundred believers in Hirado. The three companions went by boat to Hakata and from there to Yamaguchi, where Francis was received in audience by the *daimyō* Ōuchi Yoshitaka. From Yamaguchi the party traveled by land and again by boat through the Inland Sea to the major commercial port of central Japan, Sakai. Here Francis secured from a rich merchant a letter of introduction to an important friend in Kyōto, an incident which illustrates Francis' remarkable power to win respect for his person and character. The party arrived in Kyōto in the middle of January of 1551 and spent eleven days there.

In Kyōto Xavier soon learned that his hope of winning Japan by dependence upon the "king" was futile. Kyōto was then in a state of extreme confusion and physical desolation. Francis could not secure an audience with the emperor and learned that neither he nor the resident *shōgun* had any effective power in the government of Japan. He was also told that their poor clothes and unassuming appearance encouraged the Japanese in the capital to consider them unimportant.

Francis then returned to Hirado and prepared to visit Yamaguchi again, where he had been received with courtesy and whose *daimyō* was the most powerful lord of western Honshū. Taking advantage of the lesson learned at Kyōto, Francis visited Yoshitaka in ambassadorial pomp, dressed in silk and with a retinue, though small, equally well fitted out. He brought two beautifully illuminated letters on parchment from

---

had transferred their authority to others who themselves became autonomous powers.

[32] Converts were regularly given a "Christian" name at baptism; a name, however, which was invariably derived from the Western European cultural tradition. There is no evidence that any of the European fathers or brothers saw potential cultural offense in this practice.

the viceroy of India and the bishop of Goa and, most significant for the future of the mission in Japan, a number of precious gifts, objects nearly all unknown in Japan. These included "a grandfather clock which chimed the hours day and night, a musical box, a fine glass mirror, an elaborately worked musket with three barrels, bales of brocade, two pairs of spectacles or goggles, books richly bound in the European style, some beautiful crystal vases, various pictures in oils, and an unstated quantity of port wine."[33] From this time the Christian movement was associated with the most advanced European scientific knowledge and technology and, later, medical-surgical skills. Yoshitaka granted the missionaries an unoccupied Buddhist temple for their residence and gave them freedom to preach. He believed they were Buddhist monks from India, albeit of a different sect from those known in Japan; in the document of 1552 granting Father Cosme de Torres permission to build the famous Daidōji Church in Yamaguchi of Suō province, the language specifically states that the priests had come from the West (India) to proclaim the Law of the Buddha.[34] Xavier, however, remained in Yamaguchi for about five months, from April to September of 1551. Here he did his most creative and also numerically most successful work in Japan. He and his companions had suffered greatly from the cold and from the unaccustomed food during their journey to Kyōto, and now they were able to evangelize in relative comfort and security.[35]

Twice a day the missionaries preached a formal sermon to large crowds, and each sermon was invariably followed by a discussion which lasted in some cases for several hours. In fact the Christian workers spent most of their time answering questions or preaching. Buddhist priests and others came to hear

[33] Broderick, op. cit., p. 433. Cf. Obara Satoru, "Kirishitan Jidai no Kagaku Shisō," Kirishitan Kenkyū, vol. 10, pp. 101-273.

[34] Okada, op. cit., pp. 27-28. The missionaries were of course then unable to read this document, since it was composed in the Chinese language.

[35] Xavier had evidently not anticipated the severity of the Japanese winters. As for food, besides rice, only wheat, vegetables and a few other items of little nourishing value were available. Dairy products were not then consumed in Japan, nor, except surreptitiously, was beef. Fish was to be had, but in deference to Buddhist monastic rules, Francis ate almost no fish. Okada, op. cit., p. 23; Broderick, op. cit., pp. 416-417.

them, as well as laymen of every class, "so many in fact that the house was nearly always full and often could not contain all who wanted to come in."[36] The visitors asked penetrating questions, especially about the Creator, as the concept of purposeful creation was foreign to all sects of Buddhism. They objected to the notion that God was good, because if he were, he could not have created the demons which in fact existed. When the questioners were told that God had made the demons good but that they made themselves evil and would be punished forever on this account, they objected that a God who punishes so severely must be without mercy. God could not be good or he would not have made something so bad and merciless as an eternal hell. They pointed out that according to the teaching of all Buddhist sects men can be delivered out of hell and this teaching, therefore, is more rooted in mercy than the law of God.

These perceptive objections did not admit an easy answer. The missionaries had unbounded confidence in their ability to refute all opponents, but perhaps more effective than their theological explanations were their persons. The selfless sacrificial love and concern which they showed to every man gave to their answers an existential force beyond their rational power. For Francis Xavier, the perceptive intelligence of the Japanese manifested the mercy of God, and he rejoiced in the opportunities given to answer their questions. He was also able to tell them that the earth is round and to give them the latest views of the University of Paris on astronomical and meteorological phenomena. These explanations highly pleased the Japanese, and they considered the missionaries learned men, a fact which helped to gain credence for their sermons. The association of Christian faith with the most advanced scientific knowledge thus gained further strength. In consequence, about five hundred converts were baptized at Yamaguchi within two months, and baptisms continued daily, a large proportion of the candidates being of the *samurai* class. The new Christians became "most devoted friends" of the missionaries and showed them "an extremity of love."[37] Among them were a few Bud-

---

[36] Schurhammer and Wicki, *op. cit.*, vol. 2, p. 263.
[37] Broderick, *op. cit.*, pp. 434-437.

dhist priests and a half-blind minstrel who, as Lourenço, became the first Japanese lay-brother of the Society of Jesus, serving the movement faithfully for many years as a quick-witted and zealous catechist.

At this point Xavier received an invitation from the young Lord of Bungo (Ōita Prefecture in northeastern Kyūshū), Ōtomo Yoshishige. He left Yamaguchi in the middle of September in 1551 and went to the harbor city of Funai (the present city of Ōita), where a Portuguese vessel had arrived. Yoshishige gave the missionaries freedom to preach in his territory and promised them his protection. He did not become a Christian himself until twenty-seven years later, but he was a faithful protector and friend of the missionaries from this early period. Funai became for many years the chief center for the evangelization of all of Kyūshū.

Xavier, however, did not remain long in Bungo. He had received no letters from India since his arrival in Japan, and he was concerned over possible events there. He accordingly sailed from the port of Hiji in November of 1551, after a stay in Japan of no more than two years and three months, taking with him two Japanese converts whom he wished to send to Goa and eventually to Rome. He returned to Goa, and in the following year he came back to the Far East hoping to realize his long-cherished desire to evangelize China, which he believed was the best way to win the Japanese. He died on the island of Sanchuan near Canton on December 3, 1552, at the age of forty-six years and eight months, one of the most dedicated and heroic figures in the history of the Christian church and mission.[38]

---

[38] Cf. Francisco Perez, "Sei Furanshisuko Sabieru no Shoryokō to sono Rekishiteki Shimei," *Katorikku Shingaku*, I/1 (1962), 120-149.

B. THE GROWTH OF THE CHURCH

1

FOLLOWING THE DEPARTURE OF FRANCIS XAVIER, COSME de Torres was the only priest remaining in Japan. He and Brother Juan Fernandez, however, continued to work at Yamaguchi with considerable success. At the end of 1551 civil war erupted, and the original protector of the missionaries, Ōuchi Yoshitaka, was forced to commit suicide. Ōtomo Haruhide, a younger brother of Ōtomo Yoshishige of Bungo (Ōita), became the new lord of Yamaguchi, and, taking the name of Ōuchi Yoshinaga, promised to protect the missionaries. The piece of land which had been donated by Yoshitaka but confiscated during the rebellion was restored in 1552, and a new church and rectory were built.

Many converts were made in Yamaguchi; during the seven years of de Torres' stay the Christian community is said to have grown to 2,000. Among the converts were two Buddhist priests, Kyōzen, baptized as Paul, and Senyō, baptized as Barnabas. The greatest enemies of the missionaries were the priests of the Zen and Nichiren sects, but the quality of the missionaries' persons and work was in part indicated by the considerable number of Buddhist priests who were converted, the most numerous of whom were of the Zen sect.[1] This school practiced perhaps the most rigorous personal and academic discipline of all the Japanese sects, so its followers were best equipped to understand and appreciate the theological witness of the missionaries. In 1557 Yamaguchi again suffered the ravages of war, and Yoshinaga was defeated and then killed by the most powerful lord of western Honshū, Mōri Motonari. Both church and rectory were destroyed by fire and de Torres compelled to flee. The church property was confiscated, and the Christians were left without a priest until 1586.

The experience at Yamaguchi was representative of the work elsewhere, slow and difficult but yet hopeful. The small number of priests was a major problem. Fr. Balthazar Gago and

[1] Okada Akio, *Kirishitan Bateren,* p. 167.

two lay brothers arrived at Kagoshima on April 14, 1552. From 1552 to 1564 there were only two to four priests in the entire mission, from 1565 to 1570 no more than six. In consequence few communities had a resident priest.

Gago and his party were courteously received by Shimazu Takahisa, the *daimyō* of Kagoshima, who had evidently come to see how unpractical it was to be hostile to the missionaries. The three men, however, were under orders to proceed at once to Bungo and left Kagoshima after only two weeks. In Bungo they were granted living quarters by the *daimyō*, Ōtomo Yoshishige, who also had food sent daily to their house. Upon hearing that the missionaries arrived in Bungo, de Torres sent Brother Fernandez from Yamaguchi to serve as their interpreter.

Gago had brought a letter and presents from the Portuguese viceroy of India and using Fernandez as interpreter offered them to Yoshishige. Five days later he called on the *daimyō* to explain the letter and hopefully to win him to the Christian faith. He visited the lord frequently thereafter to the same end. Ōtomo responded to the personal appeal only with evasive answers but wished to see the Christian faith spread among his subjects. He also regretted that there were fewer Christians in his territory than in Yamaguchi. He then requested the missionaries to remain in Bungo. They replied that they had received orders to go first to Yamaguchi but asked for formal permission to preach and baptize in Bungo. Yoshishige was ready to grant permission at once, and on the basis of this understanding the men proceeded to Yamaguchi, where all the fathers and brothers of the mission met together on Christmas in 1552.

It is proper at this point to ask more precisely why *daimyō* with the political power and cultural sophistication of Ōtomo Yoshishige and Shimazu Takahisa were so ready to welcome foreign missionaries proclaiming an alien faith. For one thing, since the missionaries came from India, they were thought to possess the special aura of *Tenjikunin,* men from the birthplace of the Buddha, and, as we have seen, they were first widely believed to be priests of another Buddhist sect. They were courteously received by many Buddhist monks and priests, often entertained and plied with questions. Given the polemical instincts of the missionaries, however, not much time was required to disabuse the Buddhists of this notion of kinship, but the *daimyō* continued to ask for missionaries to come to their lands. What was the reason for their openness?

This period of Japanese history particularly welcomed a new religious faith. Buddhism had not acquired the sociological power that it later had in Japanese society of the Edo period. Knowledge of Confucianism was limited to but a few scholars, and Shintō had by no means kept pace with the developing cultural sophistication of the nation. No recognizable political power as yet unified the land, and the many *daimyō* were continual rivals to expand the wealth and power of their separate fiefs, and if possible, to extend them at their neighbors' expense. But in spite of the territory and income which many possessed, they were actually quite poor in terms of the relation between income and financial responsibility toward their retainers, as the missionaries testified. In the second half of the sixteenth century a *daimyō's* most promising source of substantial extra income, apart from territorial conquest, was Portuguese trading ships coming regularly to one of his ports. In no other way can we explain the repeated efforts of many *daimyō* in Kyūshū over several decades to secure Portuguese trade.[2] This fact, however, does not tell the whole story. Permission to preach and win converts in Yamaguchi was not granted to secure Portuguese trade; and, as we shall see, the growth of the church in the larger area around Kyōto was not thus motivated. One important element in the larger political and social situation has already been alluded to: the lack of political unity and a consequent cultural fluidity and openness that Japan was not to see again until the latter half of the nineteenth century. Even then the openness never equalled that of the sixteenth century.

It is necessary to explain further regarding the aura borne by the missionaries as men coming from India. For Japanese of the mid-sixteenth century, this aura conveyed more than a vague spiritual and cultural prestige; the common view of

---

[2] Alessandro Valignano's *Sumario* of 1580. C. R. Boxer, *The Christian Century in Japan*, pp. 93, 95.

Tenjikunin was that of magicians and wonder workers. When Francis Xavier met a Japanese traveler on his overland journey through deep snow to Kyōto, the exasperated Japanese said that if the missionary were indeed from India, he would like to have him stop the heavy snowfall.[3] We shall see later that this reputation of having supernatural powers had negative as well as positive aspects, but, as in the introduction of Buddhism into Japan in the sixth century, the reputation of possessing foreign, superior spiritual power was significant in the wide acceptance of Christian faith in an open and fluid culture.

2

The role of Portuguese trade in the Christian mission in Japan also requires further elucidation. So vital was this that even Francis Xavier was deeply concerned for the financial success of the enterprise. He suggested the establishment, for instance, of a trading factor in Sakai, the major commercial city of central Japan, and advised limiting the quantity in imports of pepper so that it might sell at a higher price and bring a correspondingly high profit.[4] The missionaries depended upon the traders for their (normally gratuitous) passage from India, but more significantly, the major financial support of the mission with its increasingly multifarious activities, social and educational as well as ecclesiastical, depended upon the success of the Portuguese trade with Japan.

The missionaries were considered by both Portuguese and Japanese as indispensable agents in the trade. Only they could serve as interpreters to the satisfaction of both parties; the deep and consistent respect accorded the missionaries by Portuguese traders and sailors was not lost on the Japanese. Indeed, the relationship differed markedly from that which existed in later centuries when both traders and missionaries in Asia and Africa were more from Protestant lands. The Jesuit participation in trade, however, went beyond the stage of serving as interpreters.

The sources of the Jesuits' funds for the Japan Mission were

---

[3] Okada, *op. cit.*, pp. 158-159.

[4] *Tenka Tōitsu, Nihon no Rekishi*, vol. 7, p. 63. Cf. Matsuda Kiichi, *Nihon Kōshōshi*, pp. 9-19, 189-198.

in fact many. They received considerable sums from at least two laymen who entered the order in the Orient and gave all their wealth to it, Mendes Pinto in 1554 and Luis d'Almeida probably in the same year. The latter spent one thousand *cruzados* to erect and equip a home for children who might otherwise be killed as a method of birth control then common among the poor. Dom Pedro da Silva da Gama, one of the six sons of the explorer Vasco da Gama, was the generous captain of Malacca at the time of Xavier's departure for Japan, and we learn that he gave from his personal fortune sufficient monies for a fund for Xavier and his companions to live during their entire stay in Japan.[5]

These personal contributions were later augmented by the Japanese. Ōtomo Yoshishige granted an annual allotment for the hospital at Funai equivalent to three to five hundred *cruzados*. Other *daimyō* occasionally gave a house or piece of land for a church, and Japanese Christians collected small gifts for the poor. All these contributions, however, were not sufficient to meet the financial needs of the mission. Before 1574 the Portuguese king made an annual contribution of five hundred *cruzados* from the crown customs revenue at Malacca; this sum was doubled in that year, but the payment was both "irregular and tardy" and 30 per cent was lost on the necessary exchange through Macao. As monarch of the later dual kingdom of Spain and Portugal, King Felipe increased this annual grant by an additional one thousand ducats. From 1583 Pope Gregory XIII promised a yearly allotment of four thousand ducats. The Jesuits' landed property in India designated twelve hundred ducats for the Japan Mission. All of these sums suffered in transmission from the same tardiness and irregularity as well as loss in exchange. At best they produced a total income of seventy-seven hundred ducats at the time when the minimum expenses of the Japan Mission varied from ten to twelve thousand *cruzados* annually.[6] In consequence the mis-

---

[5]James Broderick, *Saint Francis Xavier*, p. 349. Xavier wrote that while in Japan he received in alms, presumably from this fund, over a thousand *cruzados*. In India at that time one *cruzado* bought thirty-six plump chickens. Prices in Japan, however, were perhaps one-third higher.

[6]Boxer, *op. cit.*, p. 117.

sionaries felt themselves compelled to take advantage of the Portuguese trade between Macao and Japan, even though engaging in trade was contrary to canon law.

As we have seen, Portuguese trade with Japan probably began in 1542. For the first few years, three or four ships came each year, but from 1550 the annual voyage from Goa, by way of Macao, was usually limited to one or two ships. The ships used were mostly of the type called *Nao*, or Great Ship, by the Portuguese and *Kurofune*, or Black Ship, by the Japanese. Although various other items were involved, the essence of the trade was the exchange, through the use of Portuguese intermediaries, of Chinese silk for Japanese silver, a transaction profitable for all parties concerned.[7]

The financial participation of the missionaries in the trade was manifold. After the Great Ship began to come to the (at first) small village but splendid harbor of Nagasaki in 1571, the maintenance of the padres there was paid for by the Christian *daimyō* Ōmura Sumitada out of the annual customs of one thousand ducats which the traders paid the lord. The Jesuits, however, also participated more directly as partners in the trade. From 1582 they were allotted a regular share of one hundred piculs of the cargo of white silk floss, bought with the interest from the money given the order by d'Almeida, from which they received a profit of from four to six thousand ducats a year.[8]

In 1567 Francis Borgia, the superior general of the Society of Jesus, wrote to the provincial at Goa that he strongly disapproved of the methods used by the Japan missionaries to finance their work. His successor Claudio Aquaviva was also distressed, but finally supported the padres after Alessandro Valignano, the vicar general and visitor of the order in the Orient and in Europe, explained that as no other source existed for the funds

---

[7]A single voyage could bring to a captain with this privilege a clear profit of as much as 50,000 ducats, a sum sufficient to enable him to set up a household of distinction in Portugal for the rest of his life. Contemporary political tension between the Chinese Ming Dynasty and Japan largely as a consequence of the pirate activities of the Japanese *Wakō*, made direct commerce between the two nations practically impossible.

[8]Boxer, *op. cit.*, pp. 117-118.

which they needed for their growing activities in Japan, their
participation in trade must continue.

The odium which the Jesuits received for their activities
was however mostly unmerited. In principle their participation in trade was no different from that of the later Protestant
Basel Mission, and their income was spent wholly to support
the institutions, workers and needy laity of their growing Christian communities. By 1580 the Christians numbered 150,000,
served by two hundred churches. The clergy consisted of eighty-
five Jesuits, twenty Japanese brothers and one hundred catechists, called *dōjuku* in Japanese. In 1590 there were 136
Jesuits in Japan, 170 *dōjuku*, and the number of caretakers
and servants came to about three hundred, a total of more than
six hundred persons, who were primarily supported by the
mission rather than the churches. The growing number of
local schools, seminaries, hospitals and the new mission press,
though aided by Japanese contributions, also depended largely
upon mission support. Another burden was the support of
refugees who had been compelled to flee the territories of anti-
Christian *daimyō*. The Christian movement was proportion-
ately more active than the Buddhist sects yet without the fixed
incomes from land which most temples had.

The problem of the financial support of the mission and its
participation in trade is so intrinsically important that I have
devoted to it what may appear to be undue space. Of even
greater significance, however, was the role of this participation
in the complex events which led to the final expulsion of the
missionaries and the virtual extermination of the church. However pure the motives of the Jesuit fathers appear to have been,
their role in Portuguese trade colored all of their relationships
with Japanese rulers and subjects; this must be kept in mind
as a significant factor in the entire history of the first century of
Roman Catholic missionary activity in Japan.

3

At the meeting of the small band of workers in Yamaguchi
during the Christmas season of 1552, the men received their
assignments. Brother da Silva was to remain with Father de

Torres in Yamaguchi, Father Gago and Brother Fernandez were to begin work in Bungo. All felt that Brother de Alcaçova should return to India to report on the work and seek more helpers. He went with Gago and Fernandez to Bungo from whence he was to proceed to the port of Hirado and sail for India. He remained in Hirado, however, until October 18, and during this stay he was most graciously received several times by the *daimyō*, Matsuura Takanobu, who strongly wished to have Christian missionaries come to spread the faith in his land. He gave de Alcaçova a letter to the viceroy of India to this effect, as had Lord Ōtomo of Bungo. Fr. Gago, who came from Bungo for a short visit while de Alcaçova was in Hirado, was instrumental in the conversion of many Japanese, including three close relatives of the *daimyō*. Within three years there developed here a community of nearly five hundred Christians.

No resident priest served in Hirado until 1555 when Fr. Gago was assigned to this parish. He was succeeded in 1557 by the energetic Gasper Vilela, who also began Christian work in the nearby islands of Takushima and Ikitsuki. Here the work so prospered that within a short time about six hundred persons were baptized. This success was due in no small part to the patronage of the Christian nobleman Koteda Saemon. At this point the Christian community, evidently with the approval of both Koteda and Vilela, destroyed some Buddhist temples, an action understandable in terms of missionary methods in medieval Europe, but in Japan it and similar incidents portended sorry consequences. The opposition of the Buddhists in Hirado was such that in 1558 Vilela had to leave the city. The church building was demolished and was not rebuilt until 1564. The Christian community, however, continued to grow even without the presence of a priest.

This pattern of growth and opposition and further growth was followed with some variations in other fiefs in Kyūshū. The center of the work was in Funai (Ōita), where under the warm patronage of the *daimyō* Ōtomo Yoshishige the work prospered to the extent that by 1556 the Christians numbered about two thousand persons. Here, alongside the building which had been donated for a church by Yoshishige, the Jesuits purchased a large piece of land and built a church and rectory. They then used the older structure as a hospital and erected a separate building to serve as an isolation ward for the care of lepers and syphilitics. Many of the funds for the hospital as well as for a foundling home were donated by Luis d'Almeida before he entered the Society of Jesus.[9]

European medical and surgical science in the sixteenth century was not significantly advanced beyond the best of Asia; indeed, Portuguese viceroys in India apparently preferred native Indian physicians to their own compatriots. In the Far East, however, the Portuguese had gained some reputation as skilled healers. Several factors contributed to the effective medical work of the Japanese mission. Luis d'Almeida evidently had a considerable knowledge of surgery and as a lay brother devoted himself particularly to this work and the training of Japanese helpers. He established a pharmacy with a large stock of medicines and herbs which he had ordered from Macao, and he made Japanese physicians chiefly responsible for internal medicine. Perhaps the chief original contribution of this medical work was the Christian concern for the poor and humble classes. The hospital was the first of its kind in Japan and so successful in effecting cures that patients came to it from far and near, including Portuguese merchants and sailors.[10]

While the main thrust of the work remained in Kyūshū, important growth was taking place in the five provinces about Kyōto, termed Gokinai in Japanese. Xavier and his companions had been unable to work in Kyōto. After a fruitless attempt to secure entrance through the help of the monks of Mt. Hiei, the Jesuits made a third attempt in 1559 with Fr. Vilela and two Japanese brothers. On this occasion they were aided by Buddhist monks and an elderly nun. Helped by another monk,

---

[9]Johannes Laures, *The Catholic Church in Japan*, pp. 22-23.

[10]Boxer, *op. cit.*, pp. 203-204. It must be noted that in the generation after d'Almeida, Jesuit policy was changed to give primary attention to upper class Japanese and is to be sharply contrasted with the generous care given the poor in the Franciscan hospitals of Kyōto in the last decade of the sixteenth century. Cf. Ebisawa Arimichi, "Zezusukai Funai Byōin no Setsuritsu oyobi sono Tōji," *Kirishitan Kenkyū*, vol. 1, pp. 43-108.

Vilela was received in audience by the *shōgun* Ashikaga
Yoshiteru and obtained official permission to reside in the city
and preach. Considerable opposition developed from Buddhist
monks, and yet, as Luis Frois relates, at least seventeen asked
for and received baptism. Men of high social rank were also
baptized.[11]

The opposition of the monks became so strong that Vilela
left Kyōto in the summer of 1561 and began work in Sakai,
the chief port and commercial city of the area. Here he was
warmly received by the son of the wealthy merchant who had
given hospitality to Francis Xavier on his journey to Kyōto
ten years previously. Here, too, the character and message of
the missionaries impressed Japanese at every level of society;
and Vilela, although he was in Sakai for little more than a
year, baptized the four children of his host, Hibiya Ryōkei,
and about forty others. Hibiya himself was baptized in 1563,
and his home became the meeting place of the Sakai Christian
community for eighteen years.

Vilela returned to Kyōto in September of 1562, but in the
spring of the following year another significant incident occurred. The Buddhist monks of Kyōto tried again to expel
the missionaries from the city. Since the latter had an official
permit from the *shōgun*, the minister of justice, Matsunaga
Hisahide, decided to appoint two scholars as judges to determine whether the new teachings were in fact harmful to the
state. At the suggestion of his vassal, Takayama Hida no Kami,
he asked that the investigation be held at the ancient Buddhist
center of Nara, about fifty miles distant. Vilela had also been
asked, apparently not commanded, to appear; but only Brother
Lourenço, the half-blind minstrel who had become one of the
most skilled of catechists and the first Japanese lay brother of
the Society of Jesus, went to Nara. His answers were so per-
suasive that both judges as well as Takayama himself decided
to become Christians. They received further instruction and
then asked Vilela to come to Nara, where he baptized them
and all of their families. Takayama requested Lourenço to

---

[11] Joseph Jennes, *A History of the Catholic Church in Japan*, p. 26. Cf.
Johannes Laures, *Die Anfänge der Mission von Miyako*, pp. 20-65.

preach to his own retainers. As a consequence about 150 became Christians. The son of Takayama, Ukon, was to become perhaps the most winsome and representative Christian personality among all the Christian *daimyō*.[12]

This pattern, by which a feudal lord was either won to the faith personally or consented to give positive patronage, and then numbers of his retainers and his commoner subjects were converted, was the method by which most of the members of the churches were won. It must not be thought, however, that conversions by this method were entirely or even mostly insincere; the process was considered sociologically natural by almost all concerned.

The greater part of the mass conversions took place in Kyūshū. Perhaps the principal motive, at least initially, for the conversion of most of the *daimyō* was the benefit which they expected to receive from Portuguese trade drawn by the missionaries and a substantial Christian community. Another important factor, which we shall consider later in another context, was the friendship between the missionaries and the first of the great military dictators and unifiers of the country, Oda Nobunaga. Even though Nobunaga had no actual authority in Kyūshū, he was the sole figure to emerge as a symbol of unity, and the mass conversions in Kyūshū began during his military rule.

The sociological mobility of the period is strikingly seen in the person and influence of Nobunaga. As the several centuries of warfare were ending in the process of unification primarily initiated by Nobunaga, much of the social open-endedness and change of the preceding period was still manifest, and in some ways heightened, under his rule. Nobunaga's attitude and public posture toward the institutions of the old order was one of implacable opposition, even studied mockery. This policy included also bitter opposition toward Buddhist monastic institutions of political and military significance, some of which, especially the True Pure Land (*Jōdo Shinshū*) be-

---

[12]Cf. Paul Pfister, "Towards the Beatification of Takayama Ukon," *The Japan Missionary Bulletin*, XVIII/7 (August-September, 1964), 447-450; Ebisawa Arimichi, *Takayama Ukon, passim.*

lievers, took military action against him.[13] Nobunaga, who was probably an agnostic himself in religious matters, expressed at once his personal openness and his anti-Buddhist bias by friendliness to the missionaries in Kyōto, especially Luis Frois and Gnecchi-Soldi Organtino. In this context conversion to a new, foreign faith like Christianity was a wide sociological possibility as it had not been before and was not to be again for several centuries.

As an example of these conversions, in 1571 there were about five thousand Christians in the entire fief of the Christian *daimyō*, Ōmura Sumitada; fifteen hundred of these were in the port city of Nagasaki. In the two years 1575 and 1576 Fr. Gaspar Coelho baptized about forty thousand people, and by 1577 the total number of Christians in the fief came to approximately sixty thousand. The mission in Amakusa which had been begun by d'Almeida in 1569 comprised only forty Christians in 1570. In 1571 the whole fief was converted, to the number of over ten thousand persons.

In 1570 the territory of Arima Yoshisada contained about three thousand Christians. The number increased to fifteen thousand in a very few years after Yoshisada's baptism in 1576. This process, however, worked with almost equal ease in reverse. When the successor of Yoshisada, Harunobu, began to persecute the church, about seven thousand of the Christians apostatized. When Harunobu himself was baptized in 1580, the apostatized returned to the church and about four thousand of Harunobu's *samurai* became Christian. In Bungo, as a result of the notable medical and social work, the number of Christians rose to about two thousand during the early years of d'Almeida's work there. Most of the Christians, however, were of the lower classes, and this fact kept the *samurai* and the nobility aloof, with the result that the number of adherents remained approximately the same for twenty years. But after the conversion of Ōtomo Yoshishige in 1578, the number rose from twenty-five hundred to six thousand in one year.

The missionaries were well aware of the problematical na-

---

[13]*Tenka Tōitsu*, pp. 14, 24. Cf. pp. 30, 36-37, 50. Cf. also Yoshida Shōgorō, *Kirishitan Daimyō*, pp. 64-89.

ture of these conversions and adjusted their methods of instruction and organization to meet the needs. Perhaps the most unfortunate aspect of the mass conversions, however, particularly in terms of later political consequences, was that social pressure and even physical force were on occasion used by the lords to compel their subjects to become Christians. If this was not done at the instigation of the missionaries, it at least occurred with acquiescence on their part. Both Ōmura and Arima ordered all the Buddhist priests of their fiefs to become Christians and to marry or to leave. Of equally portentous consequence was the decision to destroy all the Buddhist temples in these territories.[14]

The concern of the missionaries over the spiritual content of these conversions is well expressed in the 1580 *Sumario* of Alessandro Valignano. He recognized fully the role of commercial self-interest in the conversion of the *daimyō* especially of Kyūshū. He noted that in the Kyōto region, where such considerations did not apply, the lords who were converted were moved mainly because "having heard the things of our Law they seemed good to them." Even though their vassals followed suit in order to please their lords, they and their lords, Valignano affirmed, had a better understanding of the faith and were better Christians than those in Kyūshū. But, compared to India, even those in Kyūshū had little tendency to return to their "idols" once they were converted, and Valignano gratefully acknowledged that once won to the faith, many if not most subjects remained faithful and preferred death or exile to recantation.[15]

With respect to comprehensive statistics, in 1570 the total number of Christians in Japan was about thirty thousand, an extraordinary achievement in terms of the short period of twenty years of missionary activity, the few clergy and the many difficulties. By 1582 the total number of Christians in Kyūshū rose to about 130,000 and in Gokinai (Kyōto area) about twenty thousand. The highest relatively reliable figure for

[14]Jennes, *op. cit.*, pp. 37-39. Cf. Laures, *op. cit.*, pp. 88, 93, 100.
[15]Boxer, *op. cit.*, pp. 93-95. Cf. Hiyane Antei, *Nihon Kirisuto Kyōshi*, pp. 117-131.

Christians in Japan during this century of Roman Catholic activity is 300,000 in the year 1614, although Fernão Guerreiro in his *Relaçam Anual* of 1605 claimed a total of 750,000 at this date and later writers have asserted even larger figures. In the free atmosphere which characterized the beginning of Tokugawa Ieyasu's rule in 1600, the rapidity of the church's growth is indicated by the fact that thirty thousand converts were baptized within six months in the single fief of the Christian *daimyō* of Higo (in Kyūshū), Konishi Yukinaga.[16] The question is, then, what were the methods of evangelization used by the missionaries, who numbered no more than 143 in 1614, to achieve this phenomenal numerical success? As C. R. Boxer has indicated, since the total population of Japan at this period was approximately twenty million, probably no other case in the history of Christianity exists where the faith expanded so rapidly in both numbers and influence in a highly civilized country.[17]

4

Both the success of the mission and its later tragic failure are related to the persons, attitudes and methods of the missionaries as much as to the circumstances of contemporary Japanese history. If the missionaries had little or no influence upon the forces leading to the unification of Japan under Nobunaga and Hideyoshi, they had much influence on the form that unification took under Ieyasu and in the subsequent policy of exclusion (*Sakoku*).

Perhaps the first point to observe is that it was the second half of the sixteenth century, and the missionaries from the time of Francis Xavier were the immediate heirs not only of medieval Christianity but in particular of the notions of what constituted proper missionary methodology characteristic of the Middle Ages in Europe. Although men of the stature of Xavier and Valignano were by no means without racial prejudice, especially as seen in their views of the natural potential of the

[16]Boxer, *op. cit.*, pp. 320-321, 180.
[17]*Ibid.*, p. 321. Cf. Miki Tomokaze, *Nihon Katorikku Kyōshi*, pp. 95-100.

darker races of India, both were quickly compelled to recognize
that in the case of the Japanese they were dealing with their
cultural equals.[18] They and the other missionaries, however,
were the heirs of an ideology and methodology developed over
long centuries in Europe: the governing concept was that the
church proclaimed an obviously superior civilization as well
as the eternal gospel to tribal peoples whose culture was acknowledged by themselves, as by the "Romans," to be inferior.
Almost completely gone, at least in the context of missionary
expansion, was the memory of early Christian witness in the
face of great and ancient civilizations. In the Middle Ages of
Europe, missionaries dismissed the idols of the pagans as dumb,
the vain inventions of men. They were not compelled, as the
early Christian apologists, to acknowledge through the doctrine
of the Logos the possible authenticity, in terms of salvation
history, of certain of the ethical and even religious insights of
the great philosophers of the Hellenistic past.[19]

We shall see that this heritage led to certain tragic mistakes
of understanding and tactics. It is clear from the history of
Luis Frois that the missionaries aimed at a total religious
displacement, in accordance with the medieval European experience; and when the political conditions favored, even
temporarily, this procedure, they were willing to compel conversions and to destroy non-Christian temples and shrines.[20]
Nevertheless, it must be acknowledged that in terms of their
background, the Jesuits made extraordinary adjustments to
meet the new and different situation in Japan.

Padre Valignano, after his arrival in 1579 as vicar-general
and visitor of the Jesuit order in the Orient, insisted that the

---

[18]Boxer, op. cit., p. 81. Francisco Cabral, the superior of the Japan Mission
at the time of Valignano's first arrival in 1579, was transferred to Macao
because he did not share Valignano's views; he insisted that the missionaries
treat the Japanese as inferiors. Valignano noted that the Japanese would
not submit to compulsion of any kind: "they will not suffer being slapped
or beaten, nor imprisonment, nor any other similar methods commonly used
with other Asiatic Christians." Ibid., pp. 73, 87, 79. The Portuguese consistently classified the Japanese, together with the Chinese, as belonging to
the white race.

[19]Cf. James Thayer Addison, The Medieval Missionary, p. 140.

[20]Okada, op. cit., pp. 60, 65-66.

European missionaries conform, as much as they possibly and properly could, to Japanese cultural forms and customs. In contrast to most of his co-workers, he frequently cited the Buddhist priests as models to be followed in external deportment. He advised new missionaries not only to strive to be learned and virtuous but dignified in their behavior, since the Buddhist priests are "distinguished by their dignity and gravity." Valignano greatly stressed the importance of language study and encouraged the production of Japanese language grammars and dictionaries. He noted the bodily cleanliness of the Japanese and the neatness as well as beauty of the temples and shrines. He consequently stressed the importance of neat housekeeping among the fathers and brothers. As to personal cleanliness, the closest adjustment his medieval background permitted him to make to the Japanese custom of a daily hot bath was to allow the mission personnel, both European and Japanese, to take a bath once in eight days. In short, Valignano came to agree with the principle held by the Japanese that they were willing to make allowance for the foreigners' ineptness in following their cultural ways for two years, but that if the Jesuits were then unwilling or unable to adjust, they would be despised as "ignorant louts." So far as humanly possible, in all matters of external deportment, conformity to Japanese custom was the rule.[21]

Another principle which Valignano stressed, following Xavier, was to develop as soon as possible a native Japanese clergy. He urged that Japanese Christians, preferably of *samurai* or higher rank, be received into the Society of Jesus, not only to become lay brothers or temporal coadjutors but priests on a par with the Europeans. A majority of Valignano's colleagues in Japan agreed with his views, but the principle was difficult to implement swiftly.

When Valignano wrote his first *Sumario* in 1580, the mission was already over thirty years old. Up to this time there

---

[21]Boxer, *op. cit.*, pp. 83-84. The Jesuits came to dress as Buddhist priests, and, perhaps unwisely, to adopt the social distinctions of the Zen Buddhist monastic hierarchy. *Ibid.*, pp. 162, 210.

were as yet no Japanese priests.[22] In the clerical hierarchy the brothers (*irmãos*) came next, most of whom were Europeans, but in 1592 there were about seventy Japanese brothers. Last were the *dōjuku* or native catechists, who corresponded to the category of *akoluthoi* in the early church; there were about a hundred of these in 1582 and two hundred and sixty in 1604. The *dōjuku* were, strictly speaking, not members of the Society of Jesus but integral members of the mission organization. Furthermore, it is clear that the actual work of preaching, catechization and leadership of the local churches was borne by the Japanese brothers and *dōjuku*. Since, however, the first Japanese brother was ordained as a priest in 1602, the control of the mission remained firmly in European hands; and, as padres were to be treated as social superiors by brothers and *dōjuku* by virtue of their rank (evaluated according to Zen Buddhist monastic practice), a potentially explosive situation was in the making. Many and increasing complaints came from the Japanese lower clergy, but the great majority continued with remarkable faithfulness to practice the faith and to serve the mission.

In the early days of the mission the Jesuits used "fixed and standardized sermons prepared in Japanese," probably written in letters of the Roman alphabet. Some of the catechumens took notes, and all wrote down the daily prayers and memorized them. Until the installation of a European movable type printing press in 1590, the Jesuits in Japan, in contrast to China, apparently made little use of the ancient Oriental device of wood block printing and generally circulated their literature in manuscript. The missionary and his Japanese colleagues usually gave instruction three times a day: early in the morning and the evening for adults, and at noon mostly for children

---

[22]A major problem in the first generation was that the Japanese, however well educated they were in their own culture, coming into the Society as most did as adults, found it exceedingly difficult to learn Latin to meet the standards of the Society in Europe, standards developed among men whose native tongues were direct derivatives of Latin. Regarding the first seminary and village see Hubert Cieslik, S.J., "Nihon ni okeru Saisho no Shingakkō,"*Kirishitan Kenkyū*, vol. 10, pp. 1-55; Arcadio Schwade, S.J., "Funai no Korejio ni tsuite," *Kirishitan Kenkyū*, vol. 10, pp. 56-66.

and perhaps some women. Inquirers were given baptism after fifteen or twenty days of such instruction, following a personal examination of the catechumen's knowledge of the faith and his spiritual intent. Even in the first generation baptism was frequently conferred on groups of fifty to 250 people. When the missionary went on to another place, he frequently left behind a *dōjuku* to give further instruction. Even though the latter could not administer the sacraments, he in fact became the temporary pastor of the community and frequently did yeoman's service in building it up.[23]

The two chief contemporary sources for the content of the catechetical teaching of the missionaries and their Japanese colleagues are Luis Frois' *Historia de Japan* and Valignano's report of 1583. The teaching consisted essentially of three parts. First, an apologetical introduction designed to prove the existence of God who is creator of the universe, the spiritual nature and immortality of the soul, and a refutation of the "falsities and errors" of the Buddhist and Shintō faiths. Secondly, there was an exposition of Christian doctrine primarily following the historical order. That is, after consideration of the fact of the triune God and the creation of the world, the teachers explained the fall of Lucifer and the sin of Adam. From this point they led the catechumens to the "Incarnation, the holiness of Christ's life, His death, Resurrection and Ascension, the power of the mystery of the Cross, the Last Judgment, the pains of Hell and the happiness of Heaven."[24] All this instruction was by means of "fixed and standardized sermons" in Japanese that had evidently been formulated following the example of Francis Xavier's first efforts and translated into Japanese by the most literate Japanese brothers. There was, however, also a certain

---

[23] Luis Frois relates that in a few cases instruction of women and children was conducted by married women. Jennes, *op. cit.*, p. 28. Cf. Murakami Nanjirō, "Dominika no Sekkyō ni tsuite," *Kirishitan Kenkyū*, vol. 3, pp. 1-25.

[24] Jennes, *op. cit.*, p. 29. The similarity of this methodology and that of the early church in the Roman Empire is striking. Cf. John Foster, *After the Apostles*, p. 54. A recent study of the catechetical work of the Japanese mission is Jesús López Gay, *El Catecumenado en la Mision del Japan del S. XVI*.

differentiation by which instruction was modified according to the intellectual caliber of the hearers, the better educated evidently being given more extended explanations.

Thirdly, additional instructions were given about the Ten Commandments, the necessity of avoiding non-Christian superstitions and practices and the need for perseverance in the faith according to Catholic devotional practice. After the meaning and necessity of baptism were explained, the catechumens were baptized. Instructions on the other sacraments were given later; in some places five periods of instruction were devoted to the sacrament of confession and five to holy communion. According to Valignano, converts were admitted to communion only after they had attended church, had made confession and had heard sermons and mass for a considerable number of times.

Most of these Christian communities, however, did not have a resident priest and could only rarely attend mass or take communion. The custom was for the faithful to meet together on Sundays in the church, if there was one, or in the home of a Christian to worship under the leadership and with the sermon of a *dōjuku*. If there were no *dōjuku* present, there may have been reading from a religious book by a layman. In any case, an integral part of the service was the recitation of the prayers which the people had learned by heart. All catechumens were taught the Apostles' Creed, the Lord's Prayer, the Ave Maria and a few other prayers, such as the Rosary, the Hail Holy Queen and the Litany of the Saints. The effectiveness of this capsular mode of teaching was such that, according to Valignano, those who progressed to the point of memorizing these symbols and prayers seldom or never returned to their idols.[25]

The substance of Christian devotional life thus consisted of these services and the daily family prayers, such as the Rosary, the Hail Holy Queen and the Litany of the Saints. From the early days of the mission the custom was also introduced of reciting twice a day five Our Fathers and five Hail Marys for

[25]Jennes, *op. cit.*, pp. 28-29. Cf. Boxer, *op. cit.*, pp. 220-221. The catechetical procedure was simplified somewhat after the mass conversions began. Cf. Alice E. MacDonald, "A Kirishitan Prayer Book-Catechism," *The Japan Christian Quarterly*, XXVIII/1 (January, 1962), 55-60.

the conversion of Japan. Church festivals were celebrated with great solemnity and the use of processions. Hymns were composed, probably by Japanese brothers or *dōjuku*, and sung with much fervor on these and other occasions. The history of the Passion and stories from the Old Testament were told in verse form, possibly by chant, to groups large and small. Dramatic plays and dialogues illustrative of biblical history were performed. In the context of traditional Japanese reverence and/or fear of the dead, funeral services were held in most solemn fashion and became an impressive means of witness to non-Christians.

Something of the tone of the Christian community in Japan was indicated by wide use of flagellation during Lent as an act of penance. Although separated from the men for this exercise, women also flagellated themselves. Among the Christians great devotion to the Passion of Christ was evident. In short, the intense Iberian Christianity characteristic of many of the missionaries was reflected with even greater fervor among this emotionally intense people. The zeal of so many thousands during the later times of persecution had its roots in this kind of devotional life.

Other forms of lay religious life and organization served the needs of the Christian communities. In several places local branches of the Sodality of the Misericordia, the Rosary or other confraternities were formed and flourished. In addition to encouraging Christians to faithful devotional practices, the members of these groups visited the sick and poor and collected donations for their help. They gave hospitality to Christians from other places, especially refugees, and in various ways served the community in the absence of a priest.[26]

The work of the priests consisted largely of occasional visits to the growing number of Christian communities. A brother

---

[26]Certain institutional expressions of these confraternities appear to derive from the *Casas da Misericordia*, the institutions which the Portuguese established in Asia and Africa during the sixteenth and seventeenth centuries for the poor, the sick, orphans and other needy, whether Christian or non-Christian. Cf. Broderick, *op. cit.*, p. 117. Regarding the funeral services see Hubert Cieslik, S. J., "Kirishitan to Sōrei," *Kirishitan Kenkyū*, vol. 5, pp. 32-58.

or *dōjuku* was customarily sent some days in advance to give preliminary instructions and to prepare the people to make their confessions and receive communion. Where the community was large, the priest had to hear confessions every day, possibly for a month. The relative infrequency of these visits may be seen from the fact that in 1566 the Christians of Hirado had not been able to make their confessions for four years. For a long while Funai was the only place with a resident priest.

Certain emphases in the teaching and practice of the missionaries were basic to their entire work; we must note these in order properly to evaluate their work. These men of the late Middle Ages reflected their heritage not only in their attacks on idols but also in their use of certain traditional practices of Christian faith. According to the dominant understanding of medieval Christianity, the missionaries saw salvation as deliverance from the power of demons, which granted happiness, safety and protection in this life and blessedness in the life to come. They saw the power of God at work in the world aiding men concretely: in healing and in working of other miracles, in supplying physical as well as spiritual needs, in giving victory in battle. They also envisaged the punishment of God, both temporal and eternal, upon disbelief and disobedience.[27]

Balthazar Gago in his letter of 1552 writes of cases where evil spirits were exorcised from people through the pronouncement of the name of Christ and the use of holy water. Among the miracle stories handed down by Japanese *Kirishitan* (from the Portuguese *Cristão*) are numerous accounts of this and other kinds of healing through prayer and the use of crosses, sacred images and other holy objects. To take one instance, in Francisco Cabral's letter of 1576 he reports how in Bungo the spirit possessing the wife of a *yamabushi* (charismatic shaman) could not be exorcised by her husband, but she was immediately healed through the prayer of a missionary who held in his hand an image of the Virgin. In a similar vein are the many miracle stories which originated later in connection with the persecutions.[28] In this context, however, it must be noted that, rela-

---

[27]Cf. Addison, *op. cit.*, pp. 140-154.

[28]Okada, *op. cit.*, pp. 56, 64, 184, 190; *Tenka Tōitsu*, p. 64.

tively speaking, the Jesuits distributed sparingly their relics, medals, rosaries and the like. The Franciscans, however, who came later, made much freer use of these sacramentals among the faithful; they were severely criticized by the Jesuits for distributing relics of dubious authenticity.[29]

Contemporary Japanese historians also particularly emphasize the aura of supernatural power associated with foreigners, especially since the missionaries were regarded as *Tenjikunin* (from India). The common man often believed that all pain and suffering could be relieved through these miracle workers; and, at the same time, if viewed with hostile eyes, as we see in the later stories of the period of persecution and subsequent public hostility, the missionaries were believed to cause the trees and grass to wither and disorders to occur wherever they walked. They were said to have the form of human beings but in reality were devils and workers of black magic. They ate human flesh and in their houses lay piles of dead men's bones. This kind of folk belief was apparently a significant factor in creating wide public support for the Tokugawa policy of exclusion and persecution.[30]

5

The educational methods of the missionaries were not especially noteworthy. Temple schools, called *terakoya*, conducted largely by Zen Buddhists, flourished all over the land and taught at least a modicum of reading and writing not only to children of the *samurai* but in certain cases to those of merchants, craftsmen and farmers.[31] A school for Christians was started early in Funai, and evidently schools of the level of the *terakoya* came to be established elsewhere as Christian communities developed.[32] The Jesuit religious instruction, however, did not require a high level of literacy in the con-

[29]Boxer, *op. cit.*, p. 232.

[30]*Tenka Tōitsu*, pp. 67, 71.

[31]Furuno Kiyoto, *Kakure Kirishitan*, p. 4.

[32]Since Valignano in his *Sumario* of 1580 urged the establishment of these schools, it is probable that up to that time their presence was by no means universal in the Christian communities.

verts, and while efforts for the creation of a Christian literature were made especially after the coming of Valignano in
1580, there was no attempt to translate into Japanese the Bible
as a whole or in substantial portions. The most significant
educational ventures were those to train a Japanese clergy.

Francisco Cabral, who was the superior of the mission from
1570, contended that the Japanese Christians with their pagan
background and environment were not spiritually mature
enough for the priesthood, that as priests they might become
proud and refuse to accept the direction of the missionaries. He
and other Jesuits — even Valignano had some concern at this
point — feared that because the Buddhist Pure Land schools
(*Jōdo-Shū* and *Jōdo-Shinshū*) that taught salvation by
faith in Amida alone were strong. Luther's doctrine of justification by faith alone might be readily accepted by less instructed Christians if a native clergy should rule.[33] Cabral
therefore did nothing for the higher education of the Japanese
lay brothers and *dōjuku*.

Valignano, however, rejected this principle of operation and
insisted that Japanese candidates be taught all that the Jesuits
were able to teach, with the proviso that all textbooks be
"purified" so that no mention of heresies and related problems
which had emerged in European history should mislead the
minds of the pupils. Since Cabral did not favor this proposal,
he was later removed to Macao and replaced by the more cooperative Gaspar Coelho. The plan of Valignano was for three
seminaries to be established, one for young men over eighteen,
the other two for boys under that age, both groups to be drawn
exclusively from the sons of the nobility or the *samurai*. The
curriculum was to include reading and writing in Japanese
and Latin, with the humanities and other sciences, virtue, deportment, and good manners, "which is the chiefest of all";
this latter was also to include Japanese social manners.

Only two seminaries in fact were established. The first was
opened in Arima of Kyūshū in October of 1580 with twenty-
two students. The other seminary with about twenty-five stu-

[33]Jennes, *op. cit.*, p. 51. Cf. Josef Franz Schütte, *Alexandro Valignanos
Ringen um die Missionsmethode in Japan*, p. 41.

dents was built also in 1580 in Azuchi, the new castle town
erected by Oda Nobunaga on the shores of Lake Biwa opposite
Kyōto. After the death of Nobunaga and the sacking of Azuchi,
this seminary was moved to Takatsuki (between Kyōto and
Ōsaka) at the invitation of Takayama Ukon. A novitiate with
the more specific and educationally higher purpose of training
priests for the Society was founded in 1582 in Usuki of Bungo.
Japanese of priestly rank were particularly needed to teach the
humanities and sciences in the seminaries and to create a
Japanese Christian literature. A college was later established in
Nagasaki, where a special course, according to João Rodriguez
Girão's letter of 1604, had been organized to train selected
Japanese brothers and *dōjuku* in anti-Buddhist polemics.
During the Keichō period (1596-1611) a small number of dis-
guised Japanese brothers and *dōjuku* were placed in Buddhist
temples to study Buddhist and Shintō texts not otherwise
available.

The first Japanese Jesuits, however, were ordained no earlier
than 1601, and in terms of the size of the Christian community
the educational projects were hardly impressive. Furthermore,
when Valignano returned to Japan in 1590, he was taken aback
by the prompt execution of his plans by Coelho so that seventy
Japanese novices were in training to become members of the
Society. Even Valignano was unable to welcome such momentum
emerging from Japanese clergy and, although he favored expansion of the training of *dōjuku*, he slowed down the process of admitting candidates to the Society and the priesthood.
Dōjuku who reached the age of twenty and were not admitted
to the Society became discouraged, but the Jesuits were never
able to resolve this problem satisfactorily both to Japanese
Christians and their own fears.

Mention should also be made of the literary work done by
the missionaries and their Japanese colleagues and of the printing presses set up in Kyūshū and elsewhere from 1590. Valignano had already written from Goa in 1584 to request a printing press with movable type in roman script and matrices for
printing Japanese *kana* (syllabary script) from Europe. A missionary brother and a Japanese *dōjuku* received training in

the craft for four months in 1590 in Goa, and for twenty years a remarkable series of booklets and books — catechetical, devotional, linguistic and even Japanese classics (an abridged version of the *Heike Monogatari*) — were printed. These books were designed to serve both missionaries and Japanese Christians. The Jesuits were the first to develop a system of romanization for the Japanese language, and books intended primarily for missionary use were generally written in this script. Some of these, however, were evidently read also by Japanese students in the colleges and seminaries. Books for Japanese were written with the use of Chinese ideograms and *hiragana*; for the sake of the less literate, *kana* were set alongside the ideograms to give the proper reading of the latter, a device that came to be adopted by Japanese printers in general and is still in use to this day. However, no translation of the Bible as a whole or even of the New Testament was included among the books printed.

This printing and publishing activity had considerable influence upon later Japanese cultural history; the *Kirishitan* literature composed by Japanese *dōjuku* and brothers has been judged by the Japanese historian Anesaki Masaru to be among the finest products of the era.[34] Comparably influential were *Kirishitan* contributions in the fine arts. The early missionaries had brought to Japan some paintings in the Flemish style to decorate altars, and a considerable number of Japanese Christian painters were trained through an Academy of Fine Arts established in association with the first printing press at Shiki in Amakusa in 1591. (It was later moved to Arima and then to Nagasaki.) Although most of the works of these men were perhaps copies of European originals, *Kirishitan* artistic activity contributed distinctly to the development of Japanese pictorial art. It is certain that the Jesuits first introduced into Japan the techniques of oil painting and of copperplate engraving. The magnificent *Namban Byōbu,* or colored screens depicting scenes of the activity of the European missionaries

[34]Cf. Doi Tadao, *Kirishitan Bunkenkō*, pp. 1-18. For a survey of the Christian artistic contributions of the period see Okamoto Yoshitomo, *Namban Bijutsu, passim.*

and traders, are particularly significant examples of the stimulus to Japanese pictorial art furnished by the missionaries.

Another event which may be mentioned in this context apparently had little influence on the course of events in Japan at the time, but it reveals the policy of Valignano and the attitudes of the highest levels of Catholic leadership in Europe at the time. Shortly before he left Japan on his first visit Valignano planned to take to Europe with him some Japanese Christian nobles as envoys to the pope and the king of Spain from the Christian *daimyō* of Arima, Bungo and Ōmura. Valignano hoped both to secure more dependable financial support for the Japan Mission from European Catholics and to give the Japanese envoys a favorable impression of the Catholic Church and of European civilization in general so that they, as Japanese of high rank, could communicate with authority to their fellow countrymen.

The four Japanese envoys who left Nagasaki on February 20, 1582, with Valignano and their teacher Diogo de Mesquita were only boys in their early teens. They were, however, all relatives of *daimyō* of the highest rank, and they were received together with their teacher — Valignano did not go farther than India, as he received there his appointment as provincial — by the highest prelates of the Catholic Church in Lisbon, by King Philip II in Madrid and, after an impressive trip through the chief cities of Italy, by Pope Gregory XIII in Rome on March 23, 1585. This pope died only a few days later, but his successor, Sixtus V, at whose coronation the young envoys were present in a representative capacity, was equally warm in his welcome and granted them the title of Knights of the Golden Spur. The senators of the city of Rome, as part of their welcome for the Japanese boys, conferred upon them the title of Patricians of Rome.

As a result of these meetings the envoys received a considerable sum of money for the work of the mission. They finally returned to Japan on July 21, 1590, and with Valignano were received in audience by Hideyoshi in Kyōto on March 3, 1591. Hideyoshi asked many questions of the young men, and it is possible that this experience was one factor in leading him not to enforce the edict of expulsion of July 25, 1587, of which we shall take further note later. The effect of the trip on the young envoys themselves, however, may be partly discerned from the fact that all four were received into the Society of Jesus in July of 1591.

A final word in this section regards the quality of life and spirit of the Japanese Christians. In spite of the apparently mechanical way in which many were converted, a surprising number held their faith with fervor and tenacity. The missionaries forthrightly proclaimed the righteousness as well as the mercy of God, and considerable evidence exists that Japanese Christians took their ethical responsibilities very seriously.[35] Valignano reported in his *Sumario* of 1580 that in spite of the "many iniquitous customs and laws so unjust and contrary to natural reason," the Japanese, when they do become Christians, "leave off cultivating these vices and are much addicted to religion and the celebration of the divine cult." He considered Japanese Christianity already the finest in the East. Particularly was this true of the merchants and the peasants, and the majority of the converts were of the peasantry. As one of the missionaries put it, the farmers were like slaves, laboring always for the *samurai* and the Buddhist monks, and receiving for themselves only the worst of things. Reflecting Christian concern, the churches erected in many rural villages served as centers not only for worship but also for medical and other social services; they contributed greatly to the general elevation of rural life. In consequence the converts were highly respected by their non-Christian compatriots.[36]

---

[35]Okada, *op. cit.*, pp. 67, 74. Jesuit practice with regard to human slavery was less commendable. They had both free and bond servants among their domestics, drawing the latter from various Asian and African peoples. The majority of their free and salaried servants were Japanese, but apparently none of their slaves.

[36]Boxer, *op. cit.*, pp. 76, 79, 94, 228. There were considerable numbers of Christian merchants in both Sakai and Nagasaki, but one of the primary reasons for the smaller number of Christians among the merchant class was the missionaries' strong criticism of usury and the self-indulgent life of wealthy merchants. At the same time there were a few noteworthy examples of Japanese of this class who, after becoming Christians, released their debtors

Thus while the Christians expected practical advantages and even miracles from their faith, they strove mightily to fulfill the ethical responsibilities involved in that expectation. As we shall see, many were faithful to death. Their supreme reverence for the God who created the heavens and the earth and all life thereon made them able and willing to criticize the structures and practices of Japanese feudal society in so far as they were hurtful to human life. Deep also was their respect for the foreign padres. If they reflected too faithfully certain elemental medieval expressions of Christian faith communicated by their mentors, they crowned these practices with ethical zeal, social concern and purity of devotion hardly surpassed in the history of the Christian faith.[37]

The paucity of clergy in comparison with the growing number of Christians served to develop lay responsibility, leadership and appropriate organizational structures deeply rooted in the social as well as religious life of the communities. Where there was no priest, brother or *dōjuku* in residence, care of local churches was entrusted to a guardian who was called *kambō* and shaved his head; some of these were certainly married. These guardians served as readers for Sunday services, instructed children and catechumens, visited the sick, conducted funerals, baptized in cases of emergency and communicated with the priests as necessary.[38] In many cases the local churches were divided into smaller groups called *kumi,* which were in turn divided into several *kogumi* (child groups) and a smaller number of *oyagumi* (parent groups). Other groups were called *kō,* which probably designated the local branches of the confraternities or sodalities of which mention has been made. Each *kumi* had its own name, as *Santa Maria Kumi, Misericordia Kumi* or, taking the name from the day of the week on which it met (e.g. Friday), *Sesuta Kō.*

In a manner similar to the church in the Roman Empire, a single church consisted of distinct groups in a relatively ex-

---

from all obligations, and restored the high interest which they had previously demanded.

[37]Okada, *op. cit.,* pp. 65, 101, 173-174, 181-182.
[38]Cf. Furuno, *op. cit.,* p. 38; Jennes, *op. cit.,* pp. 114, 239-240.

tended geographical area. There thus coexisted intimate local fellowships with clear consciousness of wider relationships. The various *kumi* strove to deepen the faith of their members, co-operated in arranging for baptisms, weddings and funerals and encouraged one another by vowing to follow the Ten Commandments, particularly in avoiding adultery or the killing of unwanted children. There were also many examples of concrete help to people in every kind of need. One example is the aid given during the terrible crop failure in Yamaguchi which occurred in 1558. Cosme de Torres had rice purchased from a distant province and under the cover of night with great difficulty brought the food into the church and gave it to the hungry in large numbers. The Christians not only acted to relieve the needy in times of famine but took various preventive measures of saving and storage. They developed institutions also for the aged, widows and orphans without support, all to the astonishment of the non-Christians who could not believe that in this world there could be those thus concerned with the needs of the poorest in society.[39]

C. THE PERSECUTIONS: THEIR REASONS, EXTENT AND CONSEQUENCES

1

AS WE HAVE NOTED, THE CATHOLIC MISSIONARIES arrived in Japan in the middle of the sixteenth century at a time when, as a result of a long period of civil wars and increasing dissatisfaction with the political, social and religious conditions resulting from them, there was a spiritual and social openness perhaps unique in Japanese history. Deep-rooted forces of growing strength, however, were at work to bring

---

[39] *Tenka Tōitsu*, pp. 73-74.

unity and peace to the warring land; the merchants of Sakai and other centers of trade and industry were a considerable part of this effort. The person who first responded to the widespread yearning for unification was the *daimyō* of Owari, Oda Nobunaga (1534-1582). He was the son of a feudal lord of obscure antecedents who in the early sixteenth century had expanded his holdings and military strength at the expense of his neighbors to become a figure of power near the present city of Nagoya.

By bold and skillful strategy Nobunaga developed this heritage until he became one of the major lords of the land. The Ashikaga *shōgun* of the time, Yoshiteru, was killed after his palace had been set afire by attacking *daimyō*. In this situation the emperor Ōgimachi secretly appealed for help to Nobunaga in 1562 and again in 1567. The latter gradually extended his power in the direction of Kyōto and in 1568 occupied the city. Nobunaga installed Yoshiaki, the brother of Yoshiteru, as *shōgun* but deposed him when he tried to oppose his military protector. Nobunaga became the actual ruler of central Japan, aided in no small measure by his exceptionally able associates, his general Toyotomi Hideyoshi and his ally Tokugawa Ieyasu, each of whom came to succeed him in turn as supreme ruler.

The friendship of Nobunaga for the Catholic missionaries is a most interesting and in some ways most significant phenomenon of Japanese history. He nominally adhered to the Hokke or Nichiren sect of Buddhism but was apparently as close to being an agnostic as a man of the sixteenth century could be. He knew well the political and military activities of the Buddhist warrior monks; this was his primary reason for strong hostility to organized Buddhist militancy, and as ruler he attempted to suppress these threats to his power and the peace of the land. Because the monks of the great monastic center of Mt. Hiei in Kyōto had made an alliance against him with his enemies Asai and Asakura, he attacked their headquarters in September, 1571, and burned to the ground its more than four hundred buildings and killed the three thousand monks and villagers caught in the attack. Nobunaga's difficulties with the followers of the True Pure Land Sect (*Jōdo Shinshū*)

were of longer duration, largely because they were rooted in
legitimate aspirations of the lower classes for political and
social reform; in the provinces of Echizen (Fukui Prefecture)
and Kaga (Ishikawa Prefecture) where these believers of the
single mind (*Ikkō*) had achieved temporary political control,
farmers' taxes were cut in half.[1] After recourse to further frightful measures Nobunaga finally succeeded in breaking the military power of this sect in 1580 by the capture of their central
stronghold, the fortified monastery of Ishiyama in Ōsaka.

Through the good offices of Wada Koremasa, acting on the
request of Dario Takayama, the father of Ukon, Fr. Luis Frois
was presented to Nobunaga in April, 1569, in an interview of
momentous consequence. Frois was warmly received by this
autocrat who addressed the other lords and nobles of Japan
over his shoulder as if they were his inferiors and whom all
his subordinates greatly feared. Padre Organtino also enjoyed
the intimacy of this man, and the missionaries were soon given
legal as well as personal assurances of his favor. The significance of the situation is seen in the fact which we have previously noted, that the mass conversions in Kyūshū and
elsewhere began after these events. As G. B. Sansom has suggested, perhaps the reason for Nobunaga's friendship was that
an autocrat of his stamp could not afford intimacy with his
vassals; thus he welcomed the company of "men of strong
character and high attainments from whom he had nothing to
fear." His hatred of Buddhist activities doubtlessly also pre-
disposed him to friendship with the Christians.[2] Nobunaga
was clearly interested in learning of European civilization; he
respected both its men and its products, certainly its guns, but
he feared neither one.

When Nobunaga was urged by his advisors to refuse to receive Luis Frois, he scornfully rejected the advice on the grounds
that only a mean-spirited and narrow-minded man could
imagine that a single unarmed foreigner could disturb the
peace of the empire in a great city like Kyōto.[3] Japan was

[1] *Tenka Tōitsu, Nihon no Rekishi*, vol. 7, pp. 30-37.

[2] G. B. Sansom, *Japan, A Short Cultural History*, pp. 417-418. Cf. Miki
Tomokaze, *Nihon Katorikku Kyōshi*, pp. 101-104.

[3] C. R. Boxer, *The Christian Century in Japan*, p. 60.

then the greatest military power in East Asia even in its divided state; toward the end of his life Nobunaga even contemplated the invasion of China. No one in Japan as yet had any knowledge of the fact and methods of Portuguese or Spanish colonial expansion.

As a result of an unexpected revolt led by one of his generals, Akechi Mitsuhide, Nobunaga was caught unawares and committed suicide on June 21, 1582 by setting fire to the temple in which he and his officers were temporarily staying. At the time of Nobunaga's death, his leading general Toyotomi Hideyoshi was conducting a campaign against the great Mōri clan in the west. He retained command of his troops, and although he was for a time in considerable danger both from enemies and former allies, he was able to make a pact with Ieyasu and emerge as the real successor of Nobunaga. Hideyoshi was of the humblest social background; he was the son of a wood cutter and entered Nobunaga's service as a groom at the age of fifteen. His combination of extraordinary ability combined with bravery and martial skill, however, enabled him even in the aristocratic society of the Japan of his time to rise to the position of leadership which he held under Nobunaga.

Hideyoshi not only consolidated his power by eliminating his rivals one by one, but with consummate skill he continued the process of unification by a combination of alliances and military actions until in 1590 he had unified the entire country to an extent that it had never previously known. Because of his humble ancestry Hideyoshi could not receive the title of *shōgun*. In 1585, however, he obtained from Emperor Ōgimachi the office and title of *kampaku* (regent).

For some years Hideyoshi followed the policy of Nobunaga toward the Christian missionaries and the church. Like his predecessor, he was hostile to militant Buddhism. Fr. Valignano wrote in 1592 that Hideyoshi's severe methods of restriction reduced the number of monks residing in many temples from a hundred or more to but four or five. He was not above burning Buddhist images but was generally less iconoclastic in this matter than Nobunaga. His personal views on Christian faith were revealed in an informal visit to the church in Ōsaka during Holy Week of 1586; in his conversation with the Jesuits he compared the padres and their faith very favorably with the Buddhist monks and their beliefs. He then observed that the only thing that prevented him from becoming a Christian was the prohibition against having more than one wife. And, he added, "if you will stretch a point in this, I will likewise become a convert."[4]

This conversation should not be given undue weight, since Hideyoshi undoubtedly knew that the Jesuits would not yield on the ethical issue. But he was consistently friendly with the missionaries and came to know several with some intimacy. Furthermore, many earnest Christians were among his military leaders and in his personal service. Konishi Yukinaga was one of his most trusted generals. Takayama Ukon became chief of his household guard. Another high-ranking officer in this guard, Kuroda Yoshitaka, was baptized in 1583. Among the other figures of influence who became Christians were the distinguished scholar and court physician of Hideyoshi, Manase Dōsan, and Nobuo, a son of Nobunaga by a concubine. All in all, the missionaries had reason to view the future development of the church optimistically.

A high point of this era of good feeling was the interview which Hideyoshi granted to Vice-Provincial Gaspar Coelho on May 4, 1586, in his new castle in Ōsaka built on the site of the former Ishiyama (Honganji) castle. Among those who accompanied Coelho on this occasion were Takayama Ukon, Luis Frois, seven other Jesuits, fifteen *dōjuku* and six seminarians. Hideyoshi came down from the dais on which he was seated and through the interpreter Frois laughed and joked with the utmost intimacy, praising the missionaries for their disinterestedness in coming so great a distance to teach the Christian Law. He told them also of his ambition to leave a great name behind him after his death, and to achieve this he planned to bring Kyūshū completely under his power, especially the recalcitrant Shimazu of Satsuma, and to cross the sea with a large expeditionary force to conquer Korea and China. Hideyoshi then asked the padres to arrange for him to

[4] *Ibid.*, pp. 139-140. Cf. Miki, *op. cit.*, pp. 105-130.

charter two large Portuguese carracks for which he would generously pay.

At this point, Coelho made the kind of error of judgment which C. R. Boxer, borrowing a phrase from Talleyrand, characterizes as being worse than a crime. In 1580 Valignano had made a standing rule that missionaries should not interfere in local politics. Coelho, however, not only agreed to comply with Hideyoshi's request, but he promised to secure the aid of the Christian *daimyō* of Kyūshū to further the *Taikō's* (great leader) military plans there, and he promised other help from Portuguese India. At the moment Hideyoshi appeared grateful for the offer, but Valignano later stated that he must have thought to himself, "this father-provincial is very rich and influential. One day he will make war against me as did the abbot of the Ishiyama Honganji against Nobunaga."[5]

The Christian *daimyō* of Bungo in Kyūshū, Ōtomo Yoshishige, had suffered a severe defeat at the hands of Shimazu and had asked Hideyoshi for help. He and the other Christian *daimyō* were aghast when they heard of the vice-provincial's rashness. They were aware, as the Jesuit was not, that in the long-unsettled state of Japanese politics, no one attained or remained in power without being constantly alert and even suspicious of everyone. Quite likely Hideyoshi, like Nobunaga, had no fear of Iberian territorial aggression, even though the *Taikō* gradually came to have considerably more knowledge than his predecessor of the wider world and, in particular, of contemporary European colonial activities.[6] Both had constantly to be on the alert for local rebellions, especially from coalitions of hostile *daimyō*. Coelho's offer in fact implied missionary control over Christian *daimyō* which actually did not exist to the extent of the Jesuit's words, but which he had doubtless been led to assume because of both the great reverence of the Japanese Christians for the padres and certain aspects of European history. In any case, the possibility of Christian *daimyō* acting in concert was clearly revealed to Hideyoshi. Also present at this interview was the former Buddhist priest,

[5] Boxer, *op. cit.*, p. 141.
[6] Okada Akio, *Kirishitan Bateren*, pp. 98-99.

now personal physician to Hideyoshi, Seyakuin Zensō, a bitter foe of the Christian faith and its adherents.

Hideyoshi had already decided to intervene to bring peace in Kyūshū; he ordered his general Mōri to help Ōtomo immediately while he himself followed with a massive force of 130,000 men early in 1587. Before this combination of military power Shimazu retreated to his home base in Kagoshima, where he was compelled to surrender after a brief resistance.

In Hideyoshi's redistribution of the fiefs of Kyūshū after the campaign — which lasted but from February to May of 1587 — the Christian *daimyō* were exceedingly well treated. Ōtomo of Bungo refused with thanks the regent's offer of the fief of Hyūga, but Konishi Yukinaga, Kuroda Josui and Arima Harunobu all received additional land. The first two of these three stood particularly high in Hideyoshi's favor. All in all, the position and prospects of the Christian church in the land never seemed fairer. The blow, therefore, which fell on July 24 when Hideyoshi and his troops were resting in Hakata on their return trip to the capital seemed all the more stunning.

Hideyoshi earlier on that day had made a pleasant exchange of courtesies with Domingos Monteiro, the captain-major of a Portuguese carrack then in the port of Hirado. Later in the evening he was drinking Portuguese wine with a few of his intimates, among whom was his physician Seyakuin. The latter began to speak to the regent of Christian behavior which he considered reprehensible, particularly the undue deference of the Christian *daimyō*, and especially of Takayama Ukon, to the Jesuit padres. He also criticized the burning of Buddhist and Shintō temples by zealous Christian lords and the forcible conversion of their subjects to the faith. As Seyakuin proceeded with these points, Hideyoshi became, or pretended to become, more and more angry, until he sent a messenger to Ukon with the order to renounce his faith at once or be deprived of his fief and go into exile. Ukon, in spite of the pleas of his friends to seek some alternative, promptly replied that he would not renounce his faith and would submit to the consequences.

Hideyoshi then became utterly enraged, or simulated the same, and took steps to deprive Ukon of his fief. He next sent two messengers, one after the other, to awaken Coelho and to ask him four questions: why the padres desired so to make converts, even to the extent of using force, why they destroyed Shintō and Buddhist temples and persecuted the priests instead of compromising with them, why they ate useful animals such as horses and cows, and why the Portuguese bought Japanese people and exported them as slaves.

Coelho was of course completely taken aback by this entirely unexpected communication but at once tried to answer in as deferent and placating a manner as possible. He asserted that the missionaries themselves were only concerned to save souls and employed none but peaceful means, and that the destruction of temples was the work of zealous converts. With regard to the animals, the Portuguese, he averred, never ate horse flesh but occasionally consumed beef as is the custom in Europe, but they would refrain in the future if the regent so desired. The missionaries greatly deprecated the Portuguese slave trade in Japanese ports, but were powerless to forbid it since the trade took place on Japanese soil and the sellers were Japanese.

Hideyoshi made no direct comment to this reply but sent another messenger to notify Coelho of the sentence of exile which he had decreed against Takayama Ukon. The next morning, July 25, Hideyoshi appeared even more bitter against the Jesuits. He told the members of his entourage that the padres were "deceitful propagandists of a devilish and subversive creed." He compared them with the politically ambitious True Pure Land monks of Ōsaka, except that they were more dangerous. The followers of the *Ikkō* (Single-minded) Sect were mostly ignorant peasants, but the Christians had succeeded in winning many of the finest of the feudal aristocracy, who in turn were so submissive to their pastors that they formed a potential threat to the unity and safety of the empire.

These charges were followed by Hideyoshi's sending two more successive couriers to Coelho to notify him of the decree of banishment for the Jesuits, a copy of which was sent to Captain-Major Monteiro. In the language of the decree the only particularized charge stated was that in Japan, which is the land of the *Kami*, the padres converted people to their devilish creed and destroyed Shintō shrines and Buddhist temples. Portuguese merchants, however, or others coming from

India were not forbidden to enter Japan so long as they did not interfere with the laws of the Shintō and Buddhist deities.[7] Hideyoshi subsequently promulgated a series of anti-Christian edicts, including an order for all Japanese Christians to recant or face the alternative of exile or death. This latter order, however, he made no effort to enforce.

The Jesuits were astounded at these totally unexpected events and speculated, as have later historians, whether Hideyoshi's sudden change of manner and policy were premeditated, as he himself asserted at the time, or were the result merely of an autocrat's drunken caprice. There is some reason to believe that it derived from both factors. In support of the latter, after Hideyoshi arrived at Hakata, he desired a temporary concubine, and Seyakuin apparently offered to find a suitable girl. This territory, however, was that of a Christian *daimyō* and almost all of the inhabitants had become Christians. Although in the context of Japanese tradition and the feudal system it would have been considered an honor for a girl to be selected for this service, the Christian girls forthrightly rejected the request as immoral and evidently caused considerable embarrassment to Seyakuin and some annoyance to Hideyoshi.[8]

Furthermore, Hideyoshi made no attempt to enforce the letter of his anti-Christian edicts, including the purge of the missionaries, although he had full power to do so. Only three of the nearly one hundred and twenty Jesuits assembled at Hirado when the great ship arrived from Macao actually left the country. The rest went back to their various places, where they continued to work, although as unobtrusively as possible. This fact was of course reported to Hideyoshi.

Yet the clear formulation of reasons and the decisive nature of the action taken strongly suggest that Hideyoshi had turned these ideas over in his mind previously. It had been suggested by Buddhist priests, as Luis d'Almeida reported already in 1563, that the missionaries were merely the forerunners of Portuguese territorial aggression, and again in 1578 Luis Frois wrote that such rumors were widely circulated in Bungo.

[7] Boxer, *op. cit.*, pp. 145-149.
[8] Ebisawa Arimichi, *Kindai Nihon Bunka no Tanjō*, pp. 22-23.

Ōtomo Yoshishige and Nobunaga had ridiculed these notions as absurd, but they were repeated and of course known to Hideyoshi. The latter's military power was even greater than Nobunaga's, but then again the Christian movement had also progressed in the meantime, with a great increase of baptized believers. The most likely conclusion is that Hideyoshi, who, apart from Takayama Ukon, took no further action against Christian *daimyō*, was not seriously concerned over his position but felt that certain measures, not too severe, were in order to show his power and to check the remote possibility of unwise action by Christians in concert. He was concerned also to maintain the annual trade with Portuguese ships.

2

The great majority of the Jesuits weathered this storm by wise and discreet conduct. But some serious mistakes were made, and untoward events led to the final tragedy. The vice-general Coelho was so unsettled by the unexpected purge order that, contrary to the explicit instructions of Valignano, who was in India at the time, he strove to get Arima to persuade the Christian *daimyō* to unite in armed resistance against the order. Failing in this, he wrote to Macao, Manila and Goa asking for two or three hundred soldiers and firearms with which to back up his requests for military action. He got nothing from Manila; the Portuguese in Macao sent some arms but no troops. Valignano was exceedingly angry when he heard of these proceedings and sent the arms back to Macao when he arrived in Japan again in 1590, but it is very likely that some word of all this was brought to Hideyoshi by one or more of his many spies.

Valignano's return to Japan was made possible by a promise of safe-conduct from Hideyoshi, and the regent received the visitor general in Kyōto on March 3, 1591. He revealed that he would countenance the non-enforcement of his anti-Christian edicts if the Jesuits continued to act with subdued discretion and committed no overt iconoclastic acts against the older religions in Japan. The generosity and openmindedness of Hideyoshi were further symbolized by the singular trust which Hideyoshi had long placed in the Portuguese Jesuit whom he used frequently as his interpreter and confidant, João Rodriguez, named the "Tçuzzu" (*Tsūji*), or interpreter.

It is impossible for us to trace in detail the complex events which followed the halcyon days after the initial shock of the expulsion edict. We can only consider the outlines. The Christian community quickly recovered from its early fears, and its numbers increased daily, for Hideyoshi himself, defying his own order against *samurai* in his army wearing Christian insignia, was seen to walk about his palace of Juraku in Fushimi near Kyōto in Portuguese dress and wearing a rosary. But a series of events occurred which caused the political position of the Christians to worsen. And at the same time it must be noted that Hideyoshi's knowledge of the world outside of Japan steadily increased, including the geographical extent of the Spanish and other colonial empires.

One of the most significant events in the light of its subsequent effects was the coming of mendicant friars, Franciscan, Augustinian and Dominican, to the Japan Mission, the Franciscans from 1593 and the other two orders from 1602. The goal of all the early European traders and colonizers was to secure a monopoly of trade in any land. The Roman Catholic orders each preferred to have sole rights at least in specific districts, and a kind of comity policy was worked out for most areas of the world. Valignano in his *Sumario* of 1583 wrote why it was not convenient for other orders to come to Japan, citing especially the unfavorable impression of sectarian diversity that the different dress, customs and life style of other orders might give. Valignano was also afraid that the friars' experience with "inferior races" had unfitted them to deal with people of high culture like the Japanese. In consequence of his appeals and the approval of the general of the Society, Pope Gregory XIII in his bull *Ex Pastorali Officio* of January 28, 1585, forbade all other orders to undertake missionary work in Japan.

With the founding of Manila in 1571, the Spaniards became strongly established in the Philippines, and Manila soon came to rival Macao as a trading port. Trade and communications between Manila and Mexico greatly strengthened the former's strategic position and power. And although Valignano's views were firm, Coelho, when he wrote for military help from

Manila in 1584 and 1585, asked that Franciscans should be
sent to Japan because the number of Jesuits was insufficient.
Requests for Franciscan missionaries were also made by the
Christian *daimyō* of Hirado, Matsuura, in 1584, by another
group of Japanese Christians in 1587, and again by the Christian
adventurer Harada Magoshichirō in 1591 or 1592. The
last request was made sometime after Hideyoshi in 1591 had
sent his extraordinary letter to the Spanish governor of the
Philippines demanding that the governor recognize Hideyoshi's
sovereignty over the islands.

As a result of all these communications, representatives of
the religious orders in Manila met on May 18, 1593, and decided
that in spite of the Brief of Gregory XIII, the Franciscans
should initiate missionary work in Japan. Although stray
mendicants had come to Japan before, the first planned enterprise
followed in consequence of this decision, and a group
of Franciscans left Manila on May 30, 1593, under the leadership
of Fr. Pedro Baptista Blasquez, who served in the capacity
of ambassador and representative for the governor of the
Philippines. Anxious to have Spanish trade to relieve him of
sole dependence on the Portuguese, Hideyoshi, though arrogant
at first, offered an alliance of friendship and safe conduct
for Spanish trading vessels. He also granted the Franciscans
permission to go to Kyōto — he received them at Nagoya in
Hizen of Kyūshū — and promised them property there for
a church and a monastery.

The Franciscans received a suitable site and built a small
monastery in Spanish style and a church which opened on
October 4, 1594. Other Franciscans arrived as ambassadors and
remained as missionaries. Within a few months the friars built
a hospital for the poor next to the church and shortly afterward
another of the same size, with facilities for about fifty
patients. The financial means to build and maintain these
institutions were raised largely in Japan, apart from some support
given by the governor of the Philippines. Hideyoshi sent
some rice each year for the hospitals, and Hidetsugu, his
nephew, contributed both money and rice. Many Christians
of the Kyōto area (Gokinai) also made contributions, as did
Portuguese merchants in Nagasaki.

The anomaly of this situation was that while the Franciscans wore religious garb in public and carried on this relatively ostentatious work, the Jesuits in Kyōto felt compelled to labor almost in secret and with the utmost caution. The latter were horrified at what they felt was the friars' grievous lack of prudence, based on ignorance of the real situation in Japan. The friars in turn criticized the Jesuits for their alleged lack of concern for the poor and for their personal ungraciousness to themselves. These and other matters of dispute, all related to and sharpened by the political and commercial rivalry between the Portuguese and Spaniards, created a protracted state of animosity that harmed the mission.[9]

The next event of major importance was the so-called *San Felipe* incident. A Spanish ship of that name, richly laden and bound for Acapulco in Mexico from Manila, was driven ashore by a storm on October 19, 1596, and stranded at Urado on the coast of Tosa in Shikoku. According to Japanese law, all stranded vessels became the property of the government. The local lord, however, ordered nothing to be touched and urged the ship's captain to send an envoy to Hideyoshi, while he himself sent word separately recommending that the ship's cargo be confiscated.[10] Hideyoshi hesitated at first, concerned to maintain good commercial relations with Spain. He finally decided, however, to confiscate the cargo. The pilot-major of the ship protested the confiscation to Masuda Nagamori, the minister of Hideyoshi sent to Tosa to consummate the action. In the communications between the pilot-major and Masuda, the former, evidently with intent to impress if not to intimidate the Japanese, showed him on the map the colonial possessions of the king of Spain. Masuda then asked if Christian missionaries had prepared the way to obtain these possessions.

[9] Joseph Jennes, *A History of the Catholic Church in Japan*, pp. 74-82. Not all Jesuits were Portuguese nor Franciscans Spanish, but most of the two missions followed these national lines. Cf. Okamoto Yoshitomo, "Nihon Yasokai to Firippin no Shoshūdōkai to no Ronso," *Kirishitan Kenkyū*, vol. 3, pp. 225-319.

[10] Local *samurai* had evidently already appropriated much of the cargo, as the coastal inhabitants of any European country would have done. Boxer, *op. cit.*, p. 164.

The affirmative answer of the pilot was at once communicated to Hideyoshi and served to confirm his suspicions of the ultimate aims of the Christian missionaries.[11]

This incident, however, was by no means the only factor which moved Hideyoshi again to take decisive action against the Christians. As he clearly stated in his letter to the Philippine governor in 1597, he was piqued by the success of the missionaries, particularly the Franciscans in Kyōto, in winning adherents from the lowest classes of society. Other provocative factors were also at work. But the *San Felipe* incident was clearly the turning point, and from this time Hideyoshi's policy toward the missionaries became one of implacable but restrained hostility.[12] His first step was to order the arrest of all the Franciscans, foreign and Japanese, who were in Kyōto and Ōsaka. The consummation of this action was the public exposure and execution by crucifixion in Nagasaki on February 5, 1597, of a total of twenty-six, of whom twenty were Japanese and six Spaniards. Of the twenty Japanese, however, three were Jesuits; the seventeen Japanese Franciscans were apparently all laymen. The group later came to be known as the twenty-six martyrs of Nagasaki. We may note here that the twenty-six were proclaimed as martyrs by Pope Urbanus VIII on July 10, 1627; Pope Pius IX announced the canonization of the twenty-three Franciscans on December 23, 1861, and of the three Jesuits on June 8, 1862. The other Franciscan missionaries were forced to return to Manila. One month later Hideyoshi decreed the banishment of all Jesuit missionaries except Rodriguez Tçuzzu and two or three priests to minister to the spiritual needs of resident Portuguese traders. In 1598 large numbers of churches were destroyed in Hirado, Ōmura and Arima, as was the seminary in Arima, but Japanese Christians were as yet unmolested. This period of persecution, however, came to an end with the death of Hideyoshi on September 16, 1598.

11 Jennes, *op. cit.*, pp. 82-83.
12 Okada, *op. cit.*, pp. 114-115. Cf. Kataoka Yakichi, *Nagasaki no Junkyō-sha*, pp. 88-89.

3

Hideyoshi had been greatly concerned in his last days to insure the succession to power of his son Hideyori, who was only six years old, and appointed his foremost ally, Tokugawa Ieyasu, as chief of the regents to carry out this responsibility as well as the administration of the government. This plan, however, did not reflect the real division of power, and Ieyasu moved to consolidate and strengthen his position. Two factions developed, one consisting of Ieyasu and his supporters, the other of those aligned under the name of Hideyori. They resorted to arms, and the decisive battle was fought at Sekigahara (Gifu Prefecture) on October 21, 1600. The forces of Ieyasu won a complete victory.

Christian *daimyō* fought on both sides, although perhaps a larger number opposed Ieyasu. The outstanding Christian casualty was Konishi Yukinaga, one of the most loyal of Hideyoshi's generals, who supported Hideyori and was beheaded, because as a Christian he refused to commit suicide by *harakiri*. Ieyasu further strengthened his position and requested and obtained from the emperor in 1603 the title of *shōgun*. He set up his residence and administrative headquarters at Edo. the present site of Tokyo, which soon became the cultural as well as political capital of the land. In 1605 Ieyasu passed the formal title of *shōgun* to his son Hidetada, while he withdrew to build a new castle for his retirement at Sumpu, the present city of Shizuoka. He retained, however, the actual power, and all ultimate decisions apparently were referred to him until his death.

Ieyasu unified the country to a new degree of completion in furthering the aim of his two predecessors. After the final disposal of the supporters of Hideyori in 1615, Ieyasu refined the administrative system of his predecessors into a more effective instrument of control over the feudatories of the land. He divided the *daimyō* into the two categories of hereditary (*fudai*) and outer (*tozama*) nobles. The former were his traditional allies, and he placed them in the most strategic fiefs; the others were excluded from all administrative functions in the central government and compelled to live alternate periods

of six months in Edo and six months in their fiefs. The operation of the whole system rested upon unremitting surveillance,
based on suspicion and carried out by espionage. One aspect
of this program was that Ieyasu rigorously enforced the edict
of Hideyoshi that no *daimyō* might receive baptism.

Ieyasu, like Hideyoshi, promoted foreign trade and also
created a merchant marine so that Japanese ships and crews
might share in the process. He negotiated with Spanish and,
later, Dutch and English ships to participate in the Japan
trade, but as the trade with Macao through the Portuguese
remained the most important and profitable single enterprise
until 1609, he governed his policy toward the missionaries and
the church so as not to interfere with this trade route. His early
policy was for this reason more moderate than that of the later
Hideyoshi. He continued to use João Rodriguez as his interpreter with the Portuguese traders. A number of factors, however, caused the dictator to change this moderate religious
policy to a more severe repression of the church.

One factor was the incident of the *Madre de Deus*. The
crew of a red-seal ship of the Christian *daimyō* Arima Harunobu, while in port at Macao in late 1608, had behaved so
disorderly that they provoked armed action by the Portuguese
authorities.[13] Loss of life occurred on both sides, but those of
the crew who surrendered were released after signing a statement admitting full responsibility. The acting governor of the
city, Andrés Pessoa, landed in Nagasaki in July, 1609, as captain of the great ship of the year, the *Madre de Deus*. He at
once had the Macao statement sent to Ieyasu. The Japanese
ship, however, arrived in Nagasaki shortly after and reported
a different view of the incident. Both Arima and the administra-
trator (*bugyō*) of Nagasaki accepted the Japanese version and
reported that to Ieyasu. He then ordered Arima to seize the
ship and cargo and to arrest Pessoa. The Portuguese captain
refused to allow the Japanese to board his ship or to go himself to Shizuoka and explain his case to Ieyasu personally. When

---

[13] A document bearing a red seal was given those ships of Japanese or
foreign ownership which were officially licensed to engage in overseas
trade. Cf. Boxer, *op. cit.*, p. 261.

he attempted to set sail, the Japanese blocked his passage, and the fighting caused fire to break out on the ship. Pessoa ordered the torch put to the ship's powder store and went down with his ship and cargo. Ieyasu was greatly angered by the incident, especially because of the loss of the main trade of the year, but he took no further action at the time.

This bare recital of facts, however, needs to be amplified by reference to the conflicting interests, intrigues and mutual accusations which marked the relationships of competing European traders, Japanese merchants, and administrators in this and other affairs of the period. Evidently Ieyasu decided to risk the future of the Portuguese trade with his summary handling of the *Madre de Deus* because he was assured, while he tried to make up his mind, by the Spanish captain Don Rodrigo de Vivero y Velusco that the Spaniards could send, in lieu of the Portuguese, not one but two or three ships yearly.[14]

The Spaniards never in fact carried out this promise, but other prospects were at hand. The first English ship, the *Clove,* arrived at Hirado in 1613 and received permission to conduct regular trade. The major competitors of the Portuguese, however, were the Dutch. From the first years of the seventeenth century with their larger investments in ships and men, and methods that did not stop short of piracy, they greatly expanded their trade in the Far East and came in many places to supplant the Portuguese. This fact, combined with the increasing activity of Japanese-owned red-seal ships, led Ieyasu to believe that he could dispense with Portuguese trade and hence treat the missionaries as he wished. Spanish ships regularly had missionaries on board, but neither English nor Dutch had anything to do with Christian missions. As a symbol of this change of mind, Ieyasu replaced his Portuguese interpreter Rodriguez with the Englishman, William Adams, who was the pilot of the first Dutch ship to arrive in Japan (1600); he became one of Ieyasu's most trusted advisors in commercial and maritime matters. The further meaning of this event is that an Englishman with apparently no missionary concern

---

[14] *Ibid.*, p. 277.

took the place of the linguistically most skilled of Portuguese missionaries as the confidant of the supreme ruler.

From this point on the mutual accusations of the European traders before Ieyasu and other Japanese administrators deepened, perhaps more than any other single external factor, the suspicion of the autocrat and his advisors and led to the decisive step of the edict of persecution in 1614. After the arrogant envoy of the viceroy of Mexico, Sebastián Vizcaino, had been given permission by Ieyasu in 1611 to survey the east coast of Japan from Uraga northward to Sendai to determine the safety of the harbors for Spanish ships, Adams told Ieyasu that such a survey in Europe would be considered as preparation for a military invasion. Adams, the English factor at Hirado, Richard Cocks, and other Englishmen, apparently did everything they could to traduce before Ieyasu the Portuguese and Spaniards, their rivals both in trade and religious affiliation. The Catholics of course answered in kind and tried to have the Protestants excluded from Japanese trade, but their previous record of colonial activity was singularly vulnerable, especially for the Spaniards. The recurring theme of Protestant insinuation was that Roman Catholic missionary work was but preliminary action to territorial aggression.[15]

As a possible confirmation of these charges, we may note the letter dated December 18, 1610, which the Dutch king, Mauritius de Nassau, is supposed (*lettre supposé*) to have sent to the Japanese government; in this letter the king asserts that the Roman Catholic padres wear a cloak of piety but intend in fact to divide the body politic and create internal disorder. Clearly an important factor which influenced the mind of Ieyasu and his advisors in the *Bakufu* was the report of Richard Cocks that the Jesuits had been banished from England for political interference.[16] In short, the religious and political

---

[15] Okada, *op. cit.*, pp. 118-145. Cf. Hiyane Antei, *Nihon Kirisuto Kyōshi*, pp. 200-218.

[16] Okada, *op. cit.*, pp. 129-130, 134. *Bakufu* is the Japanese term used since the Kamakura period to denote the military government actually ruling the land. In this case it refers to the authorities in the administrative structure which had been created by Ieyasu and lasted until replaced by the Meiji Restoration of 1868.

rivalries of Europe were reflected most virulently in the Far East and greatly strengthened the determination of the feudal leaders to banish the missionaries and extirpate the Christian faith from the land.

A noteworthy consequence of the unique freedom which Japanese scholarship has enjoyed since the end of the Second World War is the consensus of historians of almost every school concerning the interpretation of the events of this period which we are considering. Perhaps without exception Japanese specialists in the field agree that the charges of hidden motives of territorial aggression leveled against the Roman Catholic missionaries by both Japanese Buddhists and Protestant Christians of the time, and later believed widely throughout the two hundred and fifty years of isolation, were almost entirely without foundation in fact. Nobunaga clearly feared no such possibility, and Hideyoshi, who was able to launch a massive invasion of Korea and contemplate the conquest of the Philippines, was clearly in no real danger from foreign aggression. Valignano in his *Sumario* of 1583 wrote that "Japan is not a place which can be controlled by foreigners, for the Japanese are neither so weak nor so stupid a race as to permit this, and the King of Spain neither has nor ever could have any power or jurisdiction here."[17] Ieyasu was more cautious than his predecessors, but his possession of military might was not less. The primary reason for Hideyoshi's initial hostility to the Christian movement, as well as that of Ieyasu and his advisors, was evidently not fear of external military aggression.

Japanese government and society had had long experience with militant Buddhist monks, but, devastating as were the ravages of these men in Kyōto and its larger environs, they had little significance beyond this area; their turmoil was primarily the expression of the ecclesiastical rivalries of monastics. Far more serious ideologically as well as militarily were the uprisings of the True Pure Land (*Jōdo-Shinshū*) Buddhists. Their monotheistic faith in transcendent Amida had enabled them to move beyond the traditional social, political and religious alignments of Japanese society. Their military

[17] Boxer, *op. cit.*, p. 157. Cf. Ebisawa, *op. cit.*, p. 34.

actions, nearly twenty of which took place in the sixteenth
century, often against professional soldiers and by no means
without success, were primarily movements of the underprivi-
leged segments of Japanese society. We have noted the savage
reprisals which both Nobunaga and Hideyoshi took against
these *Ikkō-ikki* (uprisings of the single-minded believers).
On the other hand, although Buddhism itself was a foreign
import, and, to Nobunaga and Hideyoshi, the Pure Land Buddhists were particularly obnoxious, the tradition over several
centuries was so indigenous that it was politically impossible
to reject it totally, as could be done to the more recently foreign Christian faith with its numerous and contemporary
foreign missionaries.

The unification and pacification of the land which all three
of the great dictators attempted was naturally conceived in
terms of traditional Japanese concepts of political and social
order. Throughout the history of Japan a strong and frequently
dominant trend had been to express and require loyalty to
that order in religiously ultimate terms.[18] In this context the
Pure Land Buddhists were perhaps the first in Japanese history
able to base their social criticism and movements of protest
upon theological rationale. The Christians were able with equal
theological justification to question all human pretensions to
absolute power. In the political and social mobility still characteristic of Nobunaga's rule, the issue did not come to the
fore; but as the Christian movement grew in number and
social momentum under the all-victorious Hideyoshi, it was
perhaps inevitable that this issue be raised. Far more than foreign invasion, therefore, Hideyoshi and Ieyasu feared an effective radical questioning of the principles of the feudal structure then being reconsolidated with new clarity and rigor.
These men clearly aimed at absolute power in the fullest sense
of the word, religious as well as political. Concretely, they
feared a coalition of Christian *daimyō* who, under the banner
of the transcendent God, could theologically question human
pretensions to absolute power and could presumably launch a

[18] Cf. Nakamura Hajime, *The Ways of Thinking of Eastern Peoples,*
p. 352; Sumiya Mikio, *Nihon Shakai to Kirisuto Kyō,* pp. 20-21; Okada,
op. cit., p. 181; Boxer, *op. cit.,* p. 338.

resistance movement of unified ideological power.[19] The Christian *daimyō* in fact never, so far as we know, intended to form such a coalition and movement, but in the context of the suspicion and intrigue characteristic of Japanese ruling circles, the very possibility caused grave concern. In any case, in this situation the notion of Spanish or Portuguese military participation was clearly of secondary concern.

From an early period the Christian faith furnished the instruments to criticize and reform the flaws of the emerging feudal order. The pope's religious authority over the kings and princes of Europe appeared symbolic of Christian qualification for all political rule. If Christian reverence for life and concern for all classes of society struck at the roots of feudal principles of social subordination, Christian apparent lack of concern for death nullified their ultimate sanctions.[20] The supreme and uncompromising reverence of Christians for their "foreign" God, as also their "undue" respect and deference to the foreign padres, were seen as wedges that perilously divided the religiously unqualified obedience to parents and feudal overlords which traditional Japanese society held as its ideal of life and social order and which the new central governments promoted with uniformity and thoroughness. Fear of Christian criticism of the structure and moral values of feudal society helped to develop the suspicion, hostility and subsequent repressive actions of Hideyoshi and his successors.[21]

The result of this process, which in fact took several decades to mature, was the edict of persecution promulgated on January 27, 1614. Other incidents and factors confirmed Ieyasu in his determination, which he had already expressed in a letter sent to the Spanish viceroy of Manila in 1612, first to end all Christian missionary work in Japan, and then to extirpate the

---

[19] Cf. Boxer, *op. cit.*, pp. 311, 332-338; Ebisawa Arimichi, *Kirishitanshi no Kenkyū*, pp. 15-39, 128-184.

[20] At the same time, Christian rejection of the *samurai*'s privilege of *hara-kiri (seppuku)* as sinful suicide was seen as a flagrant offense to feudal standards of value.

[21] Okada, *op. cit.*, pp. 142, 181-182. This fact comes out with particular clarity in the *Refutation of Deus (Ha-Deus)* which the apostate Jesuit *dōjuku* Fabian Fukan published in 1620. Cf. Boxer, *op. cit.*, pp. 337-338; Miki, *op. cit.*, pp. 149-189.

faith from his subjects. Ieyasu's suspicions were strengthened by the hostility to Christianity of a number of his advisors, the Zen monk Suden, the Confucianist scholar Hayashi Razan, the administrator (*bugyō*) of Nagasaki, Hasegawa Sahyōe, as well as by the anti-Catholic posture of William Adams. A few Christians, although by no means typical, were implicated in certain political intrigues, and this fact greatly antagonized Ieyasu. The mass demonstrations of thirty thousand Christians who gathered to pray and sing hymns in the presence of their fellow believers being burned alive in Kyūshū on October 7, 1613 under the young *daimyō* Arima Naozumi, also disturbed the autocrat. The report of this event, where the Christians were grouped in successive and orderly rows according to their confraternities, furnished additional confirmation to Ieyasu that Christianity was a potentially subversive religion. According to the text of the edict itself, the gathering of Christians to pray at the execution of their fellow believers was interpreted as wanton approval of that which is evil and illegal.[22]

4

Persecutions, as we have seen, began already in the last years of Hideyoshi's reign. After the *Taikō's* death, however, the missionaries generally returned to their stations, and in the next two years remarkable progress took place especially in the domains of the Christian *daimyō*. In southern Higo, the fief of Konishi Yukinaga, mass conversions took place. Baptisms for the entire Japan Mission over the two years 1598-1599 numbered seventy thousand, according to a letter of Bishop Cerqueira. After Konishi's death in the brief civil war, however, his successor, Katō Kiyomasa, vigorously persecuted the new converts. Many apostatized, others went into exile, a few were executed for their faith. The Christian community in that territory was cut to less than half, only about twenty thousand being left in 1603.

But Ieyasu took no action against the missionaries after the

---

[22] Jennes, *op. cit.*, pp. 124-128; Boxer, *op. cit.*, pp. 315, 330.

civil war. In fact, he issued in 1601 official patents legalizing the churches of Nagasaki, Kyōto and Ōsaka and directed that the churches of Arima and Ōmura be left unmolested. In consequence, from 1601 on the church in Japan enjoyed for over a decade more freedom and prosperity than it had known for years. Since ruling *daimyō* were now strictly forbidden to receive baptism, the period of mass conversions was over, and local persecutions did occur. Nevertheless, the number of both Japanese and foreign missionary personnel reached its height in this first decade of the seventeenth century. Never were the workers more experienced and better organized to do the most effective catechetical and pastoral work. New missions opened at Hiroshima, Yamaguchi and Shimonoseki in the fief of the Mōri clan. Effective work continued to be done in central Japan. Consequently an average of five thousand baptisms was reported each year, and the Christian communities had more thorough instruction and deeper corporate as well as individual experience in the Christian life than they had known before. The deep roots of the faith in these communities are important to understand their response to persecution, which was increasingly severe after 1614. By this latter date the most influential Christian *daimyō* were dead, and the younger Arima Naozumi and Ōmura Yoshiaki had apostatized. Christians were then without political support, and their response had no other support than their faith.

The Edict of 1614 directly charged the Christians with intent to change the government and to obtain possession of the country. It also proclaimed the necessity of expelling the foreign missionaries and of extirpating the faith from Japanese soil. To implement the edict the *daimyō* were ordered to send all foreign and Japanese professional religious personnel to Nagasaki pending their deportation to Macao or Manila, to destroy all Christian churches, and to compel Japanese Christians to renounce their faith and return to the ancient religions of the land. An important element of the later enforcement procedure was that the local Buddhist priesthood was to supervise certain aspects of the religious life of every Japanese. For the first time in the history of Japan, each individual was compelled to belong to a specific Buddhist temple, which be-

came his family temple *(danna-dera)*, and to possess a document which certified this *(tera-uke)*. The chief priest of each
temple was to evaluate the religious conformity of his parish-
ioners to the authorities several times a year. Buddhist priests
in effect became government spies.

On November 7 and 8, 1614, four ships carried the bulk of
the clergy and religious, both Japanese and foreign, to Macao
and Manila. Some missionaries, however, had gone into hiding
shortly after the edict, and others had managed to escape em-
barkation to Nagasaki. In all, thirty-eight priests (eighteen
Jesuits, seven Dominicans, seven Franciscans, one Augustinian
and five of the diocesan clergy) remained in Japan to serve
the troubled Christian communities. By the end of 1614, apparently all of the churches and related buildings had been
either destroyed or closed. From this point, the government concentrated on measures to cause Japanese Christians to return
to their native religious traditions.

Leading Christians like Takayama Ukon, Naitō Tadatoshi
and their families were deported with the missionaries, some
to Manila and some to Macao. Other prominent Christians
of Kyōto and Ōsaka were sent into exile in the northern province of Tsugaru (Aomori Prefecture). In other places the Christians were brought together in a Buddhist temple and urged
to join one of the Buddhist sects like all other Japanese.
Ieyasu was opposed to shedding blood to carry out his directives, and except for some executions and tortures in Bungo
and Arima, violent measures were generally not employed. In
Ieyasu's final military action against the son of Hideyoshi,
Hideyori, Christians were in the armies of both sides; this
shows the fluidity of the situation. They were more numerous,
however, in the army of Hideyori and there boldly displayed
their banners bearing images of the cross, the Christ and Santiago. Since the effective rule of the *Bakufu* was still limited
geographically, as persecutions of Christians intensified in central Japan the mission was extended into the northern provinces of Honshū from Sendai and from the exiles in Tsugaru.
Indeed, a number of new Franciscan missionaries arrived in
1618 and 1620 and worked with considerable success in this
northern area. The Jesuits also had important mission stations

in Ōshū north of Sendai. In other areas, in spite of the persecutions, churches continued to grow, and in the years from 1617 to 1621 the Jesuits alone reported as many as two thousand baptisms a year.

In connection with northern Honshū, mention should be made of a second important embassy from Japan during the period of *Kirishitan* activity. The son of Ieyasu, Hidetada, as acting *shōgun,* arranged to send the Franciscan Luis Sotelo as his envoy to the king of Spain in order to consummate the commercial treaties with Spain, the Philippines and Mexico which Ieyasu himself evidently desired. Sotelo was also to serve as the personal envoy to the pope of Date Masamune, the powerful *daimyō* of Mutsu (the area about Sendai), who evidently had plans to enrich his fief through foreign trade. Sotelo left Uraga on this mission on October 3, 1612, but the ship on which he sailed was wrecked the same night, and he barely escaped with his life. Sotelo was then condemned to death in the persecution of Christians that was initiated in Edo in August of the following year. He was saved from this danger by Masamune, who still wished to use the Franciscan as his envoy. Shortly thereafter, on October 28, 1613, Sotelo left Japan, together with the Japanese Hasekura Tsunenaga, as the envoy of Masamune to the king of Spain and the pope. Their party consisted of 150 Japanese, and they landed in Acapulco, Mexico, on January 25, 1614.

The fact that seventy-eight members of the party were instructed in the Christian faith in Mexico and baptized there indicates that many of the Japanese in the party, and possibly to a certain extent Masamune himself, had sincere religious interests. The two envoys, however, went on to Europe accompanied by only twenty-eight Japanese, while the others returned to Japan. Hasekura was himself baptized in Madrid while staying at the court of King Philip III. The envoys and their party were received by Pope Paul V in solemn audience on November 3, 1615. On this occasion the letter of Date Masamune to the pope was publicly read and presented to the pontiff. The essence of Masamune's letter was a request that the pope send religious men of the Franciscan Order to his territory and appoint a prelate for the pastoral care and direction of all Christians there. Masamune promised to provide the financial support necessary for this work.

Another letter written by 116 Japanese Christians of the Kyōto and Ōsaka area, evidently persons associated with Franciscan work, was read to the pope in a private audience the following month. The most significant request contained in this letter was that instead of only one bishop in Japan, who resided in distant Nagasaki and did not know the language of the land, bishops who knew the language and customs of Japan be appointed from each religious order serving in Japan and one be appointed archbishop over the others. Both of these letters clearly reflect the intent of Sotelo and Franciscan partisan interests, but they also show that even at this late date some in other parts of Japan wished to repeat the procedures employed by influential *daimyō* in Kyūshū a generation earlier.

There is reason to believe that Paul V took these letters with the utmost seriousness and even promised to appoint Sotelo as archbishop of Japan with four suffragans under him. However, this plan could not then be effected apart from the advice, in effect the approval, of the Spanish king and the Council for the Indies; and since the resident Bishop Cerqueira and the Jesuits were opposed, nothing came of the matter. In fact, Hidetada's edict of banishment was promulgated on January 27, 1614, only two days after the Hasekura-Sotelo party had arrived in Acapulco, so the entire embassy had no practical effect upon the course of events in Japan. This event is significant, however, in revealing the continued openness to Christian witness and foreign contacts in other parts of the country, even after the strongest expressions of disapproval had been manifested by the central rulers. Japan had by no means yet been welded into effective political and spiritual unity.

Ieyasu died in July, 1616; after his death Japan came under the rule of a succession of men who lacked the personal greatness and statesman-like qualities that kept both Hideyoshi and Ieyasu from carrying out the full logic of their anti-Christian policies. Hidetada had possessed the title of *shōgun* since 1605, but when he came to hold full power after his father's death, he lacked the latter's sense of the importance of foreign trade to Japanese economic prosperity, and he favored a more vigorous course of persecutions. His neurotic son Iemitsu, who succeeded him as *shōgun* in 1623, carried this policy to even more frightful lengths.

In September, 1616, Hidetada promulgated a new decree whereby any Japanese men, women or children who offered refuge or shelter to foreign missionaries would be subject to penalty of death. In order to insure full control of all foreigners in Japan, he decreed the limitation of all foreign trade to the two ports of Nagasaki and Hirado and a strictly supervised trip once a year to Edo. Apart from the earlier martyrdom of foreign missionaries among the twenty-six at Nagasaki in 1597, no foreigners had been put to death during Ieyasu's lifetime. Hidetada made no such distinction and approved the execution of missionaries as well as Japanese Christians who refused to recant. The great number of martyrs, however, during his rule consisted of *dōjuku* and *kambō* who remained faithfully at work and those laymen who had tried to help imprisoned missionaries or to obtain relics of the martyrs.[23] The number of those martyred until 1622 did not exceed one hundred a year, and even in that year, which included the famous Great Martyrdom of Nagasaki (September 10, 1622), the figure was only slightly more than 120.[24]

The terror created by these events, however, can be better imagined than described. Yet in this period no record exists of mass defections, although considerable numbers of families and small groups renounced their faith. Apparently a much higher proportion of commoners (merchants, artisans and especially farmers) than of the *samurai* remained faithful to death.[25] The sodalities and confraternities established by the missionaries were singularly effective in preparing the Christians to keep their faith under fear of death and torture.

Under Iemitsu torture was employed in its most exquisite forms, and the *shōgun* appeared to take a "personal if sadistic" interest in the proceedings which neither his father

[23] The government considered Christian reverence for relics to be particularly offensive to feudal mores.

[24] Jennes, *op. cit.*, pp. 142-144.

[25] Boxer, *op. cit.*, p. 339.

nor his successors showed. In consequence of his policy, persecution spread rapidly to all parts of the country. Previously those *daimyō* who had little taste for persecution could and did confine themselves to minimal acts of restraint, but now in the light of Iemitsu's attitude, it became impossible to do anything but participate actively in his program. In spite of these most unfavorable circumstances, however, converts continued to enter the church. The Jesuits reported baptisms of fifteen hundred in 1624, eleven hundred in 1625 and about two thousand in 1626.[26] These were the last statistical reports in the communications of the missionaries, since the years 1627-1634 were the most frightful of all the years from the beginnings of persecution, both as to the number of victims and the atrocity of the tortures inflicted upon them. Especially were the Christians concentrated in Kyūshū subjected to a veritable reign of terror.

The intent was almost always to induce the Christians to apostatize, and at first less ultimate methods were used, such as deprivation of property and employment. Others were driven from their homes and compelled to live in the hills until many died of hunger and exposure. Only the relative failure of these methods led to the use of torture.

In the fiefs of Nagasaki and Arima some of the most terrible methods came to be used, with the objective always not to kill, but to force the most steadfast Christians to recant in order that the rest would follow their example. Branding, burning at the stake, and sawing off limbs with a bamboo saw were some of the devices employed. Victims with one or more fingers cut off were paraded through the villages naked. The *daimyō* of Arima, Matsukura Shigemasa, tortured and finally executed about forty Christians in the hot sulphur springs of Mount Unzen in Shimabara Peninsula in 1627 and 1628. The next year, he had hot water from these springs poured into incisions of the flesh of the Christians, while a physician stood by to treat the wounds so that the process might be repeated if the victims did not recant. This method was so effective that in August, 1624, when sixty-four Christians, of whom

---

[26] Jennes, *op. cit.*, p. 153.

twenty-seven were women, were subjected to this torture for several days, all but one or two apostatized. In the same year, over seventy Christians were beheaded but without torture at Yonezawa in the present Yamagata Prefecture in northern Honshū.

The records report other forms of torture, some of which were evidently new to Japan. The Japanese historian Anesaki Masaharu supposed that some kinds may have been suggested to the authorities by apostate Christians who were acquainted with stories of the persecutions of the Roman Empire. A unique form of torture, however, was that of the *ana-tsurushi*, or pit-suspension. This method was first used in 1633, particularly for missionaries, *dōjuku* and those Christians known as most zealous. In this device the victim was suspended head-downwards from a crossbeam into a pit which usually contained excretions and other filth, the top of the pit being level with the knees. The forehead was slashed to give vent to the victim's blood. Some of the stronger survived more than a week; most, however, did not last more than a day or two.

This method of *ana-tsurushi* became popular with the authorities when on October 18, 1633, Fr. Christovão Ferreira, the aged Jesuit provincial, recanted after five hours of this torture. Yet one Japanese young woman endured it for fourteen days before she died a martyr. These methods compelled a large number of Christians to apostatize, but to the chagrin of the authorities an astonishing number refused to recant and witnessed to their faith to the end. The English factor at Hirado, Richard Cocks, described the scene which he saw by the Kamo River in Kyōto in October of 1619: fifty-five persons of all ages and both sexes were burnt alive, and among them were little children of five or six years of age in their mothers' arms, who cried out with the adults, "Jesus receive our souls."[27]

C. R. Boxer has properly reminded us that the methods employed were little different from those used in contemporary Europe by Catholics and Protestants upon each other or upon the Jews. Indeed, it is unlikely that in Europe the demonstra-

[27] Boxer, *op. cit.*, pp. 349-350.

tions of sympathy would have been allowed which were still seen in Japan in the early years of the second decade of the seventeenth century. The most remarkable of these scenes was at the burning of the missionaries Pedro Zuñiga and Luis Flores, who had tried to enter Japan in 1620 but were captured by the English and handed over to the Dutch, who in turn delivered them to the Japanese authorities. The two men were burned alive with the Japanese captain of the red-seal ship on which they had come. The event was witnessed by a great crowd of at least thirty thousand people, who began to sing the *Magnificat,* followed by the psalms *Laudate pueri Dominum* and *Laudate Dominum omnes gentes.* When death came to the martyrs, the crowd intoned the *Te Deum Laudamus.* Other instances are reported where Christians in great throngs surrounded the martyrs without demonstration of hostility toward the authorities and upon their knees chanted the Apostles' Creed, the Lord's Prayer, Ave Maria and other prayers.[28]

During the years 1623-1637 the number of Christians martyred for their faith was somewhat under thirteen hundred. From 1614-1643, except for the loss of life in the Shimabara rebellion, which we shall consider next, the estimate of the number of martyrs varies from two to five thousand, of whom less than seventy were European. The number of clergy and religious personnel, Japanese or foreign, who apostatized was exceedingly small. Among the laity, although there were many examples of extraordinary heroism, the threats of torture and execution caused increasingly large numbers to recant. Evidence, however, indicates that most, perhaps the very great majority, of the "recantations" were only verbal and that the Christians continued to hold their faith and in many cases to transmit it to their children. The church, as we shall see, went "underground."

Thus the *bugyō* of Nagasaki, Mizuno Kawachi, was able in 1627 by using the most extreme measures of torture to compel 370 out of a total of four hundred to recant, Fray de San Francisco reported in November, 1629, that of the Christians

---

[28] *Ibid.,* pp. 342-343.

of Nagasaki about a thousand had fled the city but that of the remaining ten thousand families all but two hundred had recanted. Earlier, however, in 1615 Fr. João Rodriguez Girão reported from a census taken in Nagasaki in that year that the local population had decreased by twenty thousand in comparison with the statistics of two years previously. Since the number of martyrs for these two years was less than two hundred and there is no record of mass apostasies, the drop in population clearly indicates that large numbers of Christians fled to other parts of Japan, especially to the northeast, as we have seen.[29] Other evidence also confirms this. In short, the great bulk of the Christians responded over the years to the pressures and persecutions of the authorities by using every method they could to avoid apostasy. Only when every other recourse but death by torture was closed did they recant, and that was mostly verbal. The Christian faith rooted unbelievably deep in a large segment of the Japanese population and, to the astonishment and consternation of the authorities, had created heroes of steadfastness out of men, women and children belonging to classes hitherto despised and scorned.

Brief mention must also be made of the heroic role of the Japanese and European clergy and religious during the period from 1614-1637. In the early years from 1615-1619, the instructions given to the believers was that concealment of the faith was a mortal sin. This followed perhaps in some measure the relative restraint shown by the authorities in the execution of Ieyasu's edict, especially in the largest concentration of Christians at Nagasaki. Various works, such as the *Exhortations to Martyrdom,* were written from 1615 onwards to encourage the faithful to stand firm. The glories of martyrdom and the supernatural aid of God were stressed, as well as the spiritual danger of cherishing any evil thought toward judge, torturer or executioner. That these instructions were widely accepted with the utmost seriousness is evident both from the number of martyrs and the complete absence of

---

[29] *Ibid.,* pp. 352, 353. For a detailed account of the *Kirishitan* in the northeast, see Urakawa Wasaburō, *Tōhoku Kirishitanshi.*

force, even when the Christians who were assembled at scenes of executions greatly outnumbered the government representatives and soldiers.

After the mass apostasies forced by the commissioner of Nagasaki in 1626-1630, the Christian movement went "underground" completely, and almost all subsequent perseverance in the faith was in secret. But from 1614-1637 the constancy of Christians was nourished and strengthened especially by two institutions. One was the religious confraternities, which to some extent coincided at the local level with the *gonin-gumi,* or groups of five households. The other institution was the clergy and religious. European missionaries as well as Japanese co-workers were passed on secretly from one group of Christians to another, usually at night, throughout all of Japan. The Europeans traveled in disguise, sometimes as women, and certainly, as C. R. Boxer says, with sublime audacity. Through the *gonin-gumi* the Christian "underground" was also able to circulate news, letters and other communications, sending some of its reports to the pope. This was the structure which enabled the church to survive in secret for more than two centuries even when all clergy, both Japanese and foreign, were gone.

In all, the maximum figure for the martyrs for the period 1614-1637 was between five and six thousand. This number constituted perhaps two percent of the whole, but probably neither the brutality of the methods employed nor the heroic constancy of the victims has ever been exceeded in the sad history of such events in all human history. The proportion of martyrs in comparison with the total Christian population is probably greater than that of any other period or place in the history of the church, including in the Roman Empire. Furthermore, it must be remembered that by 1614 almost all of those who had become Christians for political or other non-religious reasons had already left the church. A large proportion of those who recanted did so only under duress, from direct pain or fear of torture. The fact that their apostasy was but external is indicated by the reappearance of nearly thirty-seven thousand Christians in the Shimabara rebellion of 1637-1638 and the discovery of hidden Christians

(*Kakure-Kirishitan*) communities in all but eight of the sixty-six provinces of Japan in the following two decades.[30]

5

The final event to note in this period of persecution is the Shimabara rebellion of 1637-1638. Christian faith was, as we have seen, generally understood by the conservative ruling groups as subverting the feudal Japanese expectation of loyalty to one's social superiors transcending every other obligation in heaven or on earth. But Christians were taught to respect and obey, as much as was religiously possible, legally constituted authority. The missionaries had also expressly taught that only by passive resistance could Christians gain a martyr's crown. The Christian communities were thus considerably less disposed to resort to armed resistance than the Pure Land Buddhist groups of the sixteenth century. Only extraordinary circumstances could have led to military activity in the Shimabara Peninsula of northwestern Kyūshū.

The evidence is strong that the primary reason for the uprising was economic and political oppression. The *daimyō* of the fief of Amakusa from 1633 was Terazawa Katataka, a profligate whose personal excesses were equalled only by his rapacity and his cruel methods of exacting taxes from the peasants. Matsukura Shigeharu, the lord of Shimabara, was similar, "stopping at nothing to exact the last grain from his tenantry."[31] The particular incident which sparked the revolt was an example of this policy. The daughter of one of the leading farmers was stripped naked and burnt with flaming torches by a tax collector. The farmer and a few of his neighbors killed the official and his helpers. The whole vil-

---

[30] Boxer, *op. cit.*, p. 361. Cf. Josef Schütte, "Genwa Sannen (1617 nen) ni okeru Nihon Kirishitan no Shu na Shūdan to sono Minkan Shidōsha," *Kirishitan Kenkyū*, vol. 4, pp. 3-18. Note may be taken that the name Shimabara is pronounced in Kyūshū as "Shimabaru," and the Hara of Hara no jō as "Haru."

[31] Boxer, *op. cit.*, p. 377. A more detailed account of the Shimabara rebellion, drawn primarily from Japanese sources, may be found in M. Paske-Smith, *Japanese Traditions of Christianity*, pp. 49-100. Cf. also Ebisawa, *Kirishitanshi no Kenkyū*, pp. 189-202.

lage immediately rose en masse in support, and as the news spread, the rest of the district followed in a general insurrection which began in December, 1637.

Not all the insurgents were Christians, but the movement speedily took on a religious character which all seemed to share once it had begun. The participants openly proclaimed their Christian faith and their determination, if need be, to die for it. They used banners with Portuguese inscriptions such as *"Louvado seia o Santissimo Sacramento"* (Praised be the most Holy Sacrament) and shouted the names of Iesus, Maria and Santiago in their attacks. The rapidity with which the revolt spread from Shimabara to Amakusa suggests that at least some anticipation of such an event existed. A young man of eighteen named Masuda Shiro, the son of one of Konishi's *samurai*, was chosen as commander, but the real leaders seem to have been five or six *rōnin* of mature military experience.[32] Very few weapons were available at first, apart from farming tools, but a few thousand weapons were gained by the utter rout of the first small punitive contingents of *samurai* sent against them.[33]

After their initial success, the insurgents in Amakusa and Shimabara tried to capture the castles of Tomioka and Shimabara, respectively. Failing in these efforts, they joined forces in Shimabara and, learning that more government troops were being sent, they decided to concentrate all their forces of about twenty thousand men with seventeen thousand women and children in Hara no jō, the abandoned castle of the former *daimyō* of Arima, which was surrounded on three sides by the sea and perpendicular cliffs and on the fourth separated from the land by a large swamp.

The government in Edo became alarmed as successive re-

---

[32] The term *rōnin* was used to designate the masterless *samurai* who had lost their position as a result especially of the many changes of fiefs since the time of Hideyoshi; many had served under *daimyō* who fought against Ieyasu at Sekigahara. Some formed themselves into outlaw bands that terrorized the countryside, but many became farmers distinguishable from the peasantry only by their indelible consciousness of past social status and military skills.

[33] Boxer, *op. cit.*, pp. 378-379.

ports were brought of the religious as well as economic aspect of the rebellion. Although not a *daimyō* of the highest rank, Itakura Shigemasa was given full power to levy troops from all the fiefs of Kyūshū; eventually he mustered fifty thousand *samurai*. The Christian forces had few trained men — only about two hundred *rōnin* and a few hundred commoners capable of using matchlocks. As long as their ammunition lasted, however, this handful of *samurai* and poorly armed commoners were able to worst the invaders in every kind of encounter. The *Bakufu* then replaced Itakura with Matsudaira Nobutsuna, a member of the Great Council, and dispatched additional forces. Before Matsudaira's arrival, Itakura was killed in a second major attack on February 14, 1638, which was again repulsed with great loss of life. Matsudaira then decided to dig in for a long siege, with the intent to starve out the defending garrison rather than to engage his approximately one hundred thousand men in a direct attack. The Dutch were asked to help by bombarding the castle from the ship *De Ryp*, which they sent from Hirado.[34]

By early April, it was apparent from the reports of deserters and from the bodies of the slain that the besieged were in desperate need of food and that their ammunition was exhausted. A general attack was made on April 12th, and although the first assault failed, a second attack a few minutes later broke the outer of the three circles of defense. Two more days, however, were necessary to overcome the last remnant of fighting men, who used even cooking utensils in lieu of better weapons. By April 15th every man, woman and child had been killed, the only exception being an ex-*dōjuku* painter who had apostatized some years before and was apparently a government supporter.

The astonishing bravery and military prowess of Christian peasants and a handful of old *rōnin* against the best troops that the *Bakufu* could muster shocked the government leaders.

---

[34] The Dutch probably complied only with reluctance; after doing minor damage, they were dismissed. The government forces were not able to endure the mockery of the defenders, who shot messages into their lines about the brave *samurai* who had to call upon the aid of foreigners against peasants.

A reassessment of policy was made with the consequence that previous ambitions, such as the projected invasion of the Philippines, were abandoned or revised. Iemitsu apparently felt that the Portuguese must have been involved in some way in the rebellion, and the decision was made to close all trade involving the Portuguese.[35] Trade with Manila and the Spaniards had been prohibited for over twenty years; the commercial activities of Japanese red-seal ships had more recently been forbidden. With the exception of severely limited trading allowed the Chinese and the Dutch at Nagasaki, Japan cut off all intercourse with foreign nations and became a closed country *(Sakoku)*.

The remaining Christians went completely "underground." In March, 1623, there had been thirty-three or thirty-four priests, both Japanese and foreign, in Japan. Over the next decade and a half about fifteen priests, including several Japanese from Manila, managed to reach Japan. Most were captured and executed. By 1638 apparently no more than five had managed to survive, and these, again both Japanese and foreign, were all captured in the north and tortured at Edo in 1639. One of the Japanese Jesuits died from *anatsurushi,* and two Franciscans were burned alive. Two Jesuits, one Japanese and one European, recanted under torture, but died a few years later in prison. The Japanese "underground" church had to carry on without the assistance of clergy for more than two centuries.

---

[35] No foreigners were found at Hara no jō after its fall, nor any priests, Japanese or foreign.

D. THE *SEMPUKU KIRISHITAN* (HIDDEN CHRISTIANS)

1

THE CLOSURE OF THE COUNTRY, AN EXTREME MEASURE, motivated primarily by fear of Christian contacts and influences, had consequences for the life of the nation far beyond that of the suppression of Christianity. A government office was established in 1640 to institute a kind of permanent religious inquisition.[1] As we have noted, the chief local agents to enforce the Anti-Christian Edict of 1614 were the Buddhist priests. Part of their responsibility in visiting every family in their parish during the *o-Bon* festival in the seventh lunar month was to look for any indications of Christian faith or practice. Although the fulfillment of this duty apparently varied widely according to time and place, the policy was at least formally in force until 1868. The effect upon Buddhism as a religious force for good in the nation was little short of disastrous.

Buddhist priests in effect became government spies, and if Christianity was almost completely eliminated, Buddhism was largely emasculated; feudal values reigned supreme. In spite of lip service to Buddhism, the *Bakufu* increasingly encouraged and drew upon Confucian studies to support the ideology of its regime. Even the Pure Land Buddhists, the former major threat, both theological and practical, to the feudal concept of the absolute superiority of political authority, were in effect sociologically broken. Their movement became one of the chief bulwarks of the power structure of Japanese society, with a hereditary hierarchy and close ties with the imperial family. In consequence of the *Bakufu* policy of seclusion and religious inquisition, the quality of religious faith and life of the common people degenerated gravely.[2]

[1] This office was called *Kirishitan-shūmon-aratame-yaku,* or Office for Investigation of Christians.

[2] Okada Akio, *Kirishitan Bateren,* pp. 147-148. Kagawa Toyohiko wrote in 1934 that in his youth, thirty years before, he had failed to find in the Buddhism of that day a single Buddhist priest who commanded his respect.

Their chief, perhaps their only recourse was to develop later in the eighteenth and nineteenth centuries popular religious movements that drew upon all the spiritual influences that the nation had experienced, including Christianity.[3]

The pattern of Christian response to government persecution during the first decades was for the believers not to conceal their faith, as we noted above. Under the rule of both Hideyoshi and Ieyasu, however, many people emigrated to other areas, at first to adjoining areas and later to more distant places, like the northeast. A few Japanese Christians left the country. But as the ferocity of the terrorism increased, Christians everywhere were forced to go "underground." The government was aware or suspected that the apostasy of many Christians was only external; one of the principal responsibilities of the inquisition office, therefore, was the detection and prosecution of hidden Christians. Its policy was to offer substantial monetary rewards for information leading to the apprehension of a Christian.[4] Notices of these rewards were posted in temples and in public places.

The *gonin-gumi* or five family structure, the old Japanese communal device for mutual help, which the Christians had also used so effectively for their own purposes, helped the *Bakufu* to control and supervise the activities of all Japanese, down to the smallest details of family and personal living. To help detect Christians, it was particularly useful, because if a Christian were found in a *kumi,* all the other members were liable to similar punishment. In consequence, Christians could exist only if all members of a *kumi* were of their faith.

He acknowledged, however, that Buddhism later in the twentieth century increasingly came to produce priests who inspired esteem. *Christ and Japan,* pp. 97-98.

    [3] Cf. H. Neill McFarland, *The Rush Hour of the Gods,* pp. 54-59. There is considerable evidence that Hirata Atsutane (1776-1843) was influenced by Chinese Christian works in his leadership of the Shintō renaissance in the early nineteenth century. Cf. Ebisawa Arimichi, *Namban Gakuto no Kenkyū,* pp. 412-422.

    [4] In 1682, 500 *ryō* in silver were promised for the arrest of a priest, 300 for a brother, 300 for an apostate who retracted, 100 for a *dōjuku* and 100 for an ordinary layman. Joseph Jennes, *A History of the Catholic Church in Japan,* p. 170.

The practice of *fumi-e* or *ebumi* was another device developed by the inquisition office. The term literally means "picture treading." The pictures referred to were plaques of Christ on the cross or of the Madonna — made first of paper, then of wood, copper or bronze. As early as 1631 Christians under torture were urged to trample on a crucifix, and the act was also demanded of apostates or suspected Christians. After 1640 it became a regular practice, and then primarily in areas of Kyūshū where there had been large concentrations of Christians. Here *fumi-e* was a regular ceremony as part of the New Year celebrations. Government officials went from house to house and compelled all members of the family to place their foot upon the plaque. In the villages the ceremony was more commonly held in a Buddhist temple or in the office of the local political leader. This practice was only part of the extensive system of surveillance carried on throughout the country, but perhaps more than anything else it symbolized the government's hostility toward Christianity, from which in turn an abhorrence of the faith as an evil thing developed among the general populace.

This methodology of inquisition was very effective. In the years from 1640 to 1658 well over two thousand Christians were detected in all but eight of the sixty-six provinces of Japan, and in the following decades many were arrested, often in substantial groups. In 1658, 609 were arrested at Kōri in the province of Hizen in Kyūshū. Of these 411 were executed at different places, seventy-eight died in prison, twenty were condemned to life imprisonment and ninety-nine were released after they apostatized. Again in the decade between 1660 and 1670 more than five hundred Christians were arrested in the province of Bungo. Many of these were put to death or died in prison, while others recanted and were released. The increasing thoroughness of the government's methods is seen in the introduction in 1687 of the *Kirishitan* family investigation *(Kirishitan-ruizoku-aratame)* by which the relatives of detected Christians, whether the latter had apostatized or not, were watched to the extent of the seventh generation of their male descendants or the fourth of the females.[5] And yet the *Bakufu* was not able to eliminate all of the hidden Christians.

Small groups of missionaries succeeded in entering the country even after 1640. A group of five European Jesuits entered in 1642, and a second group, consisting of four European priests, a Japanese brother and five laymen, of whom three were Japanese and two Chinese, entered at about the same time. The last missionary to enter Japan was the Sicilian secular priest Giovanni Battista Sidotti, who landed on August 22, 1708. Of the first two groups all were captured almost immediately, imprisoned and tortured. The Japanese, except the brother, were probably summarily executed; the others apparently apostatized and were given wives, but sooner or later they seem to have revoked their apostasy. The facts of the matter, however, are difficult to ascertain.

2

From the Roman Catholic standpoint, the church ceased to exist in Japan as a hierarchical community. The first ruling bishop of the church· in Japan had been Pedro Martinez, S.J., who was resident in the country only from 1596 to 1598. Luis Cerqueira, S.J., became his successor as bishop of Funai and remained in Japan, with his residence in Nagasaki, until his death in February, 1614. After Cerqueira's death the church had no further resident bishop. Two men were nominated, first in 1618 and again in 1633, but neither was able to assume the post. After 1614 resident priests became steadily fewer, and as time passed even visits were rare. From 1637 onward the Christian communities were completely dependent on lay leadership, since the subsequent attempts of missionaries to land resulted only in their immediate apprehension by the authorities.

The Christians complied outwardly with the requirements of the government. They registered in their respective family temples *(danna-dera)* and after fulfilling certain other du-

---

[5] *Ibid.*, pp. 173-174.

ties were given a temple certificate *(tera-uke-shōbun)*. They were required, as were all Japanese, to participate in certain temple ceremonies, to visit the local Buddhist cemetery with prescribed regularity, to conduct worship before the Buddhist home altar twice a year, to submit to examination the bodies of the deceased, and in other ways to demonstrate that the primary ceremonies of life and death were conducted under Buddhist auspices and without Christian alterations.[6] They even performed the *fumi-e*, believing that if they made an act of contrition afterward and kept the faith in their heart they were not guilty of sin.[7]

The faith was preserved, however, as a supreme treasure in many Christian families and transmitted from generation to generation within the relatively narrow confines of some farming and fishing villages in northwestern Kyūshū. But elsewhere in the land the faith was in fact eliminated, and by the end of the seventeenth century the *Bakufu* was convinced that it had succeeded in its complete extirpation. In consequence, after 1697 the intensity of investigations considerably abated, and during the eighteenth century Christians were largely undisturbed in their clandestine practice of the faith. The inquisition office was finally closed in 1792.

Isolated Christian families or even groups of families were particularly susceptible to a loss of faith from inadequate instruction, from intermarriage with non-Christians, or from the fear of consequences. Corruption of faith also occurred in varying degrees through syncretistic adaptations (apparently unconscious) or debasement into magical practices. In those areas, however, where all or most of the inhabitants of the villages remained Christian, Catholic faith and practice were better preserved.

The hidden Christians developed a particular structure for the continuity of their religious life and communities, evidently adapted from the older institutions of the confraternities and *gonin-gumi*. The chief figure in each larger geo-

---

[6] Furuno Kiyoto, *Kakure Kirishitan,* p. 17.

[7] Joseph Jennes, C.I.C.M., observes that from the standpoint of canon law they erred in this belief. *Op. cit.*, p. 195.

graphical unit was the *chōkata* (elder), who kept the records of the church calendar and communicated to the others the days for the proper festivals and liturgical events. He was also responsible for the correct transmission of the prayers and the teaching of the faith. In each next smaller geographical unit (*kōri*) there was a *mizukata* (baptizer) who, in addition to administering baptism, was responsible for communicating the festive days, prayers and teaching received from the *chōkata*. Then, in each *aza* a *kikikata* (or *kikiyaku*-hearer) was responsible for passing on the communications which he received to a smaller number of homes. The evidence suggests that the structure was definitely hierarchical, but it evidently varied in different places. We have record also of the office of *oshiekata* (catechist). These offices still exist today among the *Hanare-Kirishitan*.[8]

The sacrament of baptism was held in the greatest reverence, and each *mizukata,* who was normally appointed (or elected) for ten years, taught his successor the precise forms of the rite and the exact formula in Latin. By 1865 some of the formulas in use in the different districts had been appreciably distorted, but others were held by the Congregation of the Holy Office in Rome to be valid. A document written by Japanese government officials in 1806, with reference to the practices of the Christians then found at Amakusa, describes their form of administering baptism: "They offer water to Deus, recite a prayer, make the sign of the cross on the forehead of the child, give him some of the water to drink and assign him a strange (Christian) name."[9]

Not a single copy of the religious books printed by the

---

[8] The term *Sempuku-Kirishitan* (hidden Christians) is used to denote all the Christians who maintained their faith throughout the more than two centuries of national isolation. *Hanare-Kirishitan* (separated Christians) designates those of the former group who, after the coming of Roman Catholic missionaries beginning in 1859, did not return to communion with the Roman Catholic Church. *Kakure-Kirishitan,* which also means "hidden Christians," is another term used by Japanese scholars to designate the latter group, the content of whose faith has now come to be distinctly syncretistic. Cf. Kataoka Yakichi, "Saigo no Michi," *Kirishitan Kenkyū*, vol. 8, pp. 87-105.

[9] Jennes, *op. cit.*, p. 197.

Jesuit mission press was found among the *Kirishitan* at the end of their isolation, but a number of manuscript copies of summaries of Christian doctrine, the Apostles' Creed, the Ten Commandments and some prayers were circulated. The Christian communities consisted largely of poor and uneducated people, but the *oshiekata* and other leaders were evidently able to read these materials. In this way some communities maintained considerable knowledge of the Trinity, the incarnation and redemption through Jesus Christ; rather clear concepts of original sin, heaven, hell and purgatory were also held. In other communities, however, such as Kuroshima and some of the Gotō islands, doctrinal knowledge was very limited.

Except for baptism, the hidden Christians could not administer any sacraments. Marriage was therefore not celebrated as a sacrament, but we may regard as doubtful the assertion made by Francisque Marnas and repeated by Joseph Jennes that marriages were contracted without any religious ceremony.[10] Divorce, however, in keeping with male freedom in this matter in Japanese society, was apparently relatively frequent.

Unable to participate in the Catholic sacrament of penance, the *Kirishitan* relied upon the act of contrition as their primary means of obtaining forgiveness of sins and a peaceful death. One of their most treasured manuscripts, of which many copies were made, was the *Summary of Contrition (Konchiri-san no Ryaku)*, originally published as a book by the mission press in 1603. Terms equivalent to the Eucharist and Mass were preserved among the Christians, but in general they had no knowledge of this sacrament and of course did not administer it.

In spite of the need to call in Buddhist priests to perform funeral rites, the hidden Christians recited their own prayers in another room, either at the same time as the Buddhist reading of the scriptures or after the priests had departed. In their days of freedom the Christians had preferred to bury their

---

[10] *Ibid.*, p. 199.

dead, but this practice probably became impossible except in the most remote areas.[11]

The center of Christian devotional life was the daily recitation of prayers (orashio). The responsibility to teach these prayers correctly belonged to the oshiekata, and the Christians memorized them. In 1865 many were able to recite in Japanese the Lord's Prayer, the Apostles' Creed, the Hail Mary, the Hail Holy Queen, the Sign of the Cross, the Act of Contrition, the Rosary and other prayers. Some could recite the Ave Maria and the Salve Regina in Latin although with faulty pronunciation. Daily prayers were also said by families in Urakami and probably in other districts.

A strong devotion to the Virgin Mary was maintained by the hidden Christians. Because the possession of Christian devotional objects was strictly forbidden, only a few images of the Virgin were preserved. The Christians, however, frequently used small statues of Kannon (Chinese: Kwan-yin), the Buddhist goddess-symbol of mercy, especially those which, made of white porcelain and imported from China, represented the goddess with a child on her arm similar to the Madonna and Child. Certain representations of Kannon bore the mark of a swastika on her breast that resembled a cross. These statues, which are now known as Mariya Kannon, could be venerated by Christians without unduly arousing suspicion. Very few other devotional objects were preserved.

The great festivals of the church year were also faithfully remembered and celebrated, of course in complete secrecy. Many manuscript copies of the liturgical calendar are extant, and the kikikata was important in enabling the isolated Christians to maintain with extraordinary fidelity the outward forms of their faith. In the calendars mention is made of the holy days of Christmas, Circumcision, Epiphany, Palm Sunday, Easter, Ascension, Pentecost, Holy Trinity and All Saints.

---

[11] The oldest form of funeral rite in Japan, prior to the introduction of Buddhism with its preference for cremation, included burial of the dead, a practice continued in the custom still followed of burying members of the imperial family.

Festivals of many saints are also recorded. Lent and ember days seem to have been faithfully observed. The memory of a celibate clergy was kept in some communities.[12]

In this way, despite complete isolation from Christians in other lands, amid historically unparalleled continuity of persecution and hostile surveillance from government officials, Buddhist priests and a majority populace of other religious orientation, thousands of poor and generally uneducated Christians preserved faithfully the main content of their faith and lived by it for more than two centuries. This feat is not matched in the entire history of the Christian church. These hidden Christians provided continuity between the old and new expressions of the Roman Catholic Church in Japan.

E. CONTRIBUTIONS OF THE *KIRISHITAN*

1

THE THOROUGHNESS OF THE *BAKUFU* REPRESSION OF CHRIStianity would appear to have completely eliminated from the life of most Japanese any residual influences from the century of distinctly Christian activity in Japan. Such, however, was not the case. The missionaries had brought new concepts, scientific as well as religious, that were to germinate and later to bring forth fruit. In fact, the way in which Japan, uniquely among Asian nations, responded to the nineteenth-century incursion of Western culture, by transforming much of its way of life and at the same time maintaining its political independence, was due in considerable measure to its slow digestion of the contributions of the Catholic missionaries.

---

[12] Jennes, *op. cit.*, pp. 199-201. For an account of contemporary practices among the *Hanare-Kirishitan* see William D. Bray, "The Hidden Christians of Ikutsuki Island," *The Japan Christian Quarterly*, XXVI/2 (April, 1960), 76-84; Kataoka, *op. cit., passim.*

Japan, as we have noted, was a highly civilized country when the missionaries first arrived, a fact frequently attested by the most perceptive among them. But the discipline of medieval scholasticism, enriched by Muslim science and philosophy, which in turn had drawn upon the heritages of Hellenistic and East Indian civilizations, had enabled European thought to reach conclusions about man and the universe which were new to Japan.[1] Central to the teaching of the Christian missionaries was the concept that God created the phenomenal universe and that man as God's creation possessed an immortal soul. The world-encompassing missionary activity of the Roman Catholic orders in fact practically exemplified these convictions. These concepts, however, were previously unknown in Japan and were vigorously rejected by Buddhist polemicists. But the idea of the distinctive and immeasurable value of the individual person amid the overwhelmingly corporate orientation of feudal society remained to germinate in some of the intellectual circles of the Edo period.

Many of the missionaries in Japan were highly cultivated men, and the course of studies at the Jesuit colleges which they established included the latest European science. The man who was chiefly responsible for the execution of the new Gregorian calendar, Christopher Clavius, taught mathematics at the Jesuit Collegium Romanum in the second half of the sixteenth century. The friendship of Clavius and other Jesuits with Galileo Galilei also shows that the Jesuits were in the forefront of the scholarly work of the day. Both Matteo Ricci in China and Carlo Spinola in Japan had been pupils of Clavius. This was also the age of Tycho Brahe, Johann Kepler, Giovanni Antonio Mazini and the other great pioneers in science. Perhaps the chief scientific contribution of the missionaries to Japan was the communication of the latest European discoveries in astronomy and geography; this information greatly enlarged the world view of the entire educated com-

---

[1] Cf. Alfred North Whitehead, *Science and the Modern World*, pp. 12-13. Whitehead observes (p. 6) that in the year 1500 Europe knew less (scientifically) than did Archimedes, who died in 212 B.C., but an enormous expansion of knowledge, due largely to the voyages of exploration, occurred in the course of the sixteenth century.

munity in Japan, including the dictators Nobunaga and Hide-yoshi. Knowledge also came concerning the methodology of scientific inquiry and experimentation. The Japanese scholar Ebisawa Arimichi regards the work of the early Catholic foreign missionaries and Japanese Christians as a major element in the long process of the modernization of Japan.[2]

The history of Buddhism in Asia, and in Japan in particular, by no means lacks accounts of noble, sacrificial efforts to help the needy. But the Japan of the Period of Wars (Sengoku Jidai), in the context of Buddhist eschatological notions of the Age of Degeneration (Mappō), had seen nothing to compare with the quality and range of Christian service to the poor, orphans, widows, the sick, lepers, released prisoners, and, in short, the last and least of Japanese society. Various means adopted through the confraternities and the gonin-gumi also insured some measure of mutual social and economic security.

The church in Japan strove mightily to purify and elevate the moral standards and conduct of the Christian communities. At a time when, as a result of the wars and prevailing materialism, the standards of family morality had considerably broken down, the Christians emphasized the holiness of marriage and family life. Attempting to establish a higher level of social harmony, they taught the equality of both sexes before God and free monogamous marriage as the only sexual relationship possible for Christians. The near lack of unfavorable reports regarding the sexual morality of the celibate clergy, as contrasted with the relatively wide practice of homosexuality among the Buddhist priesthood, indicates that their personal conduct contributed greatly to the force of their teaching. Their understanding of the nature of man and of the family also led to a new appreciation of children in their own right. In the feudal environment, which uncritically used women and children as political hostages or marriage part-

---

[2] Ebisawa Arimichi, Kindai Nihon Bunka no Tanjō, pp. 10-12. Epitaphs on Kirishitan tombs appear to have been the first instances in Japanese history of the combined use of Chinese and Japanese script, a device which has become standard practice in the language during the past century. Winburn T. Thomas, Protestant Beginnings in Japan, p. 46.

ners as mere objects for barter, the Christians proclaimed the sacred value of persons and protested against the degradation of women and children in the confusion of the wars.

The Jesuits did not object to social stratification and, as we have seen, maintained a firmly structured hierarchy in their own society and in the churches which they founded. They introduced into Japanese feudal society, however, a radical qualification that it had not known before. Thus the Christian nobility and knighthood, in spite of their political and social rank, recognized in considerable measure the common people as having the same essential worth before God as they had. The Christian *daimyō* Ōmura Sumitada refused special seats for himself and his family in the church and knelt in prayer together with the commoners. Takayama Ukon is said to have assumed the responsibility of the funeral expenses of the poor in his fief. On at least one occasion he took part in a funeral procession, clearing away with his own hands some timber lying in the path.[3]

The point which I would emphasize is that this experience of ethical teaching and practice could not be utterly eliminated from the corporate memory of the Japanese people. The very violence of official opposition testified to its reality and depth, and however dim and distorted the memory, it served slowly to train the nation for the next stages in its history. We have noted the educational efforts of the missionaries and their introduction of new scholarly perspectives and areas of study. The virtual extirpation of the church did not result in eliminating these perspectives from the learned world of Japan. When, for example, later in the Edo period (1720) it was necessary to revise the calendar in use, which showed many discrepancies, permission was asked and obtained from the eighth *shōgun,* Tokugawa Yoshimune, to suspend the law against the importation of Christian books so use could be made of Chinese scientific works written by Jesuit missionaries.[4]

---

[3] Ebisawa, *op. cit.,* pp. 14-15.

[4] The *Seiyō-rekikei* was composed by Johann Adam Schall von Bell in China in 1645. Other books were by Ricci and Sabatino de Ursis.

The continuity of this scholarly tradition (*Namban-gakuryū*) was strengthened by Arai Hakuseki's careful questioning of the last missionary to enter Japan, Giovanni Sidotti, not long after his capture in October of 1708. Hakuseki visited Sidotti four times and questioned him minutely not only about the Christian religion but also about European science and customs. He wrote an extensive account of these interviews in the famous *Seiyō Kibun*. Hakuseki, a famous Confucian scholar, was profoundly impressed by the learning of Sidotti; but, more importantly, through the written report of these meetings the Japanese scholarly world received a new vision and new impetus for their work.

From the middle of the eighteenth century a distinct scholarly group emerged in Japan with the name of *Rangakusha*, or Dutch scholars. The study of the Dutch language was permitted only to the few interpreters at Nagasaki, but in the somewhat more relaxed atmosphere of this century these scholars obtained some Dutch books and learned enough of the language to translate several volumes on astronomy, botany and medicine into Japanese. A particularly noteworthy consequence of this work was that Japanese medical specialists realized that their own notions of anatomy differed greatly at some points from the charts in the Dutch books. In the year 1771 they dissected an executed criminal and fully demonstrated the correctness of the Dutch material. This incident convinced the larger scholarly world of Japan of the superiority of Dutch science, and it was important in creating the degree of understanding that enabled Japan in the nineteenth century to absorb Western learning with such astonishing rapidity. It also developed a growing appreciation in scholarly circles of Western achievements, and a distaste for the *Bakufu*'s policy of isolation.

These scholars, however, as we now know, inherited much of the scholarly tradition of the *Kirishitan*. Especially in medical science, which was also the primary area of the Dutch contribution, the scholars continued the tradition of medical knowledge and work begun by Luis d'Almeida and developed largely by Christian Japanese physicians. The *Rangakusha* preserved part of this tradition under the façade of

Chinese and Dutch studies, to the extent that an unbroken continuity in the transmission of the *Kirishitan* scholarly and cultural heritage prevailed until the reopening of Japan in the second half of the nineteenth century.[5]

Mention has been made that popular memories of Christianity, or perhaps accounts from even more direct sources, possibly influenced the leaders of the three most prominent new religions of the common people founded during the nineteenth century, Tenrikyō, Konkōkyō and Ōmotokyō. It is impossible to prove or to disprove this thesis, but the virtual monotheism, or at least strongly theistic position, which emerged in the case of each of these religious movements suggests some such influence. Theistic faith had been known in Japan before the advent of Christian missionaries, most notably in the Pure Land sects of Japanese Buddhism, but the national experience with Christianity had created a new religious climate. Furthermore, the home district of Kawate Bunjirō, who founded Konkōkyō in 1859, had contained numerous *Kirishitan* in the Catholic period. In general, the ethical level of these religions was high. They emphasized purification from ethical failure and social responsibility and had universalist perspectives far beyond those of the older Shintō.[6] In Shintō proper the great scholar and reformer Hirata Atsutane (1776-1843) developed theistic concepts under Christian influence, primarily, it would seem, from reading Chinese works of the Jesuit missionary Matteo Ricci.

Another area of possible *Kirishitan* influence is the Japanese school which developed from the teachings of the Chinese philosopher Wang Yang-ming (1472-1529), known in Japan as Ō-Yōmei. This school, at some points similar to Zen Buddhism, emphasized the intuitive perception of truth by meditation and self-control and the rule of conscience. The founder of this school in Japan, Nakae Tōju (1608-1648), however, living during the most intense persecution of

---

[5] Ebisawa, *op. cit.*, pp. 88-100. Cf. Ebisawa Arimichi, *Namban Gakuto no Kenkyū*, pp. 114-258.

[6] Clark B. Offner and Henry van Straelen, *Modern Japanese Religions*, pp. 63-70.

the *Kirishitan,* taught that man was created in the image of *Ryōchi,* the prime or universal Conscience. In one aspect this view can be understood in terms of the Zen Buddhist concept that the conscience of the individual man shares in the universal Reality, or that its essence *(hontai)* is identical therewith. Nakae, however, taught that man's relationship to this Reality is filial and that ethical life is the proper spiritual response of devotion to the Father of the universe.[7] Concomitantly, all men are ultimately equal. Furthermore, Nakae taught that the most important of all duties was not loyalty to one's feudal lord but dutifulness toward parents.[8]

Nakae's teachings later experienced some changes and accretions, but it is highly significant that, as G. B. Sansom writes, the most celebrated Japanese followers of the Ō-Yōmei school were resolute men of independent mind and reforming spirit. Presumably Confucian in tradition, the school opposed the authority of the approved Confucianism of the *Bakufu.* It tended throughout the Edo period to develop positions critical or contrary to the interests of the government. Among its followers were not only great scholars but leaders of specifically revolutionary movements such as Ōshio, who led an insurrection of hungry poor in Ōsaka in the year 1837, and Yoshida Shōin, who transgressed the exclusion edicts in 1859.[9]

2

Of equally great significance, however, in the history of Christianity in Japan is that the *Bakufu*'s policy and propaganda created pervasive attitudes of hostility toward Christian-

---

[7] Kagawa Toyohiko argues convincingly that Nakae had received Christian influences, specifically from a retainer of the Christian *daimyō,* Konishi Yukinaga, and that the events of his life demonstrate him to have been at least a covert Christian. Kagawa affirms essentially the same situation for Nakae's disciple Kumazawa Banzan; he suggests that the Confucianist Itō Jinsai (d. 1705) developed the Confucian concept of benevolence in a way reminiscent of the Christian concept of love. *Christ and Japan,* pp. 90-92.

[8] James Murdoch, *A History of Japan,* vol. 3, part 1, revised by Joseph H. Longford, p. 128.

[9] G. B. Sansom, *Japan, A Short Cultural History,* pp. 507-508.

ity among most of the people. Several refutations of Christianity were written to persuade men of learning that Christianity was false, such as the apostate Fabian Fukan's *Ha-Deus,* published in 1620. Other examples of such literary work are the *Taiji Jashū-ron* (Arguments for the Elimination of the Evil Religion) written in 1648 by Sessō, a Zen monk of Kyōto, and the *Hai-Yaso* (Against Jesus) by the Confucianist Hayashi Razan, written much earlier but published in 1671.

Other works were published to be read by the common people. An instance of this was the *Ha-Kirishitan* (Refutation of Christians), composed by another Zen monk, Suzuki Shōsan, and published in Kyōto in 1662. More widespread, however, in their influence were the generally anonymous anti-Christian stories which in both printed and manuscript form were circulated throughout the country and read by or to people of every class. These were often wildly improbable tales which dealt largely with two main themes, the history of the *Nambanji* (The Church of the Southern Barbarians) in Kyōto under Nobunaga and Hideyoshi, and the Shimabara rebellion.

These stories were not entirely devoid of historical fact, especially those about the Shimabara event, but most were written a hundred years or more after the events described and were often grotesque in their portrayals. Their bias was deeply anti-Christian and anti-foreign. Above all they created a folk memory of aversion and fear of both the Christian faith and its adherents. The sensitive authoress, Sugimoto Etsuko, has written about the pertinacity of the memory of the persecutions, extending to the time when she was a child in the seventies and eighties of the nineteenth century. In Nagaoka, a city in northwestern Honshū, the people knew little of Christianity. There existed, however, especially among the old, a strong distaste for the evil sect (*jakyō*), although this feeling apparently had no vital bitterness in it. "The people of Nagaoka looked upon the stories of Japan's Christian martyrs as a distant and pitiful thing; but they had none of the shuddering horror felt in some communities of southern Japan, whose memories of the tragedies of four centuries ago had reason to live."[10] Legends among the common people went even beyond these tales in telling of infanticide and cannibalism among the foreign missionaries as well as their designs to colonize the land.

Tension steadily increased in Japan in the latter part of the Edo period between the generally uncritical supporters of this anti-Christian and anti-foreign tradition and the growing number of advocates of Western thought, who generally favored a policy of intercourse with foreign nations. In the first half of the nineteenth century the latter group began to proclaim openly that free trade and intercourse with other peoples were necessary to the cultural health and military security of the nation. Feelings became so strong that a number of these progressive spirits were assassinated or forced to commit suicide by the isolationists who still dominated opinion and political power in the country. The pressure of outside forces finally resolved the issue. This pressure was supplied by the arrival of the American Commodore Matthew C. Perry, who first arrived in Edo Bay with a squadron of four warships on July 8, 1853, and in fact demanded diplomatic intercourse and the initiation of trade relationships. The *Bakufu*'s policy of exclusion, especially as it expressed itself in capricious and sometimes cruel treatment of shipwrecked sailors and in refusal to aid ships in distress, had become intolerable to the seafaring nations of the West.

---

[10] Sugimoto Etsu Inagaki, *The Daughter of a Samurai*, pp. 145-146. English translations of some of the popular anti-Christian stories are to be found in M. Paske-Smith, *Japanese Traditions of Christianity*, pp. 1-48. Cf. Ebisawa, *Namban Gakutō no Kenkyū*, pp. 259-269.

III

THE CHANGED POLITICAL AND SOCIAL SITUATION

THE CHANGED POLITICAL AND
SOCIAL SITUATION

1

THE SECOND HALF OF THE SIXTEENTH CENTURY, THE PERIOD
of greatest Roman Catholic missionary expansion in Japan,
was characterized by singular national activity in many areas.
Extensive military action, development of the structure and
quality of administration of government, the building of
castles and temples, painting and sculpture: in these the
achievements of the era were noteworthy. While in Europe
between 1550 and 1650 no military commander directed a
force of more than sixty thousand men in the field, Hideyoshi
and Ieyasu on several occasions mustered more than two hundred thousand. In the years 1592-1593 Hideyoshi had two
hundred and fifty thousand soldiers in Korea, the largest
military force ever dispatched by any nation for service overseas until the year 1900. Administrative and technical skills
of the highest order were of course required for these enterprises, and men of energy, ability and imagination emerged
in response to these needs.[1]

The age, however, was not one to foster scholastic learning.
As we learn from the instructions of Katō Kiyomasa, the
daimyō of Kumamoto under Hideyoshi, knowledge of letters among the *samurai* was primarily to read military trea-
tises and books espousing the spirit of loyalty and filial piety.

---

[1] James Murdoch, *A History of Japan,* pp. 93-94.

As contrasted with the Nara, Heian or Kamakura periods, the number of men of high attainment in Chinese studies was exceedingly small. The Ō-Yōmei scholar, Nakae Tōju (1608-1648) was virtually self-taught and was able only with great difficulty to secure a relatively meager library. Yet we note in his case and that of his energetic disciple Kamazawa Banzen a spirited originality and practicality characteristic of men who endeavored to express the heritage of the active sixteenth century in the early seventeenth.

This energetic way of life, however, was precisely the most contrary to the interests of the *Bakufu* system as Ieyasu and his successors developed it. Order was their ideal of social life, control their political goal, and repression their method. The *Bakufu* administrative structure with its strategic disposition of feudal domains, alternate residence of the *daimyō* and their retainers in Tokyo and their fiefs, and the *metsuke* system of surveillance in fact constituted one of the most efficient devices for political and social control ever known. The transformation of Buddhist religious institutions into tools of government and patronage of a form of Neo-Confucianism emphasizing feudal loyalty and social conservatism as the ideological rationale of its authority were pillars of the policy of state. The *Bakufu* thus appeared to have achieved a total spiritual as well as physical control of the nation.[2]

The burden of the system rested most severely upon the peasant class, who were often compared to sesame seeds — the harder they are squeezed, the more oil they give. G. B. Sansom has summed up the two and a half centuries of feudal rule during the period of seclusion as "pitiless oppression of the weak by a class whose rule was founded in violence."[3] Note must be taken that not all *daimyō* were tyrannical and unjust; especially among the "outer lords" there were cases of enlightened zeal to improve conditions in the villages. The emergence of towns and growing mercantilism especially in the eighteenth century provided some economic and social

---

[2] Cf. Murdoch, *op. cit.*, pp. 132-133.
[3] G. B. Sansom, *Japan, A Short Cultural History*, p. 524.

alternatives for the peasants and the lower *samurai* or *rōnin* (masterless *samurai*). But the spirit and methodology of repression were maintained by the central government as strictly as possible to the end of the period, so that an early Protestant missionary could still write in 1866 that "every Japanese is in the grasp of an iron hand, the hand of the Government."[4]

The history of the Tokugawa regime, however, is also the record of a slow but inexorable process which worked to transform and finally to unseat the regime. Frequent peasant uprisings only served to strengthen the government's hand and to keep its attention primarily upon physical control rather than upon constructive statesmanship. But other factors influenced the nation more to prepare to reopen communications with the outside world beginning in 1853.

Already by the year 1700 the rigid class structure of the feudal ideal showed signs of weakening under the somewhat relaxed discipline which inevitably followed in the wake of sustained peace. The disasters wrought by alternate famine and surplus rice crops sent landless peasants into the growing centers of government and commerce. Many of the *rōnin* created by the consolidation and change of fiefs under the Tokugawa restructuring also made their way into the cities. Here they mingled with the rising merchants (*chōnin*) to form a new middle class, a phenomenon heretofore unknown in Japanese life. Chiefly in this group the spirit of inquiry was nurtured that resulted in new literary and artistic creations and also in intellectual movements that from various points of view began to question the official policies and rationale of the *Bakufu*.

There were three primary movements: Confucian studies that at points differed from and criticized official Neo-Confu-

---

[4] Guido F. Verbeck, "History of Protestant Missions in Japan," in *Proceedings of the General Conference of Protestant Missionaries in Japan* (1900), p. 762.

cianism, the revival of "pure Shintō" (*Kokugaku*) with its focus on imperial rule, and Western studies, which, as we have seen, were based on *Kirishitan* traditions and more recent Dutch books. None of these movements was specifically revolutionary in intent or result, but they all contributed to the substantial changes in social life and world view that gradually came to be effected especially among the merchants and lower *samurai* in the cities during the latter part of the Edo period.

A recent writer on the history of the Dutch influence on Japan during this period has stressed the fact that the effect of the Dutch studies was far more than material. Early Japanese efforts in this area had to be surreptitious, but the *Bakufu* came to permit the importation of books on medicine, astronomy and military science. The government did not perceive, however, that these works were based upon the scientific world view then emerging in Europe. While not necessarily conforming at all points to traditional Christian doctrine, the European world view was opposed to the religio-natural systems of thought characteristic of traditional Chinese and Japanese learning. By the middle of the nineteenth century Western studies in Japan had achieved the momentum of a widespread intellectual movement which enabled men to attack the very foundations of the *Bakufu* system. The government resorted to various measures of repression, but such change had already taken place that when a catalyst was provided by the coming of Commodore Matthew C. Perry with his four black ships in July, 1853, and February, 1854, the process was begun that ended in the fall of the Shogunate and its replacement by the imperial government in 1868. The leaders of the Restoration movement came primarily from those "outer" fiefs which had come to sponsor Western learning officially and had sent promising scholars to schools which specialized in this learning. They were the men who had the breadth of outlook, the specific knowledge of world geography, European science, and Western government that enabled them to guide the nation on its new path of openness to foreign intercourse. They were aided in no small measure by many able administrators who had been trained under

Bakufu leadership, some by study abroad, as the *Bakufu* strove to adjust to the new situation in the country after 1853.[5]

2

The conditions which led to the opening of the country and to the overthrow of the Tokugawa regime developed slowly, and the consequence was not, therefore, a radical revolution. The term used to designate the political significance of the new Meiji government which took office in 1868 was Restoration. This meant the restoration of the power of the government to the emperor, who had for nearly a thousand years been little more than a spiritual symbol in the actual rule of the land. In fact, however, power was transferred from the *fudai daimyō*, or supporters of the Tokugawa family, to the *tozama daimyō*, or outer lords who had been kept from effective participation in the exercise of power at the national level. Among these outer lords those of Satsuma (Kyūshū), Chōshū (Honshū) and Tosa (Shikoku) were the most prominent. In terms of change of leadership personnel the change was momentous. The bulk of the new leadership in the army and navy, in education and in the emerging, partially government-subsidized large-scale industries came from the *samurai* of the outer clans. In the structure of Japanese society, however, the change was primarily from one set of *daimyō* and *samurai* to another. Sociologically considered, therefore, the change was little more than a palace revolution. Substantial measures of reform ensued, however; their intent was to reestablish national independence on the basis of industrial and military power, and the process of modernization was geared to this particular goal. The new set of leaders, however, strove to keep a firm grip on the new structures of power.[6]

There was no intent to alter the essential structure of Japanese society or the traditional emphasis of Japanese ruling

---

[5] Grant Kohn Goodman, *The Dutch Impact on Japan,* pp. 3-7, 225. Cf. Ebisawa Arimichi, *Namban Gakuto no Kenkyū,* pp. 270-431; G. B. Sansom, *The Western World and Japan,* pp. 313-315.

[6] Cf. Kami Yoshiyasu, *Purotesutanto Hyakunen-Shi Kenkyū,* pp. 13-16.

classes upon the religious ultimacy of political and social loyalty. Indeed, the Meiji government enforced these traditions
by refurbishing the ideological basis of the family system and
its concomitant political, social and economic implications.
They promoted a new mythology with the state as a great family under the divine father figure of the emperor. The new
ruling group had therefore no more initial liking than the
Bakufu for the Christian faith and its representatives. In general, its policy toward granting religious freedom was dic-
tated by the exigencies of its relationships with the great Western powers and only secondarily by its admittedly growing
confidence in the personal integrity and political harmless-
ness of especially the Protestant missionaries. Anti-Christian
suspicion and hostility continued in a substantial segment of
the ruling classes as an unbroken heritage from the *Kirishitan*
period; they formed an important element of the context of
Christian witness in Japan not only in the Meiji period but
actually until the end of the Second World War.

Christian witness in the first years after 1859 was thus
carried on amid wide hatred of foreigners and Christianity,
especially among the *samurai*.[7] The missionaries soon found
that they were regarded with great suspicion and were closely
watched; all Japanese who had any intercourse with them were
kept under strict surveillance. Consequently, all who communicated with the first missionaries were to some degree spies of
the government.[8] All foreigners were in physical danger in
the early years of residence, and during the first year, twelve
to fifteen were murdered. The English Legation in Edo was
attacked, and later the house of the American minister was
burned and his secretary assassinated. All the records of the
period refer to the danger of assault as well as insult to which
foreigners were exposed from the "intensely hostile" *samurai,*
who, "armed with two swords, cast many a scowling look at
the hated foreigners, whom they would gladly have expelled
from their sacred soil."

---

[7] The common people in either town or country hardly ever showed
such feelings. They tended to regard Christianity with fear rather than
hatred. Verbeck, *op. cit.*, p. 748.

[8] William Elliot Griffis, *Hepburn of Japan*, p. 80.

In discussing religious matters, Guido Verbeck reported in an early letter that "when such a subject was mooted in the presence of a Japanese, his hand would almost involuntarily be applied to his throat, to indicate the extreme perilousness of such a topic." The Tokugawa system of "secret espionage" by which the *Bakufu* kept the entire nation under constant surveillance still operated when the first missionaries arrived, and remained so for several years afterward. The Anti-Christian Edict was still in force, and the signboards were only removed on February 19, 1873.[9]

Japan of the 1850's and 1860's was thus paradoxically torn by feelings of attraction and revulsion toward foreigners and things foreign. Its subsequent history was significantly characterized by the alternate ascendency of one or the other of these two sets of feelings.

---

[9] Verbeck, *op. cit.*, pp. 746-748, 766.

IV

PROTESTANTISM IN JAPAN

A. EARLY PROTESTANT MISSIONS
AND CHURCHES

1

BEFORE COMMODORE PERRY ARRIVED AND JAPAN WAS opened to the restricted residence of other foreigners than the Dutch and Chinese, a few attempts were made by Protestants in the first half of the nineteenth century to share their faith with the Japanese people. Understanding and interest in the Christian world mission developed in the churches of the West in consequence of Pietism and the evangelical revivals. What was then known as the hermit nation of Japan became the object of the "prayers, contributions and efforts" of a growing number of Christians, especially in England and America. Some converts were made among shipwrecked Japanese sailors who, unable to return to their homeland, were then found in various places on the Asian coastlands, in Hawaii and the United States.[1]

In 1818 an American ship, the brig *Brothers,* entered the Bay of Edo hoping to secure permission to trade. The request was denied, but the captain of the ship gave two New Testaments and some religious tracts in the Chinese language to several among the considerable number of persons, probably all officials or their retainers, who came to the vessel. An English missionary to the Chinese, Dr. W. H. Medhurst of the London Missionary Society, had studied the Japanese

[1] Cf. Kaneko Hisakazu, *Manjiro, the Man Who Discovered America, passim (n. b.* pp. 66, 92).

language and sought permission from the Dutch to go on one of their ships to Nagasaki. The Dutch, of course, refused the request.

Seven shipwrecked Japanese sailors were living at the Macao home of the gifted and widely traveled missionary, Karl Gützlaff. An American merchant then residing in China gave the use of his ship *Morrison* to return these men to their homeland. Since the merchant, C. W. King, was hopeful that the expedition might also be a means to open Japan to Christian witness, he arranged for two other missionaries, Samuel Wells Williams and Peter Parker, a physician, to accompany Gützlaff. King himself and his wife went along with the expedition. Careful preparations for the trip were made, including explanatory documents and presents, such as a portrait of George Washington, a telescope, a pair of globes, an encyclopedia, a collection of American treaties with foreign nations, and an American history, among other things.

The *Morrison* arrived in the Bay of Edo on July 30, 1837, but although one or two hundred Japanese came aboard, no official of rank appeared. The next day the ship was fired on from the shore and finally had to leave. A similar experience was had at Kagoshima. However, when King offered to take the Japanese to Nagasaki to ask the intercession of the Dutch, they preferred to return to Macao rather than commit themselves to the hands of their countrymen. Four of the seven men were of great help subsequently to the missionaries in Macao. Two remained with Gützlaff, and two worked in the printing plant of Williams. They not only helped the missionaries gain some knowledge of the language but enabled them to translate into Japanese the biblical books of Genesis, the Gospel of Matthew, and the Gospel and Epistles of John. They were the first fruits of Protestant missionary endeavor among the Japanese people and were noteworthy both for the sustained fervor of their devotion and the nobility of their lives.[2]

---

[2]Otis Cary, *A History of Christianity in Japan,* vol. 2, pp. 12-17.

The *Morrison* had stopped briefly at the Ryūkyū island chain, and Dr. Parker was able to serve medically. These islands were a natural stepping stone to Japan proper, and in 1843 a number of British naval officers formed a society to which they gave the name of the Loochoo Naval Mission.[3] This society in 1845 sent the physician B. J. Bettelheim, a converted Jew of Hungarian birth and British citizenship, who was accompanied by his wife and two children. Another lady was also sent out as a missionary teacher. This lady, however, at the last moment declared her unwillingness to land and returned with the ship on which she had come.

The French Catholic missionary, Theodore Augustin Forcade, had been in the Ryūkyū Islands since 1844 and welcomed the Bettelheims, but circumstances impelled the latter to reside a distance away in Naha. Dr. Bettelheim made strenuous efforts to learn the local dialect, which was actually a form of Japanese, and he translated some portions of the Anglican liturgy. He composed some sermons and, committing them to memory, made heroic efforts to preach in public. At first crowds were permitted to hear him, but after the reigning monarch died in October of 1847, the treatment of both him and the French missionaries greatly worsened.[4] He found it increasingly difficult to communicate with the people, who were prevented even from receiving medical treatment from him. He was able to baptize only four persons, although a considerably larger number could be counted as believers. He was finally forced to leave in 1853, and his successor withdrew in shattered health two years later.[5]

The United States, Great Britain, France, Russia, and to a lesser extent other nations of the West had for some years increasingly sent ships into the Pacific Ocean to trade or hunt

---

[3] "Loochoo" is the form of the word which approximates more closely the Chinese pronunciation. "Ryūkyū" is the Japanese version.

[4] China had long claimed a nominal suzerainty over the Ryūkyūs. From 1846, however, the *daimyō* of Satsuma, Shimazu Nariakira, came to have largely effectual control of the islands.

[5] Cary, *op. cit.*, pp. 18-27, 34-35.

whales. The hope of most was also to trade with Japan, whose high culture, relative wealth and intelligent and industrious people were at least partially known even in the final years of seclusion. They greatly regretted that the Japanese government continued to rebuff all attempts at communication, but it was hardly possible even with the spirit and methods of nineteenth-century imperialism to force the issue with a people so resolutely independent and, as Westerners would put it, bellicose as the Japanese. Additional factors were necessary to lead to the confrontation made by the American naval squadron commanded by Commodore Matthew C. Perry.

Ships of Western nations in the Pacific, most frequently American and English, were often compelled to sail before a storm until they ran out of fresh water and fuel. If the nearest land was Japanese territory and the captain requested permission of the authorities to buy fresh supplies, even offering a hostage for the period of stay, the authorities regularly showed great hostility and flatly refused assistance of any sort. Sailors shipwrecked off Japanese coasts were usually imprisoned or otherwise maltreated.[6] In consequence, Commodore Perry was dispatched with two frigates and two sailing vessels bearing a letter from President Fillmore to attempt to induce the Japanese government to establish diplomatic and trade relations with the United States. In his mind, he intended "to demand as a right, and not to solicit as a favor, those acts of courtesy which are due from one civilized country to another." He entered Edo Bay and anchored off the shores of the fortified city of Uraga on July 8, 1853.

We cannot consider thoroughly the events and consequences of this and the following expedition of 1854. Perry's first treaty between Japan and the United States on March 8, 1854 merely assured better treatment of shipwrecked seamen and permitted American ships to obtain coal and other supplies at two Japanese ports. But Perry's display of military force — he returned in February, 1854, with a total of ten ships and a

---

[6] Kaneko, op. cit., p. 91.

complement of sixteen hundred men — aided by the fact that the Russian Admiral Putyatin had made two visits to Japan in the meantime demanding settlement of boundaries in the Kuriles and Sakhalien and the opening of a port for trade — induced the Shogunate to conclude a treaty first with the Americans.[7] The larger consequence of Perry's expeditions, however, was the demonstration of the Shogunate's inability to enforce its traditional policy of isolation, a fact which greatly contributed to its own collapse as well as to the opening of Japan.

The first Protestant service of worship in Japan proper was held on the deck of Commodore Perry's flagship on Sunday, July 11, 1853. Perry had refused to conduct negotiations on that day, and with the aid of the brass instruments of the band the voices of the crew rang out, to the tune of Old Hundred, in the singing of "All people that on earth do dwell."[8] A few days later, after the death of a seaman, a Christian burial service was conducted on land at Yokohama by the chaplain of the fleet. The interpreter brought by Perry was Samuel Wells Williams, who had come on the *Morrison* to Edo in 1837. Another fact of missionary significance was that one of the marines was a Jonathan Goble, who had joined the expedition to gain knowledge of the country and returned in 1860 as the first Baptist missionary. After Commodore Perry successfully concluded the treaty with the reluctant Shogunate, Townsend Harris was dispatched as the first representative of the United States, with the rank of consul general. The Japanese government had understood Article XI of the treaty to mean that such a representative would be sent only if both countries desired the exchange; they neither wanted nor expected Harris. The new consul, however, was equal to the situation. With immense patience and great skill he established authentic diplomatic relations and got the more

---

[7] Hugh Borton, *Japan's Modern Century*, pp. 35-36.
[8] Perry was not always so careful in his formal observance of the Sabbath, but he intended on this expedition to play his role of American representative with rigorous consistency. Cf. Cary, *op. cit.*, pp. 31-32.

formal treaty, known as the Convention of Shimoda, signed on June 17, 1857. Harris was a man of deep Christian convictions and exemplary life, and his journal often testifies to his reading the Protestant Episcopal service with his Dutch interpreter H. C. J. Heusken as both "clerk and congregation."[9]

The treaty of 1857 provided in the second article that Americans should have the right of permanent residence in the ports of Shimoda and Hakodate.[10] Americans were to be exclusively under the control of their consuls and to be tried by American law. This right of extraterritoriality was also granted in the treaties concluded with the Dutch and the Russians, respectively, on October 16 and 24, 1857; but it was later to become, together with the limitations set on Japanese control of customs duties, a matter of long dispute with considerable implications for the Christian movement as well as for diplomatic relations between Japan and the Western powers.

Townsend Harris noted in his diary that since no class of Americans was specified in the second article, missionaries might actually come and reside in Japan.[11] This possibility, however, was only realized in consequence of the Treaty of Amity and Commerce between the United States and Japan concluded at Edo on July 28, 1858. According to this latter treaty, further ports were to be progressively opened for residence and trade: Kanagawa (Yokohama), Nagasaki, Niigata and Hyōgo (Kōbe), as were Edo (from January 1, 1862) and Ōsaka (from January 1, 1863). In the ports, with the exception of Shimoda, which was to be closed after the opening of Kanagawa, Americans were to have the right to lease ground and purchase or erect buildings. According to Article VIII Americans in Japan were to be allowed the free exercise of their religion and to erect places of worship for this purpose in the open ports. No mention was made of permission to engage in religious propaganda among Japanese, but note was taken

---

[9] Mario Emilio Cosenza, *The Complete Journal of Townsend Harris,* pp. 270-271, 432; cf. pp. 153, 227, 341, 465-468.

[10] This article alone was to go into effect at a later date, on July 4, 1858. Cosenza, *op. cit.,* pp. 571-572.

[11] *Ibid.,* pp. 373-374, 466.

that the government of Japan had already abolished the practice of trampling on religious emblems. Permission was granted to import anything for sale to Japanese except opium and munitions of war (the latter could be sold to the Japanese government and to foreigners). There was thus no prohibition of the importation and sale of books, including religious books.[12] On the basis of this treaty, which went into effect on July 4, 1859, the first Protestant missionaries entered the Japanese empire.

2

Guido Verbeck in his *History of Protestant Missions in Japan,* written first for the Ōsaka Conference in 1883, divides the history up to that time into two periods. The first period, extending from the summer of 1859 to the end of 1872, he calls the time of preparation and promise; the second, from 1873 to 1883, he calls a season of progressive realization and performance.[13] Previous to the summer of 1859, when four ports of the empire were declared open to foreign commerce and permanent residence, a few missionaries, as we have noted, had made transient visits to Japan. The first Protestant missionaries with a regular appointment were the Rev. John Liggins and the Rev. Channing M. Williams, both members of the Protestant Episcopal Church, who after three years of service in China were transferred to the newly established Japan Mission of their church. Liggins arrived at Nagasaki on May 2nd, before the formal opening of the ports, and Williams toward the end of June.

On October 18th of the same year the physician James C Hepburn and his wife, of the Presbyterian Church, U. S. A. arrived at Kanagawa, near the present port of Yokohama The Rev. Samuel R. Brown and D. B. Simmons, M.D., both of the Reformed Church in America, reached Kanagawa on

---

[12] *Ibid.,* pp. 578-584.

[13] Guido F. Verbeck, "History of Protestant Missions in Japan," *Proceedings of the General Conference of Protestant Missionaries in Japan* (1900). For the history of these periods see also Frank Cary, *A History of Christianity in Japan, 1859-1908, passim.*

November 1st. The Rev. Guido F. Verbeck, also of the Reformed Church, arrived at Nagasaki on November 7th. The wives of these three, who had temporarily remained in Shanghai, rejoined their husbands at their respective locations by December 29th.

The Rev. Jonathan Goble and his wife, of the American Baptist Free Mission Society, arrived at Kanagawa on April 1, 1860. Goble had joined Commodore Perry's expedition as a sailor for the express purpose of viewing Japan as a mission field. After returning home, he continued his studies hoping to be sent to Japan as a missionary for his church. For the next ten years, although there were a few replacements and additions of personnel, these four Protestant missions were the only ones in Japan. During this period, the members of these missions and their families experienced the most difficult conditions of living, physical, mental and spiritual. Mention may be made here, however, of the arrival at the end of the decade, on November 30, 1869, of the Rev. and Mrs. D. C. Greene as the first missionaries of the American Board of Commissioners for Foreign Missions, the agency of the Congregational Church in the United States. After a brief stay in Tokyo they moved to Kōbe in March of 1870. The area of central Japan, centering in Kōbe, Ōsaka and Kyōto, became the focus of the work of this board, later one of the most effective in Japan. Four other couples joined this mission, including the physician J. C. Berry and his wife, before the close of 1872. Stations were opened and well established by that time in both Kōbe and Ōsaka, but the work of this mission belongs primarily to the second and following periods of missionary activity.

Mention should be made of the ability and character of these and other early missionaries. They combined to a remarkable degree a high order of talent with breadth of experience and achievement prior to their arrival. Dr. Hepburn was forty-five when he reached Japan, having served as a medical missionary in Singapore and Amoy and again for a number of years as a physician of distinction in New York City. Samuel R. Brown had served as a missionary to China, as a pastor, and then as headmaster of a school in Connecticut; he was forty-nine when he arrived in Japan. The two Episcopalians were men of maturity as well as high ability. Verbeck was the only young man among the first six; born and educated as an engineer in Holland, equally conversant in German and Dutch with considerable knowledge of French, he received his seminary training in Auburn Seminary, New York, and became thoroughly at home in English. Owing also to his position as a stateless person, he enjoyed an unusual degree of confidence from the Japanese government, and, with the consent of his board, he served for many years as a special counselor to the government at its highest levels, especially regarding educational policy.

Although not a missionary, William S. Clark, president of the Massachusetts Agricultural College, accepted the call of the Japanese government in 1876 to establish in the northern island of Hokkaidō a higher school of agriculture. In accordance with his contract, Clark remained less than a full year, but his Christian influence was most weighty, and all of the first class of fifteen students committed themselves to Christian faith and discipleship before he left. When he arrived he was fifty years old and at the height of his powers, having served as a colonel in the American Civil War and most acceptably as an educator and administrator. A comparable figure was Captain L. L. Janes, a graduate of West Point, who had been asked in 1871 to establish a school in Kumamoto (Kyūshū) by the *daimyō* of that place. His powerful Christian influence was responsible for the committal of the bulk of his students to Christian faith and the creation in 1876 of the Kumamoto Band of thirty-five young men, one of the most creative and effective forces in the life of the young Japanese church.

This maturity and generally high level of ability of the early missionaries was of vital and enduring significance to the life of Protestant Christianity in Japan. As in the case of the early Roman Catholic missionaries, the sending lands gave their best in talent, quality of education and spiritual dedication. This fact, coupled with the particular stage then reached in political and cultural developments in Japan, accounts, perhaps more than any other single human factor,

for the extraordinary influence which the Protestant missionaries were able to exert upon large areas of Japanese life
in the last third of the nineteenth century, one of the most
formative periods in the entire course of Japanese history.

3

The missionaries during their first years in Japan were
limited in their activity not only by the suspicions of government and people, by confinement to the treaty ports and their
immediate environs, but also by their ignorance of the language. They were aware of some of the history of the early
Roman Catholic missionaries and of their literary work, but
at first they assumed that nothing of it had survived. It was
also not an era when Protestants ordinarily could or would
make use of the Vatican archives or other Roman Catholic
repositories in Europe. Consequently, no linguistic aids were
available, no dictionaries, grammars or phrase-books of any
kind. "Pantomime, gesture, pointing to objects to obtain their
names and to build up a working vocabulary, were the first
methods."[14] And in the circumstances of the day it was exceedingly difficult to obtain teachers. Five months elapsed before
Dr. Hepburn secured a teacher, and afterward he had reason
to think that this person was a government spy. Japanese
teachers had no knowledge of linguistic principles to explain
their very difficult language to educated men of the West.[15]

The acquisition of the language was therefore a principal
part of the responsibility of the missionaries in the first years.
Dr. Hepburn, however, soon rented a Buddhist temple not
far from his residence in Kanagawa, fitted it up as a dispen-

---

[14] William Elliot Griffis, *Hepburn of Japan,* p. 91. Dr. Hepburn later
knew of the existence of the Japanese-Portuguese dictionary published in
1603 and a small Japanese vocabulary list published by Dr. Medhurst in 1830
in Batavia. An English-Japanese dictionary was compiled in the early sixties
by Japanese scholars of Satsuma, primarily with Japanese needs in mind.
Ibid., p. 131.

[15] Sherwood Eddy concluded, on the basis of his long experience with missionaries in every part of the world, that if one were to include reading and
writing as well as speaking, Japanese is probably the most difficult language
in the world for a foreigner to learn.

sary and made himself available for service. The physical needs of the populace, especially of the commoners, were at that time particularly great. The knowledge of *Kirishitan,* Dutch, and Chinese medicine in the country was not sufficiently applied to large segments of the population. No hospitals existed in Japan. Every third person was pockmarked, for smallpox was always endemic and frequently epidemic. Blindness was "shockingly common";[16] sores on head and body were everywhere visible, and tuberculosis made "frightful ravages." The rule and policies of the Tokugawa *Bakufu* caused Japan to be at some points in a worse state physically and spiritually than it had been for several centuries.[17] Dr. Hepburn's dispensary soon came to be thronged by sick people; within the first three or four months about thirty-five hundred patients were treated, including a few surgical cases. The government, however, at first hindered and then stopped the work altogether, shutting the gate of the temple and stationing a guard before it. Thus even the physician had to give himself wholly to the study of the language and later to compiling his great dictionary.

During the first decade the missionaries also felt responsible to provide those linguistic aids which could enable subsequent workers to learn the language more rapidly than they themselves.[18] They began to make translations of parts of the Bible. They were also able to sell to members of the learned class copies of the Scriptures and other religious books and tracts in the Chinese language. As their own knowledge of Japanese improved, they were able to discuss the content of this material with at least a few persons. They were able to sell to the same group a large number of the historical, geographical and other scientific works prepared by Protestant

[16] Dr. Hepburn frequently reported on the large proportion of patients who came to him with diseases of the eye.

[17] Cf. Griffis, *op. cit.,* pp. 89-90, 106-107.

[18] Cf. "The Twenty-Fifth Annual Report of the Board of Foreign Missions," *Minutes of the General Assembly of the Presbyterian Church in the United States of America,* 1867, XVIII, p. 39. Dr. Hepburn's Japanese-English, English-Japanese Dictionary was published in 1867 in Shanghai, the result of years of arduous, careful labor; it was at once recognized as a definitive work, and subsequent dictionaries were largely based on it.

missionaries in China. Thus they prepared the minds of the learned community better to understand and appreciate the developing scientific world view of the West and the efforts of Christian thinkers to relate their faith to this view. Frequently contemporary reports refer to the wide degree of literacy among the people and to their avid desire for knowledge, particularly about other countries, and of "geographical, historical and scientific subjects."[19] The missionaries were, of course, equally conscious of their responsibility to witness by deed and life. "By their Christian work and conversation, by acts of benevolence to the poor and afflicted, and by kindness and courtesy to all," they endeavored to weaken and dispel the prejudices against them and to win men to a more favorable consideration of the Christian gospel.[20]

An important area of service in which the missionaries could engage almost from the beginning was education. After the opening of the country, Japanese leaders came increasingly to learn that Great Britain and the United States had a far more dominant role in the Pacific waters and in the world than Holland. Growing numbers of Japanese were anxious to learn English, and the missionaries could provide suitable books in this language as well as teach them personally and thus facilitate personal intercourse. Even though the *Bakufu* government in Edo was being severely criticized by its political opponents for acceding to the pressures of the foreign governments to open the country ("expel the foreigners" was coupled with "revere the Emperor" in their opponents' cry [*Jōi-Sonnō*]), they increasingly saw the need to prepare a limited number of Japanese youth to cope with the demands of the future.[21] As early as 1861 the Edo government sent nine of their best young men to Dr. Hepburn for instruction in English and mathematics. The students were recalled after less than six months, owing to the growing political difficul-

---

[19] *Minutes of the General Assembly*, 1862, XVI, p. 56.

[20] John Liggins' letter, in Verbeck, *op. cit.*, pp. 751-753.

[21] At least part of the animosity in the slogan "expel the foreigners" was politically motivated, as is evidenced by the fact that the new Meiji government from the beginning (in 1868) followed an "open country" policy which went beyond that of the *Bakufu*.

ties in Japan which led to the fall of the Shogunate. When they left, however, most of them took copies of the Bible in English and in Chinese, besides copies of the American Tract Society's school books. Some of these young men lost their lives in the civil war which followed, but others occupied high offices under the new government.[22]

The Hepburns lived in Kanagawa from 1859 to 1863 and then moved to nearby Yokohama, which had come to be the chief port and foreign settlement. Here Dr. Hepburn was permitted to reopen his dispensary, and he continued his work there until 1879, when it was closed because of his own ill health. He treated from six to ten thousand patients yearly and had regularly a group of five to ten young Japanese who assisted him and studied medicine and surgery under his tutelage. He instructed these and other medical students in formal classes three days a week, and practicing physicians sometimes came from Edo to consult with him. After the move to Yokohama the number of operations he performed greatly increased and patients came to him from all parts of the country.[23] On the walls of the dispensary were hung scrolls bearing verses from the Bible in Japanese sufficiently colloquial for most of the patients to read. Dr. Hepburn often explained these personally to those who inquired. Most significantly, the care of patients was conducted with a singular benevolence and sympathy which made a profound impression upon both patients and students. This work, as of other medical missionaries in subsequent years, evidently strongly influenced a lessening of the generally strong opposition to Christianity.

Educational work, however, was to be of more lasting significance. Mrs. Hepburn had taught a class of five small boys during her brief stay at Kanagawa. In 1863, at the request of a Japanese physician who, contrary to the general desire or expectation in Japan, wished an education for his granddaughter, she began a school for girls at Yokohama.[24] She

[22] Griffis, op. cit., p. 91.

[23] Minutes of the General Assembly, 1866, XVIII, p. 38.

[24] Griffis, op. cit., p. 113. Verbeck, however, reports that Mrs. Hepburn first began this work by forming a small class for girls and boys in 1867. Verbeck, op. cit., p. 758.

later was aided in this work by Miss Mary Kidder of the Reformed Church Mission. From this work the Isaac Ferris Seminary developed, one of the finest Christian schools for girls in Japan. This school was "the mustard seed of women's education in Japan"; within twenty-five years of its beginning a million and a half Japanese girls were receiving instruction in public or private schools.[25] The nature of Mrs. Hepburn's contribution to this great change may be seen in that as late as 1871, the Imperial Rescript of that year referred to Japanese women as "without understanding," a notion radically rejected, at least by implication, in the Imperial Rescript on Education of 1890.[26]

Schools for boys had their beginnings in equally humble settings; small classes were held in the homes of missionaries where English and other subjects were taught. The first formal school was conducted in the Yokohama Customhouse from about 1865, in which Dr. Samuel R. Brown, Dr. Hepburn, J. H. Ballagh and David Thompson taught. A number of missionaries occasionally were engaged as instructors in local government schools, as Dr. Brown at Niigata in 1870 and in Yokohama for a longer period, beginning on September 11, 1870. The class of students which had been taught by the Rev. and Mrs. J. H. Ballagh formed the bulk of the membership of the first Protestant Christian church, which was organized on March 10, 1872, and from this year these students began to receive theological instruction from Dr. Brown in a little room appended to his house in Yokohama. This work began Protestant theological education in Japan, and from it grew the present Meiji Gakuin University in Tokyo.[27]

As the years passed, the educational institutions begun by the Protestant or Roman Catholic missionaries, especially the

[25] It should be noted that in Japan the educational work of Protestant missionaries was almost entirely confined to the level of secondary education, expanded later to include college and university levels. Elementary education was not comparably necessary nor practicable.

[26] Griffis, op. cit., pp. 113-114. Cf. Mrs. W. J. Chamberlain, Fifty Years in Foreign Fields, pp. 30-31.

[27] William Elliot Griffis, A Maker of the New Orient, pp. 208, 221-231, 266-268.

boys' schools, were surpassed by government-sponsored institutions in terms of physical facilities and possibly in formal academic excellence, but the enormous contributions of Christian schools to the long-range development of the Japanese educational system must not be minimized. They pioneered in introducing the content and methodology of Western education in the nineteenth century; and, as we shall see, the first government institutions depended to a large extent upon missionary personnel. In the twentieth century they have maintained, at times as almost the sole exponents, the spirit of liberal education, of education that aims to develop humane qualities of understanding and character, as contrasted with that which gives priority to technical competence and uncritical patriotism.

A surprising number of the "makers of New Japan" had been pupils of Guido Verbeck in his early school in Nagasaki, and it will be helpful if we take note of his educational work at this point for both its intrinsic and representative significance.

Shortly after his arrival in Nagasaki on November 7, 1859, Verbeck began to give "gratuitous instructions" at his home in the English language and other branches of knowledge. With two of the young men who came for this instruction he also began to teach young men outside of his own house in a school established by the governor of Nagasaki for the training of interpreters. The attainments of the men whom he taught was such that the governor proposed to the Shogunate in Edo that a school of foreign languages and science be founded in Nagasaki with Verbeck as the principal. The proposal was approved, and through the United States consul in Nagasaki, under whose "care" the Verbecks were registered, Verbeck was asked to accept the responsibility. From the time of his acceptance until 1878, when he officially returned to the Reformed Mission, he served under the pay of the Japanese government in this and other capacities.

A schoolhouse was built and was soon filled with over one hundred students, Verbeck himself teaching only the advanced classes. These young men, all of *samurai* rank, came to the school not only from the various provinces of Kyūshū and southwestern Honshū but also from more distant parts of the land. They included two sons of the court noble Iwakura Tomomi, who was to head a special mission to the West in 1871 and later became prime minister. They were driven in part by their own ambition and that of their families, but they were impelled in no small measure by Verbeck's fame, for his name had already acquired magnetic powers of attraction. The two documents in the English language which Verbeck used most and longest in teaching the more promising of his students were the New Testament and the Constitution of the United States. Scores of those who became the most influential men directing the destiny of Japan from 1868 to the end of the century — most of whom were drawn from this southwestern part of the empire — were pupils of Guido Verbeck, including future members of the cabinet such as Ōkuma Shigenobu and Soejima Taneomi.[28]

During the middle sixties Verbeck was invited to open similar schools in other provinces by some of the most powerful *daimyō* of Shikoku and the Southwest. He was, of course, unable to accede to these requests, as his personal presence was required in each case. After the Restoration of 1868 a new imperial school was founded in Nagasaki alongside the older one which continued under the auspices of the *daimyō* of Hizen, and Verbeck taught on alternate days in each one. Then in 1870 he received an invitation from the imperial government to assist in establishing in Tokyo another "school for the Western languages and science," but one which in fact was intended from the beginning to be an imperial university, the highest educational institution in the empire.[29] Verbeck's key role in the development of what became Tokyo Imperial University (he served as its first president), in the establishment of new laws and structures of government at a time of critical transition, and above all in the creation of the understanding necessary prior to such establishment, was such that it is not amiss to call Guido Fridolin Verbeck the

---

[28] William Elliot Griffis, *Verbeck of Japan*, pp. 141, 102-103, 123-125.
[29] *Ibid.*, pp. 184-185.

single most influential foreigner in the history of modern Japan.[30]

Many of these missionaries, both men and women, were veritable giants in the earth. Their linguistic achievements in the midst of the greatest obstacles, their patience and nobility of character, their endurance of physical hardship and, in the early decades, no little physical danger, their continued growth in understanding as well as in love of the people among whom they wished to serve, all deserve honest recognition and appreciation. The perspectives of the present, however, compel us to recognize their limitations, especially those of their age and of the general understanding of the churches and societies from which they came.

Almost without exception the Protestant missionaries had a low view of the Roman Catholic Church and its representatives. They professed "deep interest and sympathy" in the previous history of Catholic Christianity in Japan and showed a "wholehearted sympathy" toward the Catholics, who were persecuted again from 1867 to 1873.[31] However, even as cosmopolitan a person as Verbeck was wont to compare the "corrupted Christianity" of Catholicism, even if it had produced "such marvelous results" in Japan in earlier centuries, with the "Gospel in its purity" as introduced by the Protestant missionaries. The Anglican John Liggins referred to the Catholic missionaries of former days as "intriguing Jesuits."[32] It was anticipated that "a people so quick-witted and discriminating as the Japanese will readily learn the difference between the Roman and the true religion." For to the Protestant missionaries theirs was a very different religion from Ro-

---

[30] *Ibid.*, pp. 186-188, 279-282. Another highly important contribution of Verbeck was his role in guiding Japanese to visit and study in the West. A large number were guided to Rutgers University in New Brunswick, New Jersey, where, as in New York City, Dr. J. M. Ferris of the Reformed Dutch Missionary Board arranged for their warm welcome. Cf. *ibid.*, pp. 124, 159, 214.

[31] Joseph Jennes, *A History of the Catholic Church in Japan*, p. 229.

[32] Verbeck, *op. cit.*, pp. 740, 749, 752, 870. William E. Griffis characterized the religion preached by Portuguese and Spaniards in Japan as being more of the "church and the corporation," i.e. the organization, than of the Heavenly Father and of his Christ. *Verbeck of Japan*, pp. 71, 136.

manism; it was "embraced by the most enlightened foreigners, with doctrines and forms of government every way benign in their influence."[33]

In keeping with the views of both evangelical Christianity and popular opinion in the West, most of the missionaries brought with them and generally retained low notions of the state of man in the heathen world.[34] In the admittedly confused and, as compared to other times, relatively degenerate Japan of the 1860's they found evidence to confirm these views. There are many references to promiscuous sexual practices, "shockingly" open compared to Western mores, for "Christian countries are not quite free from similar immoralities, but it is in darkness, a work of darkness and shame. Here vice stalks about at noonday."[35] One is compelled to observe that the hypocrisy of this mode of comparison was apparent to few in the West at the time, but indubitably relations between the sexes in Japan of the 1860's had certain disreputable aspects which were alien to the best standards of Europe and America. There was much danger to life and limb from the *rōnin* and other "swash-bucklers and ruffians," who increased in number with the disturbances before and after the Restoration of 1868 and created a situation as perilous as in any frontier town in the American West of the same period. As late as 1895 Dr. Hepburn wrote of the Japanese that "in morals, they are like all pagan peoples, untruthful, licentious and unreliable."[36] Many were the statements of the business and diplomatic community regarding the untruthful and unreliable character of the Japanese with whom

[33] *Minutes of the General Assembly*, 1869, XVIII, p. 41.

[34] The sentiments expressed by Alfred Tennyson in his poem Locksley Hall may be considered typical of even the most sensitive and humane thinkers of the day:

"But I count the gray barbarian lower than the Christian child."
". . . with narrow foreheads, vacant of our glorious gains,
like a beast with lower pleasures, like a beast with lower pains."
"Thro' the shadow of the globe we sweep into the younger day:
Better fifty years of Europe than a cycle of Cathay."

[35] Griffis, *Verbeck of Japan*, pp. 85, 162.

[36] Griffis, *Hepburn of Japan*, p. 97.

they had dealings. The feudalism which tended to produce qualities of this kind was still strong although its days were numbered. An even more grievous heritage of feudalism was the apparent absence of a sense of the "nobility of all human-ity," so that in the public bathhouses, which were carefully graded accorded to classes, one pool was for "beggars and horses." And in the sixties the common enumerator used for laborers was still the same as that for animals.

The missionaries, with the sole exception of the Unitarians and perhaps the Germans of liberal theological tendencies, regarded all non-Christians as in spiritual darkness. Refer-ences were made to "the darkness, the uncleanness and the delusion of heathenism." A contemporary report in the United States refers to the religion of the Japanese as "worthless and injurious."[37] The victory of Christianity, whose cultural ex-pressions in Japan they expected to be little different from that in their own homelands, was predicated upon the "down-fall of idolatry, Buddhism and all false religions and philoso-phies."[38] Verbeck, like other missionaries of scholarly inter-ests, studied Japanese thought, history, customs and popular beliefs widely, but this was primarily to understand the back-ground of the people in order to preach the gospel to them through skillful use of "their own proverbs, gems of speech, popular idioms and the epigrams of their sages." He appar-ently felt no need to study the traditional Japanese religions for their own meaning and value. A corollary of these views was the concept of the church as a "body of believers gathered out of the world," a concept representative of large segments of American Christianity of the period.[39]

Nevertheless, the experience of living among the Japanese altered somewhat the harshness of these views, however much they had been sanctified by the theological interpretations

[37] "The Twenty-Ninth Annual Report of the Board of Foreign Missions," *Minutes of the General Assembly*, 1886, XVIII, p. 39.

[38] Note must be taken in this context of the abounding optimism which characterized not only evangelical Christianity but the whole of Western culture during the second half of the nineteenth century. Cf. Winburn T. Thomas, *Protestant Beginnings in Japan*, p. 61.

[39] Cf. Verbeck, *op. cit.*, p. 808.

and habits of mind derived from centuries of Western geographical and cultural isolation. A significant example of this change is the long letter written by Verbeck on April 21, 1870, to J. M. Ferris of the Reformed Church in America's Board of Foreign Missions, wherein he recounts with obvious admiration the extraordinary changes which he himself had witnessed in the land and the people since 1859. He was compelled to confess, "let them come out of their darkness to the light, let the spell be broken, and forthwith they are fine, clever men."[40] Verbeck was clearly not speaking only of those who became Christians. Even earlier, however, the 1860 report of the Presbyterian Mission to Japan, which was without doubt prepared on the basis of material submitted by Dr. Hepburn, reflected a high degree of appreciation of the people and civilization of Japan. Although "there are abundant proofs of human depravity among them, . . . they have reached a much higher grade of industry, ingenuity and taste for the beautiful than is commonly found amongst modern heathen nations."[41]

There was recognition that all men are children of the Father and the affirmation that "amid the general wreck of morals, many pleasing remains of the original divine workmanship were also met with. Among these may be mentioned many instances of warm family affection, of genuine kindness, and of real sympathy, honesty and faithfulness, the general peaceableness of the common people, and the politeness and suavity of the manners of the people, down to the lowest classes."[42] Deeper study of Japanese writers of the past suggested that "their own great men had groped after the essential, even as he (the missionary) was leading them to the historic, Christ." There was, however, apparently no intimation that the traditional religions had been in any sense vehicles of divine revelation or that they had contributed in any appreciable degree to the building of "useful and beneficent institutions" or had been "a power for good in society."

[40] Griffis, *Verbeck of Japan*, pp. 200-206.

[41] "The Twenty-Third Annual Report of the Board of Foreign Missions," *Minutes of the General Assembly*, 1860, XVI, p. 92.

[42] Verbeck, *op. cit.*, p. 750.

The first Japanese Christians of Protestant persuasion were drawn largely from the company of the students who studied under the missionaries or their wives and from the few men who aided them as language teachers or translators. The first formal fruit of the witness was the baptism of Yano Ryū, a respected physician and the teacher of the Reformed Church missionary J. H. Ballagh, in October, 1864. Yano died not long after this event, but he had been baptized at his own request, in the presence of his whole family and with their full consent. Another early baptism of very different origin was that of Murata Wakasa no Kami, the *karō* (minister) of the *daimyō* of Hizen, who on a trip to Nagasaki had picked up a copy of the Scriptures in Chinese floating on the waters of the harbor. For three years he had communicated through a personal messenger with Verbeck regarding the Bible and the Christian faith.

In the spring of 1866 C. M. Williams, who later that year became the American Anglican bishop of China and Japan, baptized his first convert, Shinmura of Higo. In the summer of 1868 Verbeck baptized a young Buddhist priest named Shimizu. This man was imprisoned for his faith after Verbeck was called to his new work in Edo, and he spent five years in various prisons with much suffering. He was later released and became a faithful member of a church in Edo. In 1867 the first tract in Japanese was printed, a translation of Dr. D. B. Mc-Cartee's Chinese work, *An Easy Introduction to Christianity*.

Until the spring of 1872 only ten persons had received baptism from Protestant missionaries, five in the North and five in the South of Japan. This small harvest was discouraging to many, but it is necessary to remember the conditions in Japanese society until the edict prohibiting Christianity was finally removed from the public notice-boards by virtue of a decree of February 19, 1873. As an early missionary put it, "For years there hung over every native Christian convert, as by a silken filament, the suspended sword of the executioner. I felt this when I was with them, and I never knew finer courage even in our Civil War."[43]

---

[43] Griffis, *Hepburn of Japan*, p. 172.

It is significant, therefore, that the first increase of converts and the organization of the first Protestant Japanese church occurred before the anti-Christian notices were removed. In January, 1872, the missionaries and English-speaking residents of all denominations in Yokohama united to observe the annual Week of Prayer under the auspices of the World Evangelical Alliance. Some Japanese students from among those studying under the missionaries attended the meetings. Sections of the book of Acts were read in order day after day, and for the sake of the Japanese the Scripture of each day was translated extemporaneously into their language. The meetings grew in interest and were continued until the end of February. After the first week some of the Japanese prayed in their own language and their prayers were characterized by intense earnestness; with tears streaming down their faces they prayed that God would give his Spirit to Japan as to the early church and the hearers of the apostles. English and American naval captains who witnessed the scene later reported: "The prayers of these Japanese take the heart out of us."[44]

As a direct result of these prayer meetings, the first Japanese Christian church of the Protestant tradition was organized in Yokohama on March 10, 1872. It consisted of nine young men who had participated in the prayer meetings and were baptized on that day, and two middle-aged men who had been previously baptized, one by David Thompson of the American Presbyterian Mission at Yokohama and the other by George Ensor of the Episcopal Mission at Nagasaki. These latter two men became the first officers of the church, Mr. Ogawa the sole elder and Mr. Nimura the deacon. Some of the nine young men had previously received special instruction from J. H. Ballagh of the Reformed Mission, who together with Mr. Ogawa and others was chiefly instrumental in organizing the young church. Ballagh acted as temporary pastor. The members chose what men of the period called a catholic name: The Church of Christ in Japan (*Nihon Kirisuto Kōkai*). The intent of both the Japanese Christians and cooperating

---

[44] J. M. Ferris, in Verbeck, *op. cit.*, pp. 764-765.

missionaries was to establish a Japanese national church not specifically identified with any denomination in the West. For this reason a simple creed was accepted, largely taken from that of the World Evangelical Alliance, supplemented by other articles of ethical purport. The polity of the church was government by the pastor and elders, with the consent of the members.[45]

In September of this same year, 1872, a "Convention" of missionaries was held in Yokohama consisting of representatives from the Presbyterian, Reformed and Congregational Missions. Among other things, they appointed a New Testament Translation Committee to unify and consummate the scattered efforts at translation which had been made up to this point.[46] Action was also taken to commend the spiritual basis of the new Japanese church and of its name and polity. From an early time the view had been widely held that it was a "consummation devoutly to be wished" that the separate missions, although representing different denominations at home, cooperate to form one Japanese church.[47] At the time of the organization of the first Japanese church, this subject was frequently discussed by the missionaries as well as by the Japanese Christians.

The text of the resolution is as follows:

> Whereas, the Church of Christ is one in Him, and the diversities in denominations among Protestants are but accidents which, though not affecting the vital unity of believers, obscure the oneness of the Church in Christendom and much more in pagan lands, where the history of the divisions cannot be understood: and whereas we, as Protestant missionaries, desire to secure uniformity in our modes and methods of evangelization so as to avoid as far as possible the evil arising from marked differences: we therefore take this earliest opportunity offered by this Convention to agree that we will use our

---

[45] Charles W. Iglehart, *A Century of Protestant Christianity in Japan*, pp. 43-44.

[46] This committee did not begin to meet until June, 1874, when representatives of the Methodist Episcopal Mission, the American Baptist Mission, the Church Missionary Society and the Society for the Propagation of the Gospel were invited to participate in the committee and its work.

[47] Only one Japanese Christian was constituted a member and sat with the Convention, the elder Ogawa.

influence to secure as far as possible identity of name and organization in the native churches in the formation of which we may be
called to assist, that name being as catholic as the Church of Christ
and the organization being that wherein the government of each
church shall be by the ministry and eldership of the same, with the
concurrence of the brethren.

We shall see that while it was not possible to realíze this
aim of a single Protestant church in Japan, a majority of the
missionaries continued to hold this ideal and strove to realize it.[48]

4

The second period of Protestant missions in Japan began
with the year 1873; it was the decade of "progressive realization and performance." This demarcation of periods seems
justified not only by the differing extent and momentum of
the work in the second period but by significant events in the
land which marked its beginning. The Meiji Restoration had
been effected in 1868, and the new government was beginning
to move with more forthrightness toward opening the country
to Western science and culture. One indication of this direction was the reform of the calendar by adopting the Gregorian system, beginning on January 1, 1873. Another was
the event which I have already mentioned, the removal of
the anti-Christian edict from the public notice-boards on
February 19, 1873. This act was not accompanied by any
statement that prohibition of Christianity was ended and religious freedom granted, but in the context of other related
events, it was clearly intended to show that the government
was prepared to countenance within certain limits the propagation of Christianity in the land.[49]

Another event of great significance was the return of the
Iwakura Mission on September 13, 1873. This embassy, which

[48] Verbeck, *op. cit.*, pp. 792, 855, 865-866, 885.
[49] Missionaries were not permitted freedom of travel outside the open
ports until the treaties with foreign governments were revised during the
1890's. They were, however, able to receive passports for such travel with
increasing leniency, and after 1873 many were tacitly allowed to reside in
the interior.

evidently had as its aim the investigation of Western lands and cultures as well as diplomatic overtures, had left Japan on December 23, 1871, and was led by Iwakura Tomomi, the second or third person in rank in the empire, a man of great intelligence and experience and accustomed to command. He was sent at the behest of the emperor himself and given four vice-ambassadors, all men of ability and distinction. Their leisurely trip through the United States and Europe gave these astute men ample opportunity to observe and reflect on the developments that had taken place in the Western world since the beginning of Japan's period of isolation. The policy of Westernization which the Meiji government came to follow with such forthrightness and determination was due in no small measure to the experience and subsequent leadership of the men of this mission.

With reference to the Christian movement, the Iwakura Mission was abroad at the very time that the government was persecuting the Catholic Christians *(Kirishitan)* who had come to light in the vicinity of Nagasaki and beyond as a result of the return of Roman Catholic missionaries. Numbers had been imprisoned, subjected to torture or deported to other parts of the country. The diplomatic representatives of the Western powers strongly and repeatedly protested, but to no avail. These events were widely reported in the press of the United States and Europe and aroused much public indignation. The mission was rather coldly received in America, and in Europe popular feeling ran so high that in Brussels a large crowd assembled along the route of the carriage of the envoys and with shouts called for the liberation of the persecuted Christians. In France the matter became an issue in Parliament. The consequence was that Iwakura cabled the Japanese government from Berlin that the mission would end in failure if the government did not cease the persecution of Christians and free the exiles. Soejima Taneomi, the Japanese Minister of Foreign Affairs, on February 21, 1873 delivered to the Italian minister, who was then dean of the diplomatic corps, a written attestation that secret orders had already been given to the governors of the provinces to stop the harassment of Christians and that the anti-Christian edict notices would be removed.[50]

These events, while important in themselves, were also symptomatic of wide and deep changes occurring in the land. Not only did the process of Westernization advance with astonishing rapidity, but there were also changes in the general understanding and climate of opinion. Toward the end of the 1860's we note repeated reports by the missionaries that less hostility existed than had been previously experienced.[51] By the middle of this decade the former frequent calls by government officers at the homes of the missionaries, ostensibly as friendly visitors but in fact as investigators, had entirely ceased. In this context the first Protestant church was able to organize at Yokohama without any attempt at secrecy and consequently with the full knowledge of the Japanese authorities. This relatively favorable environment, however, was not without grave dangers for individual Japanese converts. As late as 1871 in Kōbe, a Japanese teacher of O. H. Gulick of the American Board Mission was arrested at night with his wife and put in prison. He had for some time been an earnest student of the Bible and wished to be baptized but had not yet received the sacrament. His wife was then not regarded as a Christian. Every effort was made to obtain his release, but neither the requests of the missionaries nor the offices of the American minister were of any avail. The Japanese, Ichikawa Yeinosuke, died in prison on November 25, 1872. His wife was released shortly afterward. Significantly, she was later baptized and became a member of the well-known Reinanzaka Church in Tokyo.[52] This kind of treatment, while rare, only ceased with the removal of the anti-Christian edict from the public notice-boards.

Highly significant for the growth of the Christian church in Japan is that in the single year 1873, a larger number of Protestant missionaries arrived than in any one year of the

[50] Jennes, op. cit., pp. 227-228; Joseph L. Van Hecken, The Catholic Church in Japan Since 1859, p. 18.

[51] E.g. Minutes of the General Assembly, 1867, XVIII, p. 39; 1868, XIX, p. 35.

[52] Verbeck, op. cit., pp. 748-749. Cf. Iglehart, op. cit., p. 42.

nineteenth century. Indeed, this number of twenty-nine was only two less than the total number of thirty-one who had come in the fourteen years from 1859 to the end of 1872. Most of the new missionaries came to augment the forces of the missions already on the field. Since these were now established and possessed experienced personnel, various linguistic aids, and personal contacts not available in the earliest years, the newcomers were able to progress rapidly in the study of the language. They were also able to fit with relative ease into the developing institutions and other patterns of work. Almost all missionaries taught regular Bible classes, at first in the English language and later with increased use of Japanese. Public preaching was first begun in the early months of 1873 in the city of Kōbe.

It was now possible for missionaries to live in Tokyo, and the Rev. David Thompson, who with the Rev. and Mrs. Christopher Corrothers, also of the Presbyterian Mission,[53] resided there from the end of 1869, baptized the first convert in Tokyo, Takahashi Tōru, in September, 1873. With seven members from the original Yokohama Kaigan (Seashore) Church, Thompson was instrumental in organizing the first Protestant church in Tokyo on September 20, 1873, becoming himself the first pastor, on a temporary basis. This church was organized as a sister church to the one in Yokohama, having the same basis in faith and polity. It soon became exceedingly active in its life and witness and grew rapidly in membership and influence.

On December 30th of the same year the Presbyterian missionaries resident in Yokohama and Tokyo, following instructions received from America, organized a presbytery, of which the two Japanese churches became members as well as the missionaries themselves. Japanese churches which were organized by missionaries of the Presbyterian and Reformed tradition during the next three or four years all eventually came to belong to this presbytery.

---

[53] The first school which deserves the name of mission school was that begun by Corrothers soon after his arrival in Tokyo. By 1872 it had already become a substantial institution.

In the spring of 1873, the New Testament Translation Committee, which was appointed in September, 1872, began work and continued steadily until its task was completed in 1880. The chairman of the committee was Samuel R. Brown, who, with Dr. Hepburn, was largely responsible for the steadiness and diligence with which the work was carried on. As Shimada Saburō, the Japanese editor, historian, critic and reformer, wrote in 1901, Brown was in a particular way one of those missionaries who by their "humane and warm sympathies" helped to remove the antipathy and skepticism held earlier by almost all Japanese toward Western people, their culture and religion. He was noted for his kindness and noble-heartedness; "his pure and noble character," as one of Brown's students wrote, "had an unspeakable influence over us." A pioneer educator in three lands, he was also one of the first men to believe in a first-class academic education for girls. "He was one of those rare men who mold and shape the character of the age through the men whom they have trained."[54] Brown's long service as pastor of the Protestant foreign community in Yokohama may also be regarded as one instance of the extensive range of services, religious, medical and educational, which the missionaries, especially in the first decade, provided for the foreign communities in all the open ports.

At this point it is in order to observe the formation of the famous Christian "bands" which constituted vitally important nuclei in the growth of the Protestant church in the second and following decades. The first in point of time was the Yokohama Band, constituted by the company of young Japanese Christian men who studied under Dr. Brown from 1872 in Yokohama. Among these were some who were to become outstanding Christian pastors and educators over the next two generations, men such as Ibuka Kajinosuke, who was to succeed Dr. Hepburn as president of Meiji Gakuin, Uemura Masahisa, who was to become, as pastor of Fujimichō Church in Tokyo, the most influential pastor of his day in the Presby-

---

[54] Griffis, *A Maker of the New Orient*, pp. 104, 127, 319-320. Dr. Brown's linguistic work, *Colloquial Japanese*, was published in 1863 in Shanghai and proved a great help to all students of the language.

terian-Reformed tradition, and Honda Yōichi, later to be the first Japanese bishop of the Methodist Church.

The similarity of social and educational backgrounds, the closeness of the new spiritual tie of Christian faith binding these young men together, and their presence as a small minority in a still largely anti-Christian society, all worked together in the Yokohama and other bands to create an exceedingly strong cohesiveness. This went beyond the ordinary ties of students, who in Japanese history frequently formed close associations around the figure of a noted teacher. Their similarity in background, however, needs further explanation.

It will be recalled that until the formation of the first Protestant church on March 10, 1872, only ten Japanese had been baptized in the entire empire from the coming of the first Protestant missionaries in 1859. This means that the spiritual awakening as well as the formation of the church took place in a distinctly new historical and sociological situation, the Meiji Era. As we have seen, the Meiji Restoration of 1865 constituted little more than a kind of palace revolution from the standpoint of the participation in political and social power of the lower classes.[55] But it effected a radical displacement of the personnel in power. The coalition of clans which backed the imperial restoration and wielded effective power in the land after 1868, behind the façade of imperial dignity, were the outer (tozama) clans, especially those of the southwestern fiefs of Satsuma, Chōshū and Tosa. They filled almost all the administrative posts, high and low, of the new government with their adherents of samurai rank. Men from Satsuma tended to dominate among the officers of the new imperial navy, and those from Chōshū were more numerous in the army. Apart from the men of these three clans, however, or those whom they specifically approved, office in the new government was effectively closed. And in the emerging close ties between the government and the rapidly developing financial and industrial corporations (zaibatsu) of the empire, severe limitation was placed upon advancement of people in

[55] Cf. Sumiya Mikio, Nihon Shakai to Kirisuto Kyō, p. 9.

the world of industry and banking other than those of the new "in" group.

This situation meant the effectual exclusion from political, and to a lesser extent from economic, life of most of the supporters of the Tokugawa government. The limited but intense military battles which were fought following the Restoration in 1868 and 1869 strengthened the determination of the victorious clans to keep the main lines of power in the hands of their own supporters. The abolition of the system of fiefs and thereby of the social structure of lord and vassals, for which the new government substituted a national conscript army and navy, resulted in the loss of livelihood and much of the social position of the samurai.[56] Both daimyō and samurai were liberally pensioned with lump sum payments. In time, however, owing as much to their inexperience in economic affairs as to the rapid changes occurring, many lost most or all of these monies in unfortunate or unwise investments. This loss of means of support occasioned economic hardship and, added to generally effective disbarment from political life and relative decline in social position, created much personal frustration, and in many cases strong resentment against the new regime.

To understand the history of Protestant Christianity in Japan is to realize that the bulk of the leadership and a relatively large part of the membership of the church until well into the twentieth century were drawn from these samurai, many of whom were to a considerable extent socially and economically dispossessed.[57] Some of them, to be sure, did not long remain sociologically or economically helpless and became leaders in various educational, journalistic and other

---

[56] The old social structure of four classes was abolished in favor of the new one of three: nobility (kazoku), gentry (shizoku) and commoners (heimin). The samurai thus retained formal social recognition as constituting shizoku. I was informed by a Japanese friend that until the end of World War II, it was still customary to append to the name of a pupil in the teachers' class roll book in elementary schools the first ideograph of shizoku if the pupil were of that class. As a concrete instance of the early Meiji experiences see Kega Kenzō, Honda Yōichi, pp. 9-52.

[57] Kami Yoshiyasu, Purotesutanto Hyakunen-Shi Kenkyū, p. 16.

intellectual activities. They were active also in founding political parties, especially to oppose the government, and were leaders in the movement for popular political rights. The Christian church was to find its easiest access to people within this class. Among farmers and laborers, who on the whole were effectively kept apart from these movements of modernization by government policy, the church had increasing difficulty in gaining a hearing.[58] Statistically, in the year 1892, the Congregational missionary D. C. Greene estimated that 40 percent of the total body of Protestant Christians in Japan were of the *samurai* class, although the latter constituted only 5 percent of the total population. Among the Christians of Tokyo nearly 75 percent were of this class.[59]

The next band to be formed was that of Kumamoto in Kyūshū, the devoted group of young men who became Christians under the influence of Captain L. L. Janes. Janes, a graduate of West Point and for some years an officer in the United States Army, was invited in 1871 (or 1872) by the *daimyō* of Higo in Kyūshū, through the secretary of the Board of Foreign Missions of the Reformed Church, to open a school in the castle town of Kumamoto. This school, however, was by no means intended by its sponsors to be Christian; indeed, they represented the anti-foreign party in the southwestern provinces. Janes, however, spoke of Christianity as soon as was prudent, and thereafter for five years he gave religious instruction as a part of the academic program of the school. About two years after his arrival he proposed to the students of the advanced class a systematic study of the New Testament. The school authorities approved the plan with the understanding that such knowledge would help the students better to oppose the progress of faith. In consequence of Janes' teaching and personal character, about forty of the young men who had received his instruction went to the top of Mt. Hanaoka near the city on January 30, 1876, and pledged solemnly their loyalty to Jesus Christ as Lord, to whom they looked for the emancipation of their nation.

[58] *Ibid.*, pp. 15-18.
[59] Griffis, *Hepburn of Japan,* pp. 224-226.

This commitment later brought severe persecution upon the young men, estrangement from families and friends for most, and in some cases the abandonment of planned careers. Their food supplies were cut off by the school, and the whole band of professed Christians organized a private mess under the direction of Captain Janes and with the use of his food. When Janes' term of service was ended, his contract was not renewed, and the school was abruptly closed. He then, in June, 1876, recommended the students to Niishima Jō, better known in the West as Joseph Hardy Neesima, who had returned to Japan in December, 1874, after his years of education in the United States. From November, 1875, he proceeded to begin the Dōshisha (Same-purpose-society) School in Kyōto.

The coming of these young men, about thirty in number, to Kyōto in 1876 was of momentous significance for the growth of the Protestant church in Japan. For one thing, it was at once possible to constitute the Dōshisha as a theological school as well as a Christian college. Jerome D. Davis, who was associated with Niishima in the Dōshisha even from before its inception, has written of the change wrought by the men from Kumamoto: "The coming of these young men at that early day, with their earnest Christian purpose, gave a tone to the school; and their influence was felt in moulding the Dōshisha morally and in shaping its course of study from that time." Davis felt that at the time he wrote, the work of these men had already changed the history of Japan. Among those best known were Kozaki Hiromichi, who succeeded Niishima as president of the Dōshisha and later became pastor of Reinanzaka Church in Tokyo, Yokoi Tokio, distinguished pastor and Christian journalist, Ebina Danjō, pastor, educator and theologian, and Kanamori Tsūrin, author and one of the most effective evangelists in the years before and after the turn of the century.[60]

The third Christian band was formed in the capital of the northernmost island of the Hokkaidō and hence called the

---

[60] Arthur Sherburne Hardy, *Life and Letters of Joseph Hardy Neesima*, pp. 207-212. Kanamori and Yokoi both left the church in the 1890's under the influence of the new liberal theology, but Kanamori later returned and served most effectively as an evangelist for the rest of his life.

Sapporo Band. In 1876 the national government called William S. Clark, president of Massachusetts Agricultural College, to act as head of the higher school for scientific agriculture which they wished to establish in Sapporo. Clark took a leave of one year from his school and was in Japan for only eight months. His influence upon Japanese Christianity, however, and indeed upon an important segment of the moral life of the nation, went far beyond what the mere tally of time would normally indicate.

Clark, too, had been a military man, serving as a colonel in the Union Army in the American Civil War. As in the case of Janes, the combination of zealous Christian faith with ethical rigor and the formal discipline of a military background proved to be an almost irresistible attraction to the young men under his care. Like the Kumamoto youth, they had been selected with care from a variety of clans; they represented the highest intellectual quality and spiritual vitality of the *samurai* class. Owing in part to the relative freedom of the remote Hokkaidō and in part to Clark's firm insistence, the government authorities reluctantly gave him permission to teach ethics with the use of the Bible as a textbook. Before Clark left, all of the first class signed the "Covenant of Believers in Jesus" which Clark himself had written. The depth of their commitment was such that, even in the absence of Clark, they succeeded in winning the entire next class to sign the same covenant.

In this remote frontier town, apart from close parental supervision, the young Christians did not experience the bitter persecution received by the Kumamoto Band. They were baptized, the first class and then the second, by an American Methodist missionary, M. C. Harris, who had been in the Hokkaidō since January of 1874. From this Sapporo Band came some of the most distinguished of Japanese Christian leaders, Satō Shōsuke, who long served as president of Hokkaidō Imperial University (the institution which developed from the Sapporo Agricultural School), Nitobe Inazō, writer, educator and statesman, under-secretary general of the League of Nations, Uchimura Kanzō, great leader of the Non-Church (*Mukyōkai*) Movement, whom we shall consider more in

detail later, Miyabe Kinga, Ōshima Seiken, Itō Katsutake
and others.[61]

Other Christian bands, generally less known, were also of
great influence in the history of Christianity in Japan. One
of these came to be associated with the city of Hirosaki in
northern Honshū. Honda Yōichi, who was a member of the
Yokohama Band, had originally come to the port city to secure an English teacher for the Tō-ō Gijuku, a clan institution to train the sons of *samurai* with a history of seventy-
five years. Honda was able to persuade John Ing, an American
Methodist missionary en route with his wife to China, to accompany him to his remote home in the north. Within a few
months they were able to gather about fifteen students request-
ing baptism from Ing and Honda, who had been ordained an
elder in the Yokohama church. Failing health obliged the
Ings to return to the United States in 1878 after having served
in Japan but a year, but the American Methodist Church
continued to support the work, first through the presence of
the Rev. and Mrs. W. C. Davison and then with others. With
the permission of the Yokohama church, the Hirosaki fellowship affiliated with the Methodist Episcopal Church, U.S.A.,
and Honda received ordination from Bishop Wiley to the office of deacon.

Another circle of young men formed around the bishop of
the Anglican Church in Japan, C. M. Williams, who had
first served in Nagasaki, then in Ōsaka, but from November
1873 had made his residence in Tokyo. This group became
the nucleus of the later Japanese leadership of the Anglican
Church.

From Yokohama and then from other churches, witness to
the gospel was carried to the interior of the land. The second
decade was marked by a notable increase in the number of
churches established and in the size of their congregations.
Church buildings were constructed; many of them were large
and built with such substantial materials that they are still
in use. In the single year of 1879, the total membership of

[61]Raymond P. Jennings, *Jesus, Japan and Kanzo Uchimura*, pp. 12-15;
Kitasawa Sukeo, *The Life of Dr. Nitobe*, p. 10.

Protestant churches increased by 60 percent. This growth was not achieved, however, apart from much opposition and often severe persecution. Report was made, for example, in 1876 by the American Board Mission that as the missionaries and Japanese theological students made tours of various places in central Japan, the fear and opposition of the people made it very difficult to find settled places for preaching.[62]

A second characteristic of this decade was the gradual emergence of Japanese leadership in the churches. In the first decade the missionaries had necessarily carried the responsibility alone. But as compared to other lands, within a surprisingly short time leaders of the highest caliber came from the Japanese Christians. By the end of the second decade missions reported with great appreciation concerning their "native pastorate." In 1882 the American Board Mission wrote: "Many of its [the mission's] Japanese workers bring to their work great ability, natural and acquired; and they show it in such faith, zeal, tact, and self-denying devotion as not only makes their work successful, but gives earnest of an able and faithful pastorate."[63] The missionaries continued to bear great responsibility, and generally relations with their Japanese disciples were characterized by deep mutual respect and affection. Most of the missionaries were from the United States, and the New England Puritan tradition predominated. They represented the best of Protestant, evangelical Christianity of their period, they almost all had a strong church-centered approach, and in consequence they were worthy spiritual mentors to the generally young Japanese Christians.

The influx of new missionaries in 1873 included the founders of new missions as well as reinforcements for those already established. It is impossible to cite details of all the missions or similar organizations which have worked in Japan since 1859, but at this point mention should be made of some important new arrivals. The Methodist Episcopal Church, U.S.A., began its mission in 1873; on August 8 and 9, with Bishop W. L. Harris presiding, then on an episcopal visitation

---

[62] Verbeck, op. cit., p. 789.
[63] Ibid., p. 847.

to Japan, a general mission meeting was held in Yokohama. Tokyo, Yokohama, Nagasaki and Hakodate were selected as the places for central stations. The mission of the Methodist Church of Canada was inaugurated in 1873 by the arrival of two missionary couples.[64] The British Society for the Propagation of the Gospel in Foreign Parts established its Japan mission also in this year. The American Mission Home, an institution for work among women, had been established in October, 1872, under the auspices of the Women's Union Missionary Society of America for Heathen Lands. In 1874 a physician and his wife, Dr. and Mrs. Theobald A. Palm, were sent as representatives in Japan of the Edinburgh Medical Mission. In the same year five missionaries, including a physician and his wife, arrived to establish the Japan Mission of the United Presbyterian Church of Scotland. The Scottish physician, Henry Faulds, opened a medical dispensary in the Tsukiji district of Tokyo and continued his work along with his language studies. As in the case of Dr. Hepburn in Yokohama and Dr. Berry in Ōsaka, the dispensary became very popular, and Dr. Faulds gathered around him a number of medical students.

The next church to begin work in Japan was the Evangelical Association of North America, which sent its first contingent of four missionaries in 1876. The first missionaries of the Cumberland Presbyterian Church, Rev. and Mrs. J. B. Hail, arrived in Japan in February, 1877. The Baptist Missionary Society of London began its work at the end of 1878 with the arrival of the Rev. W. J. White, who, however, had previously served for several years in Japan as a teacher both in private and in government schools. The Reformed Church in the United States commenced its mission in Japan on June 6, 1880, when the Rev. and Mrs. A. D. Gring arrived. The Methodist Protestant Church began work by sending a single missionary, Miss H. G. Guthrie, who arrived in Yokohama on September 23, 1880.[65]

---

[64] At this period wives were not appointed as missionaries and were, therefore, not officially voting members of the missions. Since, however, the practice was later changed in most missions so as to include them in this category, and since wives generally performed yeoman's service in various kinds of Christian work, I count them as missionaries in my enumeration.

[65] Verbeck, op. cit., pp. 775-776, 779-781, 791, 800, 816, 827.

These churches were without exception responsible institutions in their homelands and, in the context of the day, relatively non-sectarian. Their missionaries on the whole maintained the high standards set by the early pioneers. Among them were outstanding scholars, linguists, musicians, skilled teachers and winsome preachers. The missionaries themselves, like the Jesuits of old, stressed the point in their communication with their home churches that Japan was no place for mediocre men.[66] Evaluation of missionary personnel and methods, we may note, should include reference to the levels of understanding and practice of the churches which send them. Candor compels us occasionally to offer criticism, but the same candor requires us to note that faults, especially those that are more than individual weaknesses, are with few exceptions the projections of the life of the home churches. Guido Verbeck wrote in 1883 that it is not to be expected that "missionaries, individually or collectively, should be vastly superior and wiser than their constituencies, the home churches who produce and commission them."[67] To this statement, however, may be added the important qualification that, given time, experience in foreign service has frequently given missionaries perspectives from which to rise above the limitations of their background; in turn they have often contributed to the correction and enlightenment of their home churches and homelands.

The missionaries developed close friendships among themselves and across denominational lines in the forced intimacy of the port cities. They knew and confided in one another to an extent generally not comparably possible in their homelands at this time, and they were able to share this large-mindedness — what we would now call an ecumenical spirit — with their Japanese converts. This understanding was due in no small measure to the wide theological agreement which prevailed among most Protestant missionaries. Until the year 1890 theological differences were of far less significance than those of church government and ministerial orders.[68] In this context of

[66] Thomas, *op. cit.*, p. 169.
[67] Verbeck, *op. cit.*, p. 874.
[68] Thomas, *op. cit.*, pp. 70-71, 136-137.

understanding and amity the missions made various attempts to achieve cooperation among themselves and union among the growing Japanese churches.

We have noted the strong action taken by the missionary convention of September, 1872, in favor of ecumenical cooperation and the unity of the Japanese churches to be established under their care. A committee of three was appointed on April 7, 1874, by the Presbyterian Mission to confer with the Congregational and Reformed Missions concerning cooperation in Christian work and, specifically, union of the Japanese churches emerging in association with the missions. This committee later reported, however, no definite result.

The Congregational Mission at its annual meeting in Kōbe on May 29, 1874, took formal action as unequivocally in favor of union on the basis of the convention of September, 1872. The two churches, however, which were established in Kōbe and Ōsaka in April and May of 1874, while they adopted the same name and creed as the churches of Yokohama and Tokyo, had voted rules of church government to conform with the Congregational tradition of the associated missionaries. The rules of polity of the Yokohama and Tokyo churches, on the other hand, were essentially those of the Presbyterian-Reformed tradition. The Japanese Christians in the four congregations assumed that they were in fact one church. However, since no disposition existed among the missionaries to alter the differing rules of government and since they considered them as constituting a barrier to union, it came to be an accepted fact among the missionaries that organic union could not exist between the churches of the two traditions.[69] The Japanese Christians, though not without some demur, were in general willing to follow this principle of action, and the churches established thereafter came sooner or later to belong to Japanese ecclesiastical structures which largely perpetuated the confessional and, in some cases, the sectarian distinctions brought by the Western missionaries. We shall see, however, that the determination of

[69] Verbeck, *op. cit.*, pp. 792-793. For a Japanese history of the entire course of Protestant efforts toward church union, see Miyakoda Tsunetarō, *Nihon Kirisuto Kyō Gōdōshikō*.

the churches of Congregational association to maintain the distinctiveness of that tradition was influenced considerably by the independent convictions of the Japanese leaders Paul Sawayama and, perhaps more strongly, Niishima Jō.

Beginning in April, 1876, the missions of Presbyterian-Reformed background, however, being one in their concepts and practice of polity, took steps which led to a specific program of cooperation. The missions of the Presbyterian Church, U.S.A., the Reformed Church in America, and the United Presbyterian Church of Scotland retained their separate identity with reference to certain matters concerning missionary personnel, but on June 21, 1876, they constituted themselves as a Council of Three Missions, by which they agreed to act as a single unit in mission work. They further agreed as a majority that the Japanese congregations under their care, then numbering eight, should constitute one church, in which the male missionaries who assented to the standards of doctrine and rules of government of this church should be ex officio members of the ecclesiastical body in its structure as a presbytery (*Chūkai*).[70] It should be noted that missionaries were thus able to participate as full voting members in the deliberations of presbytery, but Japanese Christians could not participate, except by specific invitation, in the meetings of the Council of Three Missions.

On June 21, 1877, the union of the eight Japanese churches in cooperation with the three missions was consummated, and the name adopted by the Japanese was the United Church of Christ in Japan (*Nihon Kirisuto Itchi Kyōkai*).[71] The standards of doctrine which were adopted by the Japanese Christians, in spite of serious opposition from some, were the Shorter and Heidelberg Catechisms, the Westminster Confession of Faith, and the Canons of the Synod of Dort. The heavy hand of missionary pressure, in conformity with the spirit at home, was clearly recognizable in this action. At this time the total mem-

---

[70] The church at this stage consisted of only one presbytery, but as the number of presbyteries grew, one missionary could of course belong to only one presbytery. Membership in the General Assembly (*Daikai*) came to be by delegation.

[71] The "official" history of this church from its beginning is *Nihon Kirisuto Kyōkaishi.*

bership of the eight churches was 623; of these twenty-five were students for the ministry. On April 5, 1881, the churches, which had then come to number twenty-five, were constituted into three presbyteries according to geographical locations, eastern, northern, and western. At the first meeting of the eight, action was taken to establish a theological school in Tokyo. The same day three candidates who had been prepared without a formal theological education were examined and ordained to the gospel ministry.[72] One of them was Okuno Masatsuna, at this time fifty-five years of age and already a preacher of rare and winning power. Okuno was one of those *samurai* who had supported the *Bakufu* at the time of the Meiji Restoration and with the defeat of his lord was left without means of support and in spiritual despair. In his extremity he sought employment as a language teacher with the Reformed Church missionary Samuel R. Brown, by whom, after being much influenced also by the preaching of J. H. Ballagh, he was baptized at the risk of his life in July, 1872.

Okuno's calligraphy was greatly admired, and he prepared the manuscript for the wood blocks of the first edition of the New Testament in Japanese. He was the first poet of the Protestant church in Japan and the beginner of authentic hymnology. Okuno increasingly impressed those who knew him by the strength and purity of his loyalty to Jesus Christ. He represented to men of that day the transmutation of *samurai* loyalty into the morally purified, spiritually ennobled dedication that characterized not a few of the Christian leaders, clerical and lay, of the first generation. Toward the end of his life Okuno seemed to grow in physical energy as in spiritual purity. Something of the effect of his preaching is shown in the words, albeit somewhat extravagant, of a missionary who had often heard him: "I listened to torrents of eloquence. I was led into vast chambers of imagery. I was melted by tenderness of appeal, that bore me in imagination to angelic realms, until I felt no longer on earth, but amid the choirs of heaven."[73]

---

[72] Verbeck, *op. cit.*, pp. 792-796.

[73] Griffis, *Hepburn of Japan*, pp. 168-176. Cf. Kuroda Yasunobu, *Okuno Masatsuna Sensei Ryaku Den oyobi Kashū;* this book includes a collection of Okuno's poems.

From 1875, Methodist missionaries, with the aid of the Yokohama church, began work in the interior. The first church established under these auspices was in Aichi Prefecture on June 10, 1877; a second was founded later the same year in Kanagawa Prefecture. Extensive work was started to the northwest of Tokyo, and a girls' school, begun in Tokyo, prospered greatly. In conjunction with this and other schools, the church in Hirosaki led in stimulating a large number of young men and women to devote themselves to professional Christian service.

In central Japan, focused in the cities of Kōbe, Ōsaka and Kyōto, the work of the mission of the American Board (Congregational) proceeded apace. By the end of 1876 seven churches had been established, a girls' school at Kōbe was in successful operation, and two buildings had been erected for the Dōshisha. By the end of 1882, this mission was operating three girls' schools, and the Dōshisha had become one of the major educational institutions of the land. The first theological class of fifteen, consisting mostly of men of the Kumamoto Band, was graduated in 1879. Missionary and Japanese workers cooperated in large monthly meetings which became possible from 1880 in the gradually improving atmosphere of openness; they were held in the largest theatres in the city of Kyōto. Calls came from far and near to preach the gospel, to the extent that the mission did not have half the Japanese workers needed to respond.

This mission had carried on extensive medical work in the Kansai (central Japan) under the leadership of Drs. Berry, Taylor, and Adams, as had the American and Scottish Presbyterians in the Kantō (eastern) area. However, as opportunities for the direct preaching of the gospel opened and were multiplied, more attention was given to this part of the work. This shift in emphasis was also due to the very rapid increase and improvement of Japanese medical facilities. Some Christian medical stations were closed, and within another decade the need for missionary support of this kind of work largely ceased.

The outstanding work in Christian literature of the Congregational Mission deserves notice. It had begun the printing and distribution of tracts expounding the fundamental principles of Christianity in 1873 and expanded the work to include the sale and distribution of Christian books, at first Chinese and English, then Japanese translations of Chinese and English works, and finally books and tracts written by Japanese Christians. This mission issued what was the first and for a time the only Christian periodical in the country. This was the *Shichi Ichi Zappō* (Weekly Miscellany), a family journal of eight pages. Another important periodical was the monthly magazine edited by Kozaki Hiromichi and Uemura Masahisa from 1880 called the *Rikugō Zasshi*. The *Maishū Shimpō,* a weekly, was begun in 1882. A monthly for women and children, the *Yorokobi no Otozure* (Joyful Tidings), was begun in 1877 by Miss S. B. McNeal of the Women's Union Missionary Society; Miura Tōru was the associate editor.

In this and other missions, direct work among women was always regarded as of great importance, and the single women missionaries of course gave much of their attention to this responsibility along with their service in schools for girls. Increasingly Japanese girls were trained for this work and were generally known as Bible women. Many, perhaps most, of this splendid body of dedicated women married pastors and continued to aid the work of the church with their professional skills and quality of spirit.

In keeping with the strong spirit of independence and self-reliance among the Japanese pastors, almost all of whom were of *samurai* origin in the first generation, and in keeping with the principles of most missionaries, strong emphasis was laid upon the financial self-support of the Japanese churches. Of the nineteen churches reported by the Congregational Mission at the end of 1882, ten were able wholly to support their pastors. This spirit came to be particularly strong in the United Church of Christ (of Presbyterian-Reformed tradition). A noted example of the zeal and self-denial characteristic of this spirit is the case of Paul Sawayama, who returned from study in the United States in 1874 to establish the first church in Ōsaka, giving up opportunities to enter government service at far higher pay. His resolve to live on the salary that his congregation could pay may have been a factor contributing to his poor health and early death, but his spirit of self-denial was so contagious that he led his congregation in the establishment of the Baika Girls' School without any financial assistance from the mission. This congregation, under Sawayama's leadership, was also responsible for starting another church in Ōsaka which shortly became self-supporting and began work in nine other places. The church was also a major force in the inception of the first Japanese home missionary society (in the *Kumiai* or Congregational Church).[74]

The work of the Anglican missions also showed much progress from 1873. Although their missionaries were the very first on the field in 1859, the American Episcopal Mission had suffered loss in personnel. During the first decade, perhaps the most important work had been in study of the language and the preparation of literary materials, including the translation of important portions of the Prayer Book. In 1872 and 1873, however, considerable reinforcements arrived, and substantial work was carried on in Ōsaka and Tokyo. A boys' school was started in Ōsaka in 1872, another in Tokyo in 1874. A dispensary was begun in Ōsaka by Dr. H. Laning, where more than a thousand patients were treated in the first six months. The reports of this mission speak frequently of the urgent need for single women missionaries. The Protestant Episcopal Church appointed in June, 1877, a Japanese who had studied medicine for six years in the United States, Isaac K. Yokoyama, as a missionary and full member of the mission. This was a situation somewhat different from that of Niishima Jō, who received a yearly financial allowance from the American Board but was not classed as a missionary.[75]

We shall have to conclude consideration of the work of the separate missions and churches in this period with a brief account of the activity of the American Baptist Mission. The Rev. Jonathan Goble had returned to America at the close of the first decade. The work had to be recommenced almost from the beginning when in 1872 the American Baptist Missionary Union took up the responsibility for Baptist work in Japan and sent the Gobles and another couple who arrived in Japan in February, 1873. A third couple arrived in October of the same year, Rev. and Mrs. J. Hope Arthur, who began a girls' school in Tokyo

[74] Verbeck, *op. cit.*, pp. 841-848; Thomas, *op. cit.*, p. 143.
[75] Cf. Hardy, *op. cit.*, pp. 212-213.

in 1874. A Baptist church was organized in Yokohama in the month following the missionaries' arrival in 1873, composed at first only of the two missionary families. The first Japanese convert was baptized and united with this congregation in July of the same year. Two single women missionaries arrived in November, 1875, and were able to strengthen greatly the work among women through education and in other ways. The work of this mission was carried on very faithfully, but again owing to loss in personnel during the 1870's, the activity and external fruit was less than in the larger missions. The first Japanese Baptist pastor was ordained in November, 1879. In the winter of 1879-1880 work was begun in the Tōhoku (Northeast), which was somewhat more backward, economically and culturally, and therefore a more difficult area; this became, however, one of the most fruitful enterprises of Baptist activity in Japan. In 1881 work was started and a small church organized on the island of Shikoku. Similar work was begun in Kōbe in 1882.

Independent Christian churches were also established. One was the exceedingly important church which was established separately in Sapporo as an off-shoot of the original Sapporo Band. Seven members of this group became dissatisfied with the structure of the local church and the methods of the Methodist pastor M. C. Harris. They decided to form their own fellowship according to what in their understanding was the way of the New Testament. All seven members of the church were held equal in authority and all took turns in assuming the responsibilities of leadership, including preaching. Harris was wisely sympathetic with the boys and helpful in various ways. With the coming of missionaries of other denominations, however, misunderstanding arose, and in consequence the young men became incensed with what they felt were the evils and folly of denominational rivalry. An unfortunate incident in the use of money from Western churches impressed upon them the necessity of financial independence from Western missionaries. One of these young men was Uchimura Kanzō, and from this modest beginning grew the great Non-Church (Mukyōkai) Movement in Japan. Another independent church was started in Tokyo under the leadership of the Rev. Awazu Kōmei, who had been baptized by J. H. Ballagh in May, 1868. This congregation later united with the *Kumiai* (Congregational) Church in Tokyo.[76]

By the end of the second period, one could reflect on the course of events and evaluate persons, institutions and methods. The missionaries themselves had become increasingly competent in the use of the language and familiar with the ways of the people. Churches had been widely established; a relatively large number of Japanese pastors had been well trained and were serving with distinction. The number of Japanese Protestant Christians at the end of 1882 was 4,987.[77] The New Testament as prepared by the Permanent Translation Committee was completed in November, 1879, and published the following April. Progress was being steadily made in the translation of the Old Testament.[78] Other literary work was being carried on with vigor and great improvement in quality. Schools had been established in many parts of the country, and through them increasingly large numbers of students were being reached with the message of the gospel and, further, being trained to lead the nation in the period of transition into the complexities of modern life.

The missionaries came to see with new clarity the need to "naturalize the Church of Japan and transform foreign missions into home missions." They saw that the responsibility for the conversion of Japan must lie primarily with the Japanese Christians. Their goal was to raise up churches taught and trained to be self-supporting, self-governing and self-propagating, although they may have understood this slogan in too narrow and individualistic a way. For the implementation of these goals home missionary societies had been formed in both the *Kumiai*

---

[76] Jennings, *op. cit.*, pp. 15-18; Verbeck, *op. cit.*, p. 824.

[77] A continued hindrance to the formal practice of the Christian faith concerned the burial of believers. Most burial grounds were in the precincts or under the control of Buddhist temples.

[78] Note should be taken of the support of several Bible societies in the work of translation. The American Bible Society had been the pioneer in support through a local committee, although its first appointed agent did not arrive until January, 1876. The National Bible Society of Scotland commenced operations through its first agent in 1875. The British and Foreign Bible Society operated from January, 1876, through a committee of missionaries, its first agent arriving in March, 1881.

Church and the United Church of Christ in Japan. Indeed, the Japanese churches had already come to form several societies independent of the foreign missions. Among these were the *Shinbokukai,* a kind of Christian fraternization society, the *Seinenkai,* a young people's society, a Young Men's Christian Association, and certain local associations for the purpose of holding assemblies for preaching or lectures. A Japanese branch of the Evangelical Alliance was early organized, and before the end of the second period the Week of Prayer had come to be observed annually.

5

The next period in the early history of Protestantism in Japan has been called the era of rapid advance (1883-1889). On the basis of the institutions and methods developed in the early decades, but with Japanese Christians increasingly emerging into positions of leadership in both name and fact, the Christian movement grew and was strengthened to an astonishing degree. The zeal of the converts was such that large numbers willingly sacrificed both time and money to serve the cause of Christian witness.[79] The profound and sustained sense of liberation experienced by many of these Christians must be considered in any attempt to understand the ethos of the church of that day. We have noted that the Christian faith gave meaning to life and opportunities for significant service to many people, especially to those of the *samurai* class, many of whom were in effect the losers in the shift of leadership involved in the Meiji Restoration.

But quite apart from this situation of political and social displacement, many Japanese of various classes came through Christian faith to experience a profound spiritual liberation from what they felt to be the tyranny of Confucianism and the family system *(kazoku seido)* as these had been developed in Japan over the centuries of isolation and had been essentially

---

[79] The policy and tone of most missions, and to an even stronger extent of most Japanese pastors and congregations, were strongly on the side of financial self-support. The Anglican missions, however, were a deliberate exception to this practice.

reaffirmed by the new Meiji government.[80] By the term "tyranny of Confucianism" I refer not to the teachings of Confucius, who in fact predicated the obedience of the people ultimately upon the justice of rulers,[81] but to the way in which Confucianism was taught in Japan. It was taught to be the ideological basis for absolute submission to the structures and personages of traditional Japanese society, and these in turn were held to constitute religious ultimates. Niishima Jō frequently referred to the Confucian doctrine of filial duty taught in Japan as tyrannous; he contrasted his new-found Christian freedom with the slavery of those bound to obey without understanding or love.[82] Kozaki Hiromichi in his famous work *Seikyō Shinron*, published in 1886, emphasized the politically and socially liberating power of Christian truth as compared to the enslaving, dehumanizing characteristics of traditional Japanese expressions of Confucianism.[83] Christian faith was thus experienced by many Japanese as bringing liberation, but it was in fact liberation from the primary element of the Japanese tradition, absolute submission to political and social superiors. Thus it constituted, as had the faith of the *Kirishitan*, a radical challenge to the tradition.[84] It was not to be expected that this challenge would fail to generate reaction, and the rapid Christian advance of the 1880's was followed by resurgent and hostile nationalism among much of the nation with retardation of Christian growth in the 1890's. In fact, as we shall see, this pattern of challenge and hostile response was to be the repeated experience of the Christian church in Japan during the twentieth century as well as the nineteenth.

The motivation to Christian faith of many of the young men who came to believe even though their experience of faith was substantially one of liberation, was by no means entirely or even

[80] Kami, *op. cit.*, p. 20.

[81] Cf. E. R. Hughes, *Chinese Philosophy in Classical Times*, pp. 24-25; Akamatsu Toshihide, *Shinran*, p. 214.

[82] Hardy, *op. cit.*, pp. 118-122.

[83] Sumiya, *op. cit.*, pp. 7-22. Cf. *Kindai Nihon to Kirisuto Kyō*, Meiji Hen, pp. 66-76.

[84] Cf. Kanamori Tokujirō, "Common Sense and the Constitution," *Religion and State in Japan*, pp. 1-20.

predominantly personal. In the historical context which I have just outlined, the desire of many was to build a new Japan which, with the formal (although not the actual) dissolution of the feudal system, they felt could best be constructed through the principles and standards of Christian faith. Honda Yōichi, Ibuka Kajinosuke, Uemura Masahisa and Kojima Ittō were among those for whom the welfare of the state and nation was of surpassing importance and who became Christians with the hope that they could thereby better serve their country.[85] The personal moral earnestness evident in these men they already possessed before becoming Christians; received in part at least from their Confucian training, this moral earnestness was strengthened by their missionary teachers. The result was that with few exceptions Christian faith never became for them a mere ideological tool. As they grew in understanding they were able to contribute to the welfare of the nation at deeper levels than they themselves had generally expected at first. They came to see, and to share the insight, that conversion to God in Jesus Christ meant transformation of the whole man, of his ethical standards, his concepts of man and society as well as of God, and, by no means least of all, transformation of conduct, personal as well as social.[86] The wonder of Japanese experience of Christian faith is that so many followed this process to its fullest implications.

The very first Japanese Protestants, as we have seen, were drawn from the *samurai* class. In the second decade Christianity was more associated with many of the politically and socially liberal elements of the nation, almost to the extent of identification with what came to be the Popular Rights Movement (*Jiyūminken Undō*). In this context the Christian faith and church appealed to segments of society beyond the *samurai,* and for a time great interest was evidenced and churches were built in many places in the rural districts. This phenomenon, however, was apparently confined largely to a limited number of prosperous farmers and members of the new professional

---

[85] Katakozawa Chiyomatsu, *Nihon Purotesutanto Hyaku Nen no Ayumi,* pp. 48-49.

[86] *Ibid.,* p. 52.

class of teachers and physicians who entered the country areas in ever larger numbers during the Meiji Era. Moreover, it was but temporary, primarily because the rural and urban poor were purposely excluded as much as possible from the process of modernization in political and social understanding. This was a consequence of government policy and its implementation through the elementary schools being built in every part of the land in conformity with the Education Law of 1872, which made elementary education compulsory. The Protestant Christian church, therefore, consisted largely of men and women of the transformed and expanded *samurai* class, that is, the new professional and bourgeois middle class and the students who fed their ranks.[87]

Winburn Thomas, in analyzing the reasons for the far deeper rootage of Protestantism in the cities, stresses the fact of the concentration of missionaries there, the fact that the students, who constituted the largest number of converts, tended to remain in the cities and the fact that "there was more money in the urban areas to maintain an exotic religion."[88] These were all valid although probably not determinative factors in what was a highly complex sociological situation. A word, therefore, may be appropriate here with reference to the last point mentioned by Thomas. The relative paucity of money in the rural areas in Japan is a truism with which we need not deal. But this fact, equally true in the sixteenth and seventeenth centuries, did not prevent Catholics from developing many strong rural congregations. The financial problem faced by Protestants was not primarily posed by their emphasis upon self-support — Japanese have almost always been zealous to assume responsibility in this area — but by the normative concept of a congregation, however small, supporting its own pastor solely from the free-will offerings of the members, a concept received from the Protestant missionary members. Over the years most Japanese pastors have had consequently to accept part-time remunerative

---

[87] Kami, *op. cit.*, pp. 18, 25, 27, 38. For a time members of the nobility and the financially upper class attended services in some numbers, but few were baptized. These people, however, continued in various ways to be influenced by Christianity. *Ibid.*, pp. 30-31.

[88] Thomas, *op. cit.*, p. 87.

work (usually writing or lecturing). The force of the concept, however — and it has been generally accepted — has been not only to create personal frustration and no little hardship but also, in my judgment, to hinder the growth of the church by deterring the emergence of lay leadership.[89]

During the third decade, among the Protestant missionary societies already in the field, the Edinburgh Medical Mission, the United Presbyterian Church of Scotland and the Society for the Promotion of Female Education in the East withdrew from active work in Japan. Fifteen of the societies, however, continued their work, in some cases expanding their forces. Eleven new missions established themselves, one English, one German and Swiss, one Canadian and eight American. The predominance of American Protestant missionaries in Japan thus became even more pronounced. The mission from German-speaking lands, however, the General Evangelical Protestant Missionary Society, was particularly significant in that it brought to Japan from 1885 organized expression of the new or liberal theology then gathering momentum in Germany and elsewhere in the West. One of their representatives, speaking of the "advanced theology" of the mission, wrote that their aim was "a reconciliation of Christianity with the modern view of the world, by striving after an up-to-date expression of the eternal truth of the simple gospel of Jesus, adapted at the same time to the particular needs of the Japanese, instead of offering ancient but transient formulas of Western dogmatics and worship."[90]

In this connection mention should be made that in 1877 the American Unitarian Association sent as a representative of its faith the Rev. A. M. Knapp, who preferred to be called an envoy or ambassador rather than a missionary. He had come to express the sympathy of the Unitarians for progressive religious movements in Japan. With emphasis upon the notion of the "sympathy of religions," Knapp proclaimed his mission to be what would now be called dialogue, and the sharing of faith

89 Cf. William Imbrie, "Nihon Kirisuto Kyokwai," *General Conference of Protestant Missionaries in Japan,* 1900, p. 889.
90 *General Conference of Protestant Missionaries in Japan,* 1900, p. 922.

and life in a process of mutual learning with other religious traditions.[91] Knapp and the continental European society constituted the first distinctly discordant element in the otherwise solid front of essential theological unity manifested by the Protestant missionaries. Their influence upon a minor, though important, segment of the church and upon wider ranges of Japanese liberal political thought was considerable, but they accomplished relatively little in the area of the organization of churches. Throughout this period and later, the major growth in numbers was achieved by the older missions and churches.

The American Methodist Mission in its report for the year 1882 indicated that the aim of its teaching ministry was to be biblical rather than theological.[92] The Presbyterian-Reformed missions were distinctly confessional in their formal adherence to the symbols of their tradition, but in fact they, too, as well as the Congregationalists, were more biblical and doctrinal than creatively theological in their emphasis. Thus the early period of Protestant Christianity in Japan has been described as relatively non-theological in character.[93] The early missionaries and their Japanese converts were primarily concerned with planting the church and the spiritual and ethical transformation of men. The ethical tone was rather strongly puritan in the New England sense of the term but was by no means entirely negative or repressive. A strong emphasis was laid upon keeping the Sabbath. Abstinence from smoking and drinking was, except in the case of the Anglican missions, a strong element on the whole, and has remained a vital part of the Japanese Protestant tradition long after its relative decline in North America. More important, however, was the emphasis upon monogamy and sexual purity, by which the missionaries and Japanese Christians strove through education and various movements — the former from the beginning, the latter more distinctly after the turn of the century — to purify both home and society, elevate the status of women and fight against legalized prostitution, especially as the system kept girls against their will.

[91] Cary, *A History of Christianity in Japan*, vol. 2, p. 199.
[92] Verbeck, *op. cit.*, p. 855.
[93] Cf. Charles H. Germany, *Protestant Theologies in Modern Japan*, pp. 2-3.

Japanese Christians, however, even more than the missionaries, were concerned to apply the Protestant social ethic, as
they understood it, to the building of a new society. As we have
seen, this hope was a primary motive for Christian faith among
many. From our perspective, their ethics were distinctly bourgeois in orientation and flavor, but in the context of the day
they pointed toward wider freedoms than any other significant
element in society. And, as we shall see, Japanese Protestant
thinkers contended valiantly with the traditional Japanese
tendency, now about to emerge with new force, to equate po-
litico-social structures and personages with religious absolutes.
Furthermore, the strong ethical emphasis of the early Protestant missionaries appears to have been uniquely suited to meet
the mind-set of the more earnest among the young men of *samurai* class. These men had been trained in a form of Confucianism ethically oriented toward the welfare of the state more than
of the person, but the peculiarly Japanese tradition of *Bushidō*
(the Way of the Warrior) at its best had led in the direction of
moral fervor as well as spiritual zeal. They were, in a word,
culturally prepared for the total dedication properly characteristic of Christian faith and unreservedly asked for by the early
missionaries. They expected to give themselves to a permanent
regimen of ethical as well as spiritual disciplines. Indeed, to
many of their contemporaries this prospect constituted one of
the appeals of Christian faith and distinctly differentiated it
from the traditional religions of the land. Evangelistic meetings
were sometimes successfully held in the early Meiji period in
the form of lectures on "the Reformation of Public Morals."[94]

As we shall see, some Japanese Christian pastors and theologians possessed and expressed a profound understanding of
the Christian doctrines of sin, forgiveness and redemption. But
of wider appeal and influence in the country was the majesty
of the biblical concept of God, his providence and love and
derived notions of personality and the ethics of responsible
men in society. The influence of the Christian movement was
far out of proportion to its size partly because of the appeal of
this content of faith and partly because most of the Christian

---

[94] *Ibid.*, p. 4.

community was of *samurai* origin, the traditional source of leadership in Japanese society.

By the mid-eighties a change in the mental atmosphere had occurred in a substantial segment of the educated classes, the emerging bourgeoisie. Anti-Christian prejudice decreased relative to a growing appreciation of Western religion and morality as well as science and technology. This is not to say that hostility had disappeared. If it had decreased among some, it had only become quiescent among others and, again, was unchanged in virulence among not a few. Toward the close of this decade a distinguished pastor and theologian, later president of the Dōshisha, Ebina Danjō, observed that it would be difficult to exaggerate the ill will which the average Japanese had for Christianity.[95] But thoughtful Japanese among the literate classes increasingly came to recognize that Christianity in the West was a civilizing factor that did not destroy wholesome patriotism. The social disorder and relatively widespread immorality consequent upon the many political and social changes of the past three decades led a number of leading citizens to urge that morality could not be promoted apart from religion and that Christianity constituted the best existing system of morality. A highly significant symbol of this change was the distinguished educator, journalist and leader of the liberal thought of the day, Fukuzawa Yukichi. He had been hostile to Christianity, but then in 1884, without receiving baptism himself, advocated the adoption of Christianity because of "its superiority in wealth, intelligence, virtue and ability to attract persons of rank."[96] One factor which contributed substantially to this change of view was the recognition that the missionaries both favored and worked strongly to revise the early treaties with foreign nations which were still in force and restricted Japanese autonomy in the areas of customs, duties and extraterritorial rights for foreigners.[97]

Throughout the 1880's, then, Protestant Christianity in Japan

---

[95] Thomas, *op. cit.*, p. 161.

[96] *Ibid.*, p. 179.

[97] The revised treaties did not go into effect until 1899, and, as we shall see, the failure again in 1889 to secure their revision was an important factor in precipitating the anti-foreign, nationalist reaction of the 1890's.

experienced remarkable growth in a context of unprecedented openness and public favor. Invitations to preach in towns and villages as well as in cities were so common that they were accepted as normal. It became easy to gather audiences of five hundred or more to hear the Christian gospel. "A little preparation with public notice would fill a hall or theatre with a congregation that for four or five hours would listen to one speaker after another. Christianity seemed to have the power of self-propagation. In every three years the membership of the church doubled; and churches were paying their pastors such salaries that self-support seemed a thing of the near future." The cry among many Japanese Christians became "Christ for Japan and Japan for Christ."[98] During this period itineration was widely carried on by missionaries, Japanese evangelists and theological students. Public preaching in Japanese had gradually become tacitly allowed after the removal of the anti-Christian edict notices in early 1873. Especially during the 1880's Japanese and foreign Christian workers made extended tours outside the treaty ports, some spending weeks and even months on a single trip. The general optimism among the missionaries was such that many anticipated that Japan might become a Christian nation in less than a generation. They urged their boards at home to act speedily and wisely to take advantage of the opportunities then available.

In this context a nation-wide revival with strong emotional overtones somewhat akin to the American frontier experience occurred in 1883 and 1884. As a result of the revival of 1888 which took place in the prefecture of Ōita, ten young men entered the Christian ministry.[99] The emotional intensity in many instances was similar to that of the prayer meeting which had led to the organization of the first Protestant church in 1873.

More than any other agency the American Board (Congregational) responded to the urgent appeals for additional missionary personnel, with the result that by the beginning of the year 1890 they had eighty-nine workers on the field in Japan. The

[98] Imbrie, *op. cit.*, pp. 895, 893.
[99] D. S. Spencer, *General Conference of Protestant Missionaries in Japan*, 1900, p. 917.

other of the five major families of missions — Anglican, Presbyterian-Reformed, Baptist, and Methodist — responded comparably and, in cooperation with the Japanese Christians, harvested most of the growth of the decade. By 1889 the larger part of the Protestant congregations in Japan were of these traditions. In keeping with long practice, standards for church admission were kept high throughout this period in almost all congregations.[100]

An important shift occurred in the 1880's in the developing relationships between the missionaries and the Japanese Christians. The experience of the Presbyterian-Reformed group in its relationship with the *Nihon Kirisuto Itchi Kyōkai* is typical. At the beginning of the decade evangelistic work (outside the normal activity of local congregations) was almost wholly under the direction of the missions; Japanese leadership was largely confined to the giving of counsel. From 1886, however, a new situation emerged, characterized by financial cooperation and joint controls, which finally in 1894 developed into one of financial independence and synodical control. A board of twenty members, most of whom would normally be Japanese, was elected by the highest judicatory *(Daikai)*, and the funds for the work came almost wholly from the church, the greater part of this from congregations and preaching places not receiving financial aid from the missions. At this time it was the policy of this board to select congregations and to bring them to financial self-support rather than to open new work.[101] This policy meant that the initiation of entirely new work largely remained the responsibility of the missions, but it was in almost all cases effected in consultation with the church.

Another important characteristic of the period of rapid advance was the continuing efforts to achieve cooperation and even union among the missions and churches. The Anglican missions, English and American, had conducted their activities separately, even with some friction, until 1886 when the new English bishop, Edward Bickersteth, called, in conjunction with the American bishop, C. M. Williams, a conference of

---

[100] Thomas, *op. cit.*, pp. 148, 156.
[101] Imbrie, *op. cit.*, pp. 888-889.

missionaries to consider a proposal to unite the scattered congregations formed as a result of the work of the three Anglican missions. At a second conference on July 8, 1886, a concrete plan was adopted, and on February 8, 1887, the Anglican Church of Japan *(Nihon Seikōkai),* in communion with the Anglican churches of England and America, was organized, and the previously prepared constitution and canons were accepted.[102]

At this inaugural synod Bishop Bickersteth further proposed a resolution looking toward the establishment of a single (non-Roman) church in Japan which should impose no non-essential conditions of communion. A memorandum to this effect was then sent to the non-Roman missions and churches. Bickersteth also inclosed with this communication two of his recent sermons, in which he claimed that the Anglican Communion united in itself the endowments and characteristics which had been granted to others separately and as "the only Communion which . . . has touch and contact with them all" was properly the rallying point for the other denominations. This posture of superiority naturally created controversy, and nothing came of the plan.[103]

More serious was the "painstaking attempt" to form an organic union between the Presbyterian-Reformed *(Nihon Kirisuto Itchi Kyōkai)* and Congregational *(Nihon Kumiai Kyōkai)* churches. The General Assembly of the former and the General Conference of the latter each appointed in May, 1887, a committee to confer and report concerning a basis of union. The statement of doctrine and polity drafted as a consequence of this work was adopted by both assemblies. A joint committee of twenty then conferred for nearly a year and unanimously adopted a constitution with bylaws and appendix. The great majority of laymen and ministers in both churches favored the constitutions, as did a majority of the missionaries. The General Assembly of the *Nihon Itchi Kyōkai,* which had a longer history as a church from its formation in 1877, unanimously adopted the constitution at Ōsaka on November 23, 1888. The

---

[102] A. C. Shaw, *General Conference of Protestant Missionaries in Japan,* 1900, pp. 879-881.

[103] Thomas, *op. cit.,* pp. 148-149.

Kumiai Kyōkai, however, which had only been constituted in 1886, meeting also at Ōsaka at the same time, voted for six months postponement of decision. Subsequent postponements finally led to termination of negotiations.

It is somewhat difficult to determine and evaluate the possible reasons for this failure, because no doubt exists of the dominance of a spirit of harmony and genuine desire for union among both missionaries and Japanese. Perhaps the most that can be said is that this ecumenical situation was at the time so far in advance of conditions at home that the majority of missionaries who favored union felt hesitant to press too strongly the minority who were constrained largely by denominational loyalties to oppose it. Opposition, however, was not confined to missionaries. Niishima Jō was apparently a powerful element in this movement or mood; his unique experience in America, by which he came to feel a special sense of loyalty to his "foster-father," Alpheus Hardy, to whom as well as to the Congregational Church he owed so much, evidently led him to a position of denominational loyalty beyond that held by most Japanese Christians.[104]

The ecumenical intent of the majority, however, was by no means crushed by this reverse, and in various ways it continued to influence the course of events in Japan. The consciousness of being part of a clearly demonstrated majority gave increased confidence. The entire experience was in fact of great educative value. One specific consequence was that the *Nihon Kirisuto Itchi Kyōkai,* whose name was changed in 1890 to *Nihon Kirisuto Kyōkai,* set up a committee to continue the study of creeds which had begun during the negotiations. From the beginning there were many, especially among the Japanese, who were dissatisfied with the standards adopted by the church (the Westminster Confession and Shorter Catechism, the Heidelberg Catechism and the Canons of the Synod of Dort) as not well suited to the needs in Japan. The positive aspect of this dissatisfaction was expressed in a strong desire for a simpler and more irenic creed. As a consequence of this background of

---

[104] Hardy, *op. cit.,* p. 318. Cf. *Nihon Kumiai Kirisuto Kyōkaishi, Kirisuto ni aru Jiyū wo Motomete,* pp. 207-226.

feeling as well as of the recent experience of ecumenical negotiations, the General Assembly adopted in December, 1890, a simple statement of faith which in five long sentences expressed simply and clearly evangelical faith in the atonement, justification and sanctification of man through faith in Christ, the work of the Holy Spirit and the inspiration and supremacy of the Scriptures. It concluded with the Apostles' Creed. The import of this act was clearly to further the mood and movement toward union within the Japanese church. In other ways, as in the publication of Sunday School literature and plans for a union hymnal, various missions continued and expanded their work of cooperation.[105]

B. THE PERIOD OF RESURGENT NATIONALISM AND EMERGING JAPANESE CHRISTIAN LEADERSHIP

1

WE HAVE NOTED THAT THROUGHOUT THE VERITABLE craze for things Western and the relative openness to Christianity that characterized the 1880's there still remained, often quiescent, but sometimes breaking out in minor incidents, a strong antagonism to Christianity.[1] This mood was rooted not only in the continuity of ancient hostility and the fear of the *Kirishitan*. It was also intimately connected with the deepest levels of ethnic awareness, national pride and loyalty, which in an earlier period were expressed in a rather unreasoning antiforeign policy but which, as the nation in the 1880's came to a new sense of its power vis-à-vis the countries of the West,

---

[105] Imbrie, *op. cit.*, pp. 886-887, 895; Spencer, *op. cit.*, p. 918.

[1] Cf. Ishihara Ken, *Nihon Kirisuto Kyōshi Ron*, p. 139.

emerged in the form of a resolve to reassert both Japanese political independence and the unique cultural traditions of the land.

From the first appearance of Commodore Perry and his black ships in 1853 Japan's primary concern had been to maintain the political independence of the country in the face of the overwhelming military and economic power of the Western nations. Indeed, leaders of the Meiji government became increasingly aware of Western colonial domination in the world and saw immediately before their eyes the spectacle of China's humiliation at the hands of the West. The resolve of every patriotic Japanese was that his country should not suffer the same fate. Thus, the policy of the government to develop an army and navy in the modern style found little opposition among the people.

In one sense, the period from the opening of the country to the end of the 1880's was a time of flux and uncertainty as the government and people felt their way to some kind of stability in the face of the cultural as well as political challenges posed by the West. During these thirty-five years, there were in fact several oscillations in relative favor and opposition to Western influences. It had come to be clearly seen that totally to reject the presence and influence of the West was a political impossibility. The real issue was over the degree of acceptance, as the most strenuous efforts were made to maintain national independence.

The new rulers in Japan, as we have seen, were not democrats; they constituted in fact a new oligarchy with a political and social orientation still primarily feudal.[2] When Itō Hirobumi, as the primary personage charged with the responsibility of preparing the first constitution, went to Europe in March, 1882, by

---

[2] The promulgation of the new constitution in 1889 did not appreciably alter this situation. The real rulers of the nation continued to be the oligarchs who formed the Privy Council and the Elder Statesmen (Genrō) in the new system and whose power was not substantially restricted by either cabinet or Diet. The cabinet, moreover, was not really accountable to the Diet, and the authority of the latter was little more than that of an effective organ of public opinion. Cf. Iglehart, *A Century of Protestant Christianity in Japan,* pp. 85-90.

imperial command to study foreign constitutions, he and his colleagues were most strongly attracted to the authoritarian constitutional monarchy of Prussia under the leadership of Bismarck; and the Prussian constitution and national practice became the chief model for what the Japanese rulers wanted, a modern industrial economy based upon feudal political structures and social relationships.[3] This aim came to be expressed in the phrase *Yōsai Wakon* (Western technology, Japanese spirit).

There were, to be sure, many factors working together to create the particular forms of the resurgent nationalism and concomitant anti-Christian mood of the 1890's. Winburn Thomas lists thirteen that he feels had the closest bearing upon the Christian movement.[4] There is wide scholarly agreement, however, that the event which brought to a focus all the other factors and precipitated the change in national mood was the failure of the Japanese government in the 1880's to secure revision of the unequal treaties of customs and extraterritoriality with the various Western powers. Opposition to these treaties had been steadily growing over the years, and one of the primary reasons why the Japanese were so eager for technological Westernization was to demonstrate to the Western nations that Japan had become "civilized" enough to warrant revision of the treaties. Adopting Western forms of government, even if Bismarckian, represented a further attempt to demonstrate this progressiveness. On this basis several attempts were made to secure revision of the treaties by which the inexperienced Tokugawa statesmen had on October 23, 1865, signed away two of the nation's basic rights.

The Iwakura Mission failed to obtain any change in the treaties at this point, as did the Tokyo diplomatic conference of 1882. A more ambitious attempt was made in 1886 under Foreign Minister Inoue Kaoru. A series of thirty-six conferences were held in Tokyo. But when it became known that the Japanese government had provisionally agreed to the formation of

---

[3] Cf. Borton, *Japan's Modern Century,* pp. 136-139.

[4] Thomas, *Protestant Beginnings in Japan,* pp. 182-206. Cf. *Kindai Nihon to Kirisuto Kyō,* Meiji Hen, pp. 178-225; Hiyane, *Nihon Kirisuto Kyōshi,* pp. 317-326, 337-348.

collegiate courts, consisting of both Japanese and foreign judges, for the adjudgment of cases involving foreigners, the reaction in Japan was so strong that the conferences were abandoned and in August, 1887, Inoue was forced to resign. The first treaty with Japan that abolished the unequal clauses was signed in London on July 16, 1894, to become effective in 1899. Similar treaties with other Western nations soon followed, but the damage had already been done. From 1887, Japan set itself irrevocably in the direction of the authoritarian, expansionist nationalism that, with varying kinds and degrees of emphasis, was largely to characterize its national policy until 1945.

During the 1880's Japan achieved a new national group consciousness and social cohesion. In place of the old, divisive loyalties to feudal lords, the nation had come to develop a patriotism focused on the emperor, a patriotism which for the first time in Japanese history embraced the entire country. Both contributing to and expressing this unity were the new system of compulsory elementary education and the conscript army. The popular press often opposed the government and generally supported the Popular Rights Movement and a "progressive" stance toward modernization. But, it was also strongly nationalistic and backed without qualification the government's efforts to secure revision of the unequal treaties. The conditions were ripe, therefore, for a reassertion of the traditional Japanese concept of the state as religiously absolute. This concept was given contemporary reformulation in the new constitution promulgated by Emperor Meiji on February 11, 1889, and in the Imperial Rescript on Education (Kyōiku Chokugo) promulgated in October, 1890.[5] These documents expressed essentially the political, social and cultural aspirations not only of the ruling classes but also of the bulk of the nation. As they came to be interpreted and applied in the light of this background, they occasioned a new form of Japanese cultural confrontation with the transcendent claims of Christianity.[6] The issue came to be formulated by the pro-

---

[5] Cf. Kami, *Purotesutanto Hyakunen-Shi Kenkyū*, pp. 39-41.

[6] Cf. Ernest E. Best, *Christian Faith and Cultural Crisis: The Japan Case*, pp. xiii, 33-52. Best's treatment of some of these problems is particularly perceptive.

ponents of the Japanese cultural tradition *(kokusui)* and socio-
political structure *(kokutai)* as the irreconcilability of Christianity with the mainstream of historic Japanese life.

2

One of the first signs of the difficulties the churches were to
encounter was a great decrease in the enrollment of mission
schools, in some cases as much as 50 percent of the total. Furthermore, public lectures, which had been very popular during the previous decade and a half, came to draw markedly
fewer people, first in Tokyo and later in the provincial cities
and towns. Those held were frequently disrupted by hostile and
vulgar heckling. The fact that almost all of the foreign missionaries had supported the aims of the Japanese government in
attempting to secure revision of the unequal treaties did not
prevent their coming under the same cloud of unpopularity
as all persons and things representatively Western, including
Christianity. The gain in new members for all Protestant
churches in 1889 was 5,677. In the following year the number
dropped to 1,199. Over the previous decade church membership
had doubled every three years; from this time twelve years
were required to achieve the same result. The strong opposition from outside the church weakened many within. Some
Christians in fact left the church and returned to older forms of
Japanese religious practice or gave themselves to the new cultural nationalism. And within the church there developed movements toward liberal theology or rationalism that appeared, at
least to most American and British missionaries, to betray the
faith. The boldness and zeal that had characterized so much of
the earlier witness seemed to abate appreciably.[7] The enthusiasm once marked by the cry "Christ for Japan and Japan for
Christ" was no longer comparably present within. Yokoi Tokio,
who had proclaimed in a public lecture meeting that "within
ten years Japan must become a Christian nation," wrote a
searing repudiation of orthodox Protestantism in 1894 and left

---

[7] Thomas, *op. cit.*, pp. 182-184.

the church, never to return.[8] Japanese nationalism came to be manifested in the church in various forms. A strong desire emerged to express Christian faith and life within the context of Japanese cultural traditions. Some members of the church exerted pressure to incorporate elements from the older faiths of the land, and a few advocated a "Japanese Christianity" which was in effect a Christianity without dogma or historical roots, a syncretistic fabrication.

The nationalist mood in the nation came to be reflected in the church in part by a stronger thrust toward independence, both financially and vis-à-vis the dominant leadership of the missionaries. The 1890's witnessed the vigorous emergence of new Japanese Christian leadership. This phenomenon carried certain distasteful aspects, and the effect on the missionary community can be seen in the 1900 report of the Congregational Mission (The American Board).

During the rapid growth following 1883, the number of Congregational missionaries had risen to eighty-nine. But as a result of what was then called the conservative reaction, "the work of the missionaries was so crippled by the criticism of prominent Christians that ere long it seemed to both the Mission and the Board that further increase of the force would be unwise." In fact deaths and resignations reduced the number to fifty by 1900.[9] Yet in this decade and the following were to emerge Japanese Christian leaders who would lead the church, and in some ways the nation, into extraordinarily creative endeavors, even as they remained faithful to the classic forms of Christian faith and life. Understanding of this period may perhaps best be gained by a consideration of a few of the most representative of these Japanese Christians. The earliest of these men also serve as transition figures from the first period of Japanese Protestantism to the third and fourth decades of the twentieth century.

---

[8] "*Jūnen go ni wa Nihon wo Kirisuto kyōkoku tarashimezaru bekarazu,*" Ishihara, *op. cit.*, p. 139.

[9] Otis Cary in *General Conference of Protestant Missionaries, Tokyo, 1900,* p. 912.

C. KOZAKI HIROMICHI AND
UCHIMURA KANZŌ

WE HAVE ALREADY NOTED THE PERCEPTIVE CRITICISM of the spiritual basis of Japanese government and society by Kozaki Hiromichi in his *Seikyō Shinron* (New Discussions on Politics and Religion) published in 1886. [1] Kozaki claimed that Neo-Confucianism combined social principles and secularized religion with the intent of maintaining the *status quo* of state and society. The distinction between the rulers and the ruled, between those possessing authority and those subject to it at all levels of society was absolutely fundamental to the system; the primary emphasis was upon the right of those above to rule and the duty of those below to obey. The apex of the structure, however, appeared to be under no restraint itself, from either divine or human perspective. Indeed, the social structure was seen as expressive of ultimate Reality itself (*Tennen Shizen no Chitsujo*).

Kozaki contrasted this world view and practice with Christian concern for persons as well as structures, with Christian insistence upon the rights of all men, upon the obligations of ruler to ruled as much as the ruled to ruler. He boldly asserted that it was childish to worship the emperor and the Imperial Rescript.[2] He made it clear to all who would see that a basic and at points irreconcilable conflict existed between the Christian understanding of man and society and that traditionally most beloved by the Japanese ruling classes.[3] In the context of the resurgent nationalism of this period, it was perhaps inevitable, therefore, that new modes of confrontation between the two should occur.

Singularly symbolic of the new confrontation was the inci-

---

[1] Cf. Kumano Yoshitaka, "Kozaki Hiromichi no Seikyōron Shingaku," *Fukuin to Sekai*, XXI-XXII/11-12, 1 (November, December, 1966, January, 1967).

[2] Germany, *Protestant Theologies in Modern Japan*, p. 17.

[3] Sumiya, *Nihon Shakai to Kirisuto Kyō*, pp. 7-26. The wide range of Kozaki's intellectual interests and studies may be seen in the fact that he was one of the first Japanese to lecture on Karl Marx. Cf. Kozaki Hiromichi, *Reminiscences of Seventy Years*, pp. 1-53.

dent of disloyalty (*fukei jiken*) involving Uchimura Kanzō. We noted this man as one of the ablest members of the Sapporo Band. In 1890, two years after his return from an extended period of education in America, Uchimura became a teacher in the new government academy in Tokyo, the Dai Ichi Kōtō Chū Gakkō, which was designed primarily to prepare students for the Imperial University. The American Board in its annual report on Japan for 1888 had noted that Uchimura was "one of the ablest and most devoted Japanese that has ever graduated from an American college."[4] On January 9, 1891, the teachers of the Tokyo school were compelled to participate in a ceremony which became standard procedure for all schools in the Japanese empire until the end of the Second World War. A personally signed copy of the Imperial Rescript on Education, which had been promulgated the previous fall, was placed on a pedestal; and as the students stood at attention, the teachers were expected to step forth one by one and make a low bow of obeisance. Some Christian teachers absented themselves from school to avoid the issue. Uchimura, however, was not the man to follow this course, and, as he described the incident in a letter to his American friend, the Minneapolis banker David C. Bell, "Hesitating in doubt, I took a safer course for my Christian conscience, and in the august presence of 60 professors . . . and over one thousand students, I took my stand and did not bow."[5] The result was such consternation as almost to disrupt the ceremony.

Uchimura was assured by Christian friends that bowing in this case was not an act of worship, and after reflection he decided to conform and from his sick bed sent a friend and fellow teacher to fulfill the duty for him. A newspaper, however, picked up the story and spread it across the country. It became impossible to confine the issue, and Uchimura was forced to resign his post. The incident became a *cause célèbre* and in fact furnished specific material to those who had been seeking

---

[4] Jennings, *Jesus, Japan, and Kanzo Uchimura*, p. 31. The major biography of Uchimura is Yamamoto Taijirō's *Uchimura Kanzō, Shinkō, Shōgai, Yūjō.* ——

[5] *Ibid.*, p. 32. Cf. Yamamoto Taijiro, *Uchimura Kanzō*, pp. 54-61.

opportunities to attack Christianity.[6] In a series of articles published in 1891 and 1892 on the theme of the conflict of education and religion (*Kyōiku to Shūkyō no Shōtotsu Ronsō*),
a professor of the Imperial University, Inoue Tetsujirō, attacked the loyalty of Christians and contended that Christian
faith was incompatible with the principles and duties of a
Japanese subject. The consequence was a renewed attack on
Christianity and its adherents in which both proponents of
socio-political conservatism and Buddhists joined.[7] Mention
should be made that these attacks issued frequently in more
than verbal abuse. In the 1890's as in earlier periods the
experiences of persecution in individual cases ranged from
petty annoyances from government officials to community
expulsion, disinheritance and even stone-throwing.[8]

Uchimura continued to support himself by teaching, but
from 1892 he turned seriously to writing. Few if any men of
the time were more emotionally as well as intellectually committed to patriotic service of their country than Uchimura, but
on the basis of his Christian faith he conceived and worked out
his understanding of what was his patriotic duty. Uncritical
affirmation of the socio-political *status quo* appeared to him a
perversion of patriotism, and he did not hesitate to use his
trenchant pen in boldest criticism of contemporary "feudalism,
corruption and chauvinism." He first approved the Sino-Japanese War of 1894-1895 as just but then changed his views and
accused the government and nation of making the war a means
to gain wealth and an occasion to oppress the Koreans.

Uchimura first wrote for secular periodicals, and as he increasingly attracted attention he also stimulated much discussion through his work. During this period of his life he wrote
on almost any subject of human interest, national or international. His posture, however, in considering socio-political
problems and events was consistently that of the moral prophet
even when writing for secular publications. In one of his
longer pieces in *Kokumin no Tomo* he was strongly critical of

---

[6] Sumiya, *op. cit.*, pp. 32-33.

[7] Takeda Kiyoko, *Dochaku to Haikyō*, p. 6.

[8] Sumiya, *op. cit.*, pp. 30-31.

contemporary Japanese political morality. Over fifteen thousand copies of the issue were sold on the first day, and Uchimura came to be regarded as one of the major journalists of the time.[9]

As the Russo-Japanese War of 1904-1905 approached, Uchimura opposed this war as much as the former and consequently resigned from his editorial post on the staff of the great daily newspaper *Yorozu Chōhō*.[10] His reason was that a public newspaper could not refuse to support the national policy and that he himself could not remain silent about his differing from that policy. In other part, however, Uchimura had come to feel increasingly that his own calling before God lay more in the role of religious teacher than of social critic.[11] Possibly this conviction was nourished by his awareness of the limited effectiveness of the latter role apart from wide public understanding and support of the principles underlying his social critiques. In any case, from this time forward Uchimura devoted himself to contributing to public understanding through the apparently narrower function of a religious teacher.[12]

Uchimura had begun publication in 1900 of his own magazine, *Seisho no Kenkyū* (Biblical Research), which had increasing popularity over the years and printed much of his best work. From 1905 he gave himself increasingly to this and related writings, and in 1918 he began the Sunday public lectures, first at the Tokyo YMCA and from the following year in his own lecture hall adjacent to his residence. They were attended by some of the most influential people of Japanese public life and continued until just before his death in 1930. Uchimura, it will be recalled, was the outstanding leader of the independent church movement in Japan, more commonly known as Non-Church (*Mukyōkai*). In the context of this

---

[9] Jennings, *op. cit.*, p. 42.

[10] Most of the Christians who by this time had come to form a distinct though small group concerned with questions of social reform were also opposed to the war. The great majority of Japanese Christians, however, both clerical and lay, supported the policy of the government.

[11] Jennings, *op. cit.*, p. 35.

[12] Cf. Kumano Yoshitaka, "Shinkō, Shisō, Hyōron," *Fukuin to Sekai*, XXI/8-10 (August, September, October, 1966).

movement these public lectures, which were primarily Bible
studies, constituted in fact services of worship and the focus of
Christian fellowship and service. This pattern came to be followed by many of his followers who provided similar programs
and gathered similar groups of disciples.[13] Uchimura and his
followers affirmed the concept and practice of the church in
the relatively non-organized sense of *Ecclesia;* they rejected
primarily the tendency in almost all the major confessions or
denominations of the West to give high theological value to
specific structures of church organization. Even the apparent
Mukyōkai neglect of the sacraments was only relative, as is
evident from Uchimura's request for the baptism of his beloved daughter Ruth who died in 1912 at the age of nineteen.[14]

Rugged independence characterized the career of Uchimura
Kanzō from beginning to end.[15] Symbolic of this spirit was
the masthead which appeared on the cover of each issue of the
English language periodical, *The Japan Christian Intel-
ligencer,* which Uchimura published for a brief two years. In
large capital letters appeared the words: "A Journal of Japanese Inner Life. Owned and Edited Entirely by Japanese.
Strictly Independent. No Connection Whatever with Churches
and Missions." Uchimura, however, was not anti-Western.
There was hardly a Japanese of his time who had a wider
knowledge of Western culture and perhaps none a better command of written English. He read Kierkegaard with keen
interest at a time when the latter was hardly known in English-

[13] *Mukyōkai* fellowships keep no membership rolls, but subscription to
the periodical which apparently each individual teacher-leader issues, together with attendance at the Bible study sessions, is generally considered to
constitute authentic participation in the movement. For a report on *Mukyōkai* after the war see W. H. H. Norman, *An Interim Report on Non-Church
Christianity.* Cf. W. H. H. Norman, "Kanzō Uchimura," *Contemporary
Religions in Japan,* IV/3, 4; V/1 (September, December, 1963, March, 1964).

[14] The cruel persecution from classmates and other children which Ruth
had to undergo in her childhood as a result of her family's faith reveals
much of the suffering and heroic fortitude of Japanese Christians in these
years. Cf. Fukuda Kiyoto, *Uchimura Kanzō,* pp. 254-257.

[15] Not all Christian leaders even of this period, however, were primarily
characterized by the more rugged manifestations of independence. A more
irenic type and, in his way, of comparable contemporary significance was Nitobe Inazō. Takeda, *op. cit.,* pp. 27-177.

speaking lands. Uchimura was primarily concerned for the freedom of the Christian man, and in his own context of life this meant the spiritual independence of Japanese Christians vis-à-vis the almost overwhelming cultural force of Western forms of Christianity. He wished to distinguish both theoretically and practically between Protestant Christianity and the cultural accretions of primarily Western origin that too often were considered indispensable elements of the former. Uchimura spoke with telling power to Christians and non-Christians in his time and, among the former, to members of churches as much as to those of *Mukyōkai*. Something of his influence and significance can be discerned from the experience of the veteran missionary William Axling, who reported from his numerous evangelistic journeys throughout Japan after World War II, during which he was frequently a guest in the homes of Japanese pastors, that almost without exception the *Complete Works of Uchimura Kanzō* were to be found in every pastor's library, no matter how small.[16]

The last two decades of Uchimura's life, however, led him into public activities well beyond the confines of his Sunday lectures and writing on biblical studies. In part as a result of the influence of his American friend David C. Bell, Uchimura came to have a strong belief in the Second Coming of Christ and initiated in 1918 a movement to further this conviction, a program which took him all over the country preaching and lecturing. In the 1920's he was active in a series of evangelistic campaigns in downtown Tokyo. Another campaign, particularly characteristic of the man, developed from his efforts to defend the rights and dignity of the Japanese people against what was widely felt to be an insult to Japan, and indeed the whole Orient, in the American Oriental Exclusion Act of 1924.[17] In this as in other acts the concern of Uchi-

---

[16] Jennings, *op. cit.*, pp. 42-43, 5, 3.

[17] It may properly be recalled that this law from its passage until the attack on Pearl Harbor on December 7, 1941, became one of the most effective tools of Japanese conservatives and militarists to demonstrate the American "attitude of disdain and superiority toward Japan." Borton, *Japan's Modern Century*, pp. 305-307. Regarding Uchimura and the Second Coming Movement *(Sairin Undō)*, see *Kindai Nihon to Kirisuto Kyō*, Taishō-Shōwa Hen, pp. 17-33.

mura for the dignity and freedom of men emerges as a primary element of his Christian faith and a major force behind his consistent posture of independence. Note, however, should also be taken of certain less pleasing aspects of Uchimura's character, particularly his occasionally abrupt treatment of persons, including his wife as well as his disciples.

D. UEMURA MASAHISA

ANOTHER PROMINENT LEADER IN THE 1890'S WHO CAME TO represent with singular power an important segment of Protestant Christianity during this and following decades was Uemura Masahisa. The quality of his leadership may be discerned from a statement made by Yamaji Aisan in the December, 1912, issue of the magazine *Taiyō:* "Over the past thirty years to the present time those who have held fast to the doctrines of orthodox Christianity, have defended them with learning and perception, have never yielded in their battle with the forces of the world, are only two, Uemura Masahisa and Uchimura Kanzō."[1] Yamaji was somewhat hyperbolic in stating that these two men were the only ones who maintained such a staunch position, although it is highly significant that he classed Uchimura, in spite of his variant interpretation of the church, as one of the prominent defenders of orthodox Protestantism. Uemura, however, in the eyes of his contemporaries was clearly the foremost representative of the Presbyterian-Reformed tradition.[2]

---

[1] Shimamura Kikaku, "Uemura Masahisa Hyōden," in Uemura Masahisa, *Shūkyō no Ishō*, p. 112. The great work on Uemura and his era is that of Saba Wataru, published in seven volumes from 1937 to 1944, *Uemura Masahisa to Sono Jidai*.

[2] Cf. Kumano Yoshitaka, "Uemura Masahisa ni okeru Tatakai no Shingaku," *Fukuin to Sekai*, XXI/1-3 (January, February, March, 1966); "Shingaku wo Oshieru Hito toshite no Uemura Masahisa," *ibid.*, XX/10 (October, 1965).

Uemura was a member of the original Yokohama Band. Like so many others of the first generation of Japanese Christians, he was born in 1858 in a family of *samurai* class which had supported the Tokugawa regime. In the confusions incident to the political, social and economic changes of those days the family experienced great economic hardship and moved for the second time in two years to Yokohama. Here in 1871 Uemura entered a prefectural school with at first no financial support beyond his mother's vow to abstain from fish and to sell personal articles for his sake. He next entered the Ballagh *Juku* (private school) at the age of fifteen and later became a student in the school conducted by Samuel R. Brown. The tuition for this last institution was set, for the purpose of attracting the best students, at the then high figure of ten yen per month. Uemura came to earn most of the money needed for his expenses by teaching privately as many as fifty pupils from one o'clock in the afternoon until ten at night. He also raised pigs on the side, a relatively lucrative but humiliating work for a boy of *samurai* class.

Uemura was never graduated in a formal way from any school, but in this period he laid the foundation for a remarkable breadth of knowledge which he nourished by extensive reading throughout his life. In his earlier years in particular Uemura was keenly interested in general literature and often wrote as well as spoke on themes in this area. Something of the flexibility of the early years of Protestantism in Japan is revealed in the fact of his preaching a sermon in church on Robert Browning. The subsequent life and career of Uemura were even more affected by his meeting several of the first generation of missionaries. Intimate contact with men of their faith and character opened a new world before his eyes and awakened him from the long sleep of restrictive feudalism that had held the nation in its grip for so many years. The new world of science, literature and art which these men revealed was given singular focus of beauty and spiritual power through their preaching and teaching of the Bible. A religious atmosphere surrounded the entire program of instruction, and supported as it was by life commitment and conduct, it could not but deeply move the mind and heart of Uemura as of the other

Japanese youths of impressionable age who came to the missionaries in those days for their higher education.[3]

Uemura was baptized in 1873 at the age of sixteen and almost at once committed himself to the life of a Christian evangelist. In 1877 he entered the new theological seminary that had been opened in the foreign settlement of Tsukiji in Tokyo, and in the same year he started a preaching place (dendōsho) in the city. This was apparently the first instance of formal Protestant evangelism conducted primarily under Japanese responsibility. Characteristic also of Uemura's spiritual independence was his concern, even while holding firmly to theologically classical expressions of Protestantism, to find something of the history of salvation in his own pre-Christian religious experience and that of his people. He came to regard the Neo-Confucian Bushidō (the Way of the Warrior) as a singular gift of God to Japan and a veritable Old Testament. He thought that the Christian doctrine of the redemptive sacrifice of Christ for the world was particularly comprehensible to men reared in that tradition. He criticized sharply the overweening pride and class consciousness which it frequently begot and felt that it had lost the concept of authentic humanity which he found in the gospel. But he believed that this tradition, fed by many sources including the simple piety of native Shintō, had true meaning and spiritual validity in the plan and providence of God.[4]

Uemura remained in Tokyo after leaving the seminary, and finally as pastor of what became the great citadel of Presbyterian-Reformed faith in Japan, Fujimichō Church, he found the home base for his increasingly extensive and influential Christian service. He began early to show unusual talent as a writer and was one of those responsible for the publication from 1880 of the periodical Rokugō Zasshi. In 1890, he began publication of the bimonthly magazine Nihon Hyōron, which was considered one of the top periodicals of the day and did much to introduce Christian concepts of man, society, literature and

---

[3] Ishihara, Nihon Kirisuto Kyōshi Ron, pp. 144-145.

[4] Similar views were also expressed by Kozaki Hiromichi and Ebina Danjō. Cf. Dohi Akio, "Nihon ni okeru Fukuin no Dochaku," Fukuin to Sekai, XXI/10 (October, 1966), 10-13.

art to the educated public. His first important theological work, *Shinri Ippan*, was published in 1884. He also became a member of the Old Testament Translation Committee and co-operated in the preparation of the first joint hymnal. After the founding of Meiji Gakuin he became a professor in its theological department, without relinquishing his pastoral responsibilities or literary work. He participated as a leader of growing importance in the organizational development of the *Nihon Kirisuto Itchi Kyōkai* and its later form, the *Nihon Kirisuto Kyōkai*.

Uemura showed his independent spirit when he published a statement in support of Uchimura Kanzō after the famous Disloyalty Incident in 1891 in the weekly magazine *Fukuin Shūhō*, of which he was a leading promoter and writer. The statement was signed jointly by Uemura, the Methodist leader Honda Yōichi and Oshikawa Masayoshi. In consequence of this statement the government suspended publication of the magazine. Uemura promptly changed the title to *Fukuin Shimpō* and resumed publication. In this format the magazine subsequently became the official organ of the *Nihon Kirisuto Kyōkai* and later of the *Nihon Kirisuto Kyōdan* after its formation in 1941.

In some ways even more heroic was the role played by Uemura in the aftermath of the famous High Treason Incident (*Daigyaku Jiken*). In 1910 a group of "anarchists" led by Kōtoku Shūsui were allegedly discovered in a plot to assassinate the emperor. In the context of the long-developing exaltation and veritable deification of the emperor, the incident created enormous repercussions of hostility toward all elements of the country that might be construed as non-supportive of the imperial system. Kōtoku himself was not a Christian, but he had been under certain Christian influences and represented an extreme position in the larger group of Socialists whose political and sociological orientation had been primarily developed through Christian perspectives. Some Japanese historians consider the entire incident to have been contrived by the conservatives for political purposes. It is generally agreed that most of the twelve who were executed were quite innocent of the charges.[5] One of these was Ōishi Seinosuke, who was a Christian and whose relatives requested Uemura to conduct a memorial service in his behalf. Uemura agreed and assumed full public responsibility in the midst of an atmosphere of public shock and antipathy that could well have led to his own assassination. Uemura's action in this matter was all the more significant because his personal conviction of the proper role of a Christian pastor was that he should not take a leading role in social reform movements. From this point on, however, we may say that the Christian church in Japan as a whole became more timid toward the national authorities.

Of particular importance both for the career of Uemura and for the history of Protestantism in Japan was his relationship with and developing policy toward the foreign missions in the land. Uemura, as we have noted, owed much to the early missionaries and never ceased to express his gratitude for their contributions as well as for those of their successors. He had intimate and warm friendships with several missionaries. He early came, however, to the conclusion that Christian witness in Japan after its first beginnings by foreign missionaries could be properly carried on only if Japanese Christians were primarily responsible. In the first two decades the number of missionaries, as of Japanese Christians, was small, but as the number of the latter notably increased from the late 1870's, so did the missionaries. The mission organizations were strengthened, and as their financial resources increased they came to constitute powerful, independent ecclesial structures alongside the Japanese churches. The missions were not denoted as churches, but they exercised "the ecclesiastical functions of a presbytery or synod in founding, developing, aiding and directing local churches." Uemura became the foremost leader in the movement to rectify this imbalance and to establish an authentically independent Japanese Christian church. As Charles Iglehart has pointed out, this was probably the first instance that the issue was clearly raised in the history of Protestant foreign missions.[6]

The situation was made particularly acute because the dif-

---

[5] Cf. Sumiya, *Nihon Shakai to Kirisuto Kyō*, p. 43.

[6] Iglehart, *A Century of Protestant Christianity in Japan*, pp. 121-125.

ficult years of the 1890's increased the number of churches receiving some financial assistance from foreign sources, and by 1900 four-fifths of all Protestant churches were reported in this category. The missionaries themselves at this period did not seem sufficiently aware of the gravity of the problem. Indeed, the situation had somewhat changed in terms of the nature of the missionary personnel. The first generation of pioneer missionaries of heroic mold and achievement was largely gone. In some ways as a result of the changing situation in the church and theological education in the United States in the late nineteenth century, the following and more numerous generations of missionaries did not have on the whole the same high level of cultural background and theological training as their forebears. A number of the now emerging Japanese Christian leaders were superior in cultural breadth and theological depth to almost any of the missionaries. The proceedings of the great missionary conference held in Tokyo in 1900, however, show little awareness of this situation. No provision was made for Japanese participation in the conference, and in spite of the undoubted and great devotion of these men, many of whom were the products of the evangelical revivals, particularly among students in England and North America during the late nineteenth century, adequate concern was absent for the problems of relationship between the churches and the missions in the context of the changing situation.[7] As Charles Iglehart has noted, there was indeed a curious lack of interest in questions of fundamental importance. There was almost no discussion of the content of the Christian message nor of the problems of communicating it to non-Christians. Little reference was made to the cultural context in which proclamation had to be made, or to problems of relationship to Buddhist thought, Confucian ethics or emerging Shintō nationalism.[8]

Japanese Christians, however, from an early period had become sensitive to the problem of relationships with the missions. We have noted that already in 1879 under the *Nihon Kirisuto*

[7] Perhaps the chief exception to this criticism is the discussion by William Imbrie, in *General Conference of Protestant Missionaries, Tokyo, 1900*, pp. 887-891.

[8] Cf. Iglehart, *op. cit.*, pp. 112-114.

Itchi Kyōkai a small board of home missions was formed, but as the results were unsatisfactory, the organization ceased to function after four years of effort. From 1886 cooperation with the missions was effected through a board composed of equal numbers of missionaries and Japanese (ministers or elders) and through a committee comparably composed in each presbytery. In practice the board was primarily concerned with the collection of funds, and the vital decisions were largely made by the presbytery committees. By agreement the Council of (six) Missions contributed three yen to every one contributed by the church toward the funds of the board. Increasingly, however, the Japanese objected to the program as ineffective, particularly with reference to their own goals of financial and administrative independence.[9]

Almost no one among the Japanese advocated withdrawal of missionaries, or at that time, dissolution of the mission organizations. The real issue was the authentic independence of the Japanese church and the assumption of primary responsibility for the evangelization of Japan by Japanese Christians. As an important concrete step to effect these goals, Uemura introduced in the Ninth General Assembly of the *Nihon Kirisuto Kyōkai* in July, 1894, a proposal to establish a commission or board of evangelism which would be under the direction of the General Assembly.[10] His intent in this proposal was to coordinate the various church extension activities which until then had been planned and executed in the separate presbytery committees without sufficient concern for overall strategy or the independence of the church in all of its parts. The lack of overall strategy had caused a proliferation of many small preaching places,[11] which, owing to the relatively large supply of trained and able

---

[9] Imbrie, *op. cit.*, pp. 887-891. Cf. Ariyoshi Katsuhisa, *Dr. Masahisa Uemura, A Christian Leader,* pp. 212-219.

[10] This commission *(Dendō Kyoku)* is commonly referred to in contemporary English publications as the Board of Home Missions.

[11] The question was raised then and later whether it is wise evangelistic strategy to allow such proliferation of small preaching places, many of which, humanly speaking, seemed unlikely in the reasonably near future to be capable of self-support in the sense of fully supporting a resident pastor. Protestantism in general, however, failed to question the assumption that a resident professional clergyman is necessary for every such group.

clergy which Japanese Protestantism has always been able to furnish, were able to be manned by pastors but unable either to attain local self-support in a reasonable time or be supported by the national body.

Uemura's proposal was radical. It would sever the organization between church and missions with the result that all churches receiving aid from a mission could no longer be eligible for membership in the General Assembly. The General Assembly would thus be constituted by delegates only from self-supporting churches and at one blow would lose about one-fourth the number of its congregations, although the total membership loss would be considerably less than one quarter. In a sense the proposal enhanced the ecclesial character of the missions, which in this way came to assume even greater control over the pastors and churches under their care. But Uemura properly counted on the spirit of independence possessed by almost all Japanese Christians to move those receiving mission subsidies to vigorous efforts toward self-support. Only by fulfilling this condition could they become a part of the Japanese church.

The proposal was passed after strenuous debate and no little opposition. The commission as constituted consisted of twenty members elected by the General Assembly but with all presbyteries represented. An executive committee whose members resided in Tokyo or its vicinity was responsible for the direct administration of the work. Of particular importance was the fact that none of the funds of the commission came directly from the missions. A small part was undoubtedly derived from the personal contributions of missionaries, but by far the greater part of the funds came from the Japanese church. Its income the first year (1894-1895) was only 562 yen, but the amount steadily increased each subsequent year. The policy of the commission in the early years was primarily, although not exclusively, to select congregations and to lead them to self-support rather than to open new work.[12]

In 1895, the year following passage of Uemura's proposal, in order to prevent what might have been a complete rupture

---

[12] Imbrie, *op. cit.*, p. 889.

with the missions, a new set of rules was established which permitted under strict supervision a limited amount of cooperation between the *Nikki* and the missions.[13] Following this action a system of itinerant evangelists was set up to strengthen the efforts of local preaching places as much as to proclaim the gospel to non-Christians. As a further consequence of the new commission on evangelism, Japanese missionaries were sent first to Taiwan (after the Sino-Japanese War of 1894-1895), then to Korea, Manchuria and various cities of China.

The problem, however, of cooperating with the missions was not at once solved by the actions cited. Uemura introduced in the Eleventh General Assembly of 1896 a further proposal which called for a census of all evangelistic, educational and social work carried on by the six related missions and specified that all local evangelistic work aided by a mission should be administered by a joint committee consisting of Japanese and foreign missionaries in equal number.[14] This proposal was not at first acceptable to the missions, as they preferred to maintain control over work in which their financial support was predominant. The principle, however, of administration by joint committees became standard for the church, and of the six cooperating missions three came to adopt it. The missions of the Presbyterian Church in the U.S.A. and of the Reformed Church in the U.S. were those which adopted the principle. The missions of the Reformed Church in America, however, and of the Presbyterian Church in the U.S. continued to work as before. The flexibility of the Japanese Christians is seen in the fact that they continued to cooperate with both groups of missions.

In 1909, however, a system of consultation (*mōshi-awase*) with the three missions in the latter category was established. There were differences in structure and nuance in the two

---

[13]*Nikki* is the abbreviation frequently employed in Japan for the *Nihon Kirisuto Kyōkai*. At this time there were six missions, which were working in formal cooperation with *Nikki* and had constituted themselves as a Council of Missions: two (representative of men's and women's boards) of the Presbyterian Church in the U.S.A., two of the (Dutch) Reformed Church in America, one of the (German) Reformed Church in the U.S., and one of the Presbyterian Church in the U.S. (Southern).

[14] Ishihara, *op. cit.*, pp. 153-155.

modes of cooperation, but both appear to have worked well and a relatively stable situation was reached in the relationships between Japanese church and missions in the Presbyterian-Reformed tradition which lasted until the formation of the *Nihon Kirisuto Kyōdan* in 1941. A spirit of independence, however, continued to characterize the church, and full self-support remained the condition for Japanese church representation in presbytery or general assembly.

Action in behalf of full autonomy and responsibility in church extension work was evident in varying degrees in other denominations. The Congregational *(Kumiai)* churches began in 1906 a three-year plan of gradual transfer by which they assumed responsibility for those congregations which had been receiving mission aid but were rather far along in the process of achieving self-support. The mission retained care of less developed preaching places. In the case of the Methodist and Anglican missions, the related churches in general manifested less vigorous desire for complete independence, and the ethos of relationship was somewhat different from that in the *Nikki*.[15]

Another instance of Uemura's independence was his decision to resign in 1903 from the theological department of Meiji Gakuin when he learned that objection was made to his use in class of what one missionary considered liberal textbooks. With several associates he founded in 1904 the Tokyo Shingakusha, the first seminary independently administered and financed by Japanese Christians. The institution began with over thirty students, who met for their lectures in the Ichigaya church of which Uemura was then pastor. The academic standards of the school were high from the beginning, and until its union in 1929 with Meiji Gakuin's theological department to form the new Nihon Shingakkō (Japan Theological Seminary) it continued to send into the church a steady supply of able, dedicated men who had deeply imbibed the spirit of independence characteristic of the founder. The strength of the church, however, and the essentially wholesome, non-partisan position of Uemura are revealed in the fact that graduates of both the Shingakusha and

---

[15] Cf. Iglehart, *op. cit.*, pp. 121-125.

Meiji Gakuin worked together in the church without serious rivalry or friction.

An incident of representative significance both for the career of Uemura and the history of the Christian movement was the theological debate between him and an outstanding literary representative of the Congregational tradition, Ebina Danjō.[16] This debate, which began in 1901, was carried on for several months through the pages of the two journals of which the men were respectively editors. The main points of difference concerned the doctrines of the incarnation and redemption. Ebina was a singularly high-minded man who strongly emphasized the unity of God and the moral conscience. He had drunk deeply of the liberal theology of Germany and the English-speaking world, and in his subjectively oriented thought he emphasized the role of Christ as teacher and example rather than as redeemer through his sacrifice on the cross. His theological position might be described as theistic philosophical idealism. Ebina was particularly sensitive to the need of Christian theology to relate to the scientific and cultural events of the day. He believed, for example, that a creative rapprochement between Buddhism and Christianity on the philosophical level was both possible and necessary.

The position in this controversy of Uemura, who was later, as we have seen, to be criticized by at least one missionary for exposing his students to liberal books and ideas, was staunchly on the side of classical Protestant orthodoxy. While recognizing the historical and human elements in the development of Christianity, he preferred to see its origin in divine revelation. He stressed the work of God. Over against Ebina's tendency to an adoptionist view of Jesus as the Christ, Uemura stoutly believed in his deity, in a literal incarnation. He saw Christ as a proper object of worship, as one to whom men may properly pray. He saw Jesus Christ as Savior, as the worthy object of all trust, as the one to whom we are united in life and in death.[17]

A controversy like this was hardly to be settled in any con-

---

16 Cf. Kumano Yoshitaka, "Ebina Danjō no Shisō to Shingaku," *Fukuin to Sekai*, XXII/2-4 (February, March, April, 1967).

17 Germany, *Protestant Theologies in Modern Japan*, pp. 13, 19-27.

clusive way by public statement of the differing interpretations and emphases of the two men. The positions represented by the two continued to exist in the Japanese church, but Uemura through clear and forceful expression of his own views thereby helped to fashion and strengthen what came to be the main-stream of Japanese Protestant theology. This tradition, which found its strongest expression in the *Nikki,* was nourished in the decades following Uemura's death by Takakura Tokutarō (1885-1934), who became president of the Tokyo Shingakusha in 1925, and was only slightly altered by the influence of dia-lectical theology in the 1930's.[18]

A final word should be said regarding Uemura Masahisa as a person. It would not do to leave the impression that he was only a doughty theological warrior, passionate evangelist, and multi-faceted man of culture. He had a genuine humility in the presence of truth, and his concern for the independence of the Japanese church was rooted in his respect for all men. He was a person of singular compassion and met others with little concern for their social status or learning. As he grew older there occurred a noticeable mellowing of his character, and the luminous quality which contemporaries early sensed in his per-son became increasingly pronounced. One of the most illumi-nating aspects of his career was his attitude toward women. He both loved and respected his wife, and as Shimamura Kikaku has suggested, at the time of his marriage in 1880 when he vowed to respect as well as love his wife, he may have been the only man in Japan to do so in reality.

Uemura once rather sharply reproved a younger pastor who in conversation with him referred to his own wife by the an-cient Chinese term *gusai* (foolish wife). In correspondence with his wife, Uemura on occasion employed the word *kensai* (wise wife), and in the context of contemporary views of women the practice constituted a veritable revolution in literary usage. The *Collected Works of Uemura* contain a number of his love letters, written in the extraordinary Japanized Chinese still commonly used in correspondence by educated Japanese at this

[18] Cf. Takakura Tokutarō, *Fukuinteki Kirisuto Kyō,* and Oshio Tsu-tomu, *Takakura Tokutarō Den.*

period, which reveal a combination of tender love and respect for a woman as a person perhaps unknown in earlier Japanese literature. He addressed his daughters as "Miss" (Sumie-san, Tamaki-san, Keiko-san) as they grew older, and in all his relations with women manifested a comparable respect. He was the first to propose the ordination of women as elders in the *Nihon Kirisuto Kyōkai* and in spite of considerable opposition was able to secure the adoption of this policy. This was the first instance, I believe, of the ordination of women as elders in the history of the Presbyterian-Reformed tradition in the world. Uemura's life-long efforts to elevate the status of women, however, were a natural and necessary expression of his wider concern for the freedom and welfare of human beings everywhere.[19]

E. KAGAWA TOYOHIKO AND SOCIAL CHRISTIANITY

1

THE PERIOD OF RESURGENT NATIONALISM AND RE-tardation of Christian growth beginning with 1889-90 further restricted Christian penetration among the rural and urban poor. For a time, especially during the 1880's, considerable openness existed among the more prosperous farmers, teachers and physicians of the rural districts who were attracted in part by the association of Christianity with the Popular Rights Movement and by its general thrust toward liberty and humane values. In consequence of the resurgent nationalism focused in the imperial system, however, the feudalistic social structures and restrictions of the historic family system were reformulated and strengthened. Freedom of religious or social change was thus effectively shut out from the countryside. Many churches

---

[19] Shimamura, *op. cit.*, pp. 121-125.

that had been started with high hopes and thrived for a while were forced to close. Above all, the great mass of the rural poor, the tenant farmers who as late as 1945 comprised 46 percent of the rural population, had not participated appreciably in the mental and social emancipation which the early Meiji era had brought to so many among the educated classes. They were easily led by the conservative elements in power to intensify their ancient fear and prejudice against the Christian faith and its adherents. The new system of universal compulsory elementary education became in this context a tool of ideological indoctrination and social repression rather than of enlightenment.[1]

The Protestant churches were thus forced into a further restriction of their activity. From this time forward it became sociologically more difficult to win adherents from other groups than students and the white-collar class of the cities. The very struggle for the independence of the Japanese church, with its emphasis upon local self-support of a professional pastor, encouraged the establishment of work in places that had the financial means to effect such results. This further strengthened the bourgeois trend in the Christian movement. The emergence of Japanese leadership in the 1890's and 1900's, however, produced new men and movements which worked contrary to this trend. This latter development constituted a form of social Christianity which had its greatest leader in Kagawa Toyohiko but included a wide range of persons and activities and influenced the whole course of Japanese social history in the twentieth century.

Before 1890 Japanese Christians had made only the smallest beginnings in social welfare work. As we have seen, most of the first missions instituted medical work as a part of their program and, especially in the first two decades, met a vital need in the land. As a result, however, of the background in Dutch medicinal and surgical knowledge possessed by many Japanese doctors and their assiduity in learning from the missionary physicians, the science of medicine in Japan made extraordinarily rapid progress. By the early 1880's medical mis-

---

[1]Cf. Kami, *Purotesutanto Hyakunen-Shi Kenkyū*, pp. 18, 20, 25.

sions had become primarily a benevolent service to the poor, and after the Ōsaka Missionary Conference of 1883 medical work was gradually terminated, except in the case of the Anglican missions and certain enterprises initiated much later.

One of the first Japanese Christian efforts in social welfare was stimulated by the visit to Japan in 1886 of George Müller, the German-English social worker famous for his large orphanage in Bristol. The following year Ishii Jūji, a convert from Roman Catholicism to the *Kumiai* (Congregational) Church who was then studying medicine in Okayama, began his great work on behalf of orphans by aiding a beggar woman and her children. From this simple beginning he gradually developed the Okayama Orphanage, which already by 1889 cared for fifty-five children and came to be one of the best known social institutions of modern Japan.

The Congregationalist missionary-physician John C. Berry as early as 1875 had obtained permission to visit the national prisons and made certain recommendations for reform to the authorities, some of which were accepted. Niishima Jō was one of the first Japanese Christians to interest himself in the welfare of prisoners. Gradually a number of other Christians began similar work, as Hara Taneaki in the Hokkaidō and Tomeoka Kōsuke in Wakamatsu. This activity became most pronounced after 1890 and had enormous influence upon the subsequent reform and development of the entire Japanese penal system.

As the Japanese Christian community developed in maturity of faith and experience, its conscience became increasingly sensitized, and it turned this enlightened concern to the various problems of Japanese society, which in some ways worsened considerably as the end of the century approached. Following the example of the early missionaries, Japanese Christians personally held to what may be called a puritanical way of life. As time passed they attacked various social vices such as licensed prostitution, concubinage, intemperance and smoking, in behalf of the moral welfare of the entire population. Particularly in the battle against commercialized vice they were aided by several secular journals. But above all, the concern of a number of Christians was increasingly drawn to the unfortunate victims of industrialization, which under capitalistic auspices was becoming a major element of the life of the great cities of Japan.

The rice famine of 1890, the financial crises of the late 1880's and the 1890's, the numerous commercial failures of the *samurai* and other inexperienced business entrepreneurs of the early Meiji era, all combined to create much economic suffering. However much the family system might be theoretically strengthened, its former cohesive power had been so disrupted by the social dislocations of the transitional period that it was not capable of adequately caring, especially in the cities, for the sick, aged and poor. As a part of the process of industrialization, the ownership of wealth became more and more concentrated in fewer hands with the result that between 1880 and 1887 the number of persons who owned sufficient land to qualify them to stand for public election decreased by 320,000.[2] Most of all, industrialization brought new kinds of hardship to Japanese life. A close tie came to exist between rural and urban poverty. The main burden of financing the industrialization process, the new army and navy, the new educational system and, indeed, the entire spectrum of ventures undertaken by the Meiji government was borne by the farmers, at first by both landlords and tenant farmers, but after 1878 largely by the latter.[3] To escape the pressures of this worsening situation, increasing numbers of farmers' sons and daughters came to the cities to work at low wages in factories under largely unregulated conditions. The number of women and girls in the labor force became particularly large; by 1905 of the total work force in all privately owned factories, the proportion of female workers was 60 percent and in spinning mills 80 percent. Unmarried girls were frequently employed on the basis of advance payment to their impoverished rural parents, and the system constituted a form of slave traffic. Twelve-hour work shifts were common; at times workers were compelled to labor for as many as twenty-four or thirty-six hours without respite. Night work for children was not outlawed until 1916.[4]

Japanese Christians became key leaders in the study of these

---

[2] Thomas, *Protestant Beginnings in Japan*, pp. 128-135, 198-199.
[3] Best, *Christian Faith and Cultural Crisis: The Japan Case*, pp. 33, 58-60.
[4] Kami, *op. cit.*, pp. 55-56.

problems, in the formation of the national conscience and in taking concrete steps toward reform. In 1897 the movement to form a labor union was first initiated, and as an institutional expression of concern for the problems of labor Katayama Sen founded Kingsley Hall in the same year. In 1898 the Socialist Research Society *(Shakaishugi Kenkyū Kai)* was formed in the building of the Unitarian Church in Tokyo with Abe Isoo, Katayama Sen, and Kōtoku Shūsui among the leaders. As in the case of the last not all were Christians, but Christian humanism and socialism of the type represented by the English clergymen Charles Kingsley and Frederick Denison Maurice were dominant elements in the ideology of the group.[5] Especially from 1902 and 1903 considerable numbers of Christians from several Protestant denominations participated in this movement, as did many non-Christians from the educated classes in the cities.

Following the Russo-Japanese War, especially in the years after 1907, various movements for freedom and social reform emerged, and confrontation with the now greatly strengthened forces of nationalism became more pronounced. In 1910 occurred the High Treason Incident involving Kōtoku Shūsui and others, particularly of the extreme or "Anarchist" position. Following this incident and extending until after the Second World War, Christian participation in the Socialist Movement in a formal sense greatly lessened. The shock of the event, however, had little effect upon the career of the greatest apostle of social reform among Japanese Christians of the twentieth century, Kagawa Toyohiko. But before we consider this man and his extraordinary life of evangelism and service a brief word is in order regarding another approach to the social problems of the day, the Salvation Army and its greatest leader, Yamamuro Gumpei.

2

The first group of Salvation Army officers arrived in Japan from England in 1895. The first corps (stations) were opened in

---

[5] Cf. Katakozawa, *Nihon Purotesutanto Hyaku Nen no Ayumi*, p. 83.

Tokyo and the work extended to other places later. By 1900 there were five organized corps in Tokyo, ten corps and eight out-posts in various other parts of the empire. A Naval and Mercan-tile Home was established in Yokohama and a Prison Gate Home in Tokyo to assist discharged prisoners. In August, 1900, rescue work for prostitutes commenced and an institution opened to care for girls who were willing to leave that way of life. This work gained the attention of Christians and later of wider sections of the population. In Gumma Prefecture, where Christians were an important element in the political leader-ship, the prefectural assembly outlawed the ancient system of licensed prostitution. Owing at least to stout resistance from brothel owners the reformers were not able to pass a comparable measure nationally, but an important change was effected in the laws regarding licensed prostitution so that it became pos-sible for any girl who wished to leave a brothel to do so. The workers of the Salvation Army helped the girls greatly to make and follow through with these decisions. In their hostels they effectively aided the girls in making the transition to normal social life.[6]

The great leader of this work in Japan was Yamamuro Gumpei, who was born in Okayama Prefecture in 1872 of a rural family of limited means.[7] At the age of fifteen he was ap-prenticed to a printer in Tokyo, and the following year attended a night school for English language study and heard lectures on his own at other institutions then being formed in the city. At this time he first became acquainted with the Christian faith through street preaching. At the age of seventeen he came to share this faith and dedicated himself to the service of God and especially the common people.[8] From this year (1888) he at-tended the theological seminary of the Evangelical Church in the Tsukiji district of Tokyo. Yamamuro's first contact with the Salvation Army was in 1899 when he was twenty-eight years

---

[6] Imbrie, *General Conference of Protestant Missionaries, Tokyo, 1900*, pp. 928, 958.

[7] Cf. Yamamuro Tamiko, "Yamamuro Gumpei: an Officer of the Salvation Army," *The Japan Christian Quarterly*, XXIX/4 (October, 1962), 223-243.

[8] *Kami to heimin to no tame*. Akimoto Mitarō, *Yamamuro Gumpei no Shōgai*, p. 37.

of age. His own background and particular sense of mission strongly attracted him to the kind of work carried on by the Army and he became a member of a local corps in the same year.

Yamamuro had already achieved considerable maturity in his understanding of the Christian faith and mission and particularly in the methodology of witness and service in behalf of the common man. In his first year with the Salvation Army he published his famous *Heimin no Fukuin* (The Gospel of the Common People), in which he expounded the Christian message to appeal to the heart and understanding of the ordinary Japanese of limited education. The book became one of the publishing miracles in twentieth-century Japan. A second edition had to be printed within twenty days, and the edition of 1954 in my own possession is the 484th.[9]

Yamamuro began in 1900 to participate in the work of rescuing prostitutes. His ability, understanding and zeal soon brought him recognition, and he was selected to be one of the attendants at the international meeting of the Salvation Army held in London in 1904. In 1907 he served as the interpreter of General William Booth in his great speaking tour of many Japanese cities and was promoted to the rank of major. This same year he became secretary of the work in Japan. In 1909 what became the famous as well as effective practice of street solicitation of funds for charitable purposes was begun; in consequence, the institutional work of the Army was expanded, its first hospital opened in 1912, a sanatorium in 1916. The work of the Salvation Army was increasingly recognized appreciatively by the Japanese government as well as by the general public. In 1918 as an unusual symbol of this recognition, an annual gift of one thousand yen for a period of ten years was granted to the social work of the Army by the emperor and empress.

In 1922 Yamamuro led in the initiation of a movement to prevent cruelty to children. In the great earthquake which devastated the Tokyo-Yokohama area in 1923 the Salvation Army distinguished itself by its zeal in the colossal work of relief in

---

9 Yamamuro Gumpei, *Heimin no Fukuin*, 1954.

behalf of the literally hundreds of thousands of victims of that disaster. For this work Yamamuro was decorated in 1924 by the emperor. In 1926 he was promoted to the rank of brigadier general and appointed commander of the entire Japan division. He was later made major general, in context of the tradition of the Salvation Army a rank comparable to that of members of the Booth family. Throughout his life Yamamuro led the Salvation Army to serve in every possible way the poor and needy in Japan. This service, however, was performed without neglecting to use every opportunity to proclaim the gospel, by word as well as by deed. As an example we may note the preparation and continued publication of the Common Man's Bible (Minshū no Seisho).

Yamamuro Gumpei died in 1940. Something of the ambivalence of the Japanese people to the Christian movement is revealed in the fact that the emperor, empress and empress dowager in concert sent a message of condolence, and some of the greatest men in Japanese life attended the funeral. The very same year the government suspended publication of *Heimin no Fukuin,* and the entire headquarters staff of the Salvation Army in Japan was summoned for questioning by the military police on suspicion of espionage. Later in 1940 the organization was forced to sever all international ties and to reconstitute itself under another name. In effect the Salvation Army was dissolved for the duration of the war.[10]

3

A somewhat similar ambivalence may be seen with regard to the life and work of Kagawa Toyohiko, undoubtedly one of the greatest men of the twentieth century and one of the most creative persons in Japanese history in the area of social and political reform. After his death on April 23, 1960, he was posthumously granted by the emperor one of the highest decorations open to a Japanese citizen. During his life, however, he was persecuted in various ways: occasionally imprisoned, frequently

---

[10] Akimoto, *op. cit., passim.* A biography of Yamamuro is included in the children's series of the great men of Japanese history, Abe Mitsuko, *Yamamuro Gumpei,* 1954.

questioned, often kept under surveillance. He was in general appreciated more highly by foreign Christians than by Japanese. At his funeral foreign correspondents were more in evidence than Japanese. Yet perhaps no single Japanese had more influence than Kagawa in leading the development of the thought and conscience of the nation during the first half of the twentieth century.[11]

Kagawa was born in Kōbe on July 10, 1888. His father was a man of considerable means and a political figure of importance in his day; he became secretary to the Privy Council, the select group of advisors who served Emperor Meiji. His mother, however, was a concubine. After the death of both parents, Kagawa was sent at the age of four to the ancestral home in Shikoku to be reared by his father's neglected wife and mother. Here he spent his early youth amid hostile resentment expressed varyingly by beatings, verbal abuse and studied indifference, while the financial state of the family steadily declined as a result of the profligate living of his elder brother. Kagawa tasted in these years the gamut of human sorrow to the extent that in later life there was hardly any suffering for which he did not have some affinity and understanding from his own experience.

Kagawa first encountered the Christian faith in the middle school at Tokushima in Shikoku. He was befriended by a Japanese Christian teacher in this school, but his greatest benefactors at this time were two missionaries of the Presbyterian Church, U.S. (Southern), Drs. H. W. Myers and C. A. Logan. In the homes of these men the love-starved boy received a welcome, understanding and sympathetic guidance such as he had never known. From them he learned of the God who cares and was led to look up and out of his tortured condition. He read and reread the New Testament until all the pent-up agony of his past burst forth in the prayer that was expressive at once of his new love, aspiration and dedication: "O God, make me like Christ." As Kagawa's American biographer William Axling describes the experience, "The dawn broke. His spirit was

---

[11] Cf. Richard H. Drummond, "Kagawa: Christian Evangelist," *The Christian Century*, LXXVII/28 (July 13, 1960), 823-825.

flooded with light and life. His melancholy melted away like the mist before the rising sun. Kagawa was born again."[12]

As an integral part of his experience of faith, Kagawa believed that he had been given a divine commission to serve the poor. Strong opposition, however, soon developed in the home of the wealthy uncle where he was staying in Tokushima when his committal to Christian faith became known. The result was disinheritance, and he was forced to leave with nothing but the clothes he wore. Arrangements were made, however, for him to enter Meiji Gakuin in Tokyo, the Presbyterian-Reformed school equivalent at that time to an upper high school and junior college. Here Kagawa's genius flourished as never before. He astonished both teachers and fellow students by reading in English books like Kant's *Critique of Pure Reason,* Darwin's *Origin of Species,* Ruskin's *Modern Painters,* and Max Müller's *Sacred Books of the East.* Indeed, his passion for knowledge was such that he is said to have read practically all the important books in the library.

In the midst of these rich opportunities for learning Kagawa never forgot his commitment to serve. From the beginning of his Christian life he had "a passion to practice," and his compassion included not only a beggar with whom he shared his bed and food but even stray dogs and cats. This concern for the weak, the poor, the defeated of life persisted to the end as a central element of his character and life purpose.[13] At Meiji Gakuin other leitmotivs of his life were manifested. He showed an affinity for the Hebrew prophets and fearlessly espoused various unpopular causes. He boldly advocated principles and practice derived from the new Socialist thought that was by this time well enough known in Japan to be feared and hated by conservative elements. At the height of the Russo-Japanese War he came to believe ardently in non-violence as a result of his reading Tolstoy and the New Testament, and proclaimed his views before the entire student body in assembly. For this he

---

[12] William Axling, *Kagawa,* p. 20. The major biography in Japanese is Yokoyama Shunichi, *Kagawa Toyohiko.*

[13] Axling, *op. cit.,* pp. 21, 84, 115, 125. Cf. Sumiya Mikio, *Kagawa Toyohiko,* pp. 13-14, 43, 55. Sumiya's work is more an analysis of Kagawa's thought than a biography.

experienced ostracization and one night a beating from twenty students.

In his second year at Meiji Gakuin, Kagawa contracted tuberculosis, the disease which in large part because of the dietary practices then common afflicted so many of the youth of the land. He was compelled to leave school and spent the entire year in an isolated seashore village where he came close to death and in the ordeal produced the first draft of a novel, which in his poverty he had to write with Japanese brush over the printed pages of old magazines. Kagawa made only a partial recovery during this year but gained enough strength to return to scholastic life. In his own mind, however, he was determined to spend whatever time in life he had left in the service of the needy of God's world.[14] With this intent he entered the Presbyterian Seminary in Kōbe and shortly after began his work in the Shinkawa slums of that city. He was twenty-one years of age and the time was Christmas day, 1909, when he carted his few belongings from the seminary dormitory to his one room in the slums.

The social evils which followed the process of industrialization in Japan had reached a singularly horrible maturation in the slums of Kōbe at this time. The cities of Japan had probably never before and, owing in no small part to Kagawa's own efforts, never again were to comprise such a maelstrom of human suffering and degradation. The most common dwelling of the area was a room six feet square, without windows, in which lived one or two families containing as many as nine to ten persons. Not all could sleep at the same time. One kitchen, water faucet and toilet served perhaps a score of families. The sanitary conditions were of course unbelievably filthy with "the refuse from the houses, overflow from the toilets and the backwash of overworked sewers."

Among the deepest of Kagawa's convictions was that God dwells among the lowliest form of men. He formed and honed this conviction in Shinkawa among the lowliest that Japan could then produce. In the business depression then in its worst stages the broken and defeated of both country and city

---

[14] Cf. Sumiya, *op. cit.*, pp. 9-10.

drifted into Shinkawa, and the physical degradation was compounded by the moral. Poverty was made hopeless by the widespread mania for gambling; it was defiled by prostitution, alcohol and every kind of violence. Here Kagawa learned to love — men, women, and children — and for them he unstintingly gave all his heart, his time, his meager possessions. For them he suffered personal violence and abuse, never fighting back.

For the details of Kagawa's heroic, selfless fifteen years of Christian witness and service in Shinkawa the reader is referred to William Axling's classic biography. We have space here only to consider the basic principles of his thought and action, which were forged in the burning fire of this experience. Primary was the conviction that religion is, must be, concerned with the whole of life. He came to see that the Christian gospel demands the utmost concern and effort to liberate men from every chain and the betterment of their physical, economic, social, psychological and moral as well as spiritual conditions.[15] For this reason he became a Christian Socialist, a social seer as well as an idealist. He never ceased to study, and in Shinkawa he studied the causes as well as the effects of poverty. He saw that urban poverty was related to rural poverty and that both were based on the practice of treating laborers as less than human beings. He perceived that the human relationships characteristic of the apprentice system in the ancient tradition of handicrafts were lacking in the new factories, that the legal rights were all on the side of the employer. He saw also that a direct ratio existed between infant mortality and the wages of parents, between the incidence of disease and the combination of undernourishment and long working hours.

After returning from two years of study in America, where he received an M.A. from Princeton University and a B.D. from Princeton Seminary, Kagawa soon emerged as one of the leading social thinkers of the day. His book *Studies in the Psychology of Poverty (Himmin Shinri no Kenkyū)* had been published in his absence (1915), and he came increasingly to be recog-

---

[15] Axling, *op. cit.*, pp. 44, 123, 131, 160. Cf. Cho Kiyo Takeda, "An Essay on Kagawa Toyohiko," *Asian Cultural Studies*, III/A (September, 1960), 47-68 and *Kindai Nihon to Kirisuto Kyō*, Taishō-Shōwa Hen, pp. 33-44.

nized outside Shinkawa. For Kagawa this meant increased opportunities for action. The result was his entrance into the
infant Japanese labor movements.

An event which contributed even more to Kagawa's fame and
by its financial benefits enabled him to back his causes with
greater power was the publication of the novel which he had
begun in his year of lonely illness. A publisher, aware of his
literary talent, asked to see the manuscript and recognized at
once its power and potential appeal. Kagawa revised the work
and added the story of his battle with death and his experience
in the Shinkawa slums. This frankly autobiographical novel
first appeared in serial form with moderate success, but after
publication as a book it became one of the best sellers of the
century. Within a very short time 250,000 copies were sold, and
new editions continued to be printed and sold over subsequent
decades.

The title of the book, *Shisen wo Koete (Crossing the Deathline)*, refers to the deathline that separated the more prosperous
parts of Kōbe from the slums of Shinkawa. Shimazaki Tōson,
one of the literary giants of the day, read the book in manuscript and termed it "of no account. " Other critics disdainfully
said that any schoolboy could have written it. But these criticisms rather point to the charm and appeal of the work. Simple
and straightforward, it dealt with the crucial issues of the human
heart and life.[16] It revealed to a whole nation the understanding and compassion which Kagawa had heretofore shown only
to the dwellers of Shinkawa. The book contributed much to
one of the greater achievements of his life, the education of the
conscience of the Japanese people.

With the royalties from this book Kagawa was able in more
concrete ways to improve the lot of Kōbe's poor. He entered
the labor movement at the very time his novel and his life in
Shinkawa made him known throughout the country. The
Christian Suzuki Bunji and some others had organized in
Tokyo a few years earlier the *Yūai Kai* (Fraternal Love Society, actually a laborers' mutual benefit society). Kagawa

---

[16] Drummond, *op. cit.*, pp. 823-824. Cf. Kumano Yoshitaka, "Shiteki Kirisuto Kyō," *Fukuin to Sekai*, XX/7-9 (July, August, September, 1965).

helped to form the Japan Federation of Labor and to organize the laborers of Kōbe into a branch of this national body. He was perhaps the leading figure in the great strike of the laborers of the shipyards in Kōbe in 1921.

For Kagawa labor unions were a means to liberate the workers, the poor, the slum dwellers. His goal was to restore the lost humanity of men, men whose humanity had been largely destroyed by poverty. Kagawa never became a scientific economist; there were and continued to be certain limitations in his understanding of economic processes.[17] His economics was primarily from the heart, in no small part subjective, but he understood the heart of men's needs. He fought for men and the restoration of humanity in men; he saw the building of persons as the true work of God. Therefore, he proclaimed as a primary principle of the labor union movement the fact that laborers are not things for sale but human beings. Men are not machines but persons, and the goal of the movement is the development of a society of persons, individual persons who work for the welfare of each other. The concept of men as persons was in fact the central element of his thought on social problems.[18]

In developing this theme Kagawa sometimes used bizarre expressions, such as his assertion of the worshipful quality of labor. "Worship the laborer" (Rōdōsha wo sūhai se yo), he proclaimed, "He is the first spirit to emerge out of this world." But he was primarily concerned to affirm the essential equality of men, and in the contemporary context of Japanese worship of ancient heroes, he insisted that most of these heroes had been little more than savage plunderers of their fellow men, and the whole of what men call history is nothing more than the record of the doings of such brigands.[19] The time had come for the reversal of these values and the recognition of the worth of the

---

[17] Cf. Sumiya, op. cit., pp. 38, 81-82.

[18] Kagawa had been influenced by the contention of the International Labor Organization that labor is not a commodity, but he went considerably beyond the thought of this organization in the radical consistency with which he developed the theme.

[19] Cf. Augustine De Civitate Dei 4. 4. "Remota itaque iustitia quid sunt regna nisi magna latrocinia? quia et latrocinia quid sunt nisi parva regna?"

laborer, the producer. And for the laborer he wanted life, liberty, autonomy.

In his methodology Kagawa was a thorough social evolution-ist, a strict follower of the principle of non-violence; he urged production motivated by love, creative and free. For this rea-son he strongly opposed violent revolution advocated in the older syndicalist or the newer Marxist theories. His ideal and goal was a religiously based guild socialism like that of the towns of the European Middle Ages at their best. As time passed, he was more and more drawn to the kind of socialistic thought which developed in England after the First World War. He favored constitutional procedures and hoped for a labor-dominated national Diet. The Labor party in England was long a symbol of his ideals. His specifically economic goal, however, of the socialization of capital, his contention that service should replace acquisition as the primary motive of economic life, and his concern for the establishment of international perspectives and relationships were hardly points designed to win the sup-port of the largely nationalistically oriented coalition of capi-talists, landowners and military leaders then ruling the Japa-nese state and society. Nevertheless, an important shift in public opinion occurred in the early 1920's; especially with reference to the conditions of life in the city slums, the conscience of the public was gradually aroused. Kagawa's conviction was vindi-cated that the Christian God speaks to the conscience of every man, Christian or non-Christian. In 1926 the government initi-ated a six-year program designed to wipe out the slums in the six largest cities of the empire and appropriated the equivalent of ten million dollars for the purpose, one of the earliest and most far-reaching instances of national social reform of this kind in the twentieth century.[20]

Kagawa came to see that the poverty of the urban slums was intimately related to the poverty of the rural villages. We noted the economic processes during the last decades of the nineteenth century whereby the conditions especially of the tenant farmers considerably worsened. The changes in tax structure effected by the establishment of a modern state led to deper-

---

[20] Axling, *op. cit.*, p. 86.

sonalized relationships between landlords and tenants similar to those experienced in the new factories between employers and workers. The tenant farmers who then comprised more than half of the rural population and paid from 55 to 70 percent of their crop to the landlords were forced in their destitution to send their second or third sons to the factories and to sell their daughters into prostitution. Kagawa found that most of the people about him in Shinkawa came from these villages, and he resolved to work for their liberation. In 1921 the first farmers' union in Japan was organized by a group of farmers meeting in Kagawa's room-house in Shinkawa. From this time he gave himself to this movement, and its subsequent wider range of activities such as credit unions, cooperatives and the like, with the same zeal as to labor unionism. As in the case of factory workers, he was concerned not only with the improvement of physical standards of living but even more with the remaking of men and women as persons. In spite of hostility and opposition from many quarters, he came to be loved and acclaimed as the savior of both farmer and laborer, the defender of all the poor and needy. By the early 1920's he had become a figure of national prominence.

4

I have described Kagawa's career to this point as if he were primarily a Christian reformer and social worker. He preferred, however, to describe himself — and his colleagues agreed with the judgment — as a Christian evangelist. He kept in touch with the various movements and institutions which he initiated and continued to aid them as they progressed, but he made it his policy to turn over formal leadership and direct operation to others. He preferred to work as the creative social pioneer, but above all as the Christian evangelist. Throughout the course of events which we have considered he continued to preach the gospel as he understood it, in season and out. He believed that true righteousness of conduct was achieved only as men "bring the unseen motive into God's presence and harmonize the hidden purpose with God's will." The Christian in Kagawa always overshadowed the Socialist. After World War II his friends urged him to offer himself as a candidate for the national Diet. His reply was characteristic of the man: "I must preach. My father was a politician. As a youth I promised God that I would preach. I listen only to the inner voice."[21]

Kagawa's deepest conviction was that at the center of things is a heart, and beyond darkness light. Prayer to God, who is personal, was central to his life. He regularly spent the morning hour from four to five in prayer and meditation; prayer was his greatest consolation and strength during times of illness or other trouble. Kagawa was not a theologian in the formal sense; systematic theology was hardly the proper mode of expression of a man so concerned with experience and practice. He could be called an old-fashioned liberal; he once described his own theology as a conscious application of Schleiermacher. Some of those who knew him best, however, insist that the deep biblical faith which he had learned at Kōbe Seminary remained the primary basis of his thought and life. He was a Christian man whose faith was one with life, whose theology was an expression of his experience of obedience and of communion with God, who is best known in Jesus Christ. We find in Kagawa a direct adoration as well as obedience of Jesus that places him in the tradition of Francis of Assisi and Bernard of Clairvaux. Those who knew him well detected an almost psychic power of insight into persons and situations. Kagawa believed therefore that true social reform as well as personal regeneration is rooted in religious faith, and he continued to see his own mission as primarily that of Christian evangelist. His experience of division within the labor movement and the growing advocacy within it of the methodology of class struggle and violence were undoubtedly important in strengthening his will at this point. Kagawa believed that to teach hate was a symbol of failure in any social movement.[22]

The great earthquake and fire of September 1, 1923, destroyed two-thirds of the city of Tokyo and even more of the port of Yokohama. One hundred thousand persons were killed, and the total loss in damage to property was estimated at five and a

---

[21] *Ibid.*, pp. 107-108, 113, 152.
[22] Sumiya, *op. cit.*, pp. 89-101.

half billion dollars. A special commission of one hundred and eighty of the ablest men in the nation headed by Premier Yamamoto Gombei was formed to cope with the situation. Kagawa, who up to this time had been trailed by the police as a dangerous demagogue, was asked to serve on the commission, the only member who was not a government official of high rank. For this purpose he moved his family to Tokyo and with his own hands built their modest home in the outskirts. To clarify his independence of the government, he issued a public statement that because of the nature of the emergency he had called a truce in political partisanship for the period of one year. Kagawa's work on this commission was very significant; the plan of operation finally adopted and carried out bore unmistakably the signs of his workmanship. While serving on this commission he was in considerable part responsible for the enactment of an Anti-Exploitation Land Act which served to check speculation in land.

Kagawa was then an expert in labor, and he was subsequently drafted to serve on a number of government commissions. One of his greatest services of this kind was as temporary head of the Social Welfare Bureau of the city of Tokyo during the terrible distress experienced there in the depression winter of 1930-31. Kagawa used to remark laughingly that the government was always most appreciative of his response to its calls but as soon as he worked through private organizations to serve the common man detectives began again to shadow him.[23]

Mention should be made also of Kagawa's efforts in behalf of peace. In 1928 he helped organize the National Anti-War League, a forerunner of the present Japan Union for World Federation. His activity in this area aroused great resentment and opposition from conservative and militarist groups, but Kagawa was a militantly non-violent pacifist and stoutly bore up under the vilification he received. He was denounced as a traitor and had to accept police protection (in place of the usual surveillance) because of threats against his life. He continued also to campaign against social evils, particularly against alcohol and prostitution. His experience and studies had led him to the con-

[23] Axling, op. cit., pp. 87-89.

clusion that 80 to 90 percent of public crimes are the matured harvest of alcohol and sexual sin. He included therein the hereditary effects of alcoholism and syphilis, and he had learned that almost every resident of Shinkawa had some physical or other handicap, arising in large measure from these causes, that made him an inefficient and therefore unwelcome member of society. Kagawa had learned to distinguish sociologically between this kind of hard-core group and the far larger class of poor factory workers. His approach to the understanding of every problem was always historical.

The main thrust, however, of Kagawa's career during the 1920's and 1930's was evangelistic. He had studied the Huguenot movement in France and became convinced that the power of the Christian church to stir the conscience and mold the moral, social, economic and political ideals of a nation is largely determined by the momentum of its impact. To create this momentum the church in Japan needed greater numbers, and Kagawa came to believe that if Japanese Christians, comparable to the Protestants in France, numbered a million, sufficient momentum could be achieved to effect changes of great import. He had long proclaimed the gospel of his Lord to men of every class, but as the 1920's progressed he sensed with ever stronger urgency a divine call to a concerted evangelistic campaign in which all churches and Christians would participate.

In response to this call the Kingdom of God Movement (*Kami no Kuni Undō*) was begun in November, 1926. In August of the following year a conference was held at Karuizawa to further what was also called the Movement for the Salvation of a Million Souls (*Hyaku Man Kyūrei Undō*), and in 1928 Kagawa himself went forth in a nationwide evangelistic campaign. From 1929 the Kingdom of God Movement gathered increasing momentum. In 1930 a central committee was set up to coordinate and direct the activity, and great campaigns were launched simultaneously in the six largest cities of the empire. The intent was to gather every Protestant congregation and Christian in support of an all-inclusive movement and to create thereby spiritual solidarity among them, an effort perhaps unique then in the divided state of the church in the world. Inspired by the leadership and vision of Kagawa, efforts were made to win the classes and groups of people that the Japanese church and related foreign missions had largely been unable to reach in past years: farmers, factory workers, fishermen, miners, day laborers and the like. Students were also a primary goal of the evangelistic effort.

In keeping with Kagawa's own understanding of the gospel as bringing "full-rounded emancipation" of the whole man and the transformation of all of life, strenuous efforts were made to bring Christian perspectives and standards of value to bear on the social and economic life of the nation. This fact must also be noted in the context of the day, when such understanding and activity were still largely confined to minority groups in the churches of the West.

From 1930 until the formal end of the campaign in 1934 Kagawa committed himself almost exclusively to the Kingdom of God Movement. Following the direction of the central committee's planning, he went systematically to cities and towns all over the country, speaking everywhere to capacity audiences. A total of twenty-five thousand persons were reckoned to have accepted his appeal to Christian faith during this period. Of equal or perhaps greater importance was the fact that over one and a half million people heard him speak. The movement did not result in significant additions to the official membership of the churches; the same can be said of Kagawa's evangelistic work in the years after the Second World War. Yet the Kingdom of God Movement not only helped to enlarge the range of vision and concern of Japanese Christians; it constituted a major contribution to the life of the nation as it entered a period of fifteen years of increasing dominance by military leadership. On the eve of compounding tragedy and suffering the movement became a spiritual and moral heritage of incalculable value in nourishing the "quiet people" of the land and preparing them to rise again from defeat and the ashes of war.

I do not have space to consider further the person and career of this great Christian. I refer the reader to my own article for a discussion of his efforts to preserve peace between Japan and the United States prior to the attack on Pearl Harbor on De-

cember 7, 1941.[24] A final word, however, will attempt somehow
to measure the stature of the man. To do this properly we must
see him in the context of his time and place. One of the characteristics of his preaching, especially after World War II, was
the frequent use of illustrations drawn from natural science. He
was not a scientist in the technical sense of the term, and it was
not impossible in later years for a specialist to find him inadequate at some points. Yet Kagawa's knowledge of natural science,
especially astronomy, physics and biology, reached levels rare in
non-specialists.[25] In 1920 there was probably not a man in Japan
qualified to challenge him in either the natural or social sciences. The creative nature and social value of his work in almost every case is most properly recognized as we perceive it at
its point of initial impact.

Kagawa was an apostle of non-violence almost as early as
Gandhi, and he could criticize Gandhi for his preoccupation
with India, his failure to be concerned adequately for the international aspects of movements for the emancipation of man.
Kagawa was concerned for his brothers everywhere. During the
Kingdom of God campaigns he not only went to Japanese
colonies in Asia — Korea and Taiwan; he also made repeated
trips to China over the years. In 1940 he was twice arrested and
investigated at home for apologizing in China for the Japanese
invasion of that country. His speaking tours in North America
and Europe were among the highlights of Christian witness in
the twentieth century for innumerable people.

Kagawa was the creative, dynamic initiator and promoter of
almost every movement for constructive social reform in Japan
for more than forty years. If Suzuki Bunji was the father of the
labor movement in Japan, Kagawa was early called its wise
mother; "his heart, his soul, his sympathy, his understanding
of the laborers are like that of a mother."[26] In the movements
for farmers' unions, cooperatives, credit unions, in campaigns

---

24 Drummond, *op. cit.*, p. 825.

25 A recent study reveals important affinities in the religious and scientific thought of Kagawa and Pierre Teilhard de Chardin, apparently quite
without mutual influence. Kishi Hideji, "Uchū Ishiki no Shūkyōsei,"
Koe, MC (January, 1970), 1-8.

26 Axling, *op. cit.*, p. 49.

against social evils of various kinds, in direct welfare work, he was not only an active pioneer but a spiritual guide. He was always more concerned for people than for organization; he aimed more at the reconstruction of humanity than of society. For this reason Kagawa was almost never doctrinaire; this fact in part accounts for his extraordinary creativity, his flexibility and mobility.

Perhaps the most historically significant aspect of Kagawa's career was the fact that as a Christian he informed the moral conscience of a largely non-Christian nation probably more than any other of his countrymen in the twentieth century. The ethical awareness, the social ideals, and to a very appreciable extent the spiritual understanding of the Japanese people in the present generation are, in my judgment, owed to Kagawa as a nation rarely owes its inner life to one man. He was, as my teacher John Aberly once said, one of the three greatest Christians of the twentieth century. He is, however, a man for all times, as he is a man for all peoples.

F. EVENTS AND ORGANIZATIONS, 1900-1945

1

THE CHRISTIAN MOVEMENT IN JAPAN HAS BEEN PARticularly distinguished by the spiritual quality and moral stature of its personnel. I elected to consider in some detail the careers of a number of these men because I feel that the movement cannot be properly understood or evaluated apart from a consideration of the inner as well as outer life of its representative figures. At this point, however, we must take note of some of the more external aspects of the period beginning with the year 1900.

Following the retardation of growth and enthusiasm in the 1890's, the Protestant churches were able to recoup their morale and energy sufficiently to promote the Forward Evangelistic Campaign of 1900-1904, the most ambitious joint effort of this kind heretofore made. Clearly influenced by the practices of

American Christianity, the campaign "included series of mass rallies in the larger cities, visiting teams for single meetings in the smaller places, evangelistic appeals, the signing of cards, after meetings for personal work, and the final follow-up assumed by local pastors."[1] Only a thousand persons were baptized as a result of these meetings, but three hundred thousand people were reported to have attended. The effects of the campaign were accordingly felt far beyond the confines of the churches. During this period a new Japanese evangelist became prominent, Kimura Seimatsu. Kimura had been trained in the Moody Bible Institute of Chicago, and, while by no means a man of narrow views, he was primarily concerned with religious conversion and, as compared with Kagawa, less with social issues and needs. Kimura, however, was a speaker of great power, colloquial in language, and strove with no little success to win the common man.

The separate denominations continued independent evangelistic programs, and with a certain ebb and flow of emphasis this methodology was important in Christian life until it reached a new climax in the Kingdom of God Movement, which we noted in connection with Kagawa. The Young Men's Christian Association began work in Japan as early as 1880; in 1904 the Young Women's Christian Association was established and soon developed a national organization. It particularly achieved distinction by the quality of its leadership and service. The Canadian missionary Caroline MacDonald and Kawai Michi, the founder of Keisen Girls' School, were leaders in the formative years of the movement.

The high rate of literacy in Japan early led to the development of Christian literature with emphasis in the first decades upon translation of the Bible and the establishment of periodicals. As Japanese leadership emerged in the 1890's, their thought increasingly was in the forefront of the entire literary production of the first three decades of the twentieth century. Included were some of the literary giants such as Shimazaki Tōson and Tokutomi Sohō. From 1900 trained colporteurs were used, and in 1905 and 1906 the sale of Scriptures doubled

---

[1] Iglehart, *A Century of Protestant Christianity in Japan*, p. 119.

and doubled again to reach a million copies of the Bible in whole or part per year. The Christian Literature Society was formed in 1910, with the Methodist missionary Samuel R. Wainright as prime promoter of this organization to facilitate the publication of writings and translations by Japanese Christians.

Japan's victory over China in 1895, over Russia in 1905, its participation on the side of the victorious Allies in the First World War, its consequent territorial acquisitions, all coupled with the remarkable growth of its industrial capacity as well as military power, created growing self-confidence and a sense of national greatness in the leadership of the nation that were not appreciably altered by the revelation of deep social problems by Kagawa and other reformers. A focus of this nationalism was the cult of veneration of the emperor which took on more and more the elements of religious faith. The lectures of Professor Hozumi Yasoku of Tokyo Imperial University were important ideological expressions of this position, and after the death of Emperor Meiji in 1912, Professor Kakehi Katsuhiko developed it to the status of a formal theology expressed in terms of a kind of Hegelian philosophy of national life.[2] This development was ominous for the later more direct confrontations of church and state in the third and fourth decades of the century. In the meantime, however, most Japanese Christians shared in the new sense of national pride, and the major Protestant churches, especially the *Nikki* and the *Kumiai,* began missions in the new Japanese colonies of Taiwan and Korea, in the islands of Micronesia given in mandate to Japan in 1919, and in China.

The first formal instrument among the Japanese churches to develop ecumenical relationships and cooperation was the Fellowship of Laymen *(Shinto no Dai Shimbokukai),* which held its initial public meeting in Tokyo in 1878. Japanese Christian laymen generally did not share equally in the denominational training received by the clergy and had far less consciousness of the meaning of the denominations or their historical rationale. They were most eager for union of the churches; but, as we have seen, similar views were held by most Japanese clergy, as by many missionaries. In 1883 the Fellowship was restructured into

[2] *Ibid.,* pp. 137-138.

the firmer organization of the Japanese Christian Laymen's Evangelical Alliance *(Nihon Kirisuto Kyōto Fukuin Dōmei Kai)*. The Alliance served as the primary agency for cooperation until its dissolution in 1906. In 1911 a higher level of ecumenical relationships emerged in the Japan Federation of Christian Churches *(Nihon Kirisuto Kyōkai Dōmei)*, which effected a relationship of eight churches as well as of individual Christians.[3] The great evangelistic campaigns beginning with that of 1900 were regularly planned and conducted under the auspices of these organizations and later by the National Christian Council. Union was consistently seen by many clergy and laity as essential to the proper execution of the mission of the church at home and abroad.

Another ecumenical instrument was the interdenominational Christian Young People's Society *(Kirisuto Kyō Seinen Kai)*, which was organized first in 1880. The so-called Summer Schools or youth conferences held every year under the auspices of this organization contributed greatly not only to the growth in faith and knowledge of large numbers of young people but also to the development of a consciousness of Christian unity transcending denominational allegiances. Increasingly a spirit emerged strongly critical of ecclesiastical fragmentation, as when Kozaki Hiromichi at the Tokyo conference of the Alliance in 1906 declared the preservation of meaningless divisions a tragedy and the union of the churches their greatest responsibility.[4] In 1906 the National Sunday School Association was formed. Corollary with these organizations was the Federation of Christian Missions, which was restructured already in 1902 from the Standing Committee on Cooperating Christian Missions.

The Japan Continuation Committee was a third focus of ecumenical activity, including both missionaries and Japanese Christians. This organization was formed in 1913 following the visit to Japan in that year of John R. Mott. It expressed in Japan the aftermath of the Edinburgh World Missionary Conference of 1910 and its Continuation Committee. The Japanese

---

[3] The term "Federation" is commonly used in English for this organization, but the Japanese word *(Dōmei)* is the same as for "Alliance."

[4] Nihon Kirisuto Kyōdanshi Hensan Iinkai Hen, *Nihon Kirisuto Kyōdanshi*, pp. 68-72, hereafter cited as *Kyōdanshi*.

committee continued to work for eight years to further relationships with the other churches of the world and for joint action
with missionaries. Another result of the Mott meetings was the
launching of a new evangelistic campaign, officially named the
"Cooperative Campaign of Evangelism." This activity continued with great vigor from 1914 to 1916 and included perhaps
90 percent of the entire Protestant movement. Under the auspices of the campaign work was carried on not only in Japan
but also in Korea, Taiwan and China. Five thousand meetings
were reported held with a total of 777,119 people in attendance
and 27,350 who made decisions.[5]   Again the membership of the
churches grew very little, but the educative influence of the
campaign upon large numbers of non-Christians was great, as
was the development of a new sense of unity and confidence
among Christians.

Christian witness continued to be made in new ways and
forms. Under the auspices of the YMCA about two hundred
young men were sent from North America to teach English
mainly in government schools. Perhaps the best known of
these was Merrell Vories, from whose work developed the Omi
Mission, a remarkable example of cooperative living and work
which created architectural and industrial activities with a
staff of several hundreds. Vories married a member of the Japanese nobility and became a Japanese citizen taking the name of
his wife's family (Hitotsuyanagi).[6]

Among smaller denominations, the Seventh Day Adventist
Mission began its work in Japan in 1911 with emphasis upon
medical work, the publication and dissemination of its own
Christian literature, and direct evangelistic work. The Oriental
Missionary Society began its intensive work in the same year
stressing home visitation on a house-to-house basis.

2

The 1920's constituted the heyday of political liberalism in
modern Japanese history. It was a decade which opened with

---

[5] *Ibid.*, p. 73.
[6] Cf. Hitotsuyanagi Merrell Vories, *A Mustard Seed in Japan*, 1948.

great promise for the Christian movement as the World Sunday Convention met in Tokyo in 1920 with generous support from many prominent Japanese who had no formal connection with the Christian church. A degree of freedom of speech and action existed beyond what the nation had known, although the nationalistic, militarist forces were only deterred, not seriously weakened, during the period. This was the decade of Kagawa's greatest public activity. However, future problems were predictable in that much of the liberalism of the period popularly imitated lower forms of Western culture and thus greatly increased the incidence of crime, divorce, prostitution and alcoholism. These developments in time came to strengthen greatly the hand of the primarily puritanical advocates of the policy of militaristic expansion. The gradual shift of the labor movement from the control of its early, largely Christian leaders to that of more strongly left-wing men and ideas, as the influence of Marxism grew in the land, led to increasing apprehension in almost every segment of society and tended to create support for extreme measures.

The Christian movement in Japan continued to be characterized by a small constituency of church members and a much larger body of sympathizers whose primary religious orientation may have been Christian but who for perhaps a variety of cultural reasons preferred to refrain from baptism and formal membership. Buddhist and Shintō leaders regularly count people of such position as a part of their institutional statistics, and in line with this policy Prince Tokugawa reported to the Washington Naval Conference in 1922 that the Christian population of Japan was one million. This was three times the figure of formal church membership.[7] And of this latter figure perhaps no more than a third were vitally active. Something of the nature of the churches' struggle for identity and self-support can be sensed from this situation.

From a study made in the early 1920's it was learned that of the twelve hundred Protestant churches and eighteen hundred preaching places, the average membership was fifty. In the cat-

---

[7] In similar fashion recent estimates of the size of this larger constituency range from three to ten million.

egory of churches the average membership was one hundred, but of these the number of active members was considerably less. There were only a few large congregations, such as Fujimichō in Tokyo, of which Uemura was pastor, with sixteen hundred members, and comparable churches in Kōchi and later in Sapporo. But for the most part the churches were small, and the problems of institutional life and support were great.[8]

Christian schools, however, generally continued to grow and to thrive during this period. They were often aided by the missions in capital improvements, but increasingly they developed financial resources of their own and became exceedingly important parts of the Christian movement, often overshadowing the churches in their social influence and financial power. Lack of adequate coordination in planning among and within the denominations led at times to inefficient duplication of work, notably in the case of theological schools. High quality was generally maintained in secondary education. Various attempts to improve the quality of higher education by coordination of efforts among boys' schools all failed. Notable success, however, was achieved by the founding in 1918 of Tokyo Women's Christian College (*Tokyo Joshi Daigaku*), which became a first-rate school with the backing of several denominations and missions.

Christian social institutions were less powerful in numbers and means, but as they depended for their support increasingly upon sources outside the churches and missions — in later years upon the government, local, prefectural and national — they, too, developed essentially independent organizations and traditions. New Christian social service agencies were created during this period. One example is the Japan Deaf Oral School (*Nihon Rōwa Gakkō*), founded in 1920 to teach lip-reading and speech to the deaf. Dr. and Mrs. A. K. Reischauer, together with Miss Lois Kramer, were key figures in the founding and development of this school.

The inability of great evangelistic campaigns to produce substantial increments to the membership of the churches led to some disenchantment with this methodology of witness. But

---

[8] Iglehart, *op. cit.*, pp. 178-180.

various Japanese Christians gifted as evangelists continued to attract great crowds. In addition to Kagawa and Kimura, notable names were Kanamori Tsūrin, with his famous three-hour sermon, and Nakada Jūji, an outstanding figure in the Holiness Church, which rapidly became a dynamic force in Japanese Protestantism. Nakada and Kimura, although with a distinctly different style from Uchimura Kanzō, found an ally in him in their emphasis upon the imminent return of Christ.

In 1923 the Japan Federation of Churches was superseded by the National Christian Council (*Nihon Kirisuto Kyō Remmei*), which included Christian schools, social institutions, the YMCA, YWCA, WCTU. This event not only constituted a further step in ecumenical relationships and a strengthening of the climate favoring church union; it also expressed new levels of achievement in maturity on the part of the Japanese churches. The preparation made by Japanese staff members of the NCC for the Jerusalem Conference of the International Missionary Council was particularly noteworthy for its quality and thoroughness; five persons, three Japanese and two missionaries, attended this conference from Japan. The Kingdom of God Movement was launched in a formal way in 1929 as a result of the planning of the NCC. Kozaki Hiromichi assumed the responsibility, under the auspices of the NCC, for the coordination of this work, although, as we have seen, Kagawa Toyohiko led in its execution. The NCC continued to be the focus of ecumenical aspirations and activity, and in this process it was greatly helped by the majority of missionaries, as is evidenced by the action of the Federation of Christian Missions in 1925 recommending a survey of the Protestant churches to further church union. There were, however, among both Japanese and foreign Christians not a few who disapproved of this activity of the NCC. The actual power of the NCC within the structures of the several denominations was of course limited to moral suasion, and at this time its role was primarily that of channeling the slowly growing ecumenical spirit of the Protestant churches.[9]

---

[9] *Kyōdanshi*, pp. 74-78.

3

Japan was very quickly affected by the world-wide economic depression which began in 1929. We have noted the widespread unemployment and great personal suffering which Kagawa helped to lessen, especially in the city of Tokyo in 1930-1931. The economic structures of the 1920's, in which the great industrial and mercantile aggregations of power *(zaibatsu)* constituted by the Mitsui, Mitsubishi, Sumitomo, Yasuda and a few other essentially family groupings dominated, failed to save the nation from this suffering and confusion. This failure, in turn, greatly strengthened the hands of the militarists, who had become increasingly resentful of the political and economic as well as moral and spiritual developments of the twenties. They opposed the spirit of liberalism not only from the standpoint of their own nationalistic, emperor-centered ideology. The Army and Navy had both been particularly incensed at the reduction of armaments following the Washington agreements of 1922 and the London Naval Treaty of 1929. The leaders of the Army and Navy also felt more akin economically and spiritually to rural Japan, from whose gentry their officers largely came and from whose poorer farmers the bulk of the common soldiers were drawn. Their ideal of industrial-mercantile activity was military service and territorial expansion. The emphasis upon capitalism in the twenties was not really to their liking, and the events following 1929 gave them their opportunity. Not only was there increasing unemployment in the cities; in 1930 the price of rice plummeted after an abundant harvest, and a crisis developed in the rural economy. In 1931 following a poor harvest the number of farm girls sold into prostitution considerably increased.[10]

In 1931 military leadership began to take the initiative in national affairs; the so-called Manchurian Incident first indicated the emerging dominance of this group. Domestically their policy was to assume political control, if necessary by assassination. In 1932 Inugai Ki, the last premier representative of parliamentary government, was assassinated, and other officials attacked by a small group of naval officers and farmers, and the period of

[10] Cf. Borton, *Japan's Modern Century*, pp. 321-324.

distinct military dominance began. In 1933 Japan withdrew from the League of Nations; in 1936 occurred the famous *Ni Ni Roku* Incident, in which on the 26th of February a group of young Army officers murdered seven key civilian figures in the government. This coup by the Imperial Way faction in the Army technically failed in its attempt to overthrow the government, but the situation was such that only the Army was in a position to form a cabinet and rule the nation. From this time until 1945 the Imperial Army was the controlling power in Japanese political life.[11] Under their regime increasing controls were established over the civilian population in every phase of life. Essentially every major element of the nation, the politicians, intellectuals, religious leaders, men of finance, labor and the farmers capitulated to the rule of the military. The Christian church, with some few exceptions, was compelled to do the same.

The process, however, of the development of a fascist state was gradual, and the church remained publicly active as long as it could. Indeed, in the first years of the decade of the thirties, one senses a heightening of the tempo of its activity. We noted that in the early part of this period the Kingdom of God Movement reached its height. From 1930 the Student Christian Movement became particularly active. During the decade the enrollment in Christian schools doubled, and Christian student activities were even better supported than before. Indeed, in government schools Christian student organizations outnumbered those of all other faiths combined and constituted the primary religious witness in their environment. One of Kagawa's most beloved institutional methodologies was the so-called Rural Gospel Schools *(Nōson Fukuin Gakkō)*, which were brief training institutes of perhaps three weeks, held in any convenient location, in which young farmers were trained in the Christian faith, Christian principles of community life and organization, and more efficient methods of agriculture.

---

[11] The extreme fascist elements were only one part even of the Army, and their ultimate dominance was achieved only after the use of assassination within as well as outside the armed forces. Many officers, especially in the Navy, continued to hold and at times to advocate more moderate views.

In 1932 over a hundred of these schools were being held in many parts of the country. In 1934 the Oxford Group became active among both Japanese and foreign missionaries.

Ecumenical relationships were furthered and certain concrete steps taken in the direction of church union. After the formation of the National Council of Churches in 1923, we note a series of events of this kind. The American Oriental Exclusion Immigration Law of 1924 stirred the laymen of the churches to unite and express their protest in that year. At the general meeting of the NCC in 1925 a proposal for church union was made, although nothing concrete came from it at the time. In 1927 the All-Japan Council of Christian Social Work was organized. In 1928 work was begun to prepare a new joint Protestant hymnal. In the same year the NCC published its Social Creed of fourteen items, including a pledge to support the limitation of armaments and work for universal peace. It also issued a basic draft for church union. In 1929 all the churches united in the celebration of the seventieth year from the beginning of Protestant Christianity in Japan.

In 1930 the Congregational *(Kumiai)* and Christian churches in Japan consummated union. The interdenominational nature of the youth programs of this period, such as the YMCA and SCM, of course greatly facilitated the trends toward church unity. In 1933 we note a joint meeting for consultation in Kyōto of six hundred representatives of the *Nikki* and *Kumiai* churches. From 1935 joint services of worship became popular. This trend, however, was not without certain reverses, such as the division in the Holiness Church which occurred in 1936.

The output of Christian literature reached a new height in this decade, indicating the remarkable intellectual and theological maturity of the Japanese church. About two hundred new books were published each year, mostly without subsidy, and were read widely, by non-Christians as well as by Christians. Approximately the same number of Christian periodicals were issued, and the Scriptures continued to be sold annually to the extent of a million copies in whole or part. The works of the great Japanese theological leaders had already become classics; the writings of Uchimura were published in fifteen volumes and Uemura's in eight. Translations of Calvin's

Institutes, of many of Luther's works and of Augustine were issued. Translations of contemporary European and American theologians were read by large numbers. Kierkegaard and Troeltsch continued to be studied; Barth, Brunner and Heidegger were in some cases better known and at an earlier period than in English-speaking lands. This kind of theological activity was particularly strong in the Presbyterian-Reformed tradition under the leadership of Takakura Tokutarō. Note must be taken of a fundamentalistic theological tradition to be found in Holiness and some other churches in varying degrees. A kind of biblically oriented pietism had always been strong in Japanese Protestantism and was widely to be found in the *Nikki* and *Kumiai* as well as in the Methodist Churches.

The Federation of Christian Missions responded to the situation of the day — the growing maturity of the church, its desire for independence, the need for foreign personnel and influence to be less prominent — by transferring most of its functions to the National Christian Council and restructuring itself into the more informal Fellowship of Christian Missionaries. The Congregational, Disciples of Christ and Baptist Missions dissolved their mission organizations as such.

From 1936 the pressures of the military state began to be felt with new degrees of intensity. The distinguished Christian *(Mukyōkai)* professor of Tokyo Imperial University, Yanaibara Tadao, was forced to resign from the faculty for his criticism of the government policy in Manchuria. His academic superior, Nambara Shigeru, later came under comparable disapproval for his opposition to the increasingly proclaimed thesis of religious nationalism. Significantly, both of these men in turn became chancellor of Tokyo University after the war. In various ways Christians felt the hostility of the new regime to their transcendental theology, their international ties and perspectives, and their strong stand for peace. Churches and individual Christians, however, issued various statements of concern regarding the military expansionist trend of the time; in 1936 through the NCC the churches again declared themselves publicly in behalf of peace. In general they tried to maintain a posture consistent with their historic positions and at the same time show themselves as patriotic Japanese, an increasingly difficult task.[12]

In 1937 a department was created in the NCC to coordinate work in behalf of men in the imperial forces. Christians were also enlisted in activities to combat the spread of Communism. In 1938 one of the first examples of direct theological confrontation occurred when a questionnaire was sent from the head of the military police in Ōsaka to Christian pastors in the area. Categorical replies were demanded to questions regarding Christian attitudes toward the emperor, imperial rescripts, shrine worship, etc. The Ōsaka pastors formulated a corporate reply which was accepted as satisfactory, but they were then informed that the tablets issued by the great Shrine of the Imperial Family at Ise should be placed upon an appropriate shelf in every home. This latter policy was actually ordered by the Home Ministry in 1940, but no serious effort was made to enforce the ruling. In 1940 a nationwide Christian laymen's conference was held to celebrate the 2600th year (according to the then official chronology) of the establishment of the imperial throne. During the war, officials of the Kyōdan and other Christian churches visited the Ise Shrine and offered prayers for the well-being of the emperor. They affirmed in explanation that their prayers were addressed to the one God, but these acts were apparently disapproved of by most Christians. The policy of the national government was in general to bring the Christian churches under the ideological as well as the physical control of the military state without a direct theological confrontation so as to create martyrs.

The ideology of the military government, however, was a new expression of the ancient Japanese tradition by which religiously absolute values were assigned to the structures and personages of government. In essence this ideology was no different from the *Fukoku-Kyōhei* policy of the Meiji government, but the latter, occupied with the many pressing problems of modernization, was never able to bring the religious issue to bear on the lives of most individuals in society. The Taishō liberal governments in general did not wish to raise the issue. The new

[12] Katakozawa, *Nihon Purotesutanto Hyaku Nen no Ayumi*, pp. 175-180.

military government, however, as it developed increasingly into
a totalitarian regime made use of modern media of communication to effect a personal confrontation such as had not been
known since the period of Tokugawa rule.[13] In the context of
world opinion of the 1930's various devices were employed to
camouflage the issues before the outside world, such as the interpretation that the emperor was above the state and that
state Shintō was not a religion. The NCC and prominent
Christians, such as the well-known member of the Diet, Tagawa
Daikichirō, appealed for clarification of the issues, such as
shrine attendance, stressing that if it be religious, attendance,
according to the constitution, should be voluntary. If shrine
attendance be not religious, all religious elements should be
removed. The government, however, continued to prefer ambiguity, by which it could maintain the forms of the constitution
and at the same time promote its own national policy and ideological program. Its purpose was to make the Christian church,
as all other religious organizations, a fully compliant and
cooperative tool of this policy.

Something of the tension of the time can be seen from the
experience of Kagawa. He was arrested in 1940 on the charge of
engaging in subversive propaganda for peace. In the course of
the questioning he refused to ascribe to the emperor a higher
religious status than Jesus Christ, and his refusal was construed
as a criminal act. To the surprise of the authorities, however, a
great volume of spontaneous protest arose, and both Christians
and non-Christians of national prominence worked vigorously
for his release.[14] Kagawa was set free shortly afterward, but the
incident gives a glimpse into the state of affairs at the time. As
the military regime extended and strengthened its hold upon
all segments of society as well as government, all organized expressions of democracy, peace, internationalism and rational
discussion were silenced. But there was little popular approval
of the policy of military expansion and far less for the policy of
government by assassination. Within the vast apparatus of civil
service which the military authorities had no alternative but to

---

[13] *Kyōdanshi*, p. 80.
[14] Axling, *Kagawa*, pp. 144-145.

continue to employ, there were men, even of high rank, who were sympathetic to Christianity and also a few Christians. Like the rest of the population they felt helpless to change the main course of events, but in various ways they acted to prevent general disaster from overtaking the Christian movement.

The popular mood toward Christians and the church, however, had gradually become more and more hostile under the prodding of the propaganda of the right wing nationalists and militarists. Hostility to Christians had over the years always been latently if not patently present, more in some areas, especially the provinces. The possibility was always present as the thirties progressed, given the proper occasion, of an outburst similar to that in Tokyo in 1905 when, after the signing of the Treaty of Portsmouth between Russia and Japan under the good offices of President Theodore Roosevelt, popular resentment expressed itself in the burning of Christian churches. But in spite of the revival of the old suspicions of Christians as spies, culminating in the arrest of two leaders of the Salvation Army on this charge on July 31, 1940, and a few incidents of persecution and even torture in the provinces, there was no general, wide-scale persecution, official or unofficial. Possibly some persons in government, in spite of the fanaticism of the military regime itself, had learned sufficiently from the historical consequences of the persecutions of the *Kirishitan* period so as to be determined to avoid a policy that could only result in the recurrence of martyrdoms and apostasies on a large scale. Differently from the policy of the Nazi regime in Germany, which resolved to pursue its "solution" of the Jewish question even to the extent of interference with the war effort, the Japanese government generally refrained from any action which might entail substantial diversion from its primary goal of unifying the nation to fight the war.[15]

The presence of this relative understanding and consideration among at least a few in the highest echelons of civilian government helps to explain the willingness of Japanese Christians and churches to cooperate with the government in keeping with Christian faith. Japanese Christians had always been loyal

[15] Cf. *Kyōdanshi*, pp. 109-112.

citizens and considered civil obedience and service to the state
their divinely prescribed duty. We have noted the grave mis-
givings many individuals had and expressed with regard to the
policy of military expansion, but once the nation as a whole
was committed, apparently without power of retrieval, to war
with China from 1937, almost all Christians felt that they had
no alternative but to cooperate with national policy.[16] This was
the environment in which the various steps were taken leading
to the union of all Protestant churches and the formation of the
United Church of Christ in Japan *(Nihon Kirisuto Kyōdan)*
on June 24, 1941. We shall now briefly review those steps.

4

The immediate background of the formation of the United
Church was the passage of the Religious Bodies Law in 1939.
Ruling governments had attempted on several occasions to pass
a strongly regulatory religious law from the year 1899. Each attempt met with strong opposition from Christians and liberals
of almost every persuasion, and it was never possible to obtain
sufficient support in the Diet to pass what many thought was
outside the proper province of government and an infringement
of the religious freedom guaranteed in the constitution. But by
1939 the situation in the country had changed so much that the
government was able without difficulty to pass its new bill
through the now thoroughly compliant *(Yokusan Gikai)* Diet.

One of the measures of the bill served to place all state Shintō
shrines outside the category of religious bodies and therefore not
subject to the other provisions of the act. By this means the
religious absolutism of the regime was technically removed from
the category of religion, and shrine worship, the "Peoples'
Rite" *(Kokumin Girei)* and the like could be made constitution-
ally legal and compulsory for all Japanese.

Another vitally important provision required every religious
body to fulfill certain conditions to be approved as a religious
body by the Ministry of Education, under whose jurisdiction

---

[16] The concrete steps which the churches should take were outlined in a
pamphlet issued by the NCC in 1938 under the title *The People's Spiritual
Mobilization and Christianity*. Cf. Iglehart, *op. cit.*, pp. 221-222.

such bodies were to be. In case any religious organization failed to be so approved, it was considered a mere religious association (*shūkyō kessha*) and came under the jurisdiction of the provincial governors, from whom the possibility of recognition was much more problematical. Without this recognition dissolution was almost certain. Even if recognition were obtained, nationally the religious organization came under the jurisdiction of the Home Ministry and was certain to receive far stricter supervision than from the Ministry of Education. Without the latter's protection any religious group was also far more liable to experience annoyances and even persecution from local police, the military or patriotic organizations. The advantages, therefore, of securing recognition from the Ministry of Education were great, and Christian laymen were particularly strong in their desire to comply with the conditions.[17]

The conditions, however, as announced in amended form to representatives of the Christian churches on June 12, 1940, included the provision that to qualify for Ministry of Education approval a denomination had to comprise a minimum of fifty congregations and five thousand members. This news created consternation among the Christians, because of the twenty-three denominations belonging to the NCC only seven were large enough to qualify. It became at once apparent to all Protestants that church union was the one indispensable means to save Japanese Protestantism from eventual disintegration, and after much deliberation, even the *Nihon Kirisuto Kyōkai*, from which perhaps the strongest opposition to union had come in recent years, quickly decided to move toward organic union. The great desire of most Japanese Protestants over long years, which they were not able to fulfill of themselves, was now to be realized under the pressures of a totalitarian government seeking primarily the reorganization of religious bodies into units of a size it could more conveniently control.

Interchurch discussions of an informal nature began on August 15, 1940 under the chairmanship of Methodist leader and

---

[17] Cf. *Kyōdanshi*, p. 88. The writer, Yamaya Shōgo, affirms that probably the bulk of the laymen were not sufficiently informed as to the nature of the religious and other issues which the churches faced at this time.

chairman of the NCC, Abe Yoshimune. The main problems discussed were those of financial independence from the missions, foreign missionaries, and church union. About twenty-five persons were present. The sense of pressure and rapidity of action at this time are indicated by the fact that only two days later a second meeting was held with approximately sixty present. On this occasion the main subject of concern was church union. On August 16 and 17 a group of Christian ministers and laymen who had formed themselves into an informal brotherhood *(Kirisuto Kyō Dōshikai)* and had worked for some years in behalf of church union met and brought their urgent appeal for union to the second meeting mentioned above.

Other informal discussions were held in August and September, mostly under the auspices of the NCC; some included representatives of Christian schools and social welfare organizations. On September 2 a meeting attended by one hundred twenty representative figures was held under the chairmanship of Abe which in effect constituted itself as an actual working committee for union. It took action in the light of the contemporary international situation to urge the Japanese Christian churches to sever all ties with foreign missions and to commit themselves to self-support and independence. It also in effect put a time limit on the churches' action on union by setting October 17 as the day when the churches should announce their decision to unite. The occasion would be the National Christian Laymen's Conference in celebration of the 2600th year of the founding of the imperial throne. The meeting urged the formation of a preparatory committee for church union entrusted with full power to act.

The Standing Committee of the NCC met on September 6 to discuss these recommendations and after deliberation decided to communicate them to the churches for appropriate action. It was careful to express in the warmest terms the deep appreciation of all Japanese Christians for the zealous efforts of the missions in behalf of the church over the many years.

Japanese Christians writing of these times tell of the many and great difficulties experienced as the churches moved to implement these recommendations which were clearly the *sine qua non* of their survival. Not only had the separate denominations conducted their affairs separately, some of the smaller bodies were not members of the NCC and had never communicated much with Christians of the larger denominations. To bring together into effective union these churches with their different histories, doctrines, polities, forms of worship and life style was no easy task; innumerable obstacles appeared and various objections seemed to block the proceedings. The two churches which experienced the most difficult problems were the Anglican and the Lutheran, although the *Nikki* also had to pass through troublesome negotiations.[18] But the times were not such as to permit quibbling or delay, and the churches proceeded to take action on the basis of the strong support for union among the great bulk of the clergy and laity.

The NCC was responsible for holding a number of regional meetings of an informal kind, and from early September, 1940, the various churches began to hold special general synods or assemblies. One after another took action to agree to participate in union. As a consequence, it was possible to announce the collective decision in time at the Laymen's Conference on October 17, where approximately twenty thousand Christians gathered for worship on the campus of the Methodist school Aoyama Gakuin in Tokyo. At this meeting the churches were asked to designate, in proportion to the number of their members, representatives for a Preparatory Committee for Church Union. The first meeting of this committee was held the following day with twenty-two denominations represented by sixty-four delegates. The chairman was Abe Yoshimune, and four sub-committees were formed to handle, respectively, matters pertaining to creed, polity, finance and ministry. The committee arranged to meet as a whole every two weeks.

The committee as a whole met eight times, and the sub-committees several dozen times. The problem which actually caused the most difficulty was that of finance in the event of union. Not a few of the denominations carried on their activity with

---

[18] The Anglican Church ultimately did not enter the United Church as a body, but a majority (over sixty) of the Anglican congregations applied on their own initiative and remained as integral parts of the Kyōdan throughout the war. The Seventh Day Adventists did not participate and were later dissolved as a religious organization.

very great help from related missions and hardly knew how to manage without this support. More immediate, however, were the problems of creed and polity, and there were occasions when it seemed that the negotiations would end in rupture.

With reference to the problem of creed, it was decided not to attempt a formulation of a confession of faith but to prepare only what the Ministry of Education requested, a general statement of Christian doctrine. As to polity, the preference of the majority was for a federated or bloc system, which consisted of eleven blocs with considerable autonomy in mode of worship, creed and evangelistic work, although the United Church existed as a unitary structure on a higher juridical level. The preparatory committee took its final action on March 25 and 26, 1941 to name a Committee for the Establishment of a United Church with full power to act, designating both members and officers. Tomita Mitsuru (*Nikki*) was made chairman. This latter committee immediately set to work, and as a result the general meeting of the delegates of thirty-two bodies to constitute the United Church of Christ in Japan (*Nihon Kirisuto Kyōdan*) was held in Fujimichō Church in Tokyo on June 24 and 25, 1941. The number of official delegates present was three hundred, with about fifteen others also in attendance. The church comprised eleven synods, including the synods of Korea and Taiwan, and one mission, Manchuria. It had a Board of Trustees (*Jōgiinkai*) with eleven members and nine departments of work.[19] The most significant element of the polity of the new organization was the role of its leader, who in the person of Tomita Mitsuru was elected by unanimous vote of the delegates; the other provisions of the plan presented were likewise approved unanimously.

The term (*tōrisha*) for the head of the organization had been designated in the Religious Bodies Law. It did not denote a moderator or president or even bishop according to the democratic tradition of the Protestant churches. The structure of au-

---

[19] The Ministry of Education later required the formation of a Standing Committee of seven which essentially replaced the Board of Trustees and acted in place of the General Assembly. This structure was altered again in January, 1945, as a result of the emergency conditions caused by the bombing raids.

thority of which the *tōrisha* was the apex was not democratic but centrally authoritarian, and the leader had powers of control and discipline over churches and pastors which though partially qualified by the roles of the Board of Trustees and General Assembly were far beyond that known in any Protestant church in Japan. He had authority comparable to the head *(kanchō)* of a Buddhist sect. He was expected to rule as well as to represent the Kyōdan; his was the power to convene the General Assembly or Board of Trustees and to order their adjournment. He was to be responsible for the execution of the constitution and bylaws and to settle all disputes. He was to approve the formation of congregations and changes in their rules, to determine their qualifications for legal incorporation, to order their merger or dissolution. Above all, his was the responsibility for the appointment, dismissal and discipline not only of headquarters staff personnel but also of all clergy. The approval of General Assembly was necessary for the levy and collection of funds, but the *tōrisha* administered the finances of the United Church. In short, the church was committed into his hands.[20]

The structure of the church was that most suited to the forms of control which the government wished in order to meet wartime needs. At the same time, considering the military dominance of government, the Ministry of Education was not in general, in the context of the time, unreasonable; it did protect the churches, Roman Catholic, Orthodox as well as Protestant, from what might have been much worse treatment. It may seem upon retrospect that Tomita and his headquarters staff at times overplayed the role of compliance with government directives, but his action and that of the churches must be viewed in the context of this relationship with the Ministry of Education. In any case, these men worked zealously to create an organic unity out of the Kyōdan, a church in heart and life as well as name. The moderators and vice-moderators of all the synods had already been appointed at the time of the organization of the Kyōdan. They, too, were zealous in their efforts to create a real unity out of the heterogeneous parts that constituted their

---

[20] *Kyōdanshi*, pp. 107-108.

constituencies. Synodical meetings were held in August and September of 1942, and with relative smoothness and dispatch the necessary local organizations were formed and set to work.

Note must be taken of the fact that while government pressures were an important factor in these developments, there was no foreign participation whatsoever.[21] Indeed, for the first time in the history of Protestant Christianity in Japan the church was administered totally by Japanese Christians. The severance of all formal ties with the missions was preceded and followed by the gradual withdrawal, upon the advice both of their home boards and government embassies, of the great majority of foreign missionaries to their homelands. Only a very small number were still in the country at the time of the beginning of the Pacific war, and most of these were repatriated in two exchange ships which sailed in 1942 and 1943.[22] Only about ten (apart from German or Swiss citizens) remained in Japan throughout the war; they were mostly women.[23]

It must not be thought that the severance of ties with the missions and the departure of the missionaries were casual events. Quite apart from the financial aspects, almost all missionaries had deep personal ties with numbers of Japanese, non-Christian as well as Christian. It is heart-warming to read Japanese accounts written nearly thirty years after the events which speak with much feeling of the strength of these relationships and of the profound appreciation which almost all Japanese Christians had for the persons and services of their foreign co-workers in the faith.[24]

---

[21] There is reason to believe, however, that the advice of William Axling, and perhaps of other missionaries, was sought at this time. Cf. Leland D. Hine, "William Axling and the War Years," *The Japan Christian Quarterly*, XXXIII/4 (Fall 1967), 267.

[22] Cf. William Axling, *Japan at the Midcentury, Leaves from Life*, pp. 118-149.

[23] Cf. Frances Benten Clapp, *Mary Florence Denton and the Doshisha*, pp. 358-405.

[24] *Kyōdanshi*, pp. 79-122. Most of the material in this section on the process leading to the formation of the United Church of Christ in Japan has been derived from this book, which may be regarded as a definitive history of the United Church. I consider it eminently fair as well as perceptive.

5

The origins of the war between Japan and the United States lay in the policy of Japan following the First World War to develop exclusive political and trading rights in Manchuria. This policy clashed directly with America's avowed principle of an Open Door for China. In the context of the background of European colonial and mercantile activity in China from the beginning of the nineteenth century and the concern of Japan to set a firm limit to Russian expansion in the Far East, the moral issues can hardly be said to be free of ambiguity. Subsequent Japanese military action in Manchuria, however, its expansion into northern and central China, and Japanese claims to hegemony in the whole of East Asia brought about a direct confrontation of interests and increased public resentment in the United States to Japan's policy.

Japanese historians who are critical of the policy of military expansion stress the fact that before Pearl Harbor the war with China had reached an impasse. Japanese forces had won the major battles and occupied all larger cities but were unable to conquer the country as a whole. Important Chinese military units, especially those of Chiang Kai Shek and of the Communists, eluded their grasp. The Japanese people were weary, the economy was under severe strain and it became increasingly difficult to supply the armies. But the military regime had committed the nation, and to their minds national pride absolutely forbade withdrawal under any terms that suggested defeat or dishonor. This was the context in which the United States under the diplomatic leadership of Secretary of State Cordell Hull began to exert increasing pressure upon Japan to withdraw from China. As diplomatic measures moved into economic embargo, the Japanese military responded by movement into Southeast Asia to secure the rice, petroleum, iron and other products which were vital to the war effort. The attack on Pearl Harbor was the Japanese reaction to what were believed to be intolerable pressures upon the nation's life line of supplies.[25]

---

[25] Cf. Paul W. Schroeder, *The Axis Alliance and Japanese-American Relations, 1941*, pp. 168-216. Cf. also Hiyane, *Nihon Kirisuto Kyōshi*, pp. 407-420.

Most of the Japanese people, already weary of war and doubtful of final victory, felt that to declare war upon the two powerful nations of the United States and Great Britain was indeed a rash undertaking. From the beginning serious doubts existed as to whether military planning, brilliant in its early execution, had really prepared sufficiently to succeed in the project. After the battle of Midway on June 5, 1942, thoughtful Japanese sensed defeat in the offing, and many came increasingly to doubt the official reports of unceasing victories. But to express these doubts was utterly impossible in the atmosphere of wartime Japan, and the repression of every hint of dissidence became more severe as time passed. There were many instances of arrest and imprisonment for the slightest word or deed suggestive of criticism or non-cooperation.

The government's concept of the role of every religious organization was to serve unreservedly as an instrument to further the war effort. The organizations, their members and physical facilities were to be at the disposal of every local enterprise which might serve this purpose. The government's understanding of the role of religious teaching was primarily that it should strengthen popular conviction of military victory, affirm the moral rightness of the war,[26] nourish the spirit of determination and perseverance, and encourage every kind of personal economy and generous contribution. The churches held citywide joint prayer meetings for victory and in every way possible cooperated with the program of the government. To further this purpose training sessions (kyōshi no rensei) were held in various parts of the country for what we might call the mental conditioning of pastors. A small number of ministers were sent overseas to the newly conquered territories to serve as liaison persons with local Christians; for example, a contingent of twelve ministers selected by the military was sent to the Philippines as early as November 20, 1941. The Kyōdan itself was assigned responsibility for communications and efforts for unity and cooperation among the churches and Christians in

---

[26] Official communications of the Kyōdan denote the war as holy (seisen). Cf. Kyōdanshi, p. 139. The predominance of these responsibilities appears with particular clarity in the Kyōdan's Guide to Wartime Christian Witness (Kyōdan Senji Fukyō Shishin), pp. 138-141.

all the territories in East Asia under Japanese control. Numbers of leading pastors served to this end especially in the Philippines and Indonesia. Abe Yoshimune resided for some time in central China for this purpose, and Kozaki Michio traveled extensively in northern China. It must be confessed that some men abused this trust, even as those who worked zealously for the welfare of native Christians and peoples were greatly respected and loved by them.

The churches, however great the difficulty, tried to maintain their regular schedules of Sunday worship and weekly prayer meetings. Conditions varied in different places, but it became increasingly difficult to hold Sunday morning services because of other demands upon people's time.[27] On July 18, 1944 the Evangelism Committee of the Kyōdan noted that the attendance of men at services had become almost impossible and housewives were under severe pressures. Attempts were made to counteract this situation through small group meetings and family worship.[28] It is remarkable, however, to what extent church life was able to continue in some congregations under these difficult conditions. Yamaya Shōgo writes with much feeling of his wartime experiences in Kyōto, where, although church and Sunday School attendance dropped appreciably, serious inquirers continued to appear.[29] The atmosphere was one of deep earnestness, and in the shortage of goods the Lord's Supper was celebrated with water and bread substitutes. Even as this congregation supported the program of the government and in particular sent off its young men to the front with solemn farewell ceremonies, it continued to remember the church throughout the world in prayer and to pray for the early advent of peace. At this point the church in Japan could not completely identify itself with the totally nationalistic aims of the government.[30]

[27] Iglehart, op. cit., pp. 247-248. The statistics of the Kyōdan reported as of March, 1942, give the total membership as 190,447, but these figures of course do not indicate the actual attendance at services. Reported at the Second General Assembly on November 25-26, 1943, was the figure of 174, 521, of which the same qualification must be made.

[28] Kyōdanshi, p. 163.

[29] Men and women also continued to be ordained as ministers even into 1945.

[30] Kyōdanshi, p. 133. Cf. Hine, op. cit., p. 270.

As the war progressed church activity became more and more difficult to maintain and almost ceased when regular bombing raids began in the spring of 1945. From 1944 pastors under forty-five years of age were mobilized to serve fulltime in various war production capacities. Biblical preaching or authentic religious teaching was almost completely transformed into exhortations to service the war effort.[31] The People's Rite, at first a simple moment of silence with head bowed in memory of the war dead, came to include a turning toward the imperial palace in Tokyo, singing of the national anthem and the reading of some imperial rescript. This ceremony became a compulsory part of every service of worship or public religious meeting. Even the hymnals were changed so as to delete those hymns which referred too forthrightly to God as Creator or Judge. All public or formal references to peace were forbidden. This was the time when the term "Japanese Christianity" came to be used frequently. Thoughtful Japanese Christians reflecting on those days tend to feel now that the word and work of the Kyōdan as a whole over the war years should have been marked by a more distinctly Christian, that is, biblical tone. This essentially valid statement, however, must be countered by reference to the incident in early 1945 when Tomita Mitsuru and Murata Shiro in discussion with the Ministry of Education over the Kyōdan's Catechism, which had been completed and unanimously approved by the Board of Trustees on November 15, 1944, resolutely insisted that it was impossible to alter the church's belief in the resurrection of Christ and the subordination (in effect) of the emperor to God and his Christ.[32] Tomita is reported to have said later to friends that at this point he was prepared to take his stand and die if necessary. The war ended before the Ministry was able to take further action on the matter.

As public transportation became more restricted and finally largely dislocated by the bombing, committee meetings could no longer be held, and from early 1945 the *tōrisha* and his staff conducted almost all affairs by administrative fiat. His

---

[31] *Ibid.*, p. 139.

[32] *Ibid.*, pp. 138, 140-142, 167-168. Cf. Iglehart, *op. cit.*, pp. 251-252; Aikawa Takaaki, *Unwilling Patriot*, Tokyo: The Jordan Press, 1960, *passim.*

power, however, had been steadily augmented during the course of the war. At his installation service on February 7, 1942 he had hinted at the dissolution of the bloc system, which of all the items in the constitution and bylaws of the Kyōdan had been most objectionable to the Ministry of Education and which the latter had approved only with great reluctance and with the proviso "for the time being" *(tōbun no uchi)*. The first General Assembly of the Kyōdan met in Tokyo on November 24 and 25, 1942.[33] Apart from items pertaining to co-operation with the war effort the most important proposal, strongly advocated by the *tōrisha,* was to abolish the bloc system as inconvenient to the government in its desire to integrate all religious bodies and their work to serve the war needs. Almost none of the delegates had understood the term "for the time being" to mean such a short period, but they were in no position to do anything other than acquiesce. The action, however, was clearly premature for many of the delegates and was to reemerge after the war as a serious problem.

On May 18, 1943, a ceremony was held marking the formal inauguration of the three theological schools, one for eastern Japan, one for western and one for the training of women workers, which represented a further expression of the unity of the Kyōdan by the amalgamation of all the fourteen or more theological institutions of its constituent parts. Even these three, however, were difficult to finance under wartime conditions, and in 1944 the two men's schools were united into one school, the *Nihon Kirisuto Kyō Shingaku Semmon Gakkō.* The YMCA and YWCA and other youth organizations became a part of the Kyōdan, as did the WCTU and almost every previously independent Protestant activity, but the Kyōdan took its responsibility in these areas with great seriousness. Throughout the war it strongly stressed the training of youth, even if it was severely limited in the execution of its intent.

On November 26, 1942, Tomita *Tōrisha* was received in audience by the emperor in company with forty other representatives of religious organizations. This event greatly enhanced

[33] The second and last wartime meeting of the General Assembly was held November 25-26, 1943, when Tomita Mitsuru was reelected as *tōrisha.*

his own authority, but he and other Christians made much of the affair as betokening an official recognition of Christianity by the state such as it had never had before and interpreted it as entitling the church to take a firm stand against harassments by local or military police. Tomita traveled widely about the church to report on the honor which the church had received in this way. The event also reveals the ambivalence, or perhaps more precisely the division, within Japanese officialdom toward the church, for earlier that year, on June 26, 1942, 106 pastors of two Holiness churches (blocs six and nine within the Kyōdan) were suddenly arrested and interrogated. Their teaching of the Second Coming of Christ and the Thousand Year Kingdom (Rev. 20:1-6) was considered derogatory to the dignity of the emperor and contrary to the law of the land. They were also charged with conspiracy, in conjunction with Christian laymen, to overthrow the government. This was patent nonsense, but the men were kept in detention. Their case was not heard by the Tokyo District Court until August, 1944. Eleven were finally given relatively light sentences, which they immediately appealed. The bombing raids prevented further court action, and the last of these men were freed only after the end of the war. Several men, however, of the original larger group died in prison.[34]

In some ways a deepening of faith and moral insight is discernible in the columns of the sole periodical (Kyōdan Shimpō) left to the church as the war came to its end. As the very existence of the nation and the personal lives of all the citizens, civilian as well as military, came into jeopardy, the witness of the church, however small in the country at large, was expressed with a stronger and purer spiritual tone. Christians gave themselves without stint to works of mercy and public aid. The people of God had been oppressed, even broken, but not crushed. In spite of some weakness and failure in content of faith and consistency of spiritual understanding they were able

---

[34]Kyōdanshi, pp. 148-149, 172. The authorities of the Kyōdan apparently did not forthrightly support these men as having the legal right and the theological freedom to hold their convictions but rather endeavored to change them.

to survive the experience of war and national defeat with an integrity comparable to the highest levels of the adherents of other faiths in the land.[35]

G. THE POSTWAR PERIOD

1

THE OVERWHELMING FACT OF THE LAST YEAR OF THE war for the Japanese in the homeland was the bombing raids on the cities. The devastation wrought by atomic bombs in Hiroshima and Nagasaki is well known, but sixty Japanese cities were damaged, many almost destroyed, by firebomb raids. Perhaps 80 percent of Tokyo was laid waste as a result of these terrible holocausts. Churches and other Christian institutions suffered accordingly. About one-third of the church buildings were totally destroyed. Out of a total of 1,184 Protestant churches, 507 were destroyed or severely damaged; of Roman Catholic churches, 74 out of a total of 245.[1]

After the destruction of much of downtown Tokyo in March, 1945, a new cabinet was formed by an admiral of moderate views, Suzuki Kantarō, and the process begun which was to lead to the cessation of hostilities. Already in August, 1944, a Supreme Council for the Direction of War had been created with the emperor as chairman. After the second great bombing raid on Tokyo in May, 1945, this body became the instrument by which decisive steps were taken to end the war. The emperor himself in the course of its later deliberations at least twice broke a tie to decide in favor of action toward peace; the

---

[35] Cf. Iglehart, *op. cit.*, p. 255. Cooperation among all religious groups was naturally the wish of the Ministry of Education and was proclaimed as part of the Kyōdan's Guide to Witness.

[1] *Nihon Kirisuto Kyōdanshi*, p. 205. Cf. pp. 173, 183, 202. There is some discrepancy in the figures reported.

army minister and the two chiefs of staff, however, held out to the end for resistance and non-surrender. Various attempts were made for a negotiated peace, but these were all unsuccessful. The government still felt its position strong enough to reject the Potsdam Declaration of July 26 with its demands for immediate and unconditional surrender, but the aftermath of this rejection was the dropping of the two atomic bombs on August 6 and 9.[2] The emperor then summoned the Supreme Council and by breaking a tie vote forced the decision to surrender. In spite of last minute violent attempts by Army officers and men to prevent the broadcast of the recorded message of the emperor, the announcement of the intent to surrender was heard by the nation on August 14, 1945. The adventure of military expansion had ended.

The church as an institution had cooperated with wartime government policy and program essentially without qualification, but the testimony of those who lived through those years is that perhaps most Christians as individuals, while they suffered the same experiences as their fellow citizens, managed somehow to maintain distinctive perspectives concerning the war. They had not lost their Christian consciousness, and in spite of the frightful dislocations of especially the last months they strove to live and pray as Christians even when unable to participate in the public worship of the church. However imperfect, the relatively rapid restoration of church life after the war seems to corroborate this.[3]

The condition of the nation, however, following the surrender was extremely difficult, even perilous. Almost all factories had been destroyed, and while the ability of the farms to produce food, apart from lack of fertilizer, was little damaged, the structure of wartime forced deliveries and rationing had broken down, and the nation in time had to feed perhaps an additional eight million repatriated soldiers and civilians. For a time an exchange economy existed as city dwellers went out into the

---

[2] Cf. Joseph C. Grew, *Turbulent Era,* vol. 2, p. 1426.

[3] *Kyōdanshi,* p. 174. Cf. *Kindai Nihon to Kirisuto Kyō,* Taishō-Shōwa Hen, *op. cit.,* pp. 326-356. It is reported that about two hundred Christian pastors were imprisoned for the faith during the war. Kuwada Hidenobu, *Zen to Kirisuto Kyō,* Tokyo: Chōbunsha, 1967, pp. 106-107.

countryside to give of their most precious belongings in return for food. Many had died in the bombing raids, many had been burned or were disabled without adequate medicine or care. Literally millions had been made homeless, and everywhere in the burned-out cities shacks began to appear built from the tin or corrugated iron roofing left over from the fires. In the desperate struggle for survival amid unaccustomed freedoms many persons reverted to lower levels of social living to the extent that the immediate postwar years were called the period of irresponsibility. The fundamental spiritual foundations of perhaps millions had been shattered by the defeat of the supposedly invincible "land of the gods."

The Board of Trustees of the Kyōdan first met as this situation was beginning clearly to emerge, on August 28, 1945. On this occasion the *tōrisha* warned and advised the members: the task of the church was to contribute to the rebuilding of Japan no matter what the obstacles. After long years of various forms of repression the church was now in a position of freedom and of relative importance in the land. But it must not presume lightly that "our time has come." The church must maintain its integrity in the new relationships which would emerge, and, Tomita emphasized, it must strive to insure that missions or ecclesial structures of missionaries not be created separately from the Kyōdan.

Japanese Christians are now able to evaluate the events of this period with perspectives that the leaders then could apparently not summon. They acknowledge with deep regret as well as candor that the leadership of the Kyōdan by no means gave evidence of sufficient reflection on past events, nor did it sufficiently repent for the church's uncritical complicity with the government or make adequate efforts toward a truly new start in keeping with the new situation of the nation. The statement issued by the Board of Trustees on August 28 indicated repentance more for having failed the nation than God. It affirmed the principle of the autonomy and independence of the Kyōdan and of the evangelism of Japan by Japanese, but its concept of evangelism was still heavily weighted in the direction of religious service to the empire.[4] This relative inflex-

---

[4] *Kyōdanshi*, pp. 177-179.

ibility made even more difficult the course of church life in the following years.

The Religious Bodies Law, in consequence of which the entire wartime structure of the Kyōdan had been erected, was repealed on October 4, 1945, without any immediate enactment to replace it. Shortly after this, on October 23, a deputation of four men arrived in Japan representing the Foreign Missions Conference of North America and the National Council of Churches in the U.S.A.[5] Distinguished churchmen, they came to reestablish relationships with the Christians of Japan and to enter into discussions "regarding the common tasks of the ecumenical Church." The leaders of the Kyōdan had apparently not known of their coming but at once arranged to meet them on October 25. The four had all participated in the Riverside meeting before the outbreak of war and symbolized to the Japanese that the spiritual ties between the Christians of the warring nations had not been severed.

A lengthy conference with Kyōdan leaders was held on November 6-7, and the needs and requests of the church were discussed in detail. One request was for missionaries of ability and special skills, but because of the unsettled condition of the church their numbers should be limited and their work should be primarily in the area of church reconstruction and in education. Above all, the immediate need of the Christians and, indeed, of all Japanese in the cities was to prevent starvation, and they asked the churches of North America to help. The delegation later toured the major cities of Japan and saw at first hand the enormous extent of the devastation and human need. They also held discussions and conferences with pastors in these places and were able, after their return, to present a detailed account of the situation. From this event developed the magnificent program of postwar Christian relief and reconstruction in Japan which was largely made possible by the generosity of the churches of North America. Numberless non-Christians as well as Christians benefited from this program, and it may be

---

[5] The four men were Bishop James C. Baker, Douglas Horton, Luman J. Shafer, and Walter Van Kirk.

considered as one of the major activities of the Christian church in the twentieth century.

The primary intent of the Allied military occupation authorities under the leadership of General Douglas MacArthur was to disarm and then to democratize Japan so it might become a peaceful, cooperative member of the world of civilized nations. As an important part of this program the Religious Bodies Law was abolished, and in its place came the Occupational Directive of December 28, 1945, which became a part of the law of the land under the name of the Religious Juridical Persons Law (Shūkyō Hōjin Rei).[6] The enactment of this law brought a new era to Christianity in Japan and to the Kyōdan in particular. The relationship of the government to religious organizations changed so that the government no longer had the power of authorization but simply presumed their acceptability and registered each organization according to simple rules of procedure. The freedom of religion implied in this law came to be given ultimate legal validity by the twentieth article of the new constitution, which was passed by the Diet in November, 1945, but came into effect in May, 1947. A further step of very great importance was the proclamation by the emperor on January 1, 1946, denying any quasi-divinity in himself or special superiority in the Japanese people. He stated that the ties binding him and the nation were those of mutual trust and affection. By this statement the traditional spiritual basis of Japanese government and society, the doctrine of the divinity of the emperor, which had been developed with increasing explicitness for over half a century, was at one stroke demolished. For many Japanese the act was psychically more shattering than military defeat and surrender, and it left literally millions to reconstruct their spiritual foundations and standards of value, a task for which most Japanese were hardly prepared by previous experience.

This was the context which from 1945 to 1951 led to what was called the "Christian Boom." In the physical devastation and spiritual confusion of those years, large numbers of people who had lost their spiritual moorings visited the churches, not

[6] Cf. William P. Woodard, The Religious Juridicial Persons Law, 1960. For a succinct account of the constitutional changes effected at this time see Edwin O. Reischauer, Japan, Past and Present, 1962, pp. 229-235.

only for services of worship but often at any time of night or day. The church schools of congregations across the land were filled to overflowing, and many of those who came were earnest seekers after faith. The Kyōdan took advantage of this open door by formulating and executing its first evangelistic plan after the war, the Christian Movement to Build a New Japan.

In general, however, the church was not prepared adequately to use the opportunities presented by this heretofore inexperienced influx of inquirers. Pastors and laymen alike were as physically and often perhaps as psychically exhausted as their non-Christian neighbors. Zealous efforts were made locally to give the leadership and guidance sought, but the Kyōdan itself was to pass through a series of severe trials before it could emerge with new maturity and power as a Christian church.

In light of the abolition of the Religious Bodies Law, the Board of Trustees of the Kyōdan had already created at its meeting on December 5-6, 1945, a committee to formulate proposals to revise the constitution and bylaws of the church, which had been created to conform with the wartime needs of the government. The committee was instructed to act on the basis of the principle of the catholicity of the Kyōdan and to make simple and democratic recommendations. The committee set to work at once and was able to present its draft for approval to the Board in early March, 1946; the Board promptly approved the document for presentation to the next General Assembly.

In the meantime, however, a mood of resentment toward the leadership and organizational structure of the Kyōdan was growing, especially among the younger pastors and laymen. Essentially three major foci of thought existed in the church at this time. One group frankly advocated dissolution of the Kyōdan as an unnatural union forced by government pressure. Another preferred a return to the bloc system characteristic of the first year of the Kyōdan's life. A third, probably the majority, while acknowledging the impertinent role of government, saw also the hand of God at work in the process leading the church to its proper state of unity. This group, however, was also determined to press for reform of the Kyōdan in keeping with the demands of the new situation. An important institutional expression of this mood was the formation on January 21, 1946, of the informal but influential Evangelical Fellowship *(Fukuin Dōshikai)*. In this context of events the (first postwar) Third General Assembly of the Kyōdan was held on June 7-8, 1946.

The assembly promptly elected Kozaki Michio as moderator, abolished the position of *tōrisha* and established the moderator of the General Assembly as the highest responsible official in the church. Action on the new constitution and bylaws was postponed until the next General Assembly, but the democratic intent of the church had been fully manifested. The assembly also approved the proposal to initiate the Christian Movement to Build a New Japan. Another significant act of this assembly was to give public recognition by personal introduction to those Christians who had suffered imprisonment and other indignities under the wartime government.

On the day following the assembly a great laymen's conference was held on the campus of Aoyama Gakuin in Tokyo. This conference strongly affirmed its support of the proposed evangelistic movement and emphasized the Christian profession of the gospel of peace. At this conference we note the first clear expression of repentance before God and man of the church's betrayal and neglect of its Christian mission during the war.[7] From this time crowds began to fill the church services and pack the special public meetings and lectures to an extent not experienced since the 1880's. E. Stanley Jones described the opportunity for witness as unique in five hundred years of Christian history.

From early 1947 the widespread dissatisfaction with the manner in which the Kyōdan had been formed and then administered under government dictation was expressed in secessions from the organization which then comprised essentially the

[7] *Kyōdanshi,* p. 196. A letter dated June 9, 1946, over the signatures of the moderator and of the general secretary of the Kyōdan, Hinohara Zensuke, was sent to Christians in North America as an expression of the mind of the General Assembly. In addition to warm terms of thanks and aspirations for the future the letter contains the following sentence: "Feeling a grave responsibility concerning the last great war we wish to express our profound regret and heartfelt repentance."

whole of Protestantism in Japan.[8] The first group to secede, in
April, 1947, was a segment of the old *Nikki* which left to form
the Reformed Church in Japan *(Nihon Kirisuto Kaikakuha
Kyōkai)*. This was followed by the withdrawal in April of Baptist churches related to the Southern Baptist Convention in the
United States and then of several Holiness groups, including the
Salvation Army, in September. The Anglican Church withdrew
in October, followed by the Lutheran Church. Altogether about
two hundred congregations withdrew in the years from 1946 to
1950. However justifiable the reasons were from one point of
view, the loss of these groups was a severe blow to the Kyōdan
as an organization and to those who continued to hold high the
ideal of catholicity in a united church.

The Kyōdan was further disturbed by the emergence within
the larger majority of differences regarding the formulation of a
creed, which as yet it did not possess. Some, especially those of
the Presbyterian and Reformed tradition, held that a church is
not truly a church without a creed. Others, of Congregational
or Baptist background, preferred freedom in this area and no
binding statement of faith. A third group, of Methodist or kin-
dred orientation, had no objection to a creed but did not feel
pressing need to take immediate action. These events were
evolving from 1946 when the food and the housing situation
worsened in the country, in part because of the repatriation of
large numbers of soldiers and civilians. These were exceedingly
difficult times for all Japanese, and the problems of the church
as it attempted to reconstitute itself and at the same time make
proper use of the evangelistic opportunities must be understood
in this context.

One of the first concerns of the deputation of four American
churchmen after their return to their homeland was to send
copies of the Scriptures to Japan, where the entire stock of the
Japan Bible Society had been depleted and many personal Bi-

---

[8] Cf. Richard Terrill Baker, *Darkness of the Sun,* pp. 75-100. Baker, an
American Christian journalist, records the impressions of men during the
first year or two after the end of the war. An excellent book in Japanese
that covers the war period, both frankly and fairly, is Andō Hajime, *Fukaki
Fuchi Yori,* 1959. Cf. also the collection of articles published by Dōshisha
University, *Senjika Teikō no Kenkyū,* 1962.

bles had been burned. The American Bible Society responded to this appeal by printing and shipping two and a half million copies of the New Testament by the end of 1947. Ninety thousand copies of the Japanese Union Hymnal were sent out in the same way.[9]

The next important step in renewing cooperation with related churches in North America was the arrival of a commission of six experienced missionaries to represent their own boards and in a larger sense the whole of North American Protestantism. Of the previous deputation of four only one, Luman J. Shafer, had had experience as a missionary in Japan. Every one of the six had served long in the land and was in a position at once to communicate in depth and to cooperate with Japanese Christians in initiating concrete programs of work. The policy of the occupation authorities was to show no religious favoritism, and negotiations lengthened in order to clear the way for these persons to come without either receiving logistic support from the military or adding a burden to the impoverished Japanese economy.

G. Ernest Bott of the United Church of Canada and Paul S. Mayer of the Evangelical Association arrived first. Bott, with long experience in Christian social work, was responsible for organizing a program of relief using materials from overseas churches. Mayer served as liaison person with SCAP (Supreme Commander of the Allied Powers) to arrange for the return of missionaries; he was also to communicate with the churches. By June, 1946, the remaining four arrived, and a division of responsibility was effected. Alice Cary of the American Board (Congregationalist) was to renew contacts with Japanese Christian women and their work; Henry G. Bovenkerk of the Presbyterian U.S.A. board was to specialize in relations with the Kyōdan and evangelistic work. John B. Cobb, Methodist, was to do the same in central and western Japan. Karl D. Kriete of the Reformed Church, U.S., received the responsibility of liaison with Christian schools. These six constituted the initial structure through which all cooperation between the

---

[9] Iglehart, *A Century of Protestant Christianity in Japan,* p. 281.

Protestant churches of North America and Japan was channeled. It proved to be most effective.

Also in June, technically separate from the Commission of Six, Esther Rhoades, a Quaker, and a representative of the Catholic Welfare Conference, arrived in Japan to join Bott in coordinating the work of relief based on the goods which were beginning to pour in from the churches of North America in ever increasing quantities. The largest single organization responsible for sending these goods was Church World Service; smaller agencies were those of the Church of the Brethren and the Mennonites. Notable large-scale work was also done by the Catholic Welfare Conference, Lutheran World Service, and the American Friends Service Committee. These agencies were all coordinated in the organization known as Licensed Agencies for Relief in Asia (LARA). Distribution of commodities, both food and clothing, was effected in cooperation with SCAP and the Welfare Ministry of the Japanese government. In the desperate need of the people as a whole, goods were given quite without discrimination to Christian and non-Christian alike. Note should also be taken of the large amounts of food which were bought abroad by SCAP and distributed during the worst years of 1946 and 1947 so that literally hundreds of thousands were saved from starvation.[10] About a million dollars worth of CARE packages were also sent each year from North America to individual Japanese.

In this way the Christian churches of the West contributed greatly not only to the recovery of the churches in Japan but also to the rehabilitation of the entire nation. In consequence of the early work and reports of the Commission of Six, representatives of eight Protestant churches met in New York on January 9, 1947, to create a structure of cooperation to meet the needs of the situation in Japan.[11] In the following August representatives of this association came to Japan and held extensive discussions with 150 leaders of the Kyōdan and of

---

[10] Ibid., pp. 279-284. Cf. Borton, Japan's Modern Century, p. 434.

[11] The churches were the Congregational Christian Churches, the Disciples of Christ, the Evangelical and Reformed Church, the Evangelical United Brethren Church, the Methodist Church, the Presbyterian Church in the U.S.A., the Reformed Church in America, and the United Church of Canada.

Christian schools and social agencies. As a result the Interboard Committee for Christian Work in Japan (IBC) was formed to represent and coordinate the activities of the ten boards of the eight churches, and a Field Committee was established primarily to handle the logistical needs of related missionaries. The secretary of the Field Committee became also a primary, even if informal, channel of communication between the IBC and all related work in Japan. Darley Downs served very ably in this position for over fifteen years from its inception. The Kyōdan in turn set up a Council of Cooperation (*Naigai Kyōryokukai*, COC) to deal with the IBC and to supervise all cooperation with overseas churches and missionaries. It was composed at first of eight representatives of the Kyōdan, eight from the Japan Christian Education Association, and eight from the IBC, who at that time also comprised the whole of the Field Committee. Later the Japan Christian Social Work Association also became a part of the COC.

This plan went into effect in 1948, and its structure has served to the present time without essential change to effect cooperation between the Kyōdan and the churches of North America. Through this means was begun the reconstruction of about three hundred destroyed or severely damaged churches.[12] The hope of the Kyōdan was that the Japanese churches would furnish one-half of the cost of rebuilding and the overseas churches one-half, but it was not possible for them to realize that amount. In all, the churches of North America are reported to have contributed $3,404,195 for church building reconstruction in the Kyōdan and the Japanese churches $1,143,051.[13] It is significant that the Japanese members of the COC on August 22, 1947 in expressing their deepest thanks for the beginning of this great work also voiced their conviction that prayer and concrete service in behalf of the churches of East Asia devastated by Japanese military forces were the proper responsibility of the Christian churches of Japan.[14]

---

[12] Not all churches were considered as worthy of being rebuilt. In some cases congregations were asked to unite, and one building was constructed for both. —

[13] *Kyōdanshi,* p. 202.

[14] *Ibid.,* p. 205.

2

The groups which had withdrawn from the Kyōdan reconstituted themselves as separate churches and in general reestablished direct relations with the Western churches with which
they had formerly been associated. The latter in turn had in
most cases already reconstituted mission organizations in Japan,
even if in embryonic stage at first. Thus Edwin Dozier of the
Southern Baptist Convention arrived as early as October, 1946,
and began arrangements for the arrival of a group that was to
become one hundred missionaries, a far larger number than in
the prewar period. In this and perhaps most other cases the
presence of the nucleus of a mission organization in Japan preceded the withdrawal of the various groups from the Kyōdan.
The representatives of the Anglican, Baptist, Holiness, Lutheran
and other churches overseas entered into the work of relief,
church reconstruction and evangelism in ways very similar to
those of the Kyōdan.

Some of the smaller prewar missions were also being reconstituted. One of these was the Swedish Missionary Alliance
Church, whose two or three families returned and resumed
work. In America, however, a new organization was created as
the missionary organ of this and other churches of similar theological orientation. This was The Evangelical Alliance Mission
(TEAM). A large number of missionaries came in through this
organization, and a relatively new climate emerged among foreign missionary personnel in Japan. Prior to the war all Protestant missionaries in Japan regardless of theological persuasion
had felt themselves able to participate in good conscience in the
Fellowship of Christian Missionaries. After the war the theological and, if I may so add, the sociological climate changed so
that this kind of inclusive fellowship was no longer possible.

Before the war the proportion of missionaries belonging to
what may be termed churches of fundamentalist theological
position was relatively small. After the war this proportion was
reversed. TEAM itself later comprised some two hundred missionaries, and when in 1948 SCAP modified its regulations to
admit agents of churches or societies that had not previously
worked in Japan, large numbers of theologically conservative

missionaries, mostly American, swelled the stream begun by TEAM.

After the secession from the Kyōdan of groups belonging to historic traditions in Christendom, such as the Anglicans, some Baptists and the Lutherans, it was felt necessary to reconstitute the National Christian Council in May, 1948. But at this time only four churches were included in its constituency: the Kyōdan, the Anglican Church, the Evangelical Lutheran Church, and the Baptist Convention.[15] In 1954 the total number of missionaries cooperating with the NCC was 563. They constituted less than 28 percent of the total of 2,017 Protestant foreign missionaries in Japan in that year, of whom 1,637, or approximately 81 percent, were American.[16] This meant that the large majority of foreign missionaries in Japan were now of theologically conservative, non-ecumenical orientation, mostly representatives of independent missionary societies. With few exceptions they were young, without previous experience in Japan or knowledge of the language. They began first to learn the language, and when they started evangelistic work upon leaving the language school, they usually labored without reference to older Christian activity. They accordingly had relatively little impact upon the Japanese churches or Christians. But their effect upon the missionary community was to divide it and create a climate of hostility among missionaries that had never been known in Japan previously.

These young, non-ecumenical, very largely American missionaries created a new missionary fellowship alongside the fifty-year-old Fellowship of Christian Missionaries. Under the name of the Evangelical Missions Association of Japan (EMAJ), it established a creedal basis of membership and initiated its own program of summer conferences and certain other missionary projects, including a monthly magazine *Japan Harvest*.[17] If I may be permitted my own evaluation as an American mis-

---

[15] Other Christian bodies than churches also became members of the NCC, such as the YMCA and the Japan Christian Education Association.

[16] Yanagita Tomonobu, *A Short History of Christianity in Japan*, pp. 82-83.

[17] There is also another much smaller non-ecumenical missionary fellowship called the Japan Bible Christian Council, and there are independent missionaries not affiliated with any group. Yanagita, *op. cit.*, p. 83.

sionary who lived in Japan during those years, I would suggest that the particular climate generated by these young missionaries reflected in part the emergence in the United States in the years after World War II of a generally conservative stance in political and economic matters as well as in theology. As seen in the Japan missionaries representative thereof, this stance appeared to become more belligerent as the Cold War deepened; it was hardly helped by the frustrations experienced as direct evangelistic work had to be delayed by the necessity of learning one of the most difficult languages in the world.

There were, however, important qualifications to this rather negative portrayal. Older American missionaries of this theological tradition, especially those with prewar experience, and European missionaries, young or old, tended to be more ecumenically oriented. Although they felt constrained to unite with the EMAJ, they tried to maintain at least warm personal relationships with missionaries of the older churches, as I can testify from personal experience. The Japanese pastors and laymen of the churches founded in this tradition also tended to have a mellowness different from the harsher types among the missionaries. The latter themselves as they moved out from language school into the realities of direct work in many cases came to lose much of the cocksureness that many Americans of the early postwar generation found easy to assume. In all there is great hope for improvement in the climate of understanding and even for certain kinds of cooperation in the future.

It should be noted that while in the postwar period the number of non-ecumenical missionaries greatly exceeds those of ecumenical orientation, the number of Japanese Christians in the two groups reverses the proportion. Statistics indicative of the proportion vary somewhat according to the inclusion or non-inclusion of certain groups in the respective categories, but after twenty years of postwar work, the number of non-ecumenical Japanese Protestant Christians probably does not exceed 30 percent of the whole of Protestantism. The church which has shown the highest rate of growth in the postwar period is the Pentecostal body called the Church of Jesus' Spirit (*Iesu no Mi Tama Kyōkai*), which developed from a few hundred members in 1941 to over thirty thousand by 1960. Since 1953, when other Christian groups began to show smaller rates of increase, the Church of Jesus' Spirit has grown more rapidly than before. It records an increase of from thirty-six hundred to five thousand each year. This church, however, is an entirely indigenous body which receives no aid in finances or personnel from abroad. Another indigenous movement of great vitality is that led by the able and spiritually gifted Tejima Ikuo. This group regards itself as outside the category of the regular churches but considers the church (*Ecclesia*) to be the giant of human history, the giant which at times falls asleep and needs to be awakened by groups such as itself. The name which Tejima and his followers give themselves is Original Gospel Movement (*Genshi Fukuin Undō*), and in their activity a prominent role is assigned to faith healing, prophesying, speaking in tongues, psychic perception and even walking on fire, the last a practice found in Shintō from ancient times.[18]

3

Japanese historians regard the five-year period from the end of the war in August, 1945, to the signing of the San Francisco Peace Treaty on September 8, 1951, by Japan and forty-eight Allied nations as an era of confusion, although the first three years of the period were by far the most difficult. Under the Allied military occupation government was orderly and violence almost non-existent, but the economic and general physical hardship was frightful, and there was enormous spiritual and mental confusion. When the treaty went into effect on April 28, 1952, the occupation officially ended; and while American forces remained in considerable numbers in accordance with a security pact signed on September 8, 1951, Japan became again a sovereign nation. Almost at once turbulence emerged in Japanese politics, but the steady development was begun of the political, economic and cultural life of the people. The procurement orders which were placed in Japan during the Korean

---

[18] Cf. Yanagita, *op. cit.*, p. 83; Iglehart, *op. cit.*, pp. 339-342. A large part of the membership of the Church of Jesus' Spirit is in Okinawa. For the Original Gospel Movement see Tejima Ikuo, "Genshi Fukuin Undō no Tokushitsu," *Inochi no Hikari*, IV/143 (July, 1962), p. 15.

War, which broke out on June 25, 1950, gave enormous impetus
to Japanese industry, and a new mood of confidence was apparent. The churches also shared in this mood and began to
achieve increasing success in the ordering of their life.

During the years of the Allied military occupation the Japanese churches did not have the reserve energy to serve as well
as to witness to the larger society of the nation as later reflection
would wish. But the period was well used to regain spiritual
power. Prayer meetings were frequently held and widely attended, and from the early fifties Christians began with new
earnestness to care for the orphans, the vagrants, the sick and
others who did not share comparably in the gradually
emerging prosperity of the nation as a whole. Even though
implementation lagged behind aspiration, the sense of obligation toward all classes and areas of the land emerged once
again into Christian consciousness.[19]

At the Sixth General Assembly of the Kyōdan in 1950 the
final draft of the new constitution, prepared after two years of
labor by the Committee on Structure Revision, was presented
and passed with only slight modification. By this action the
totalitarian structure of the wartime period was replaced by a
democratic constitution operating on the principle of rule by
the General Assembly and administration by committees. The
highest elected official of the Kyōdan according to the new
constitution was the moderator of the General Assembly. He
was also moderator of the Board of Trustees and had certain
executive powers, but his authority was entirely different from
the wartime *tōrisha*. The churches which had withdrawn from
the Kyōdan had in the meantime also reconstituted themselves in more democratic forms of government. The Kyōdan,
however, had to contend with the tension caused by the presence within it of substantial groups each favoring either Congregational, Episcopal or Presbyterian polities. A viable solution was eventually reached through a modified Presbyterian
structure which refrained in practice from interfering with the
freedom of local congregations as much as possible and gradu-

---

[19] *Kyōdanshi*, pp. 208-213. An unprecedentedly strong interest in music
appeared in the church in the postwar years.

ally assigned limited executive powers to certain officials, as by the appointment in 1960 by the Eleventh General Assembly of a General Secretary of Evangelism to administer the decisions of the Evangelism Committee.

The Kyōdan's most serious problem in the early 1950's was the strong pressure within its ranks to formulate a creed. As we have noted, essentially three positions on this matter existed in the church. Those of Congregational and Baptist tradition favored local freedom to profess or not profess a creed corporately. Those of Presbyterian-Reformed background regarded a creed as an essential element of an authentic church, while those of Methodist tradition had no objection to a creed but in general did not emphasize the issue. The Kyōdan in 1941 had created a simple, very short confession followed by the Apostles' Creed. This statement was slightly expanded in 1946 and "other creeds or confessions" were cited as standards of faith but not named. In 1954, however, the Eighth General Assembly voted overwhelmingly to approve the draft of the new Confession of Faith presented by the preparatory committee. This confession was a relatively brief but clear evangelical statement of faith followed by the Apostles' Creed. According to the explanation of the committee chairman, certain freedom of interpretation was to be allowed, but the term "confession" was preferred to that of "creed" to emphasize that the religious act involved in confession was primarily praise of God's grace. The confessional statement was not to be understood as a juridical formula.[20]

In the eyes of many in the church the Kyōdan first became authentically a Christian church by the adoption of this confession of faith. But apart from a consideration of the theological merit of this concept of the church, the event clearly marked the beginning of a new era in the self-consciousness and assurance of this particular fellowship of the people of God. In 1950 it had had to face in some ways the most difficult year of its existence after the war. Under the leadership of Onomura Rinzō, heroic and eloquent pastor of the Kita Ichijō Church in Sapporo, a considerable number of pastors and laymen of the

---

[20] *Kyōdanshi*, pp. 230-238.

Nikki tradition campaigned with fervor for a return to the bloc system. When the conclusion was reached in the Kyōdan not to formalize or give ecclesiastical status to the old blocs, about fifty churches withdrew from the church to form the *Shin Nihon Kirisuto Kyōkai (Shin Nikki)*. In some ways this was the most painful, even if the last, of the group secessions from the Kyō-dan, especially for the majority of the Presbyterian-Reformed tradition, who remained within the church. But out of the suf-fering of all a true if not perfect union had been achieved.[21]

During the postwar years the churches were aided in their programs of evangelism by notable foreign evangelists as well as the indefatigable Kagawa Toyohiko. E. Stanley Jones came first in 1949 and every two years thereafter by invitation of the National Christian Council. With his very able interpreter, Yasumura Saburō, he traveled the length and breadth of the land giving incisive, perceptive messages to regularly crowded meetings. Lawrence Lacour with his wife and four other young ladies created a musical troupe and toured the country in 1950, making a singular appeal, especially to youth, with marimba and harp and low-keyed but thoughtful messages. In coopera-tion with the energetic Japanese Christian leader, Mutō Tomio, Lacour returned in 1954 with a number of American pastors, some accompanied by their wives, who gave a full sum-mer to intensive evangelistic work, usually each in one location. This program was begun among several small towns in Fuku-shima Prefecture with young Japanese theological students serving as the interpreters. The hope of this plan was by inten-sive work to complement and in part to rectify the work of the traveling evangelists, who could generally speak to large crowds and obtain numerous signers of decision cards but seemed un-able to lead more than a very small number to active church life. The year 1951 was the high-water mark of the "Christian boom," and from this time Christians had to return to more "laborious" methods of witness. The Lacour-Mutō program was continued in succeeding years and by 1967 had succeeded in establishing thirty-three congregations of which over a third had become financially self-supporting. Another program of

---

[21] *Ibid.*, pp. 241-251.

public evangelism conducted over many years without much fanfare but with great spiritual effect was that of William Axling.[22]

Help from abroad of a somewhat different kind was given by the coming of a number of distinguished Christian scholars. John C. Bennett of Union Theological Seminary in New York came in the summer of 1950 to hold a series of seminars and lectures. He combined sensitivity to social problems with depth of theological perception in a way that led many Japanese pastors to new understanding of the social responsibility of the church.[23] Another scholar who contributed in this area was Edward Heimann of the New School of Social Research of New York City, who came in 1958. From this understanding emerged new concerns and activity for industrial evangelism. Emil Brunner came from Switzerland first in 1949 and then again to stay for three years from 1953-1955. In the latter period his primary responsibility was at the new International Christian University and at Tokyo Union Theological Seminary, but he lectured widely across the country and, perhaps most notably, contributed greatly to a new personal rapprochement between leaders in the Non-Church movement and in the historic churches. Other significant visits of some duration were made by John Mackay in 1950, Paul Tillich in 1960, and Hendrik Kraemer in 1961.

We may say, however, that with regard to cooperative aid in evangelism and church extension, in education and social service, the burden was borne by the far more numerous resident missionaries. Many of them were very able as well as dedicated workers. Making good use of the greatly improved linguistic techniques developed during the war and employed in the language schools in Japan afterward, many achieved high levels of skill in the Japanese language and had particularly fine and intimate relationships with Japanese, Christians and non-Christians alike. Some missionaries served in remote rural areas as well as in the urban concentrations of population. From 1952 to 1959 seventy-six new churches were started by the

---

[22] Cf. Axling, *Japan at the Midcentury,* pp. 266-276.
[23] Cf. Richard H. Drummond, "Catharsis in the Japanese Church," *The Christian Century,* LXXIX/21 (May 23, 1962), 651-654.

Kyōdan, in many cases as a result of the participation of a missionary in the work. In some ways institutional and personal adjustment was easier for missionaries related to Christian schools or social institutions than for those serving more directly in the structure of the churches.[24] Partly for financial reasons the churches did not achieve institutional self-confidence as early and to the same degree as the schools and social centers, and the working out of personal relationships with missionaries was always a delicate matter.[25] But in fact there were some remarkable instances of the finest kind of personal relationships as well as effective cooperation. The Buddhist scholar Watanabe Shōkō has compared the Japanese experience of Buddhist missionaries from China with that of Christian missionaries and noted that in spite of greater differences in language and culture Christian missionaries both in the *Kirishitan* period and after 1859 have enjoyed more intimate personal relationships with Japanese fellow-believers than has generally been the case among Buddhists.[26]

In November, 1959, under the auspices of the NCC the Protestant churches of Japan celebrated the one-hundredth anniversary of the beginning of Protestant Christian witness in the land. The celebration had been long prepared for, among other things by a Kyōdan five-year evangelistic campaign beginning in 1955, the third major evangelistic program after the end of the war. By 1959, however, Japan had moved beyond the category of "postwar." The Kyōdan, in particular, at this time was not primarily interested in reminiscences of the past, although it now had the spiritual reserves to admit its past mistakes with boldness as well as with shame. It was more concerned to gather its strength for unity, witness, and service. The position of Japanese Christianity in the world was symbolized

---

[24] An important service in the postwar years was rendered by single missionaries who came out for a period of three years (J-3's) and labored mostly in connection with Christian schools.

[25] Cf. Takasaki Takeshi, "The Function of Missionaries," *The Christian Century*, LXXXIII/1 (January 5, 1966), 19-22; Richard H. Drummond, "A Missionary 'Exodus' from Japan?" *The Christian Century*, LXXXII/21 (May 26, 1965), 672-674; *Gendai Nihon to Kirisuto Kyō*, 1961, pp. 142-164.

[26] Watanabe Shōkō, *Nihon no Bukkyō*, pp. 20-21.

by the presence at the ceremonies of W. A. Visser 't Hooft, the General Secretary of the World Council of Churches. Its position in Japan was symbolized by its fresh concern to relate itself to Japanese culture and by the presence and message of the prime minister, Kishi Nobusuke, at the Fourteenth World Convention on Christian Education held in Tokyo in the previous summer of 1958. Kishi spoke to the delegates and numerous Japanese guests of how Japanese Christians had made "signal contributions to the social progress and spiritual uplift of the nation through their exemplary conduct, their piety and their spirit of service and helpfulness."[27]

Japanese Protestants were concerned that attendance at church schools had been steadily declining for several years; in 1957, as compared to 1956, attendance in the nation as a whole had dropped to the extent of 2,000 pupils. But the church in its total program was making steady if moderate progress. At a Kyōdan conference held in September, 1959, it was reported that with regard to the five categories of number of members, attendance at Sunday worship, church school attendance, total budget, and monthly promised offering, 869 churches out of a total of 1572 had doubled the achievement in at least one of these categories over the previous five-year period.[28] If the increase in active church membership was small, the influence upon the nation was relatively great. One of the primary characteristics of Japanese Protestantism had been its power to develop persons of outstanding spiritual power and social influence. In the calmer perspectives of this time these facts were increasingly recognized and appreciated by the nation as a whole. Christians continued to be sensitive to their minority status and lamented their limitations in indigenization, but their cultural self-confidence grew apace and expressed itself in new levels of maturity in almost every aspect of church life.

This confidence and maturity were seen not only in their expressions within Japan and in developing ecumenical relationships with churches of the world beyond North America.

[27] Iglehart, *op. cit.*, p. 331.
[28] *Kyōdanshi*, p. 280. For a survey of the period see *Gendai Nihon to Kirisuto Kyō*, pp. 3-31.

They became manifest in a new sense of responsibility for overseas mission, especially in cooperation with other churches of Asia. In the prewar years almost without exception the churches established in Korea, Taiwan and Manchuria had been for Japanese citizens, who made almost no effort to bring the local peoples into their churches.[29] The influence of participation in Asian and world church conferences enabled Japanese Christians to see their own responsibility in the mission of the church outside Japan. In consequence they began to send missionaries to Brazil, Bolivia, India, Thailand, Taiwan, Indonesia and Nepal. Some of these men and women are partially or totally supported locally. The measure of Japanese church support is increasing. The largest Japanese overseas missionary enterprise is that conducted by the Japan Christian Medical Association, which was founded in 1949 and is supported entirely by Japanese Christian doctors and nurses.

4

Protestant Christians in Japan now feel a sense of having passed through the worst and having solved in some measure the most critical internal problems of the church. In the context of the relatively deep theological understanding of the Japanese church, there is renewed perception of the proclamation of the gospel as the primary responsibility of the church. Symbolic of the scholarly concern in this area was the establishment by the Kyōdan in 1960 of the Research Institute for the Mission of the Church. Mission, however, is not seen as limited to verbal proclamation. The seed sown in the early 1950's by John C. Bennett and others has borne fruit in wide concern to relate the gospel to the changing situation and needs of Japanese society and the world. The daily life of people at home, at work, and in their recreation is seen to be the primary place of Christian witness. The churches recognize as perhaps never before their responsibility before God for the whole life of the nation and the state. They are concerned for family life and the ethics of everyday living by Christians and

---

[29] A notable exception was the work of Fukui Jirō in Jehol Province in China.

all men. The Kyōdan turned to the renewal of its life *(taishi-tsu kaizen)* not only for its own sake but that it might better serve and witness to the nation.

This larger perspective coexists with the fact that many individual congregations of the Kyōdan, for example, still bear rather distinctly the tone and practice of their former denominational background. But the movement of life is in the direction of unity. In part because of their strength in unity, churches are able to act with more vigor as well as perception in their role as the "watchmen" of society and the "salt of the earth." This role has become significantly important in Christian understanding, especially among younger pastors and laymen, since 1959. Acting usually through small or informal groups, these Japanese Christians have expressed their views or undertaken other forms of action in behalf of world peace, nuclear disarmament, opposition to the Mutual Security Pact with the United States, preservation of the postwar national constitution, opposition to moves by conservative political forces to restore state support of Shintō and more recently strong opposition to American military action in Vietnam. Theologically, this activity is understood as Christian effort to participate in God's creative work in the transformation of the cosmos. Expressive of this understanding and spirit was the election in 1966 of scholarly pastor Suzuki Masahisa, formerly one of the "angry young men" of Japanese Protestantism, as moderator of the Fourteenth General Assembly of the Kyōdan.[30] In his first moderatorial address Suzuki set forth three goals for the Kyōdan: self-determination *(jiritsu),* consolidation *(sōgō),* and advance *(shinten).* These goals are indicative of the kind of responsible forward-moving church which Suzuki and a large part of the Kyōdan pastors and laymen envisaged for their future; the goals represent some of the best hopes for the Chris-

---

[30] *Kyōdanshi,* pp. 266, 273, 314-322, 331-332. Expressive of Suzuki's position is the "Confession on the Responsibility of the United Church of Christ in Japan During World War II" issued over his name on Easter Sunday, March 26, 1967. Both Suzuki and the previous moderator, Ōmura Isamu, were active in behalf of peace in Vietnam. See Suzuki's "Letter of February 21, 1968," *Kyōdan* (Tokyo: The United Church of Christ in Japan), no. 23 (March 20, 1968), pp. 1-3.

tian church in Asia. Suzuki was reelected moderator at the Fifteenth General Assembly of the Kyōdan held in October, 1968, in spite of considerable opposition to his leadership of the church, especially in the area of social responsibility. The bulk of the Kyōdan appeared to approve his twofold emphasis upon renewal of the church from within and confrontation with a rapidly changing contemporary society. At this latter General Assembly the delegates also voted to simplify the structure of the church and to unite with the United Church of Christ in Okinawa in the form of making the Okinawan body a District (Synod) of the Kyōdan.

A shift in emphasis has taken place in Japanese Protestantism away from mass meetings held, except in the case of Kagawa Toyohiko and one or two others, by evangelists from the West especially in the years from 1950 to 1960. In 1958 World Vision, Inc., under the leadership of its president, Bob Pierce, held a lavishly staged and relatively effective evangelistic crusade in Ōsaka. In 1961, however, a heated dispute arose within the Protestant churches as Japanese pastors were asked to cooperate with an even larger-scale Tokyo crusade under the same auspices. The objection was not based on nationalistic or anti-foreign prejudice, the critics averred, but in reality constituted a demand for Japanese Christians to plan responsibly.[31] The crusade was attended by many, but the discussion marked a turning point for the churches in Japan away from programs planned and sponsored by foreigners. One result was a renewed effort by Protestant churches to undertake responsible, long-term planning in evangelism on their own.

The Kyōdan formulated a Ten-Year Plan of Evangelism to extend from 1962 to 1972 with emphasis upon lay training and the continuing education of pastors. It included also a plan for cooperative parish programs (dendōken).[32] Three dioceses of

---

[31] Saeki Yōichiro, "The Christian Movement in Japan Today," *The Response of the Church in Changing Japan,* Charles H. Germany, ed., p. 82. Cf. *Kyōdanshi,* pp. 322-325.

[32] It may be helpful to cite at this point recent statistics of the strength of the Kyōdan as the largest Protestant body in Japan. As of March 31, 1968, the number of members was 201,311, of congregations 1,629, of pastors 1,997. The total number of baptized Christians of every tradition is reported as

the Anglican Church have five-year plans for lay training institutes, concentrating upon the training of the whole congregation. The personnel of the Lutheran churches were greatly
strengthened when Scandinavian missionaries came to Japan in
considerable numbers from China, and they have now turned
from emphasis upon the denomination as a whole to the local
congregation as the key element in their evangelistic strategy.
Along with the training of pastors for joint action, a new
approach is the call for pastors and people to serve and witness
to others in the context of their daily lives. In 1965 the membership of all Lutheran bodies showed a 37 percent increase
over the previous year.

The Japan Baptist Convention, related to the Southern Baptist Convention in the United States, initiated in 1960 its
Five-Year Advance Movement. By 1965 it recorded 101 churches
and preaching places, a 25 percent growth since 1960. The
emphasis in this program was to win people to faith in Jesus
Christ and membership in the church with relatively less concern for the relationship of faith to culture and the service of
the community. The Southern Baptist Mission, however,
conducts an excellent hospital and medical service in Kyōto.
The Japan Baptist Union, consisting of churches related to the
American Baptist Convention, also works according to five-year
plans. Its second was begun in 1965. During the first five-year
period seven new churches were formed, of which at least two
are now self-supporting. Several of the most substantial churches
of this tradition remained in the Kyōdan, and as distinguished
from the Japan Baptist Convention, this denomination is noted
for its outstanding indigenous leadership.

The churches of the Reformed Church in Japan and the
Shinnikki emphasize worship and doctrine under a ministry
trained to this end. In cooperation with these churches the
Southern Presbyterian Mission has been conducting the Yodo-
gawa Christian Hospital since March, 1956.[33] This mission,

965,647. There are Japanese, however, who regard the "sympathetic constituency" of Christianity to be as many as ten million.

[33] James A. Cogswell, *Until the Day Dawn*, p. 219. Comprehensive histories
of the Anglican, Lutheran and Baptist churches have been published in Japanese in recent years: Matsudaira Kitarō, *Nihon Seikōkai Hyakunenshi;*

however, and its board at home now fully participate in the Interboard Committee and cooperate with the Kyōdan as with these smaller denominations.

The Fundamentalist and Pentecostal churches are all zealously engaged in their several programs, generally with emphasis upon individual conversion and personal religious experience. A high quality of ethical and spiritual life is frequently seen in Japanese Christians of this allegiance.[34] A contemporary Japanese evangelist of this tradition, Honda Kōji, is widely respected for his cooperative spirit as well as effective work.

One of the new developments in Japanese Protestantism is industrial evangelism. An older American Presbyterian missionary, Henry Jones, was an important catalyst in leading the Kyōdan into this activity. Among the results of this work are the Kansai Labor Evangelism Fellowship, the Nishijin Labor Center in Kyōto, and the centers in Himeji and Hyōgo Prefecture for truck drivers. Anglican and Lutheran churchmen have also organized projects in industrial areas.

Another evangelistic approach of the churches is directed to the new planned cities which emerge as large communities often within a few months, such as Senri New Town in the suburbs of Ōsaka, with a population of 150,000, in which missionary J. Lawrence Driskill has played a creative role.[35] Another is the "new town" in the Tama hills west of Tokyo with about 300,000 people. The Kyōdan has pioneered in this work with programs designed to meet the special needs of families living in these massive projects (danchi).

5

A few concluding words need to be said about Christian activity in the intellectual and literary world.[36] The whole

Fukuyama Takeshi, *Nihon Fukuin Rūteru Kyōkaishi; Nihon Baputesuto Remmeishi (1889-1959)*.

[34] Saeki, *op. cit.*, pp. 80-93.

[35] Charles H. Germany, "Crucial Challenges and Strategic Ministries," *The Response of the Church in Changing Japan*, pp. 108-118.

[36] The emergence in the past decade or more of a considerable number of Japanese Christian artists, of whom the printmaker Watanabe Tadao is

Bible or portions thereof sell now nearly four million copies per year, second in total volume only to the United States. If this sale is at all indicative of reading habits, the Japanese are among the most avid readers of the Bible in all the world. There has been, also, a remarkable increase in the sale of Christian books, as much as 1500 percent in the first six months of 1966 after a new program of cooperation with secular retail bookstores was initiated. Increased use has been made of the facilities of radio and to a lesser extent of television. Newspaper evangelism has long standing in the Protestant tradition.[37] But the most singular characteristic of the Japanese church is its literary and theological production.

One of the major figures in Japanese Protestant theology between the First and Second World Wars was Takakura Tokutarō, whom we noted as the successor of Uemura Masahisa and the outstanding theological exponent of the Presbyterian-Reformed tradition until his death in 1934.[38] Indeed, we may say that he was the first systematic or scientific theologian to emerge among Japanese Protestant Christians. The many able Christian thinkers before him had almost entirely preferred to express their convictions in works of an apologetical or expository nature. Takakura read widely in liberal German theology of the nineteenth century from Schleiermacher on and was one of those mainly responsible for introducing into Japan the dialectical theology associated with Karl Barth and Emil Brunner. But Takakura's deepest affinities came to be with P. T. Forsyth, H. R. Mackintosh, and other Scottish theologians of the early twentieth century.[39] His position was in the central tradition of the Protestant Reformers, with emphasis upon the grace of God in Jesus Christ and the church as a community of faith living by grace. Ethics he saw as properly the expression of gratitude to God. Takakura distinguished his theological

perhaps the best known in the West, deserves separate treatment. For a survey of Christian literary activity before World War II, see Hiyane, pp. 357-373.

[37] Cf. *Adevangelism*, Eddie Karnes, ed.

[38] Cf. Kumano Yoshitaka, "Kyōkairon no Kisozuke," *Fukuin to Sekai*, XIX/3 (March, 1964); "Shokuzairon no Teii," *Fukuin to Sekai*, XIX/9-11 (September, October, November, 1964). For a series of essays on Japanese Protestant and Catholic theology and biblical studies see Ken Ishihara, ed., *Nihon no Shingaku*.

[39] Cf. Germany, *Protestant Theologies in Modern Japan*, p. 95.

position from extreme liberalism, and also from what is now known as conservative evangelicalism. His theology of biblically oriented, but not biblicist, evangelical Christianity contributed greatly to what I consider the essential wholesomeness of most Japanese Protestant theology, especially in the historic churches, and accounts in considerable measure for the renewed popularity of his works in the postwar years. During the same period a significant but probably less influential figure was the more philosophically oriented Hatano Seiichi.

The freedom from extremes generally characteristic of Japanese theology after World War I is also, I believe, owing to the fact that most theologians have been pastors of churches at the same time that they taught in theological seminaries. The reorganization of the theological institutions of the Kyōdan centered on the establishment on March 24, 1949, of Tokyo Union Theological Seminary (*Tokyo Shingaku Daigaku*), and the hope was that this school would serve as the sole theological seminary of the church.[40] The perseverance, however, of the denominational traditions in the church led to the reestablishment of other theological schools which, while remaining within the Kyōdan, maintained to a limited extent the flavor of their past associations. Several of these were theological departments of what after the war became great universities and were able to be largely independent of Kyōdan financial support. In consequence there are seven theological schools related to the Kyōdan. At first this phenomenon appeared to many as ecumenically indefensible, but time has shown that the multiplicity of seminaries has not contributed to divisiveness or schism but rather to the enrichment and creative diversity of theological thought in the church.

One of the most original of contemporary Japanese theologians is Kitamori Kazō, professor at Tokyo Union Theological Seminary. Within the larger context of Japanese Christianity, Kitamori is perhaps best known for his attempt to relate the Christian faith to Japanese culture. Few if any Japanese Christians have a wider knowledge of the cultural tradition of

---

[40] Cf. *ibid.*, pp. 87-122. Satō Toshio, *Nihon no Kirisuto Kyō to Shingaku*, pp. 116-175.

the nation, especially in literature, ideas, and art, and in this he may be properly considered, I believe, "the Paul Tillich of Japan." Kitamori, however, is best known in the West for his significantly original work entitled *Theology of the Pain of God*.[41] Kitamori himself had suffered for some years from tuberculosis, and his personal experience influenced his theme of the centrality of suffering as indicative of the nature and work of God. He distinguishes his position from that of the Patripassians of the ancient church by emphasizing a distinction between the suffering of the Son on the cross and of the Father as he goes out of himself in Jesus Christ. The pain of God for Kitamori, however, properly leads to its voluntary, active symbolization among men in the form of sacrificial service to others.[42]

One of the most respected contemporary systematic theologians is Kuwada Hidenobu, formerly president of Tokyo Theological Seminary, who is best known for his *Outline of Christian Theology*, which has reached its fifth printing.[43] The man, however, who may be called the giant of Japanese theology is Kumano Yoshitaka, a pastor as well as professor at Tokyo Union Theological Seminary. He has assimilated with remarkable understanding the major theological developments of the history of Christianity in the West and has also made a special study of the contributions of Japanese Protestant theological thinkers from the beginning. His articles in the scholarly Protestant journal *Fukuin to Sekai* have greatly informed the younger generation of pastors and laymen of the richness of the Japanese theological tradition. Kumano, however, has also long been taken with great seriousness by Japanese non-Christian intellectuals as one of the major thinkers of the land.

Kumano has written on the themes of eschatology and history, Christology and tradition, the Bible and the church. The doctrine of the church is central in his thought to the extent that church existence has been called the point of departure of his

---

[41] Cf. Kitamori Kazō, *Kami to Ningen, passim*. This book of essays is an example of the wide range of Kitamori's studies. *Theology of the Pain of God* was published by John Knox Press, Richmond, Virginia, 1965.

[42] Carl Michalson, *Japanese Contributions to Christian Theology*, pp. 73-99.

[43] Kuwada Hidenobu, *Kirisuto Kyō Shingaku Gairon*.

theology. But the faith of Kumano is above all centered in the sovereign God who is uniquely revealed in Jesus Christ, and his understanding is essentially in the tradition of John Calvin and Karl Barth. For him the church is the primary place where the eternal God is by grace creating the new man. Anthropologically viewed, the existence of the church is created by obedience to the Word of God. In his own *Dogmatics* Kumano leans heavily on Barth, but as the heir not only of Takakura but of all the past theologians of the Japanese church, he has his own richly creative integrity. Kumano in a special way exemplifies the remarkable intellectual and spiritual maturity of Japanese Christian theology.[44]

In the last half dozen years a new school of theological activity has emerged in the School of Theology of Dōshisha University in Kyōto. Under the leadership of Takenaka Masao, now dean of the school and editor of the journal *Kirisutokyō Kenkyū,* new areas of research and practice in the social responsibility of Christian faith have been opened up.[45] Japanese theological scholarship has long leaned heavily upon English and German publications, but under the stimulus of Dōshisha a group of younger scholars has emerged who are breaking fresh ground in the history of doctrine also through the skilled use of Latin and French materials.[46] The overall impression given by contemporary Japanese theological thought is that of perceptive and creative activity on the highest level of scholarship, intellectual activity that is at the same time deeply concerned for the relevance of theology both to worship and the life of men in society.

---

[44] Michalson, *op. cit.,* pp. 46-72, 126-162.

[45] Cf. Takenaka Masao, *Reconciliation and Renewal in Japan,* pp. 23-93.

[46] Cf. *Kirisutokyō Kenkyū,* XXXIV/1-2 (June and October, 1965), *passim.* In the future Japanese theology will hopefully become better known in the Western world through the new English language journal, *The Northeast Asia Journal of Theology,* of which the first issue, printed in Taiwan, appeared in March, 1968.

V

THE ROMAN CATHOLIC
CHURCH FROM 1859

A. THE PERIOD OF REDISCOVERY AND PERSECUTIONS, 1859-1873

THE SHOGUNATE GOVERNMENT CONCLUDED A TREATY OF commerce and friendship with France on October 9, 1858, shortly after the signing of similar treaties with the United States and Great Britain on July 29 and August 26, respectively. Fr. Eugene E. Mermet de Cachon, who had served briefly in Okinawa as a missionary beginning in 1855, accompanied the French diplomatic representative in these negotiations and became the first Catholic priest to enter Edo in the modern period. The first priest, however, to reside more permanently was Fr. Prudent S. Girard, who had also served in Okinawa. Accompanying the first consul general of France as interpreter and chaplain, he arrived in Edo on September 6, 1859. France was the only predominantly Catholic country among the first nations which signed treaties with Japan, and Girard, who made his residence in a Buddhist temple which was granted the consul general in the Mita district of Edo, thus became the spearhead of the renewed mission of the Roman Catholic Church in Japan.

Roman Catholic missionary thinkers, especially in the Sacred Congregation for the Propagation of the Faith (S.C.P.F.) in Rome, had long hoped for the restoration of the Japan Mission. In 1781 the society had urged the bishop of Nanking

"never to give up the hope of sending missionaries."[1] The
Ryūkyū Islands were attached to the vicariate of Korea in
1831 with the intent of gaining access to Japan. The work in
Okinawa during the following decade was a part of the same
strategy, as was the elevation of Japan to a vicariate apostolic
by Pope Gregory XVI on March 27, 1846. The responsibility
for the Japan Mission had been formally granted to the Société
des Missions Étrangères de Paris (M.E.P.). The arrival of the
first Catholic priests was therefore no minor incident but the
first step in the execution of plans which had long been conceived even if they lacked specific detail.

Girard at first primarily cared spiritually for Catholic foreigners who were beginning to settle in Kanagawa and Yokohama or who were members of ships' crews temporarily in port.
Mermet, who went to Hakodate, where he arrived on November
25, 1859, also could do little direct missionary work at this
time. The missionaries, however, had been well instructed in
the background of Catholic experience in Japan and were
most anxious to find descendants of the ancient *Kirishitan,*
whose existence in some form they counted on especially
because of the occasional appearance in Korea, the Philippines,
and China during the intervening centuries of various Japanese Christian objects such as religious medals. Girard had
inscribed on the façade of the large church built in Yokohama
(largely as a result of the gifts of a German layman and dedicated on January 12, 1862) the Chinese ideographs which he
hoped would reveal to any *Kirishitan* the presence of the
Catholic Church *(Tenshudō).*[2] Many Japanese visited the
church, and a few indicated their desire to become catechumens, but none declared himself a Christian.

The port of Nagasaki had also been opened to foreign residence, and the first French diplomatic representative there,
Leon Dury, was an earnest Catholic. Peter Mounicou, superior
of the mission in place of Girard, who had returned to France,

[1] Van Hecken, *The Catholic Church in Japan Since 1859,* p. 4.

[2] Cf. Joseph J. Spae, *Catholicism in Japan,* p. 13; Sakurai Tadashi, *Nihon
Kirisuto Kyōshi,* pp. 359-368; Hiyane, *Nihon Kirisuto Kyōshi,* pp. 277-287.

sent Louis Furet to serve in Nagasaki. Furet arrived there on January 22, 1863, and after a short time resided permanently with the vice-consul in the Daitokuji temple. He was able to lease some land on a hillside in the Ōura district of the foreign concession and there began the construction of a large and impressive church. It was completed after the arrival of his successor, Bernard Petitjean, in August, 1864. Furet left Nagasaki after ceding responsibility for the work to Petitjean. Joseph Laucaigne arrived later in November, 1864. Frs. Petitjean and Laucaigne walked frequently about the city and in the country-side in their cassocks to let it be known that Catholic priests had returned. The hidden Christians who still lived by the hundreds in the environs of Nagasaki, of course, took notice of these events and discussed among themselves the question of the authenticity of the fathers. Their criteria were primarily whether the fathers were loyal to the pope of Rome, honored the image of the Virgin Mary and preserved celibacy.

On March 17, 1865, only a few weeks after the consecration of the church, a small group of these Christians arrived at Ōura from Urakami. They stood in a group before the church, and sensing an interest beyond mere curiosity Petitjean led them into the church, where he knelt before the main altar in prayer. After a short while three older women came forward and knelt beside him; one of them said to him: "The heart of all of us here is the same as yours." Another woman asked where the image of Santa Maria was, and when shown the statue all were assured of its authenticity by seeing the child Jesus in her arms. Further conversation convinced both priests and Japanese that they were indeed of the same faith.[3]

Extreme caution had to be exercised, as all the anti-Christian laws were still in force. Some weeks later contact was again made by the heads of some families, who came to the rectory at night. The fathers in turn met secretly with these men and others at night in the mountains. Subsequently other Christian

---

[3] Jennes, *A History of the Catholic Church in Japan*, pp. 214-215. Cf. Yamaguchi Aijirō, "Shinto Hakken no Hyakushūnen," *The Japan Missionary Bulletin*, XVIII/4 (May, 1964), 275-278.

communities made themselves known, and by the end of 1864 the fathers had met with delegates from at least seven different Christian areas and estimated the number of believers to be about twenty thousand. We previously noted the problem for the priests regarding the authenticity of the faith and the validity of the sacramental practice of the *Kirishitan*, but apart from minor difficulties and the much larger problem of the *Hanare-Kirishitan*, who refused to acknowledge the authority of the priests, it became clear that the ancient Christians had been found in large numbers and that the church in Japan was not dead. Pope Pius IX is said to have wept tears of joy on hearing the news.[4]

Pastoral care was begun in the greatest secrecy with special intent to purify the traditional teaching and sacramental life of the Christians. The primary methods employed were to train Japanese catechists to instruct their own communities missionaries used as much as possible the traditional baptizers *(mizukata)* for this work. Petitjean made a brief pastoral visit to the community of Shittsu in September, 1865, but because of possible danger to the Christians no further visits were made until the summer of 1866 when four additional missionaries arrived, one of whom was Louis Furet. During this year Petit-jean was appointed vicar apostolic of Japan, and was conse-crated at Hong Kong on October 21, 1866. Following his return the missionaries began pastoral visitation on an expanded scale and discovered many more hidden Christians. Through their own efforts and those of the Japanese catechists, thousands received religious instruction; during the first five months of 1867 about 1200 received communion. In a catechism and a book of daily prayers which Petitjean prepared, he used much of the special terminology which had become traditional among the *Kirishitan*. The catechism was completed in March, 1866,

---

[4] Van Hecken, *op. cit.*, p. 16. The reader should note that in the compila-tion of statistics of believers it is customary for Roman Catholics to include all those who are baptized, including infants. Protestants, however, count only communicant members, in practice generally limited to those over twelve years of age.

but even before that time portions of it were copied by cate-chists and widely used.[5]

Activity of this scope could hardly remain unknown to the government. The initiative, however, was taken by the Christians who, on the basis of instruction by the missionaries, came to understand that they could no longer act externally as Buddhists as did their *Kirishitan* ancestors.[6] They no longer summoned Buddhist priests for funeral services, and in April, 1867, delegates of the Christians came to the village headman (*shōya*) of Urakami and openly requested exemption from the requirement to employ the Buddhist priests. The headman asked for and received a list of seven hundred families making the request; he took the list to the governor of Nagasaki, adding his own appeal in their behalf. The governor was both embarrassed and angry, but owing to the large number of families involved, he finally granted permission to the Christians to bury their dead without Buddhist rites. He subsequently obtained a list of three hundred names of those who had been given instruction by the missionaries.

For a time no overt action was taken by the government, but on the night of July 14, 1867, about three hundred armed policemen entered Urakami and arrested sixty-four Christians, including several women. The Christians were taken to Naga-saki and imprisoned there, where attempts were made to force them to apostatize. All except one man signed a somewhat ambiguous statement indicative of apostasy, but nearly all revoked it after they were set free in early October. This action of the government, however, began a series of persecutions which resulted in the imprisonment of many other Christians, in the death in prison of about sixty by March, 1869, and the exile in February, 1870, of almost all the Christians of Urakami,

---

[5] Petitjean wisely insisted on the use of his own catechism with its *Kirishitan* terminology even though a Japanese language catechism had been prepared and published by Mounicou in Yokohama before the end of 1865. Mouni-cou's version depended more upon Chinese terminology and, while probably more appropriate for educated Japanese in his own area, was hardly suited to the needs of the *Kirishitan*.

[6] In the light of the subsequent renewal of persecution, the ethical impli-cations of this particular teaching of the missionaries at this time deserve serious consideration.

totaling 3,404.[7] The latter were scattered in twenty-one provinces in western Japan and endured much suffering from local
government officials in their places of exile. We previously
noted the unavailing protests of the diplomatic representatives
of Western powers in Japan, but the experiences of the Iwakura
Mission in 1872 especially in Europe finally caused the government to alter its policy. The decree which removed from the
public notice-boards the edict against Christianity was issued on
February 19, 1873, and on March 14 of the same year the
return of the exiles was formally permitted.

From this point the relationship of the Catholic Church in
Japan with the state in general paralleled that of the Protestants. The actions of the government did not constitute formal
proclamation of freedom of religion, but they signified that the
government was prepared tacitly to allow a limited teaching of
Christianity, and Japanese subjects to profess the faith openly.
The renewed experience of persecution, however, effected a
policy of caution. The mission proceeded with its work forthrightly but in a low-keyed manner.

When the persecutions ended, the foreign missionary personnel consisted of Bishop Petitjean as vicar apostolic and sixteen others. Eleven new priests, however, arrived to augment
this force in September, 1873. Both the older and newer priests
were members of the Foreign Mission Society of Paris (Société
des Missions Étrangères de Paris).

The first order of religious sisters (St. Maur) had arrived
before the liberation of the exiles. Coming from Hong Kong in
June, 1872, the first contingent of five established their headquarters in Yokohama, where they built an orphanage and a
school. A woman lay helper, the mother of one of the missionaries, arrived on October 29, 1871 and settling in Nagasaki
devoted her life and much of her fortune to give religious
instruction to the women in that city. During this period only
three churches were constructed, the first in Yokohama in 1862,
then in Nagasaki in 1865, and in Kōbe in 1870. There were
residences occupied in Hakodate, Niigata, and Ōsaka, the

---

[7] Van Hecken, op. cit., pp. 17-18. Jennes cites the total exiled as 4,100. Op.
cit., p. 225.

latter two completed in 1870. In the Christian communities of Kyūshū there were twenty-seven oratories, or small prayer chapels.

A seminary to train Japanese priests was built in Yokohama at the end of 1870. Already in 1865 Bishop Petitjean had selected three boys whom he hoped to educate for the priesthood. Several boys from Kyūshū were serving as servants of the missionaries to prepare them for more specific education for the priesthood when the persecution began. Ten of these were sent to the General College of Penang on July 21, 1868, the night after the first deportation of exiles. In 1870 another group was sent to Hong Kong but returned with their teachers to Yokohama in February, 1871. The students in Penang, three of whom died, were also recalled and returned finally at the beginning of 1872. The seminary, however, was moved to Tokyo in 1873, where under the leadership of Henry Armbruster it thrived for a short time. A second seminary was begun in Nagasaki after the return of the exiles and completed in 1875. After the division of the vicariate, Petitjean recalled the Kyūshū students to the Nagasaki seminary in 1876, which surpassed the Tokyo institution in importance for the next few decades. Some students continued to be sent to Penang for a portion of their studies.

The statistics of November 1, 1873, cite the number of Catholics as approximately fifteen thousand. This figure includes only those Christians who had formally accepted the authority and returned to the sacramental life of the Roman Catholic Church, not the *Hanare-Kirishitan*. The great majority of these Catholic Christians were poor farmers or fishermen, many illiterate. Reports of the period, however, testify to their spiritual fervor and their willingness to accept the pastoral guidance of the missionaries in matters of ethics as well as doctrine.[8] The church, however, did not lay disproportionate financial burdens upon the faithful. The missionaries and apparently also the catechists were supported primarily by foreign funds. There were resident priests only in the largest places. In the smaller communities the people had the financial responsibility primarily to lodge and entertain a mis-

---

[8] Jennes, *op. cit.*, pp. 230-232.

sionary or catechist for the time that he was there, and to build
the small oratories. Sacrificial giving of the Christians, however,
over a period of twenty-five years was an important factor in the
construction of the church in Urakami, which seated six thousand persons and was consecrated in 1915; but in general the
program was geared to the financial means of the Catholic
population.

B. THE PERIOD OF RELATIVE TOLERANCE, 1873-1915

1

THE ASPIRATIONS AND PLANNING OF THE MISSION-
aries at the beginning of the period of relative tolerance was
turned toward a direct apostolate to the non-Christian Japanese. The pastoral care of former *Kirishitan* and efforts to lead
others of this tradition into the church continued to occupy the
primary attention of a number of the missionaries. Furthermore,
227 men and women catechists are reported to have assisted the
priests in this work in the 1870's. After the end of the overt
persecution a course for the training of these catechists was
instituted at Nagasaki which consisted of two lessons a day for
five months. However, others were being reached: already in
November, 1873, a total of 120 baptisms of adult non-Christians
was reported, and the missionaries looked eagerly toward wider
witness in the land.[1]

In order to effect a more suitable organization for this work
Bishop Petitjean went to Rome at the end of 1875 to request a
division of the vicariate of Japan. The Holy See approved the
request and by a brief of June 20, 1876 established the two

---

[1] Jennes, *A History of the Catholic Church in Japan*, pp. 230-231. For this
period cf. also Sakurai, *Nihon Kirisuto Kyōshi*, pp. 368-373.

vicariates of northern and southern Japan, with Lake Biwa just east of Kyōto as the point of division. Petitjean became vicar apostolic of the southern vicariate and resided in Ōsaka. Bishop Peter Osouf was appointed vicar apostolic of the northern vicariate, in which by 1875 there were five missions: Tokyo, Yokohama, Yokosuka, Hakodate, and Niigata. Fourteen priests and thirty-four catechists served 1,235 Catholics and worked to spread the knowledge of the gospel. In the southern vicariate there were but four missions: Nagasaki, Urakami, Kōbe, and Ōsaka, with the vast majority of Christians in the first two.

Roman Catholic missiological thought has traditionally seen missionary work as preeminently a labor of love. Missionaries are regarded as the instruments of God to bring eternal salvation to men and also the services of the church through its institutions of education and welfare.[2] As the Japanese government began to allow foreigners to travel into the interior of the country by special passport, the Catholic missionaries made increasing use of this privilege. They divided themselves into two categories, the itinerants and the residents. The latter concentrated chiefly on work in a particular location centered in a church of some size. The former toured cities, towns and even villages throughout the entire country. With their black cassocks and long beards the French missionaries were impressive figures and usually able to draw substantial audiences to hear their public lectures. In later years the missionaries, looking back especially on the period from 1875 to 1890, regarded them as "the finest years of their apostolic life, the golden age of the expansion of the Church in Japan."[3] By their efforts the Catholic Church was planted in almost all the important centers of Japanese life.

Fathers Francis Vigroux, Germain Testevuide, and Hippolyte Cadilhac were missionary pioneers in the plains extending north, south and west of Tokyo and along the Tōkaidō.[4] Others

---

[2] For an exposition of recent Roman Catholic missiological thought see Eugene Hillman, *The Church as Mission,* and Ludwig Wiedenmann, *Mission und Eschatologie,* pp. 194-204.

[3] Van Hecken, *The Catholic Church in Japan Since 1859,* pp. 11, 25-26.

[4] Cf. J. M. Martin, "An Itinerant Missionary in Japan," *The Japan Missionary Bulletin,* VI/5 (September-October, 1953), 146-149.

were responsible for itineration about Nagoya. In the northern part of Honshū, Urbain Faurie is perhaps most famous for introducing the cultivation of apples in Aomori Prefecture, an industry now productive of several thousands of tons annually. One of the greatest missionaries in the Hokkaidō was Alexander Berlioz. Out of their mission funds the missionaries bought property for residences and churches in central locations, although they were often compelled to purchase these under assumed names since until 1899 foreigners were not legally qualified to acquire property outside the foreign concessions. The principal method of preaching the gospel was to hold announced meetings in public places, often with the use of lantern slides, in the cities as well as in the provinces. The missionaries began to use this method in Tokyo in 1875 and from this time held regular meetings on Sundays and holidays.

In the southern vicariate the *Kirishitan* communities naturally comprised most of the church. Socially, however, they formed their own separate communities, had distinctive habits, and even used unique terminology. The methodology of the missionaries, therefore, was to approach non-Christian Japanese with an appeal geared to their more modern and intellectual way of life. This work, however, was difficult and slow, the results poor in comparison with the effort expended. A principal aim of the missionaries was to dispel the deep-rooted prejudices held against the *Kirishitan* even as they proclaimed in a positive manner the teaching of the Catholic Church.

The number of *Kirishitan* Catholics grew both from the discovery of new communities and from the numerous baptisms of children. In 1891 there were 27,909 Christians and fifty-four churches or chapels (oratories) in the larger area about Nagasaki. Some communities, such as Shittsu, became noted as particularly productive of religious vocations. Japanese clergy and religious, however, almost exclusively cared for established communities, and throughout this period pioneer work was almost entirely the work of foreign missionaries assisted by Japanese catechists. The ultimate goal — to found the church upon an indigenous clergy — was thus only very partially realized at this period.

The French missionaries of the Paris Society regulated their spiritual life in general by the seventh chapter of the rule of their society, La Regle Generale de la Société des M.E.P. In their apostolic activity they were primarily guided by the *Monita ad Missionarios* of the Sacred Congregation for the Propagation of the Faith. This latter document was apparently carried by every Paris missionary along with his breviary and almost equally revered. Other materials were also available for the guidance of the missionaries both in personal conduct and pastoral and apostolic methodology. From an early period the missionaries of Tokyo and Yokohama met periodically to discuss practical problems related to their apostolate. The reports of these conferences were published in a single volume in 1883 and served as a rule of conduct for the missionaries of the Paris Society for a long time. Details concerning the proper use of time, care of health and the dress to be worn were given as well as directives on pastoral procedure.[5]

The Japan Mission was restructured in 1888 by the creation of a third vicariate, that of central Japan. It comprised the section of Honshū west of Lake Biwa and included also the island of Shikoku. On June 15, 1891, the pope instituted the episcopal hierarchy of Japan. The see of Tokyo, where Bishop Osouf had resided since 1878, was elevated to the rank of metropolitan, and its head became properly an archbishop. Nagasaki, Ōsaka and Hakodate were constituted dioceses with suffragan bishops in charge. This action followed the creation of the vicariate apostolic of Hakodate on April 17 of the same year, by which the northern provinces of Honshū, the whole of the Hokkaidō, and the Kuriles became a separate mission.

The first regional synod to consider various missionary and ecclesiastical problems was convened by Bishop Osouf on March 2, 1890. This synod, which lasted until March 29, included also the missionaries of Korea. The entire range of problems confronting the Catholic Church in the Far East was considered at this meeting; the acts and decrees were later published and served as a guide for the missions. In order to deal with the special problems which emerged as a result of the Imperial Rescript on Education of October 30, 1890, and the

---

[5] Van Hecken, *op. cit.*, pp. 112-114.

general anti-Christian milieu, another synod was convened in Tokyo on April 28, 1895. Attendance at this meeting was limited to the ordinaries in Japan and their advisors. The acts and decrees of this synod were also published and were added to the authoritative material available to guide missionaries in their work.

The faithful work of the itinerant and resident missionaries was reflected in church growth until 1890. In that year there were 3,110 Catholics in the city of Tokyo, and 247 persons were baptized during the year. In the south and west, according to the statistics of 1889, Kyōto recorded a Catholic population of 520 with forty-eight baptisms for the year, Kōbe 512 with twenty-one baptisms, Okayama 555 with 104 baptisms.

2

The crisis in the church following the change in political climate in 1889-1890 which we noted in connection with Protestant experience was equally catastrophic for Roman Catholics. Men wrote that a primary shift in popular interest seemed to occur; now enthusiasm for politics existed where formerly, at least among some, there had been enthusiasm for the church. Antipathy to things foreign was very strong in some quarters, and in 1905 after public announcement was made of the provisions of the Treaty of Portsmouth with Russia, zealous patriots burned down the Catholic church, school and rectory in the Honjō district of Tokyo. From 1890 attacks on the Christian religion appeared frequently in newspapers and books. In consequence the number of catechumens decreased notably, and not a few Christians turned from the faith or at least from participation in the public life of the church. As the center of political life and every current of thought, Tokyo was most noticeably affected by the change in mental climate. For twenty years there was almost no growth; in 1891 there had been 9,660 Catholics, in 1914 no more than 9,804.

There was much heart searching among missionaries during these years. For one thing, apart from the large communities in Kyūshū mostly comprised of the descendants of *Kirishitan,* the Catholic missionaries were not winning as many converts as the Protestants. We noted the anti-Catholic bias of the early Protestant missionaries. The Catholics were not behind in their depreciation of Protestant faith and preaching, although both generally refrained from public denunciation of each other's faith. It must have been particularly galling to Frenchmen that they were less effective in winning Japanese of the educated classes than Protestants. A number of missionaries suggested that one reason was the many fine educational institutions related to the Protestant churches, then as now considerably more numerous than the Catholic. Some missionaries advocated new methods in the apostolate, better use of books, magazines and newspapers, better training of the missionaries especially in the language and culture of Japan. At the time, however, differences of opinion among the missionaries prevented appreciable change in methodology. This had to wait until the coming of missionaries from other societies than that of Paris.

The older methods, however, continued to bear fruit in Kyūshū, among non-Christians as well as among the *Kirishitan*. The man noted as the greatest apostle in northeastern Kyūshū in the last decades of the nineteenth century and well into the twentieth was Emil Raguet. Several Japanese priests, such as Shimauchi Yōsuke and Ariyasu Hidenoshin, did effective work among non-Christians. Raguet composed a large Japanese-French, French-Japanese dictionary and began a translation of the New Testament which he completed in 1910. On the island of Amami Ōshima, south of Kyūshū, by far the most successful work among non-Christians was that conducted by Joseph Ferrié with the assistance of other missionaries and Japanese priests. By 1904 about four thousand people in a dozen towns and villages had become faithful Catholics. In spite of the difficulties experienced elsewhere, the number of baptized Christians in the diocese of Nagasaki rose from 26,060 in 1889 to 41,458 in 1904.

Growth was slower in the central diocese of Ōsaka but the trend continued steadily upward. Much of this may be attributed to the multiplication of secondary parishes or stations which became centers of new growth while in their early stages remaining under a mother parish. In this way the Catholics were also able to make the widest use of their missionary personnel. The two churches, fourteen chapels and 2,185 Christians of this diocese in 1888 grew to thirty-two of the former and about four thousand of the latter in 1904. Heroic work was done in the Hokkaidō, where Fr. Urbain Faurie had traveled and labored alone for twenty years, making his frequent journeys almost entirely on foot. A half dozen missionaries assumed one by one the work of the various stations which he had started in his pioneer travels. Two monasteries were founded in the Hokkaidō, that of the Cistercians in 1897 and the Trappistines in 1898, but until 1904 the Foreign Mission Society of Paris was the only Roman Catholic missionary society working in Japan.

An important event, therefore, of the following decade (1904-1914) was the arrival in Japan of fifteen new orders of men and about thirty of women. The church in France was undergoing a crisis in vocations, and the Paris Society was unable to supply the replacements and new workers needed for the expanded prospects in Japan. These many orders came on the basis of the principle adopted by the Sacred Congregation for the Propagation of the Faith that each society be assigned a separate territory and have its own ordinary in charge. This policy, however, required changes in the old dioceses and considerable shifting of personnel.

We do not have space to consider the details of the names and particular assignments of the many orders which arrived in Japan after 1904. They came from many lands of Europe and North America and gave a variety of methodology as well as of tone to the work, in particular a cosmopolitanism which the mission in Japan had previously lacked. Spanish Dominicans came from the Philippine Islands. Germans of the Society of the Divine Word (Steyl) arrived principally to carry on educational work. Franciscans were sent from six different provinces of Europe. Jesuits were sent from Germany, and later men and women of many orders came from the United States and Canada.

As time passed, problems emerged concerning the need to shift both hierarchical and pastoral responsibility to the Japanese clergy, but the system of separate geographical assignments to the respective orders had many advantages especially in the pioneer stages of mission work. The practice meant that each district had a homogeneous group of workers with close personal ties and relatively small-scale local organizations. Not only were Roman Catholic workers less likely to suffer from the loneliness of isolation, but their system also allowed most decisions to be made on the field and enabled direct, rapid communications with the home bases of their orders.

3

We noted among the first literary works of the Catholic missionaries the publication of catechisms in Yokohama and Nagasaki. In the earliest decades the missionaries were too busy to engage in or promote literary work. Many were aware of the need, however, and on May 1, 1881, the first Catholic newspaper was published in Tokyo, first under the title of *Kōkyō Bampō* and then of *Tenshu Bampei*. It continued until the end of 1889. Beginning in November, 1889, a monthly periodical was issued, but it lasted only three years. The magazine which had a far longer life was *Koe* (The Voice), which was continued with only a brief suspension to the present day. The purpose of *Koe* from the beginning frankly included polemics. It was intended to "instruct the Christians, fortify them against the prejudices hostile to Christianity which everywhere steal into the press, conversations, teachings and penetrate in some sense the whole atmosphere." The intent was also to answer attacks from every quarter and "to fight against the invasion and influence of the heretics."[6] This magazine was later published by the Central Catholic Bureau of Publication, which was founded in 1929. In 1931 Sauveur Candau, M.E.P., became director of the bureau, and served in this capacity for a number of years. Candau was one of the finest of Roman Catholic apologists as liaison with the intellectual and wider non-Christian world of Japan. He became unusually skilled in the Japanese language, and making use of the rare opportunity of a daily column in one of the great metropolitan newspapers, he wrote with such perception, humor and winsomeness as to create much goodwill toward Christianity and the Catholic Church in particular.[7]

[6] *Ibid.*, pp. 132-133.
[7] Cf. Sauveur Candau, "Apostolate Among the Japanese Intellectuals,"

In the first decades after 1859 Catholicism in Japan, in spite of being represented by cultivated French priests, suffered considerably, perhaps largely through its association with the poor and mostly illiterate *Kirishitan,* from the reputation of being "the poorest, most ignorant, lowest of the Christian sects." As we have noted, some missionaries chafed under this burden and a few were even prepared to give up direct missionary work in order to prepare a more favorable climate, especially among intellectuals, for later conversions. These men accordingly began in 1898 a periodical called *Tenchijin* (Man of the Universe), which intended to treat philosophical and moral problems on a high intellectual plane and without predominant sectarian concerns. The magazine soon came to be highly respected and was an important element in the long process by which finally, after the Second World War, the Roman Catholic Church was associated by many Japanese with scholarship and the arts. Another periodical of this caliber which had a limited but welcome circulation among those able to read French was the *Mélanges japonais;* it was published from 1904 to 1910. [8]

Of religious books the most numerous were catechetical or those explaining in more detail the doctrine of the Catholic Church. Contemporary Catholics, however, are frank to report what they consider a long delay in the translation and publication of the Scriptures in the early period. We noted that Emil Raguet was responsible for the first translation of the entire New Testament published in 1910. Portions of the Bible, especially translations of individual gospels, were published in 1895, 1897 and 1900, and scriptural knowledge was of course communicated through articles in magazines and newspapers. The primary concern, however, was for catechetical teaching and the cultivation of the devotional and moral life. Many materials, including prayer books and various guides for laymen, were

---

The Japan Missionary Bulletin, XVIII/4-5 (May-June, 1964), 245-252, 341-344.

[8] *Ibid.,* pp. 134-136. I recall seeing posters after World War II on which the Catholic Church was proclaimed as the "Mother of the Arts" *(Geijitsu no Haha).* Cf. Joseph J. Spae, "The Japanese Intellectuals," *The Japan Missionary Bulletin,* XIX/3 (April, 1965), 186.

prepared to serve this purpose. In the more intellectual area
the problem of the relation between science and religion
occasioned much interest. The Franco-Japanese Society published pamphlets on this and related problems before the outbreak of the First World War. A significant sidelight in the
area of religious books is furnished by the work of Peter Mar-
monier; as director of the Tamatsukuri orphanage in Ōsaka
he founded in 1907 the St. Joseph printing shop, which served
until 1919 both to teach children of the orphanage the printing trade and to publish books for clergy and laity.

4

The educational program of the Roman Catholic Church in
Japan is both similar to and different from that of the Protestants. Like the early Protestant missionaries, Prudent Girard in
Edo and Eugene Mermet in Hakodate began early to establish
contacts by teaching their native language. In almost every
larger town or city the missionaries of the M.E.P. were able to
gain openings by teaching French. Henry Armbruster opened a
language school in Tokyo on December 25, 1891. It came to
have 130 students, many of them from the nobility.[9] But con-
trasting with the Protestants, the Catholic missionaries soon
had, in Kyūshū, responsibility for a rapidly growing community of Christians largely of the lower classes.

The first effort to meet the general educational needs of these
people was a small school at Urakami begun after the withdrawal of the anti-Christian notices. A young woman taught a
class of girls the elements of reading and writing together with
simple catechetical instruction. Catechists instructed a larger
number of boys in the same fashion. The M.E.P. report of 1873
cites six such schools for boys with a total of two hundred pupils
and one school for girls with fifteen pupils. Various orders of
sisters, starting with the order of the Sisters of St. Maur in 1872,
began educational work in many parts of the country, and by
1880 there were sixty-seven Catholic schools with 3,159 pupils.
In 1887 there were ninety-three schools with 4,718 pupils.

---

[9] Spae, *Catholicism in Japan,* p. 48.

These schools, contrary to Protestant practice, were all of elementary level.

In the mid-1880's, however, the Japanese government reformed elementary education so that all elementary schools came under the control of the Ministry of Education, and religious instruction was no longer permitted even in private elementary schools. The Meiji Rescript on Education constituted the norm by which Shintō nationalism became the spiritual foundation of all education, and the Catholic Church found itself gradually forced out of elementary education. After 1905 all elementary schools were controlled by the government. The orders of sisters which had operated such schools responded by transferring them into institutions of secondary level. Some schools were closed, the one at Urakami became a kindergarten. As a result only twenty-six Catholic educational institutions were left in 1909, but the number of pupils was larger than before, 5,522.

The need for Catholic higher education had been felt for some time, and as a result of initiative taken by Pope Pius X the Jesuits established Sophia University on October 18, 1908, which became the center and standard of Catholic education in Japan. The sisters of the Society of the Sacred Heart first arrived on January 1, 1908, and began their work which contributed so notably to the higher education of girls in Japan.

In the education of men for the priesthood many problems existed at the beginning of this period because of the lack of uniformity in the educational facilities then available. Students entered the seminaries, especially in Tokyo, with great differences in background. Nearly all of those who were not from Kyūshū matriculated before receiving baptism. The number of students in Tokyo remained small; from 1890 Archbishop Osouf decided to send most of the seminarians to Nagasaki, and the Tokyo seminary was subsequently closed.

The Nagasaki institution became the center of the Catholic Church's program of theological education. In October, 1877, thirty-one boys had matriculated, and from 1878 the students always numbered from forty to seventy. On December 31, 1882, three men were ordained to the priesthood, the first fruits of this kind since the seventeenth century. Over a period of fifty years, 288 students entered the seminary in Nagasaki, of whom sixty-three were ultimately ordained.[10]

5

One of the essential aims of the mission of the Roman Catholic Church is the temporal as well as eternal happiness of every person. This aim is said to constitute the *raison d'être* of all Catholic institutions, but most particularly of those devoted to social welfare. The Catholic Church in Japan has an unusually large number of such institutions in comparison with other religious organizations.[11]

Eugene Mermet gave free care to the sick in Hakodate shortly after his arrival in the northern city in December, 1859. He planned to open a hospital there and asked his friend, the French vice-consul of Nagasaki, to be the first director. Leon Dury arrived to do this work, but the project had to be abandoned because of various political difficulties. From an early period medical dispensaries were founded in several places in Kyūshū; in each a pharmacy was added and sisters served as nurses. The first Catholic general hospital, however, was founded considerably later, at Sapporo in 1912.

The first leper asylum in nineteenth-century Japan was founded in 1887 at Gotemba in the mountains of Shizuoka Prefecture by Germain Testevuide, several years before a similar institution was established at Kumamoto in Kyūshū by the Anglican missionary Hannah Ridell. Testevuide enlisted the energies of the Franciscan Missionaries of Mary, a society of sisters, to found another leprosarium, also in Kumamoto, in 1898. After the Japanese government began to make provision for lepers in 1906, Catholic priests offered pastoral care also to patients in government institutions.

Work among orphans and the aged was continued and expanded. The first Catholic orphanage, as we noted, was founded by the Sisters of St. Maur in 1872 at Yokohama. After the arrival in 1877 of the Sisters of Chauffailles, orphanages were built in Kōbe, Ōsaka, Kyōto and Kumamoto. The

[10] Van Hecken, *op. cit.*, pp. 228-233.
[11] Spae, *Catholicism in Japan*, pp. 40-41.

Sisters of St. Paul de Chartres established similar institutions in northern Japan. The Paris Society missionaries also founded orphanages, some of which, as those in Sekiguchi and Tamatsu-kuri, became large institutions. The Sisters of Chauffailles founded the first home for the aged at Amakusa in 1889. In the following decade at least two priests initiated similar work, but in later years service to the aged became the exclusive respon-sibility of orders of sisters.

C. EXPANSION AND CRISIS, 1915-1945

1

ACCORDING TO THE MISSIONARY PRINCIPLES OF POPE Benedict XV and Pope Pius XI, the well-established ecclesias-tical provinces of a mission land should be transferred to the care of the national clergy as soon as possible. Already Japanese priests had long been at work, especially in the pastoral care of the *Kirishitan* churches. In 1927, however, the diocese of Naga-saki was restricted to an area coextensive with the civil prefec-ture and the first Japanese bishop was appointed as its adminis-trator. Upon the withdrawal of the M.E.P. missionaries, the Catholic population of 53,643 was served by thirty-four Japa-nese priests in seventy-eight churches and chapels. The mis-sionaries who formerly served in the Nagasaki area then turned largely to the extension of the apostolate in the burgeoning industrial cities of northern Kyūshū.[1] This process of com-mittal of responsibility to Japanese leadership gained momen-tum as the nation moved toward World War II.

---

[1] In the last decade of the nineteenth century Christians from the Naga-saki area had been moving into these cities as factory workers and to a lesser extent as merchants. This migration to industrial centers has continued to the present day, now to the extent of 1,500 per year. Cf. Paul Pfister, "The Catholic Church in Japan," *The Japan Missionary Bulletin,* XIX/3 (April, 1965), 184.

On the occasion of the consecration of Joseph Lemieux as bishop of Sendai on December 9, 1935, the apostolic delegate to Japan, Paul Marella, sensing the particular inappropriateness of consecrating a foreigner as bishop of a Japanese see at that time, gave as a primary principle of operation that the presence of foreign missionaries in a land should "not be protracted beyond strict necessity." Thus the missionaries of the Paris Society on November 9, 1937, committed to the fifteen Japanese priests of the Tokyo diocese full responsibility for the pastoral care of its 10,681 Catholics. On December 2 of the same year Doi Tatsuo was appointed archbishop of this diocese, in which notable growth had occurred in the years following the great earthquake of 1923. During these fourteen years ten new churches were founded in the larger Tokyo area. Comparable growth occurred also in the great metropolitan center comprising Kyōto, Ōsaka, and Kōbe.[2]

Brief mention should be made of Catholic work among Japanese emigrants. Japanese Catholics who moved to the annexed territories of Korea, Taiwan, or Manchuria came under the jurisdiction of the local hierarchy and missions. The major continuing responsibility of the church in Japan was for emigrants to Latin America. A mission center for migrants was founded in Kōbe in 1926 by Hermann Heuvers, who came once a month from Tokyo to speak to the emigrants at the government emigration center in Kōbe. His work was taken up the following year by a Japanese priest, Yamanaka Iwahiko of Kōbe, who supplied the emigrants with various materials as well as a thorough orientation to their life in a new land. As a result of this and extensive work in Latin America itself a very large number of the Japanese residents there became Catholics. It is estimated that perhaps 50 percent of the 244,536 Japanese who had emigrated to Brazil before World War II were Catholic.

Growth continued in both the older and newer Christian communities of Kyūshū. The older groups were remarkably faithful to the church; from the single community of Imamura in the diocese of Fukuoka there were twenty-six seminarians

[2] Van Hecken, *The Catholic Church in Japan Since 1859*, pp. 75-81. Cf. Sakurai, *Nihon Kirisuto Kyōshi*, pp. 373-385.

at one time. The number of Catholics in this diocese grew from 7,450 and twenty-three churches or chapels in 1928 to 10,927, with forty churches, in 1940. A most remarkable phenomenon was the increase in this diocese of the number of adult baptisms per year from 129 in 1928 to 1,255 in 1940, in spite of the highly unfavorable circumstances of the time.[3]

The Roman Catholic Church, however, was affected very much in the same way as the Protestants by the passage of the Religious Bodies Law and related decrees in the spring of 1940. From this time the apostolate among non-Christians became exceedingly difficult and catechumens few in number. It was seen as no longer desirable for foreign ordinaries to hold ecclesiastical jurisdiction over specified territories or groups in Japan, and the process was begun by which within a short time all foreigners, who unanimously offered their resignations to Rome, were replaced by Japanese bishops. Likewise, foreign administrators of Catholic schools turned over their authority and responsibility to Japanese clergy or religious. Foreign missionaries serving as pastors of parishes found their activity more and more circumscribed, and since Japanese priests were able to move about with relative freedom, almost all responsibility was given to them.

The Catholic Church had in a way similar to the Protestants and Orthodox great difficulty in composing a constitution and bylaws satisfactory to the Ministry of Education, which wished to change at some points both the official doctrine and the liturgical books of the church. When, however, the officials of the Ministry tried to force the Catholics to sever their ties with the pope of Rome, the ordinaries and laity, represented respectively by Bishop Taguchi Yoshigorō and Admiral Yamamoto Shinjirō, insisted that such separation was contrary to the essence of their faith and that they preferred martyrdom to obeying an order of this kind. The Ministry then backed down from insistence on this point. The church was formally authorized on May 3, 1941, as the *Nihon Tenshu Kōkyō Kyōdan*. The archbishop of Tokyo, Doi Tatsuo, became *tōrisha*. The baptized membership of the church as of 1940 was 119,224.

[3] *Ibid.*, pp. 72-73. Cf. *Kindai Nihon to Kirisuto Kyō*, Taishō-Shōwa Hen, pp. 318-326.

After the outbreak of war with the United States and Great Britain on December 8, 1941 (Japan time), most of the clergy and religious of Allied citizenship were interned or repatriated. The Japanese clergy, however, were mobilized for service either in the military or on the home front. The majority of both Japanese clergy and religious, including cloistered monks as well as seminarians, were conscripted for military service. Church life thus became greatly restricted, and, as with the Protestants and Orthodox, almost ceased to function in the last year of the war.

When in the 1930's attendance at ceremonies conducted at state Shintō shrines was made compulsory for children in elementary schools and in various ways the religio-ideological program of the military regime confronted Christian theology and practice, the Catholic Church was able to receive authoritative guidance for its people. The Propaganda in Rome sent to Cardinal Paul Marella, the apostolic delegate, on May 26, 1936, an instruction on the duties of Catholics to their country. According to this document Catholics were permitted to participate in patriotic ceremonies conducted at Shintō shrines. In effect, the Catholic Church took at face value the contention of the government that state Shintō and its ceremonies were not religious. This decision was never formally altered, although the external situation has radically changed with the effective abolition of state Shintō under the new national constitution of May, 1947. The matter continues, however, to draw the attention of Catholic theologians as a problem both of church-state relations and of missionary accommodation or acculturation.[4]

2

As new missionary societies arrived in greater numbers after 1915 the literary work of the Catholic Church in Japan expanded greatly. For the first fifteen years of this period one of the most notable phenomena was the appearance of new peri-

---

[4] Cf. Jan Swyngedouw, "The Catholic Church and Shrine Shintō," *The Japan Missionary Bulletin*, XXI/10-11 (November-December, 1967), 579-584, 659-663.

odicals, which were, however, generally aimed at constituencies limited to small geographical areas or specific interests. In all, sixty-seven new Catholic magazines were initiated in Japan between 1915 and 1945. Parish bulletins are, of course, not included in this figure. The need to coordinate these activities became ever more apparent, and in April, 1931, the first Congress of the Catholic Press was convened in Tokyo. The result was the decision to suspend the local newspapers and merge their activities in the single *Nihon Katorikku Shimbun,* which had been inaugurated in January of that year.

The publication of Catholic books greatly increased. More than four hundred titles were issued in the years between 1915 and 1930. From the latter year the rate of increase rose noticeably; an average of seventy-five books were published each year until the war compelled the suspension of almost all such activity. From 1915 to 1941 more than one thousand different books or large pamphlets were printed. Many of these were original creations of missionaries or Japanese Christians, laymen as well as clergy. The missionaries of the Paris Society and of the Divine Word Society, together with the Japanese clergy, were the groups most productive. In 1934 the Paulist Fathers began their publishing activity in Tokyo, as did Rupert Henderle, the agent of Herder and Herder in Tokyo.

During this period radio was used increasingly for missionary communication. The first recorded instance is a broadcast on September 26, 1926, by Joseph Flaujac of a discourse on the fundamentals of Catholic teaching. Other radio broadcasts of Catholic programs, frequently with music, were made in subsequent years until the situation in the country finally prevented all such religious broadcasting until the war ended. A motion picture entitled "The Twenty-Six Saints of Japan" was made by a commercial company in 1931 with the help of two missionaries. Depicting some of the deeds of witness and social welfare as well as the martyrdoms of the early Catholic period, the picture was well received, dispelled some of the ancient prejudices, and revealed the spirit of the gospel at its best. This motion picture represented the transformation into another medium of the older tradition of play-writing and production. A play of the same title had been produced with great effect as early as 1901 in Yamanashi Prefecture. Other noteworthy plays with Catholic themes were presented in the following decades with marked increase in popularity.[5]

The educational work of the church continued to expand especially after 1920, when new orders, particularly of sisters, came to Japan specifically to teach. In this way Catholic schools for girls as well as for boys were established in all larger and some smaller cities of the empire. The church acquired increasingly a reputation as a promoter of culture. Certain missionaries, especially the Canadian Dominicans, took as their particular apostolate the penetration of non-Christian universities with the witness of the gospel. The first Catholic hostel or dormitory for students at a non-Christian school had been founded in 1899 at Kokura in Kyūshū, and similar institutions were established in Tokyo and Kanazawa shortly after.

The picture of Catholic theological education in Japan became considerably more complicated after World War I with the advent of the many new orders of clergy and religious. The major societies of men maintained seminaries of their own, and as the ecclesiastical districts were altered the number of minor seminaries increased. The number of students in these schools also increased, especially after 1925. The seminary in Tokyo was reopened in 1914 with fourteen students, but recruitment for the priesthood remained difficult especially outside Kyūshū, which continued to be the area most productive of clerical vocations. Tokyo functioned as a minor seminary for preparatory studies, but the proportion of dropouts was high. Until 1929, when a new institution designed to serve as a regional or major seminary was founded in the capital city, the few seminarians who finished their studies were sent either to Rome or Saint Sulpice in Paris for philosophy and theology. In 1929, however, Tokyo became the major seminary where even the Kyūshū students completed their studies prior to ordination, although, in accordance with the wishes of Rome, each diocese sent a limited number of students to Europe. Special efforts were made by the Paris Society missionaries to recruit boys for the priesthood. They founded in a number of *Kirishitan* vil-

[5] Van Hecken, *op. cit.*, pp. 141-150, 217-219.

lages in Kyūshū what they termed "clerical schools," where they gave to selected students the kind of education best designed to prepare them for the seminaries. Every effort was made particularly to encourage vocations among the children of catechists, who were still important in the local work of the church.

Schools were also founded for the training of catechists, who came to number 370 in 1891 and 617 in 1912. Their number went down during the First World War but rose again as the new orders of missionaries coming in after the war wished to use their services. They numbered 740 in 1935, many of them being women.

Minor seminaries were or had been founded in other areas. One had been established in Ōsaka in 1879 but existed for only three years. For the following fifty years candidates from the diocese of Ōsaka were sent to Nagasaki; from 1929 Nagasaki served as their minor seminary and Tokyo as the major. A minor seminary was founded in Sendai in 1901 but lasted only five years. This school was reestablished in 1920, and although small in size is noted for the quality of its students. Of the five who were in residence in 1927 four became bishops. Other minor seminaries were also established in Fukuoka (1932), Sapporo (1915) and Miyazaki (1930).[6] Until World War II the major responsibility for theological education was carried by the missionaries of the Paris Society.

3

Welfare work in Japan also expanded when the institutes opened new activities after 1920. Orders founded in Japan also participated in such work. An order of Japanese sisters, the Sisters of the Visitation, began their apostolate in 1928 with the establishment of a general hospital in Tokyo. Other hospitals of comparable scope were founded in Tokyo (1930), Kanazawa (1932), Ōsaka (1940) and again in another location in Tokyo (1939). At the beginning of the Pacific War there were seven Catholic general hospitals in Japan and nine dispensaries.

---

[6] *Ibid.*, pp. 234-236.

Protestant Christians had pioneered in establishing sanatoria for tuberculosis patients, the first being that founded by the Salvation Army in 1919. In 1927, however, the Paris Society missionary Joseph Flaujac began visitation among especially poor patients in the Tokyo municipal sanatorium. From this humble beginning developed a remarkable procession of institutions to care for tubercular patients, some founded more directly as a result of Flaujac's work. Others, such as those in Kamakura (1930), Niigata (1931), Shindenbaru (1933), Akita (1935), Tokyo (1939) and Kusatsu (1942), were the fruit of the dedication and work of orders of sisters, Japanese and foreign.

Several Catholic hospitals were also established to provide specialized services, such as the Hospital of St. John (1939) in Tokyo, which has a ward for the mentally ill. Two other hospitals, one in Himeji, another in Kōbe, furnish similar specialized treatment for other problems. Homes for the aged continued to be established, at least four in the period from 1915 to 1945.[7]

D. THE POSTWAR PERIOD

1

LIKE THE PROTESTANTS, THE ROMAN CATHOLICS suffered enormous institutional losses as a result of the bombing raids in the last months of the war. Only the diocese of Niigata incurred no losses of this kind. Over thirteen thousand Catholics died in these conflagrations, and the 1940 number of 119,224 baptized Catholics had dropped to 108,324 by 1946. From the Catholic standpoint, however, the confrontation with the civil authorities during these years caused no essential damage upon either the dogmatic or ecclesiastical integrity of the church.[1]

---

[7] *Ibid.*, pp. 177-182.

[1] Cf. Anthony Creemers, "Christianity and the Emperor System in Japan,"

Again like the Protestants, Roman Catholics found open doors on every side at the end of hostilities. Missionaries returned, many new orders came for the first time, and as the workers traveled and settled in various parts of the country, they found ready listeners everywhere. Often priests were invited to give religious instruction in what earlier would have seemed unlikely places. By 1948 the total number of foreign missionaries was 314, and the number of Japanese priests 164. This latter figure is far fewer than that of the more than one thousand Japanese Protestant clergymen serving in the early postwar years, but results show the effectiveness of the work of the Japanese Roman Catholic priests. The number of catechumens greatly increased as opportunities for instruction were extended.

Among the most pressing needs was the rehabilitation of property: buildings of every kind, books and equipment. Many of the clergy and religious as well as the laity desperately needed food and clothing. New personnel had to help face the staggering immensity of the tasks. A committee to coordinate this work was organized in Tokyo on January 24, 1946, to serve under the direction of the Japanese hierarchy. A special appeal was made by this committee to the hierarchies of the United States and Australia for help in men, money and goods, but the entire Catholic world was requested to give aid as each country was able. The response, as in the case of Protestants, was phenomenal, one of the major events of the twentieth century. Quantities of supplies came in, especially from North America and Australia. In 1947 the bishops of Australia inaugurated a program by which they lent fourteen of their diocesan priests to Japan for a period of five years. In the immediate aftermath of the war, with physical needs so important, much good work was done with only a modicum of knowledge of the Japanese language.

In 1948 ten new religious orders of Europe and North America sent missionaries, and when, beginning in 1949, most Christian missionaries were compelled to leave China, many of the Catholics, especially Franciscans, came to Japan. They brought

The Japan Missionary Bulletin, XIX/8-9 (September, October, 1965), 505-508, 560-565.

their own financial support and thus greatly strengthened the entire program in Japan. New administrative arrangements, however, had to be worked out for this new situation. Before the war each order had its own bishop in Japan, but the replacement of all foreign ordinaries in 1940 by Japanese, who were all secular clergy, changed this system. The device employed to handle the situation was a structure of bilateral contracts worked out between the Japanese bishops in charge of the fifteen dioceses in Japan and the foreign orders serving within them. The bishops of course retained full jurisdiction, but under their aegis the superior of each foreign — or Japanese — order directed his own personnel and their activity in the territory assigned them by the bishop concerned. The orders were also responsible for their own financial support. The system, with its combination of differing levels of authority and small-scale, local groupings of homogeneous personnel, has on the whole worked exceedingly well.[2]

The expansion of churches progressed steadily in this context. There were twenty-one churches in the archdiocese of Tokyo in 1941, and fourteen of these were destroyed in the war. Not only were the latter rebuilt, but by 1963 the total number of churches had risen to sixty-six. The number of Catholics in the archdiocese in 1946 was 8,455; in 1967 it was 54,575. The other metropolitan dioceses had registered comparable growth so that the 108,324 baptized Catholics of 1946 had become 344,343 in 1968.[3]

There are, however, various problems faced by the church in spite of this relatively rapid growth. Like the Protestants, the Catholics, apart from the larger Nagasaki area, win their faithful chiefly from the middle classes, notably the white-collar groups of society. And even in Nagasaki there are serious causes for concern. In terms of faithfulness to the traditional practices of the church, attendance at Sunday mass, and reception of the sacraments, the Catholics of *Kirishitan* descent, who now constitute about one-third of the total Catholic population, manifest an unusually high level of spiritual zeal. Catholics, however,

[2] Van Hecken, *The Catholic Church in Japan Since 1959*, pp. 95-101.
[3] *The Japan Missionary Bulletin*, XXII/9 (October, 1968), 594-599.

seem more mobile than most groups in the fluid labor market of contemporary Japan, and increasing numbers of Nagasaki Catholics migrate to great industrial centers in northern Kyūshū and in Honshū. Doubt has even been raised as to whether these communities can exist as sociological units for more than two or three generations. Since the Catholic Church, like the Protestant, is physically accessible to less than half of the population and the psychological barriers between Christian faith and these millions are still formidable for most, missionary strategists are greatly concerned to extend the church's approach to wider sections of the populace.[4]

2

When the Religious Bodies Law was rescinded by the Allied occupation "Bill of Rights" in October, 1945, the former legal structure of the Catholic Church in Japan ceased to exist. To take its place the ordinaries of Japan established on November 28, 1945 the National Catholic Committee in Japan, which is the legal corporation of the church in the empire. The director of its administrative council is Peter Cardinal Doi Tatsuo, the ranking prelate of Japan. This committee is to administer the decisions of the annual meetings of the ordinaries (diocesan bishops) in April and of the religious superiors (of the orders) in October. Its various departments supervise the work of the missionaries as well as of the secular clergy, but in keeping with traditional practice much local freedom and initiative are allowed.

Mention should also be made in this context of the development of diplomatic relationships between Japan and the Vatican. An apostolic delegation had been officially established in December, 1916, but strong opposition especially from Buddhist quarters prevented Japan from sending diplomatic representation to the Vatican. On February 23, 1952, however, the Japanese government officially announced that it had established a legation at the Vatican, and on the same day the Holy See raised the status of its delegation in Tokyo to that of inter-

---

[4] Cf. Spae, *Catholicism in Japan,* pp. 30-40.

nunciature. In 1958 the rank of the Japanese minister to the Vatican, Tsuruoka Senjin, a Catholic, was raised to that of ambassador, and in turn the apostolic legation in Tokyo became an embassy.[5]

Under this administrative structure the Catholic Church in Japan has undertaken since 1945 a new range and degree of activities. In the area of literary activity and publications we note such energetic zeal that a Japanese Protestant affirmed in 1958 that while Protestant publications as a whole were double or more in quantity, in certain fields, "such as philosophy, apologetics, law, literature, etc. Catholic publications excel those of Protestants both in quantity and quality."[6] There are more than fifty Catholic publishers in Japan at the present time.

An important development in postwar literary work is the heightened activity in Bible translation. The final volume of a translation of the entire Old Testament in the literary style was published by the Franciscans of Sapporo in 1959, four years later, however, than the publication of the whole Bible in a colloquial version by the Japan Bible Society (Protestant) in 1955. Translation into colloquial language, a necessity in contemporary Japan, was begun by several scholars from different orders collaborating under the leadership of Bernadine Schneider, O.F.M. The Catholic group cooperates closely with Protestant scholars and participated officially in the Bible Translators' Seminar held at Hachiōji from August 15 to September 2, 1966 under the auspices of the United Bible Societies. Great hope exists that the Catholic Church may help prepare a joint Japanese translation of the Bible.[7]

Catholics are also more active in the area of audio-visual media, but as yet their range does not come near that of the

[5] Cf. Van Hecken, op. cit., pp. 269-273.

[6] Spae, op. cit., p. 55. Cf. Kobayashi Yoshio, "Katorikku Shingakusha toshite no Iwashita Sōichi Shi," in Ishihara, Nihon no Shingaku (1962 section), pp. 124-127. Sawada Kazuo, "Nihon Katorikku no Shingaku Gyōseki," in Ishihara, op. cit. (1963 section), p. 117.

[7] Bernadine Schneider, "The Hachiōji Bible Translators' Seminar," The Japan Missionary Bulletin, XX/11 (November, 1966), 709-711. Cf. T. S. Miyauchi, B. Schneider, "Towards a Common Bible," The Japan Christian Yearbook 1968, pp. 175-182.

Protestant AVACO, sponsored by the NCC. Rather extensive use, however, is made of local radio stations, and in television one regularly scheduled Catholic program is broadcasted twice monthly from an Ōsaka station, YTV.

Catholic educational institutions became very popular in the first ten or more years after the war, and while Catholics, like the Protestants, have experienced relatively more difficulty in Christian work since 1955, the press of students to enter Catholic schools is still very great. In some university departments, particularly in foreign languages, the ratio of applicants to those accepted has been as many as twenty to one, a phenomenon unknown in prewar years. Students are attracted by the international atmosphere of Catholic schools; their parents are impressed by the moral education given as well as by the adherence to older intellectual disciplines. One should also frankly note that the reputation of Catholic education, especially that of girls, has been greatly enhanced by the fact that the wife of the crown prince was educated in the Catholic Sacred Heart (*Seishin*) University in Tokyo. This school together with Sophia (*Jōchi*) University in Tokyo and *Nanzan* in Nagoya are the three largest Catholic universities in Japan, and all enjoy excellent reputations.

Most of the eighty-five religious orders of women in Japan conduct educational institutions, and this accounts in part for the larger number of girls' schools in the total of 769 Catholic educational establishments (including kindergartens). The heaviest concentration is in the metropolitan areas of Tokyo and Ōsaka. There are still ten times as many students in Protestant universities as in Catholic, but Catholics have become increasingly active in elementary and secondary education. From 1953 to 1964 the total enrollment in all Catholic schools more than doubled, rising from 91,201 to 218,330.[8] The importance of this trend for the future can be seen in the fact that many yearly baptisms of adults come from the student class.

In the postwar structure of theological education the various

---

[8] Nicholas Luhmer, "Catholic Schools in Japan 1964/1965," *The Japan Missionary Bulletin*, XIX/4 (May, 1965), 247-254. Cf. H. Hellweg, "Catholic Education in Japan," *The Japan Missionary Bulletin*, XX/6, 8 (June, August, 1966), 331-340, 477-482.

minor seminaries, some new and some old, are capped by two regional or major seminaries, the older one in Tokyo and the second in Fukuoka for all the provinces in Kyūshū, which was fully completed first in 1953. Until the Second World War the missionaries of the Paris Society bore almost solely the responsibility for theological education, but after the war other orders, such as the Canadian Sulpicians in the Fukuoka seminary, as well as Japanese clergy participated in the work. The importance of the program is obvious from the fact that in no other part of the Far East has the national clergy developed as rapidly as in Japan. According to the statistics of June 30, 1968 there are 412 students in all the major seminaries of Japan, 442 secular and 271 religious Japanese priests and 228 lay brothers. These figures, however, must be compared with the 1968 statistics of 6,174 ordained and licensed Japanese ministers of the Protestant churches, a figure which in proportion to the 496,948 Protestant church members of the same year represents probably the highest ratio of clergy to laity of any nation in the world. The picture of Catholic vocations, on the other hand, must include the extraordinary number of Japanese religious, especially women, which, as Joseph J. Spae avers, is "nothing short of marvelous and unique in the Catholic Church."[9] As of 1968 the number of Japanese women in religious orders was 4,984, and they are augmented by an additional 1,048 foreign women religious. The number of foreign priests, however, is 1,191, nearly twice the total of Japanese clergy.[10] This proportion of Japanese and foreign clergy, however, is more than reversed in the Protestant churches, especially in the *Nihon Kirisuto Kyōdan,* the largest denomination.

This large reservoir of religious workers enables the Catholic Church to carry on its wide range of activities. In the schools less than 20 percent of the teachers and employees are religious, but in the institutions of social welfare, which have greatly multiplied since the war,[11] the proportion of religious

[9] Spae, *Catholicism in Japan,* p. 68.

[10] *The Japan Missionary Bulletin,* XXII/9 (October, 1968), 594-599.

[11] There were in 1968 a total of thirty-five Catholic hospitals in Japan, twenty-three dispensaries, twenty-five homes for the aged, sixty orphanages, 113 day nurseries, and ten institutions for handicapped children.

is far higher. Catholic lay men and women, however, are increasingly enlisted especially in the welfare works of the church. The Society of St. Vincent de Paul has over one hundred and twenty chapters with some three thousand members who make visitation of the poor a special mission.

The church continues to guide and nourish the life of its laity through confraternities and sodalities. The Sodality of the Living Rosary was introduced among the *Kirishitan* of Nagasaki shortly after communications were reestablished, as was the Confraternity of the Scapular. The Paris Society missionaries particularly encouraged devotion to Mary as Our Lady of Lourdes and to the Immaculate Conception. The most widely circulated of Japanese Catholic magazines is *The Knight of the Immaculate Mother,* which is notably an organ of this form of religious devotion. In the postwar years, however, relatively more variety of devotional life is to be found in the church in Japan.

Properly to be included in the category of lay activity is that of the catechists. Several new schools for catechists were opened after the war in Niigata, Nagoya, the Gotō Islands, Ōsaka and elsewhere. These workers play an important role in the catechetical instruction of children and adults, often serving as invaluable agents of communication between laity and priests. In 1962 there were 779 catechists, of whom 300 were men and 479 women.

Various lay associations of Catholic Action were formed after the beginning of this century, including associations of Catholic youth and women. Catholic Action was reestablished after World War II, and one of its important subsidiary organizations is the JOC movement of young Catholic workers who include in their apostolate efforts to improve the social as well as economic conditions of Japanese workers. Many Catholics participate in the Boy Scout movement. Various societies of Catholics exist in the professions and the arts. An important new kind of organization is that of the Neighborhood Associations, which makes use of the ancient Japanese term *(tonari gumi)* to enlist as many Christians as possible in a parish to participate in small cell-groups for mutual encouragement and a more effective lay apostolate.

3

To know something of the ethos and direction of spiritual movement in the Roman Catholic Church in Japan at the present time mention must be made of two important phenomena. One is the growing interfaith dialogue and cooperation among Christians in the wake of the Second Vatican Council. We noted the cooperation developing among biblical scholars, but the range of dialogue and cooperative events extends far beyond this area. The *Japan Missionary Bulletin,* which was the bilingual organ of the National Catholic Committee and the Committee of the Apostolate but after 1961 became an independent publication, is also a highly significant channel for interfaith communications and frequently carries important articles by Protestant church leaders and theologians. On March 6-9, 1967, Bishop Itō Shōjirō participated by invitation as a Catholic observer in a consultation on Joint Action for Mission held under the auspices of the National Christian Council of Japan. Fr. Joseph J. Spae, editor of the *Japan Missionary Bulletin,* was one of three Vatican-appointed observers at the First Faith and Order Conference held under the auspices of the East Asia Christian Conference in Hong Kong October 26 to November 3, 1966. These events are representative of a new climate of spiritual understanding and amity in the Christian church in Japan and give the greatest promise for the future.[12]

A second important phenomenon is related to the spirit and documents of the Second Vatican Council but is also to be noted among Protestant Christians.[13] It consists of a new attitude which attempts to understand and appreciate non-Christian religious traditions not only as phenomena worthy of

[12] Cf. Spae, *op. cit.,* pp. 70-71; Itō Shōjirō, "NCC no Senkyō Kyōryokukaigi ni Manekarete," *The Japan Missionary Bulletin,* XXI/5 (June, 1967), 268-272. Ryōzō Hara and Paul Pfister, "Ecumenism and the Future of Christianity in Japan," *The Japan Christian Yearbook 1968,* pp. 183-189. Cf. Peter Nemeshegyi, "Fukuin ni Fusawashii Hanashiai," *Katorikku Shingaku,* II/1 (July, 1963), 208-214; Sawada Akio, "Katorikku Rutā Kan no Henkan ni tsuite," *Katorikku Shingaku,* VI/2 (November, 1967), 240-283.

[13] Cf. Richard H. Drummond, "Japan's 'New Religions' and the Christian Community," *The Christian Century,* LXXXI/50 (December 9, 1964), 1521-1523.

scientific study but also as potentially possessing religious truth and value. This means that Christian theology now considers the possibility that non-Christian religions may be instruments of the God and Father of Jesus Christ to reveal his will and save his people. It is to reckon with the possibility that non-Christian religions may in themselves have authentic significance in terms of the history of salvation as the latter term is generally understood by Christian theologians. The problem is exceedingly complex and requires historical study of the religions in depth as well as spiritual sympathy and theological acumen. The extent, however, to which attention has been given to this problem in recent years is indeed remarkable and is also highly suggestive of the climate of thought which the church in Japan will manifest in the future.[14]

---

[14] The literature on the subject is considerable, but the reader is invited to peruse the ten or more articles on the theme in *The Japan Missionary Bulletin* in volumes XVIII-XXI. Cf. *Nihon ni okeru Kirisuto Kyō to Sho Shūkyō to no Sesshoku no Mondai, passim*.

VI

THE ORTHODOX CHURCH

THE ORTHODOX CHURCH

1

THE RUSSIAN ORTHODOX MISSION TO JAPAN HAS BEEN called the most spectacular achievement in the long history of Russian missionary work.[1] Among the several reasons which may be cited to justify this bold assertion, the person and methods of the pioneer missionary, Ivan Kasatkin, better known in Japan as Père Nicolai, assume a primary place. *De jure* the Orthodox Church of Japan is still a mission church; it is not yet counted among the autocephalous national churches of the Orthodox family. *De facto,* however, it has long possessed such independence and such a distinct life that it at least deserves the designation of "younger church" in the best sense of this word.[2] The unique aspect, however, of the Russian missionary activity in Japan, in comparison with its counterparts elsewhere, consists in its almost complete separation from Russian political aims or interests. Nicolai made this separation a basic principle of his work and saw his strength therein. "L'oubli absolu de toute politique et la prédication de la pure orthodoxie catholique — voice le principe de notre travail, et là est notre force."[3]

---

[1] Serge Bolshakoff, *The Foreign Missions of the Russian Orthodox Church,* p. 75.

[2] Only in the person of its bishop did it depend, until the Russian Revolution, upon the "Most Holy Governing Synod of the Church of All the Russias." Cf. Eugene Smirnoff, *Russian Orthodox Missions,* p. 81.

[3] In Josef Glazik, *die Russisch-Orthodoxe Heidenmission seit Peter dem Grossen,* pp. 178-179.

Nicolai's policy is particularly significant in the context of the relatively long history of Russian attempts to establish diplomatic and trade relations with Japan and of the border disputes between the two countries in the nineteenth and twentieth centuries. As early as 1727 the adventurous missionary to Kamchatka, Ivan Kozrevsky, received an award from the czar for his services of "investigation" of the Japanese empire. There were various though slight contacts in subsequent years, but the interest of Russia in her Far Eastern neighbor is seen in the fact that the Russian Vice-Admiral Putyatin entered Nagasaki harbor in command of four warships in 1853, where he found Commodore Matthew C. Perry and his squadron of four ships before Perry had made his first trip to Edo. Also of interest is the fact that the first self-disclosure of a Japanese *Kirishitan* to a Westerner was to the chaplain of the Russian ship *Diana* when the latter was anchored at Shimoda in 1854.[4]

The Treaty of Shimoda, concluded in February, 1855, opened the harbors of Nagasaki and Shimoda to Russian trade. Shortly thereafter Hakodate on the northern island of the Hokkaidō was opened as a third harbor for trade. Russia chose this last port as the site of its consulate, where according to current custom a chaplain served as part of the consular staff. The first chaplain had apparently belonged to the fleet of Putyatin, but as a result of ill health he was compelled to leave after having served in Hakodate less than a year. Putyatin requested a successor, and the man chosen by the St. Petersburg Ecclesiastical Academy was Ivan Kasatkin, a young man of twenty-four, devout and with strong missionary concerns. Kasatkin had already developed a keen interest in Japan through his readings, and although the post offered him was no more than that of chaplain, he later acknowledged that he had gone to Japan with fully conscious intent to serve as a missionary to the extent that circumstances might permit.[5]

Kasatkin became a monk with the monastic name of Nicolai and received ordination as a priest. After a journey that lasted almost a year he arrived in Hakodate on June 2, 1861. Not long

---

[4] Otis Cary, *A History of Christianity in Japan*, vol. 1, pp. 375-376.
[5] Glazik, *op. cit.*, p. 180.

after this, Nicolai was visited by the great Russian missionary to the Yakuts and the Kamchadals, the Metropolitan Innocent Popov-Veniaminov, who urged him to devote himself to an intensive study of the Chinese and Japanese languages. Nicolai took this advice seriously; his studies helped him not only to become proficient in Japanese but to gain the understanding of the people and their culture which enabled the Orthodox Mission to become quickly indigenized and to raise up Japanese leaders of distinction. This understanding, coupled with Nicolai's remarkable executive ability and undoubted dedication, also explains the sustained personal influence of the priest-monk during his long life in Japan.[6]

The story of the first converts to Orthodox Christianity reads like the most engaging of adventure novels. The opposition to the faith and the dangers incident to its adoption by Japanese were no less in the Hokkaidō than on the other islands. One of the first converts, a *samurai* by the name of Sawabe, had come from Tosa in the island of Shikoku and married the daughter of a Shintō priest. After the latter's death he succeeded to his position, but he was in fact more akin in spirit to the swash-buckling *rōnin* of the time, many of whom were then to be found in Hakodate. Sawabe first went to Nicolai with intent to kill him if he could not overpower him in argument. Such, however, was the winsome manner and power of persuasion of Nicolai that by the end of this first meeting Sawabe asked to come again for further instruction in the Christian faith. It was not until 1868, however, that he and two friends were baptized secretly in the chapel of the consulate as a young Russian Christian kept watch outside.

The three men, baptized as Paul Sawabe, John Sakai, a physician, and Jacob Urano, had perhaps become Christians for reasons as much political as religious, but they remained faithful amid the many dangers which they faced during a series of harrowing adventures. These men witnessed to their families and throughout Sendai and the province of Rikuzen (Miyagi Prefecture), and saw the beginning of Christian communities in this area of northern Honshū. In consequence,

---

[6] Cf. Cary, *op. cit.*, p. 414.

when Nicolai made a trip to Russia a year later, the number of baptized Christians was already twelve, of inquirers twenty-five. In 1873 there were twenty Christian families in Sendai and about a hundred other families in which one or more persons were believers.[7]

The purpose of Nicolai's trip to Russia in 1869-1870 was to secure from the Holy Synod of the Russian Orthodox Church the formal establishment of a Japanese mission. He felt that a great change was in process, and that the time was soon to come when open evangelistic work would be possible. He felt that his post as consular chaplain was too restrictive for the missionary activity that he anticipated. Nicolai's request was at first provisionally granted, and then the Russian Orthodox Japan Mission was officially established on April 4, 1871, under the formal supervision of the bishop of Kamchatka.[8] Nicolai was made the head of the mission and consecrated as archimandrite. According to the plan presented stations were to be opened in Tokyo, Kyōto, Nagasaki, and Hakodate. The Russian personnel were to consist of Nicolai as archimandrite, three hieromonachs, and a catechist. But only one priest was able to accompany Nicolai on his return, and he became ill on the journey and returned to Russia only two months after arriving in Japan. Nicolai remained the only missionary until the coming of the priest Anatolius in late 1871.

Nicolai had already thought deeply about the methodology of mission in Japan, and evidently one of the reasons for the favorable reception of his plan in Russia was the set of rules for the proposed mission which he had already prepared before his departure from Japan. Since these rules constituted the principles of operation for the subsequent missionary activity of the next half-century and more, I shall cite at this point some of the most significant.

Nicolai stressed the importance of learning the language in its literary as well as colloquial forms so that not only verbal communication might be effected but that the Bible, liturgical books, and even primers for children might be gracefully trans-

[7] *Ibid.*, pp. 377-398.
[8] Bolshakoff, *op. cit.*, p. 77.

lated and form the beginning of an indigenous Christian literature. From the first the missionaries should seek out those among
the believers who seem qualified to become the primary agents
of proclamation, the catechists, and spare neither time, effort
nor material means in their training. The financial support of
the catechists should be provided by the mission, and stress was
laid upon the importance of witness in their own household,
among their relatives and other homes.

Inquirers should be carefully instructed, the young taught
the basic truths of the faith and the main prayers, while older
people should be further enabled to give reasons for their faith
as they have opportunity to witness to others. The missionary
should make a careful examination of all who request baptism
and baptize no one until he be fully assured of the firmness of
his Christian convictions. The missionaries are especially obli-
gated to exercise close pastoral care over the newly baptized.
They must be true shepherds of the flock of Christ.

Nicolai was particularly concerned for the education of the
children of believers in the Christian spirit as well as truth. He
anticipated that the catechists would serve as helpers in this
area, at least until circumstances permitted the erection of
schools. He hoped to train some to be catechists and others
as school teachers or interpreters. Those best qualified should
be trained for the priesthood in a seminary in Japan or sent
to an academy in Russia.[9]

Nicolai stressed that there should be two kinds of instruc-
tional meetings of Christians. One should be that of the
catechists or evangelists, together with others who already knew
the basic doctrines of the faith. They would meet twice a week,
the catechists taking turns in conducting the meetings. The
purpose shall be to pursue further study, particularly to read
and explain the New Testament. The second kind of meeting
is for those, whether men, women or children, who are beginning
the study of Christian teaching. The catechists shall divide them
into classes and explain to them the Apostles' Creed, the Lord's
Prayer and the Ten Commandments. These meetings shall also
be held twice a week. The catechists shall also be concerned to

---

[9] Glazik, *op. cit.*, pp. 181-183.

share what is learned in either kind of meeting with those who are unable to attend. They shall go about the city every day trying to win new inquirers and go to the homes to instruct those who are not able to attend meetings.

The similarities of this methodology with that of the early Jesuits are apparent, but note should be taken of Nicolai's emphasis upon teaching the New Testament as a whole, and indeed his concern for translation and dissemination of the entire Bible. Furthermore, the catechists were to be organized as a deliberative body. On Sundays the catechists of a district were to meet at the house of the priest and report as well as consult and decide future plans. The structure of the hierarchy was firm, but the hand of authority was not heavy. Also Nicolai did not delay in ordaining Japanese as priests. The number of Russian missionaries was always purposely kept small; there were never more than four in the mission at any one time.[10]

These rules reveal not only the mind and quality of spirit of Nicolai; they also give us insight into the atmosphere that pervaded and characterized the work of the Orthodox Mission and Church in Japan throughout the first half-century of its life. They tell us why Nicolai, bearing no more than these rules and plans and the singular purity of his dedication, was able to gain so quickly and maintain so long with no appreciable change the fullest support of the Holy Synod. At this time he was asked to become the bishop of Peking, but he refused the offer, saying he had no desire to be a bishop and was too concerned with the work in Japan to leave it for another country. Nicolai gained the confidence of many laymen on his first visit back to Russia, and a considerable number promised him financial support for the mission. Ten thousand rubles were brought to him by a merchant of Moscow who, when asked his name, answered only "God knows."[11]

The spirit and methodology of Nicolai were later admirably summed up in the following words of Sergius Tichomirov, who became his coadjutor bishop in 1908:

---

[10] Cary, *op. cit.*, pp. 383-384; Glazik, *op. cit.*, p. 188; Sakurai, *Nihon Kirisuto Kyōshi*, pp. 396-399.
[11] Cary, *op. cit.*, p. 390.

"Moyen d'évangelisation: prédication dans les familles, sans ce fruit des manifestations et des conférences; l'apostolat est positif (non apologétique): 'Je suis le Christ; crois si tu veux!,' sans polémique, sans critique aucune des autres confessions; sans attaque même contre le bouddhisme et le sintoisme: le Christ lui-même-comble de Vérité-n'accaparait les coeurs que par la paix!"[12]

2

After his return to Hakodate in February, 1871, Nicolai sent a letter to Sendai asking that those interested and able should come to him for further instruction. A number came and were lodged in a building belonging to the consulate, where they were formed into a kind of school. Nicolai instructed them in the faith and also taught the Russian language to those who desired. At this time he also worked on an adaptation of the Chinese New Testament to make it more readable to educated Japanese. The school grew with the addition of further arrivals from Sendai and of others in Hakodate, including Paul Sawabe and John Sakai. From among these men Nicolai found his most valuable fellow workers, Sawabe being perhaps the most effective. In 1871 fifteen Japanese were added to the church, and in the following year the number of inquirers came to five hundred, of whom fifty were baptized.

Growth of this extent could hardly remain unnoticed by the authorities, and in February, 1872, Paul Sawabe and eight other Christians were arrested and jailed in Sendai, where he had gone as a preacher. A number of others were subjected to thorough investigation. One hundred twenty persons were remanded to the surveillance of their relatives, who were made responsible for their conduct according to the historic method of *Kirishitan-aratame*. Among those examined by the authorities were several children, who "astonished the examiners by asserting their willingness to suffer punishment for the sake of Christ." Persecution broke out in Hakodate soon thereafter, and

[12] Glazik, *op. cit.*, p. 183.

Governor Kuroda had three catechists arrested and took other steps to harass the community.[13]

Before these events occurred, however, Sawabe had urged Nicolai to move his center of operations to Tokyo, saying that Hakodate was too far removed from the major currents of Japanese life to be a satisfactory place for work intended to affect the whole nation. Nicolai acknowledged the wisdom of this advice but delayed its execution for a few months owing to the pressure of work in Hakodate. He was supervising translations and with the aid of his students printed copies of the Lord's Prayer and of manuals of doctrine. He also prepared a Russo-Japanese dictionary, which his students copied by hand and which served as the sole dictionary of these two languages until one was published in 1881 by the Ministry of Education.

Sawabe was sent to Tokyo in November, 1871, to arrange to move Nicolai to the capital. Because of his social position and contacts, Sawabe was able to meet high officials of the government and learned of the swirl of opinions regarding the posture Japan ought to adopt toward Christianity now that the government had largely committed itself to the policy of Westernization particularly with regard to science and technology. Some of his acquaintances in high office even expressed their personal willingness to have Christianity publicly taught. Sawabe concluded that favorable opportunities for evangelism were at hand and asked to return to Sendai for evangelistic work there, while his Christian friend, Ono, who had come to Tokyo on private business, carried on with the arrangements for the coming of Nicolai.

After the arrival of the hieromonach Anatolius in Hakodate, Nicolai committed to his care the community of fifty Christians there and in January, 1872, set out for Tokyo with a catechist and interpreter.[14] He was subsequently able to lease, in the name of the Russian legation, a large piece of ground on Surugadai, a hill located in Kanda, a central and populous part of Tokyo; and settled down to a regime of teaching Russian by

---

[13] Cary, *op. cit.*, pp. 395-396, 398-402.

[14] The term hieromonach refers to a monk who has also been ordained as a priest. For an account of the early work in Tokyo and the provinces, see Sakurai, *op. cit.*, pp. 402-416.

day and Christian doctrine at night to those who were willing to come.

In the meantime Ono returned to Tokyo after the persecution in Sendai had broken out and sought in various ways to have the central government intervene. He was able to secure an interview with the Minister for Foreign Affairs; and through friends he got Fukuzawa Yukichi to plead his case on the grounds that at this time the persecution of Christians would bring disrepute upon Japan in the eyes of foreigners. Some *samurai* from Sendai who were in Tokyo communicated with Guido Verbeck, who was then serving as an advisor to the Council of State and who appealed to Ōkuma Shigenobu and other ministers of the government. The consequence was that when the prefectural officials presented their report, orders were sent to Sendai to release the prisoners. Those in Hakodate were released on May 1, 1872, after an imprisonment of about two months.[15] This was the end of all serious persecution of the Orthodox Mission, and, after the decree which led to the removal of the anti-Christian edict from the public notice-boards was issued on February 10, 1873, the Orthodox Church had the same freedom of work allowed, even if tacitly, to other Christian groups.

During his first year in Tokyo Nicolai revealed the scope of his plans by opening a seminary to educate priests and a school to train catechists. The liturgy was from this point on celebrated exclusively in the Japanese language. A translation commission of nine was made responsible for continued development of a Japanese religious literature. Even though the majority of students first came to learn Russian, a number asked for instruction in the Christian faith, and on September 24, 1872, ten persons were baptized. This service was performed in secrecy, as much hostility and suspicion still existed in Tokyo during this year. Nicolai later learned that several of his students were government spies, but the government at this time of transition found no reason to take action, and in December, 1872, another ten persons were baptized.

Preaching places which were opened in several parts of Tokyo

---

[15] Cary, *op. cit.*, pp. 397, 401.

were led by those who were receiving instruction from Nicolai. Some of these men also made visits to Nagoya, Kyōto, Ōsaka, and other cities and reported a favorable reception everywhere. By the end of 1874 the Orthodox Church in Japan numbered three hundred baptized members and several hundred inquirers or adherents. The community in Tokyo consisted of eighty-five persons. With the addition of two hieromonachs from Kiev the number of missionaries was four. In Hakodate, therefore, it was possible to open a boys' and a girls' school.

The work of the mission, however, developed so that it was impossible for the foreign priests effectually to order the life and work of the church. Nicolai therefore made use of the form of lay representation which was legally a part of the tradition of the Orthodox Churches. He established the rule that every two years lay delegates from each congregation, however small, be sent to a Great Synod, which would be responsible, under his presidency, for discussion and resolution of the most important matters concerning both the congregations and the church as a whole. In the intervening year the clergy, who consisted of both priests and catechists, would meet to constitute a Small Synod.

The first synod of priests and catechists was summoned in May, 1874. Several days were spent in discussing the problems and opportunities of the work, and a new set of rules was drawn up. There were to be two classes of non-priestly workers, catechists and assistant catechists or mission helpers, with their duties and salaries prescribed. Changes in their location were to be decided by the Tokyo church. Catechists should appoint in each congregation under their care two or three persons to serve as local assistants, who were to spread the gospel and strengthen the flock. In accordance with the Orthodox tradition, the catechists were presumed to marry and have families; part of the responsibility of the local assistants was to care for the families of the catechists when the latter were away on missionary tours.

Local churches were expected to manage their own affairs and to contribute to the support of the catechists. It seems, however, that much of the funds for the salaries of the catechists continued to come from Russian sources. In spite of the *samurai* background of some of the early Japanese leaders, the Orthodox communities in Japan consisted almost entirely of the poor and uneducated.[16] The catechists were expected to make the service of the gospel their chief work, but the rules allowed them to use their "spare time" in gainful employment and thus, "by their industry, be an example to believers." In spite of this freedom, however, the poverty of most of the Orthodox Christians compelled the majority of the catechists to depend substantially upon the mission, that is, upon the Russian church, for much of their financial support.[17]

The first conference of clergy was held in 1874 with eight participants, although the number of catechists was already larger than this. In 1875 the first Great Synod was convened with forty persons present, the representatives of one thousand Japanese Christians scattered in numerous communities in the land. In 1875 Paul Sawabe and John Sakai both received ordination as the first Japanese Orthodox priests.

The reports of these activities aroused considerable interest in Russia. The consort of Czar Alexander II, Maria Alexandrovna, directed the Orthodox Missionary Society to give special attention and financial aid to the Japan Mission. Nicolai made wise use of this help, and in 1878 he reported the existence of five thousand Christians who were united in a hundred congregations reaching from Hakodate to Ōsaka. There were now six Japanese priests, twenty-seven catechists and fifty-one assistant catechists or helpers. The congregations were arranged in groups so that each group of eight or ten at the most could be cared for by a catechist. Recognition of the quality and extent of this work was given by the consecration of Nicolai in 1880 as titular Bishop of Reval with assignment in Tokyo. He and the mission now came under the direct super-

[16] Glazik, op. cit., p. 185.

[17] Many of the Japanese workers preferred to support themselves by their own efforts, but as they inevitably could give much less time to formal Christian work. Nicolai appealed to them and was able to persuade some to accept help from the general fund, whose source was largely Russian. Cary, op. cit., p. 409.

vision of the Holy Synod, in place of the Orthodox Missionary Society.[18]

We have little information regarding the interior life of the Orthodox Church in Japan during the following decades. Work was carried on, however, with sturdy faithfulness, and the growth of the church reflects this fact. Until the Russian Revolution the annual number of people baptized was approximately one thousand; the annual access in membership averaged about eight hundred. In 1882 the number of believers reported was 7,611, in 1890 it was 17,614, in 1900 — 25,994, in 1910 — 32,000, in 1918 — 36,618. In 1931, however, we note no more than 40,000.

The seminary and training school which Nicolai founded in Tokyo in 1873 were relatively well attended and continued to produce workers for the church. By 1890 there were eighteen priests and five deacons. In 1912, the year of Nicolai's death, the number had risen to thirty-five priests and five deacons. The number of catechists was 125 in 1890, rose to about 150 before Nicolai's death, but dropped considerably thereafter, especially after the Russian Revolution when funds were no longer available from Russia to support these workers. In 1931 the church reported only thirty catechists at work. It was possible for catechists to become priests, as we learn that in 1878 the five men who went to Vladivostok for ordination to the priesthood were all catechists.[19]

In comparison with other Christian confessions at work in Japan, the educational activity of the Orthodox Church was relatively small. Apparently not all of the schools founded continued in existence. At the outbreak of the Russo-Japanese War in 1905 there was in Tokyo, in addition to the seminary and training school for catechists, a girls' school with eighty-one pupils. Another girls' school was located in Kyōto.[20] In all there were four schools, the other two probably being institutions for boys. Small in size, these schools evidently served chiefly to educate the children of the clergy. Church schools,

---

[18] Glazik, op. cit., pp. 186-187.

[19] Cary, op. cit., p. 409. For this period cf. Sakurai, op. cit., pp. 416-424.

[20] Bolshakoff, op. cit., p. 78.

however, for the catechetical and general religious instruction of children were widespread. Reports for the year 1902 tell of 1,168 children and for 1912 of 1,250 who participated in this instruction.[21]

We hear also of women's societies which apparently existed in all the larger congregations and met monthly not only for devotional programs but to take action in behalf of orphans and the poor. They were zealous also in encouraging faltering Christians and in witnessing to those outside the faith. As early as 1873 we learn of a women's society formed in Hakodate partially to help the poor, and their example stirred the men to action. Among their gifts of that year was a sum sent to help those in Russia who were suffering the effects of a famine. In Sendai and other places Christian societies lent money, sometimes without interest, to members of the churches. In some cases money was given outright to those who could not make repayment. In 1875 when a flood caused much distress in Sanuma near Sendai, the Christians there purchased rice and, covering their faces so as not to be recognized, brought it to those in need, most of whom were non-Christian. Other instances might be given which indicate the dedication and self-sacrifice of Japanese Orthodox Christians.[22]

In 1891 Nicolai was able to consecrate the great cathedral in Tokyo in Surugadai, Kanda, a magnificent edifice of Byzantine style which was five years in building and with its splendid cupola became one of the main attractions of the city. By the year 1893 the translation commission was able to report the publication of fourteen different Orthodox theological works in Japanese. The development and expression of Japanese religious thought were furthered by the founding of three Orthodox periodicals. By 1900 there were the bimonthly official organ of the mission, Seikyō Shimpō, and two monthly journals, the Seikyō Yōwa, primarily a devotional magazine, and the Uranishiki, a periodical especially for women.[23]

[21] Glazik, op. cit., p. 190.
[22] Cary, op. cit., pp. 411-412.
[23] Glazik, op. cit., p. 191.

3

The resurgence of nationalism and anti-Christian feeling which characterized the 1890's in Japan naturally affected the life and progress of the Orthodox Church. In some ways its association with the Russian church made its position more difficult than that of other Christian communions. A number of leaders in the Japanese government, of whom the chief spokesman was Saigō Takamori, as early as 1872 were determined to force Japanese expansion in Korea; even though the experience of the Iwakura Mission was sufficient to thwart this plan, the nation was particularly sensitive to Russian imperial activities in the Far East from this time. The rivalry over hegemony in Korea led in 1895 to a temporary predominance of Russian influence in that land, and the way was prepared for the Russo-Japanese War of 1904-1905.[24]

Nicolai was now in a very difficult position. Two Russian priests who were officially attached to the Russian legation but had been helping him in the work of the mission returned to Russia. Nicolai then called a council of the clergy and leading laymen to ask their opinion. Their unanimous request was that he should remain in Japan. The greatness of the man is shown in his subsequent communications by word of mouth and pastoral letter to the Japanese Orthodox Christians. He urged them as loyal Japanese subjects to do their patriotic duty. They should pray to God for the victory of the Japanese imperial forces, thank him for victories granted and sacrifice for the needs of the war. Those who must fight, however, should do so not out of hate for the enemy but from love for their nation. "Beyond our earthly fatherland we have a heavenly one. Men belong to this without distinction of nationality, for all men are in the same way children of the heavenly Father and brothers of one another. This our fatherland is the Church, whose members we all are in like fashion and in whom the children of the heavenly Father form one family in fact. Therefore I do not separate myself from you, Brothers and Sisters, and I remain in your family as in my own."[25]

---

[24] Cf. Borton, *Japan's Modern Century*, pp. 85-87; 216-219.

[25] Glazik, *op. cit.*, p. 192.

Nicolai resolved to take part no longer in the public prayers in the cathedral because "until now I prayed for the victory and peace of the Japanese Emperor, but now in case of war I can not pray as a Russian subject that our native country should be conquered by an enemy. I have, as you also have, an obligation to my country, therefore I am glad to see that you realize your obligation to your country."[26] Nicolai retained, however, his episcopal functions, and although he devoted himself all the more to the translation of the liturgy and kept himself as much as possible from the public eye, he continued without stint in the work of his office.

The Japanese government responded to this conduct in like spirit. It had already given assurance upon outbreak of the war that Russian residents in Japan would be given the full protection of Japanese law. It called upon all Japanese subjects to refrain from showing hostility to Russian civilians. And after Nicolai's pastoral letter of February 11, 1904, the Ministry of Education gave public assurance that there would be no restrictions upon the freedom of religion in Japan as a consequence of the war. Indeed, the government put the personal work of Nicolai under its special protection for the duration of the war and allowed him and the clergy of the Orthodox Church unusual freedom in extending pastoral care to the 73,000 Russian prisoners of war who were quartered in Japan. The War Department gave permission for Japanese priests with an understanding of Russian to be sent to all the towns where prisoners were held, and temporary chapels were erected within the camps. Nicolai supervised giving to the prisoners 68,000 copies of the Gospels in Russian and several thousand copies of prayerbooks and other religious and general literature. Winter clothes were also given to the sick.[27]

During the period of hostilities accessions to the Orthodox Church dropped greatly in number, but the growth of the

---

[26] Cary, op. cit., p. 418.

[27] Ibid., pp. 419-420. The gratitude of the Russian prisoners for these services was warm and in part concretely expressed. One cannot escape, however, melancholy reflection on the fact that these examples of civilized behavior became far rarer in the harsher atmosphere of later decades in the twentieth century, regardless of the countries concerned.

church, though hindered, was not stopped. A few years after the war with Japan the number of baptisms climbed to its former high figure. The financial difficulties, however, experienced by Russia after the war led to a considerable drop in the receipts of the Orthodox Missionary Society. This led to less support for the Japan church and the number of catechists and students aided had to be reduced in 1907.

The great services of Nicolai were recognized by his being raised to the rank of archbishop by the Holy Synod in 1906. In 1908 Sergius Tichomirov became his coadjutor bishop with residence in Kyōto. Nicolai was able to participate in the celebration of the fiftieth year of his missionary activity in 1911. He died shortly thereafter on February 16, 1912, and was succeeded by Sergius as head of the church in Japan. At this time the statistical report gave the number of Orthodox Christians as 33,017, who worshiped in 266 congregations and were served by thirty-five Japanese priests, twenty-two deacons and 106 catechists. The number of seminarians was eighty-two.

The life and life-fruits of Nicolai compel us to recognize him as one of the greatest missionaries of the modern era. In accordance with Orthodox tradition he respected highly the language and cultural traditions of the people among whom he served. He respected the people and loved them as persons. He went beyond the common traditions of Orthodoxy in freeing his work to an extraordinary extent from the political aims and interests of his homeland. His apostleship was remarkably non-polemical for the day; he was in singular fashion an apostle of peace among men. His method of evangelization was concentrated upon the family, and he stressed above all the raising up of national workers and the indigenization of the church, even as he urged it to remember its distinctive association with the Kingdom of God.

A Protestant contemporary of Nicolai relates that in places where both Orthodox and Protestant clergy were working, their relations were cordial even if not intimate. The chief cause of friction was that converts passed over from one church to another. In the case of removal from the Orthodox Church, the severe terms recited in the ban of excommunication "were not calculated to promote harmony." An instance is given, however, of the finest kind of harmony in the city of Wakayama, where thirteen workers, including four missionaries, of the Anglican, Orthodox and Presbyterian Churches had an association which met once a month. The church members also cooperated in the form of an alliance that sponsored public lectures once a month. Effective cooperation was achieved, among other goals, in a vigorous campaign to oppose the introduction of licensed prostitution into Wakayama Prefecture.[28]

4

The Russian Revolution had a devastating effect on the life of the Orthodox Church in Japan. If Nicolai had taken unusual steps to insure the predominance of nationals in the clergy of the church, he had failed to take comparable measures to secure their independence from Russian financial support. With the Revolution the heretofore rich flow of gifts from Russia completely ceased, with the result that the seminary and other educational institutions had to be closed and the number of clergy, especially of catechists, sharply reduced.

Bishop Sergius was elevated to the rank of archbishop in 1923 and made a metropolitan a few years later. The great earthquake of 1923, however, which particularly damaged the Tokyo-Yokohama area, brought a further setback to the work of the Orthodox Church. Among the church buildings destroyed was the great cathedral in Tokyo, which was finally rebuilt and consecrated in 1930 as a result of great sacrifices from the Japanese members. In 1931, however, of the former 174 church buildings there were left only thirteen consecrated churches and fifty-five chapels. Archbishop Sergius reported in 1931 the number of believers as forty thousand but acknowledged that of these only fifteen thousand "were imbued with the missionary spirit," that is, could be counted on as faithful, practicing Christians and church members. There were at this time thirty parishes with thirty-two priests, five deacons and thirty catechists. Relatively substantial church structures were to be found

---

[28] *Ibid.*, pp. 416-417.

in Hakodate, Sendai, Shirakawa, Takasaki, Nagoya, Kyōto and a few other places.[29]

The Orthodox Church in Japan had other problems following the Revolution. In spite of the ecclesiastical difficulties in Russia at this time, Sergius remained loyal to the Moscow patriarchate. This tie was formally renewed in 1927, although the relationship practically amounted to little more than an occasional exchange of letters with the patriarch Sergius Stragorodsky, who himself had served as a missionary in Japan for two periods. Even this slight tie, however, occasioned some offense, especially after the Japanese-Manchurian incident in 1932 and subsequent Japanese expansion in Manchuria and China.

Mounting pressures from the government and the nationalist spirit of the time created an even more difficult situation for the church in the late 1930's. Together with the other Christian confessions the Orthodox Church was compelled to prepare a new church constitution and submit it to the government for ratification. Of the 171 articles which the church submitted in April, 1940, the government confirmed only 159 and considerably altered the remainder. As Sergius felt himself unable in good conscience to accept the emendations, he resigned his office as metropolitan. He transferred the property of the Orthodox Mission to the national church and proposed three Japanese candidates for his post. He appointed the Japanese protopriest Arsenius Iwazawa to act as vicar-capitular until the first Japanese bishop could be elected. The Japanese national Synod (Sobor), however, which met on September 21, 1940, in Tokyo, declared its independence of the Moscow patriarchate but was unable to agree to the extent of electing a bishop.

The new church institution was approved by the Japanese government in the spring of 1941. According to its rules only Japanese could be bishops or priests in the church, and the election of bishops and some other officials had to be confirmed by the government. On the basis of this constitution the na-

---

[29] Bolshakoff, op. cit., pp. 78-79. In addition to the number of buildings cited above, the church also rented twenty houses for public worship. Cf. Sakurai, op. cit., pp. 424-432; Hiyane, Nihon Kirisuto Kyōshi, pp. 356-357.

tional Synod shortly thereafter elected the protopriest John Ono to be the first Japanese bishop of the Orthodox Church. Ono was then over seventy and had spent the last fifteen years of his ministry as a parish priest in Tokyo. As a married man, however, he could not be consecrated as bishop in that state. His wife then agreed to take vows as a nun and he himself became a monk. They both made their professions on the same day in Harbin. Ono was then consecrated on April 7, 1941, in Harbin by the Metropolitan Meletius of Manchuria, the primate of the Far East, taking the name of Nicolai in commemoration of the great founder of the Japanese Orthodox Church. The metropolitan and other bishops of Harbin were not under the jurisdiction of the patriarchate of Moscow but constituted a synodal group of bishops under the patriarchate of Constantinople.

After the entry of Japan into the Second World War, Russians resident in Japan were interned, the former Metropolitan Sergius among them. He died on August 10, 1945, shortly after his release from prison.

After the war Bishop Nicolai worked to restore relations with the patriarchate of Moscow, and on April 3, 1946, the national Synod, which consisted of both lay and clerical delegates from the entire church, took action to that end. A part of the church, however, was evidently opposed to this action from the beginning, and the protopriest Samuel Ugawa convened a new national Synod on April 5 and was apparently elected by the body as president of the Japanese consistory, that is, as presiding priest. The situation was further complicated by the interest taken in the actions of the church by both the Soviet diplomatic corps in Tokyo and the American occupational authorities.[30] Most of the church, however, perhaps increasingly with the passage of time, preferred not to be under the jurisdiction of the Moscow patriarchate, and by action of the Synod held in July, 1946, requested through SCAP that a bishop be appointed for the Orthodox Church of Japan by the *Sobor* of North American bishops. Action was taken by the latter body

---

[30] Iglehart, *A Century of Protestant Christianity in Japan*, p. 336. Cf. Alexander A. Bogolepov, *Toward an American Orthodox Church*, pp. 77, 100.

on October 31, 1946, whereby Metropolitan Theophilus (Pash-kovsky) of New York assumed jurisdiction over the Japanese church and Bishop Benjamin (Basaliga) of Pittsburgh was appointed as temporary bishop.

An extraordinary Synod of the Japanese church was then held on January 10, 1947, and it requested the North American metropolitan to make Benjamin the regular bishop of the Orthodox Church in Japan and to include the Japanese church within the spiritual jurisdiction of the Metropolitanate of New York. This request was granted by action of the *Sobor* of North American bishops in November, 1947.

Bishop Nicolai, however, claimed all ecclesiastical rights for himself and the Moscow patriarchate and entered legal suit for possession of the cathedral and all other property of the church.[31] He was not able to win the case; and at the time of what may be called an actual split in the church in 1948, he had only four priests on his side. In April, 1954, however, he returned to the larger fellowship together with three of the original four priests.

Benjamin served as presiding bishop of the Orthodox Church of Japan from 1947 to 1953. He was followed by Bishop Ireney, who served from 1953 to 1961, and then by Bishop Nikon from 1961 to 1962. The incumbent, Bishop Vladimir, who formerly labored with distinction as a missionary in the Aleutian Is-lands, was consecrated bishop on November 1, 1962. He is the sole foreigner among the Orthodox clergy in Japan, and his wise and irenic leadership has been important in the unification and renewal of the church.

The Orthodox Church in Japan is perhaps not yet flourish-ing, but evidence exists within the past few years of a renewal of life and activity. The formal membership is said to be about twenty-four thousand, but there appears to be a strong loyalty among its approximately ten thousand active members.[32] There are thirty parishes with resident priests and sixty-five chapels without clerical leadership. In addition to the thirty priests

---

[31] Glazik, *op. cit.*, pp. 194-196; Bolshakoff, *op. cit.*, pp. 79-80.

[32] According to the *Kirisuto Kyō Nenkan 1969*, the membership is 8,274, the number of clergy is thirty-three and of congregations ninety-eight.

there are twelve catechists and seven deacons. Young men continue to be attracted to the ministry of the Orthodox Church and trained in its seminary. The official name of the church in Japanese is *Nihon Harisuto Seikyōkai Kyōdan*.

The church has recently been afflicted by another small defection, which, however, appears larger than in fact it is. A Japanese priest by the name of Sayama Dairoku left the larger body to form his own church with Russian support. He was then consecrated as Bishop Nicolai in the Orthodox cathedral in Leningrad, Russia, on December 9, 1967. Probably without full knowledge of the situation, Bishop John Willebrands, secretary of the Roman Catholic Secretariate for the Union of Christians, preached the consecration sermon. Sayama, however, who was able to take with him only two priests, is said to preside over but three congregations, and his movement is of little consequence in Japan.[33] This small group, however, claims continuity with the tradition of loyalty to the Moscow patriarchate and is recognized by the patriarchate as the true Japan Orthodox Church.[34] Bishop Vladimir as presiding bishop is known to be most charitable in the matter and has made several moves toward reconciliation. He and his clergy acknowledge the legitimacy of Sayama's episcopal ordination, and there is hope that Bishop Sayama may return to the fold of the Orthodox Church of Japan.

---

[33] The *Kirisuto Kyō Nenkan 1969* cites this church as having 825 members, three congregations, and nine clergy.

[34] See the *Kirisuto Kyō Nenkan 1969*, pp. 229-230, for a brief statement by Bishop Sayama.

VII

EPILOGUE

EPILOGUE

THE HISTORY OF CHRISTIANITY IN JAPAN IS A LONG
story, now extending over four hundred years. It manifests a
richness of color, dramatic events, great tragedy, gifted and
creative personalities, heights of devotion and courage not to be
surpassed by any nation in the world over a comparable
period. Perhaps no Christian community has suffered physically
and mentally for the sake of the faith to a greater extent than
that of Japan. Indeed, one may even ask before God whether
the missionary imperative of the gospel can be ethically justified in the case of Japan when he sees the consequences wrought
by obedience to it there.

The whole history of modern Japan, however, is inextricably
linked with the presence of the Christian witness and fellowship in its midst: it is impossible to conceive of this history
without Christianity. No one of course can know the full extent
of the effects of the Christian presence upon Japanese history,
in particular upon the individual lives of the people. But this
presence has certainly contributed powerfully to the creative
energy and achievements of the nation at least over the past
century and more. In the course of this work I referred often to
particular contributions of individual Christians and organizations to the whole or large segments of Japanese society.
Viewed cumulatively, these contributions assume massive pro-
portions.[1] But clearer in outline, distinctive in quality of life

---

[1] The problem of the indigenization of the Christian faith and church in

363

and character, is the Japanese Christian community itself. The
fruit of the mission seems to justify it, in so far as the mind of
man can make value judgments of this kind. Those of Christian
faith cannot but praise God that he has wrought a work of such
notable quality in the persons of the Christians of Japan.

Concerning what I have called the persistent issue in the
history of Christianity in Japan, we may say that after the end
of World War II the Japanese nation, for the first time in its
history, formally rejected the concept of religious absolutization
of the structures of state and society. One public act by the
national Diet, which acted as representative of the people, gave
formal expression to this change in November, 1945. This was
the creation of the new constitution whereby the ultimate
authority of government derives from the will of the people.
Another was the denial by the emperor on January 1, 1946, of
any divine status appertaining to his person or office. The
twentieth article in the constitution further specifies religious
freedom to an extent never known before in Japanese history.
These acts mean that the Christian church, with all other religious bodies, now has full legal freedom to hold, practice and
propagate its faith apart from any threat of conflict with a
religiously absolutized state or society.

The heritage of Japan's past, of course, can hardly be
expected to be changed entirely by legal fiat in this or any
other aspect; the old customs and ways of thinking are but in
the process of change. Yet the nation has apparently committed
itself irrevocably to the principle of true religious freedom and
a secular state, and the rate of inward change seems rapid. The
Christian church in Japan now has full freedom in life and
witness. What it does from this point forward will depend
largely upon its own resources of vision and spiritual power
under God. There is good reason to believe that the Christian
faith and church are now accepted by the nation as an authentic part of Japanese life. Christianity probably no longer appears as something spiritually alien, at least not to most people

Japanese society needs to be considered in the light of these contributions.
For one of the many discussions of this problem, see *Gendai Nihon to Kirisuto Kyō*, pp. 276-323.

in the cities. The Christian community, therefore, no longer need face the old sociological disfavor of the past.

It would be presumptuous of me to attempt at this point a prognostication of the future of the Christian church in Japan. Theologically and missiologically there no longer appears to be any such need. The best theological thought of our time has moved beyond the notion that the "success" of Christian evangelism in a land is to be measured in terms of the size and number of its ecclesiastical institutions or the extent of their cultural dominance over society. As one, perhaps the truest, expression of the people of God in Japan, the Christian community is both sufficiently large and spiritually well endowed to fulfill its primary task under God to witness and serve in preparation for the coming kingdom of its Lord. Because, however, both Western churches and non-Christian religions very largely evaluated "success" in terms of sociological power and cultural dominance, the Christians' experience of minority status and social disabilities has left wounds and created habits of thought and action that do not always accept the free opportunities of the present. Japanese Christians face the future with a heritage that is at once glorious and, at some points, burdensome. But they have hope as well as faith, being both disciplined and chastened by their suffering. My prayer is that the new expressions of witness, service and unity which we may properly expect from this community will be informed by such levels of love for God and man that at the time of our summoning all men will rise up and call them blessed.

BIBLIOGRAPHY*

Abe Mitsuko. *Yamamuro Gumpei*. Tokyo: Kaiseisha, 1954.

Addison, James Thayer. *The Medieval Missionary*. New York: International Missionary Council, 1936.

Aikawa Takaaki. *Unwilling Patriot*. Tokyo: The Jordan Press, 1960.

Akamatsu Toshihide. *Shinran*. Tokyo: Yoshikawa Hirobumi Kan, 1965.

Akimoto Mitarō. *Yamamuro Gumpei no Shōgai*. Tokyo: Kyūseigun Shuppan Kyōkyūbu, 1954.

Andō Hajime. *Fukaki Fuchi Yori*. Nagasaki: Kirisutosha Heiwa no Kai, 1959.

Augustine. *De Civitate Dei*.

Ariyoshi Katsuhisa. *Dr. Masahisa Uemura, A Christian Leader*. Tokyo: Kyō Bun Kwan, 1941.

Axling, William. *Japan at the Midcentury, Leaves from Life*. Tokyo: Protestant Publishing Co., 1955.

——————. *Kagawa*. New York: Harper and Brothers, 1946.

Baker, Richard Terrill. *Darkness of the Sun*. New York: Abingdon-Cokesbury, 1947.

Bellah, Robert N. *Tokugawa Religion*. New York: The Free Press, 1957.

Best, Ernest E. *Christian Faith and Cultural Crisis: The Japan Case*. Leiden: E. J. Brill, 1966.

Bogolepov, Alexander A. *Toward an American Orthodox Church*. New York: Morehouse-Barlow Co., 1963.

Bolshakoff, Serge. *The Foreign Missions of the Russian Orthodox Church*. London: SPCK, 1943.

Borton, Hugh. *Japan's Modern Century*. New York: Ronald Press, 1955.

Boxer, C. R. *The Christian Century in Japan*. Berkeley: University of California, 1951.

Bray, William D., "The Hidden Christians of Ikutsuki Island," *The Japan Christian Quarterly*, XXVI/2 (April, 1960), 76-84.

Broderick, James, S.J. *Saint Francis Xavier*. London: Burns and Oates, 1958.

---

* Japanese names are listed with the surname first and the personal name following.

Candau, Sauveur, "Apostolate Among the Japanese Intellectuals," *The Japan Missionary Bulletin*, XVIII/4-5 (May-June, 1964), 245-252, 341-344.

Cary, Frank. *A History of Christianity in Japan, 1859-1908*. Tokyo: Kyō Bun Kwan, 1960.

Cary, Otis. In *Proceedings of the General Conference of Protestant Missionaries* (1900). Tokyo: Methodist Publishing House, 1901.

_____. *A History of Christianity in Japan*. New York: Fleming H. Revell, 1909.

Chamberlain, Mrs. W. J. *Fifty Years in Foreign Fields*. New York: Women's Board of Foreign Missions, Reformed Church in America, 1925.

Cho Kiyo Takeda, "An Essay on Kagawa Toyohiko," *Asian Cultural Studies*, III/A (September, 1960), 47-68. Mrs. Cho writes in Japanese under the name of Takeda Kiyoko.

Cieslik, Hubert, S.J. "Kirishitan to Sōrei," *Kirishitan Kenkyū*, vol. 5. Tokyo: Yoshikawa Hirobumi Kan, 1959.

_____. "Nihon ni okeru Saisho no Shingakkō," *Kirishitan Kenkyū*, vol. 10. Tokyo: Yoshikawa Hirobumi Kan, 1965.

Clapp, Frances Benton. *Mary Florence Denton and the Dōshisha*. Kyōto: Dōshisha University Press, 1955.

Cogswell, James A. *Until the Day Dawn*. Nashville, Tennessee: Board of World Missions, Presbyterian Church, U.S., 1957.

Cosenza, Mario Emilio. *The Complete Journal of Townsend Harris*. Tokyo: Charles E. Tuttle, 1959.

Creemers, Anthony, "Christianity and the Emperor System in Japan," *The Japan Missionary Bulletin*, XIX/8, 9 (September, October, 1965), 505-508, 560-565.

Dohi Akio, "Nihon ni okeru Fukuin no Dochaku," *Fukuin to Sekai*, XXI/10 (October, 1966), 10-13.

Doi Tadao. *Kirishitan Bunkenkō*. Tokyo: Sanseidō, 1963.

Drummond, Richard H., "Catharsis in the Japanese Church," *The Christian Century*, LXXIX/21 (May 23, 1962), 651-654.

_____, "Japan's 'New Religions' and the Christian Community," *The Christian Century*, LXXXI/50 (December 9, 1964), 1521-1523.

_____, "Kagawa: Christian Evangelist," *The Christian Century*, LXXVII/28 (July 13, 1960), 823-825.

_____, "A Missionary 'Exodus' from Japan?" *The Christian Century*, LXXXII/21 (May 26, 1965), 672-674.

Ebisawa Arimichi. *Kindai Nihon Bunka no Tanjō*. Tokyo: Nihon YMCA Dōmei, 1956.

_____. *Kirishitanshi no Kenkyū*. Tokyo: Unebi Shoten, 1942.

_____. *Namban Gakuto no Kenkyū*. Tokyo: Sōbunsha, 1958.

_____. *Takayama Ukon*. Tokyo: Yoshikawa Hirobumi Kan, 1963.

_____. "Zezusukai Funai Byōin no Setsuritsu oyobi sono Tōji," in *Kirishitan Kenkyū*, vol. 1. Tokyo: Tokyo Dō, 1943.

Foster, John. *After the Apostles*. London: SCM Press, 1951.

Fukuda Kiyoto. *Uchimura Kanzō*. Tokyo: Kaiseisha, 1954.

Fukuyama Takeshi. *Nihon Fukuin Rūteru Kyōkaishi*. Tokyo: Rūteru Sha, 1954.

Furuno Kiyoto. *Kakure Kirishitan*. Tokyo: Shibundō, 1959.

Gay, Jesús López. *El Catecumenado en la Mision del Japan del S. XVI*. Roma: Libreria dell' Universita Gregoriana, 1966.

_____, "Pre-evangelization in the Primitive Mission of Japan," *The Japan Missionary Bulletin*, XVIII/9 (November, 1964), 587.

Gendai Nihon to Kirisuto Kyō. Tokyo: Kirisuto Kyō Gakuto Kyōdai Dan, 1961.

Germany, Charles H. *Protestant Theologies in Modern Japan*. Tokyo: International Institute for the Study of Religions Press, 1965.

Germany, Charles H., ed. *The Response of the Church in Changing Japan*. New York: Friendship Press, 1967.

Glazik, Josef. *Die Russisch-Orthodoxe Heidenmission seit Peter dem Grossen*. Münster-Westfalen: Aschendorffsche Verlagsbuchhandlung, 1954.

Goodman, Grant Kohn. *The Dutch Impact on Japan*. Leiden: E. J. Brill, 1967.

Goodrich, L. Carrington, ed. *Japan in the Chinese Dynastic Histories*. Translated by Tsunoda Ryūsaku. South Pasadena: P. D. and Ione Perkins, 1951.

Grew, Joseph C. *Turbulent Era*, vol. 2. Boston: Houghton Mifflin Co., 1952.

Griffis, William Elliot. *Hepburn of Japan*. Philadelphia: Westminster Press, 1913.

_____. *A Maker of the New Orient*. New York: Fleming H. Revell, 1902.

_____. *Verbeck of Japan*. Chicago: Fleming H. Revell, 1900.

Haas, Hans. *Geschichte des Christentums in Japan*, vol. 1. Tokyo: Rikkyō Gakuin Press, 1902.

Hara Ryōzō and Paul Pfister. "Ecumenism and the Future of Christianity in Japan," in *The Japan Christian Yearbook 1968*. Tokyo: Kyō Bun Kwan, 1967.

Hardy, Arthur Sherburne. *Life and Letters of Joseph Hardy Neesima*. Boston: Houghton, Mifflin and Co., 1898.

Hellweg, H., "Catholic Education in Japan," *The Japan Missionary Bulletin*, XX/6, 8 (June, August, 1966), 331-340, 477-482.

Hillman, Eugene. *The Church as Mission*. New York: Herder and Herder, 1965.

Hine, Leland D., "William Axling and the War Years," *The Japan Christian Quarterly*, XXXIII/4 (Fall 1967), 267.

Hitotsuyanagi Merrell Vories. *A Mustard Seed in Japan*. Oakland, Cal.: Color Art Press, 1948.

Hiyane Antei. *Nihon Kirisuto Kyōshi*. Tokyo: Kyōbunkan, 1949.

Hughes, E. R. *Chinese Philosophy in Classical Times*. London: J. M. Dent, 1954.

Iglehart, Charles W. *A Century of Protestant Christianity in Japan*. Tokyo: Charles E. Tuttle, 1959.

Imbrie, William. "Nihon Kirisuto Kyokwai," in *Proceedings of the General Conference of Protestant Missionaries in Japan (1900)*. Tokyo: Methodist Publishing House, 1901.

Ishihara Ken. *Nihon Kirisuto Kyōshi Ron*. Tokyo: Shinkyō Shuppansha, 1967.

Ishihara Ken, ed. *Nihon no Shingaku*. Tokyo: Kyōbunkan, 1962, 1963.

Itō Shōjirō, "NCC no Senkyō Kyōryokukaigi ni Manekarete," *The Japan Missionary Bulletin*, XXI/5 (June, 1967), 268-272.

Jennes, Joseph. *A History of the Catholic Church in Japan*. Tokyo: The Committee of the Apostolate, 1959.

Jennings, Raymond P. *Jesus, Japan and Kanzo Uchimura*. Tokyo: Kyō Bun Kwan, 1958.

Kagawa Toyohiko. *Christ and Japan*. London: SCM Press, 1935.

Kami Yoshiyasu. *Purotesutanto Hyakunenshi Kenkyū*. Tokyo: Nihon Kirisuto Kyōdan Shuppambu, 1961.

Kanamori Tokujirō. "Common Sense and the Constitution," in *Religion and State in Japan*. Tokyo: International Institute for the Study of Religions, Inc., 1959.

Kaneko Hisakazu. *Manjiro, the Man Who Discovered America*. Tokyo: Hokuseidō Press, 1954.

Karnes, Eddie, ed. *Adevangelism*. Kōbe: World Harvesters, 1960.

Katakozawa Chiyomatsu. *Nihon Purotesutanto Hyakunen no Ayumi*. Tokyo: Nihon YMCA Dōmei, 1957.

Kataoka Yakichi. *Kakure Kirishitan*. Tokyo: Nihon Hōsō Shuppan Kyōkai, 1967.

_____. *Nagasaki no Junkyōsha*. Tokyo: Kadokawa Shoten, 1964.

Kega Kenzō. *Honda Yōichi*. Tokyo: Aoyama Gakuin, 1968.

Kindai Nihon to Kirisuto Kyō, Meiji Hen. Tokyo: Kirisuto Kyō Gakuto Kyōdai Dan, 1965.

Kindai Nihon to Kirisuto Kyō, Taishō-Shōwa Hen. Tokyo: Kirisuto Kyō Gakuto Kyōdai Dan, 1966.

Kirisuto Kyō Nenkan 1969. Tokyo: Kirisuto Shimbunsha, 1968.

Kishi Hideji, "Uchū Ishiki no Shūkyōsei," *Koe*, MC (January, 1970), 1-8.

Kitagawa, Joseph M., "The Prehistoric Background of Japanese Religion," *History of Religions*, II/2 (Winter, 1963), 292-328.

_____. *Religion in Japanese History*. New York: Columbia University Press, 1966.

Kitamori Kazō. *Kami to Ningen*. Tokyo: Gendai Bungeisha, 1956.

_____. *Theology of the Pain of God*. Richmond, Virginia: John Knox Press, 1965.

Kitasawa Sukeo. *The Life of Dr. Nitobe.* Tokyo: Hokuseidō Press, 1953.

Kozaki Hiromichi. *Reminiscences of Seventy Years.* Tokyo: Christian Literature Society of Japan, 1933.

Kumano Yoshitaka, "Ebina Danjō no Shisō to Shingaku," *Fukuin to Sekai,* XXII/2-4 (February, March, April, 1967).

_____, "Kozaki Hiromichi no Seikyōron Shingaku," *Fukuin to Sekai,* XXI-XXII/11, 12, 1 (November, December 1966, January 1967).

_____, "Kyōkairon no Kisozuke," *Fukuin to Sekai,* XIX/3 (March, 1964).

_____, "Shingaku wo Oshieru Hito toshite no Uemura Masahisa," *Fukuin to Sekai,* XX/10 (October, 1965).

_____, "Shinkō, Shisō, Hyōron," *Fukuin to Sekai,* XXI/8-10 (August, September, October, 1966).

_____, "Shiteki Kirisuto Kyō," *Fukuin to Sekai,* XX/7-9 (July, August, September, 1965).

_____, "Shokuzairon no Teii," *Fukuin to Sekai,* XIX/9-11 (September, October, November, 1964).

_____, "Uemura Masahisa ni okeru Tatakai no Shingaku," *Fukuin to Sekai,* XIX/1-3 (January, February, March, 1966).

Kuroda Yasunobu. *Okuno Masutsuna Sensei Ryaku Den oyobi Kashū.* Nagoya: n.p., 1936.

Kuwada Hidenobu. *Kirisuto Kyō Shingaku Gairon.* Tokyo: Shinkyō Shuppansha, 1961.

_____. *Zen to Kirisuto Kyō.* Tokyo: Chōbunsha, 1967.

Laures, Johannes. *The Catholic Church in Japan.* Tokyo: Charles E. Tuttle, 1954.

_____. *Die Anfänge der Mission von Miyako.* Münster-Westfalen: Aschendorffsche Verlagsbuchhandlung, 1951.

Luhmer, Nicholas, "Catholic Schools in Japan 1964/1965," *The Japan Missionary Bulletin,* XIX/4 (May, 1965), 247-254.

MacDonald, Alice E., "A Kirishitan Prayer Book-Catechism," *The Japan Christian Quarterly,* XXVIII/1 (January, 1962), 55-60.

Martin, J. M., "An Itinerant Missionary in Japan," *The Japan Missionary Bulletin,* VI/5 (September-October, 1953), 146-149.

Matsuda Kiichi. *Nihon Kōshōshi.* Tokyo: Kyōbunkan, 1963.

Matsudaira Kitarō. *Nihon Seikōkai Hyakunenshi.* Tokyo: Nihon Seikōkai Kyōmuin Bunshokyoku, 1959.

McFarland, H. Neill. *The Rush Hour of the Gods.* New York: Macmillan, 1967.

Michalson, Carl. *Japanese Contributions to Christian Theology.* Philadelphia: The Westminster Press, 1960.

Miki Tomokaze. *Nihon Katorikku Kyōshi.* Tokyo: n.p., 1929.

Minutes of the General Assembly of the Presbyterian Church in the United States of America, XVI-XIX. Philadelphia: Presbyterian Board of Publication, 1862-1869.

Miyakoda Tsunetarō. *Nihon Kirisuto Kyō Gōdōshikō*. Tokyo: Kyō-bunkan, 1967.
Miyauchi, T. S. and B. Schneider. "Towards a Common Bible," in *The Japan Christian Yearbook 1968*. Tokyo: Kyō Bun Kwan, 1967.
Murakami Nanjirō. "Dominika no Sekkyō ni tsuite," in *Kirishitan Kenkyū*, vol. 3. Tokyo: Tōyōdō, 1944.
Murdoch, James. *A History of Japan*, vol. 3, part 1. Revised by Joseph H. Longford. New York: Frederick Ungar Publishing Co., 1964.

Nakamura Hajime. *The Ways of Thinking of Eastern Peoples*. Tokyo: Japanese National Commission for UNESCO, 1960.
Natori Junichi. *Historical Studies of Christianity in Japan*. Tokyo: Hoku-seidō Press, 1957.
Nemeshegyi, Peter, "Fukuin ni Fusawashii Hanashiai," *Katorikku Shingaku*, II/1 (July, 1963), 208-214.
Nihon Baputesuto Remmeishi (1889-1959). Tokyo: Yorudan Sha, 1959.
Nihon Kirisuto Kyōdanshi. Tokyo: Nihon Kirisuto Kyōdan Shuppambu, 1967.
Nihon Kirisuto Kyōkaishi. Tokyo: Nihon Kirisuto Kyōkai Jimusho, 1929.
Nihon Kumiai Kirisuto Kyōkaishi, Kirisuto ni aru Jiyū wo Motomete. Tokyo: Sōbunsha, 1958.
Nihon ni okeru Kirisuto Kyō to Sho Shūkyō to no Sesshoku no Mondai. Tokyo: Nihon Kirisuto Kyōdan Senkyō Kenkyūjo, 1960.
Nihon no Hajimari (Nihon no Rekishi, vol. 1). Tokyo: Yomiuri Shimbun-sha, 1961.
Norman, W. H. H. *An Interim Report on Non-Church Christianity*. Nishino-miya: Kansei Gakuin Daigaku, 1958.
⸻, "Kanzō Uchimura," *Contemporary Religions in Japan*, IV/3, 4; V/1 (September, December 1963, March 1964).

Obara Satoru. *Kirishitan Jidai no Kagaku Shisō*. In *Kirishitan Kenkyū*, vol. 10. Tokyo: Yoshikawa Hirobumi Kan, 1965.
Offner, Clark B. and Henry van Straelen. *Modern Japanese Religions*. Tokyo: Rupert Enderle, 1963.
Okada Akio. *Kirishitan Bateren*. Tokyo: Shibundō, 1955.
Okamoto Yoshitomo. "Nihon Yasokai to Firippin no Shoshūdōkai to no Ronsō," in *Kirishitan Kenkyū*, vol. 3. Tokyo: Tōyōdō, 1948.
⸻. *Namban Bijutsu*. Tokyo: Heibonsha, 1965.
Oshio Tsutomu. *Takakura Tokutarō Den*. Tokyo: Shinkyō Shuppansha, 1954.

Paske-Smith, M. *Japanese Traditions of Christianity*. Kōbe, Japan: J. L. Thompson, 1935.
Perez, Francisco. "Sei Furanshisuko Sabieru no Shoryokō to sono Rekishi-teki Shimei," in *Katorikku Shingaku*, I/1. Tokyo: Chūō Shuppansha, 1962.

Pfister, Paul, "The Catholic Church in Japan," *The Japan Missionary Bulletin*, XIX/3 (April, 1965), 184.

—————, "Towards the Beatification of Takayama Ukon," *The Japan Missionary Bulletin*, XVIII/7 (August-September, 1964), 447-450.

Reischauer, Edwin O. *Japan, Past and Present*. Tokyo: Charles E. Tuttle Company, 1962.

Rugoff, Milton, ed. *The Travels of Marco Polo*. New York: The New American Library, 1961.

Saba Wataru. *Uemura Masahisa to Sono Jidai*, vol. 1-7. Tokyo: Kyōbunkan, 1937-1941.

Saeki Yōichiro. "The Christian Movement in Japan Today," in *The Response of the Church in Changing Japan*. Charles H. Germany, ed. New York: Friendship Press, 1967.

Sakurai Tadashi. *Nihon Kirisuto Kyōshi*. Tokyo: Ryushokaku, 1933.

Sansom, G. B. *Japan, A Short Cultural History*. New York: Appleton-Century, 1943.

—————. *The Western World and Japan*. New York: Alfred A. Knopf, 1950.

Satō Toshio. *Nihon no Kirisutokyō to Shingaku*. Tokyo: Nihon Kirisuto Kyōdan Shuppankyoku, 1968.

Sawada Akio, "Katorikku Rutā Kan no Henkan ni tsuite," *Katorikku Shingaku*, VI/2 (November, 1967), 40-283.

Schneider, Bernadine, "The Hachiōji Bible Translators' Seminar," *The Japan Missionary Bulletin*, XX/11 (November, 1966), 709-711.

Schroeder, Paul W. *The Axis Alliance and Japanese-American Relations, 1941*. Ithaca, New York: Cornell University Press, 1958.

Schurhammer, Georg, S.J., and Joseph Wicki, S.J. *Epistolae S. Francisci Xaverii*, vol. 1 & 2. Rome: Monumenta Historica Societatis Iesu, 1945.

Schütte, Josef Franz. *Alexandro Valignanos Ringen um die Missionsmethode in Japan*. Rome: Borgo S. Spirito 5, 1944.

—————. "Genwa Sannen (1617 nen) ni okeru Nihon Kirishitan no Shu na Shūdan to sono Minkan Shidōsha," in *Kirishitan Kenkyū*, vol. 4. Tokyo: Tōyōsha, 1957.

Schwade, Arcadio. "Funai no Korejio ni tsuite," in *Kirishitan Kenkyū*, vol. 10. Tokyo: Yoshikawa Hirobumi Kan, 1965.

Senjika Teikō no Kenkyū. Tokyo: Misuzu Shobō, 1968.

Shaw, A. C. In *Proceedings of the General Conference of Protestant Missionaries in Japan (1900)*. Tokyo: Methodist Publishing House, 1901.

Shimamura Kikaku. "Uemura Masahisa Hyōden," in Uemura Masahisa, *Shūkyō no Ishō*. Tokyo: Kyōbunkan, 1960.

Smirnoff, Eugene. *Russian Orthodox Missions*. London: Rivingtons, 1903.

Spae, Joseph J. *Catholicism in Japan*. Tokyo: ISR Press, 1964.

—————, "The Japanese Intellectuals," *The Japan Missionary Bulletin*, XIX/3 (April, 1965), 186.

Spencer, D. S. In *Proceedings of the General Conference of Protestant Missionaries in Japan (1900)*. Tokyo: Methodist Publishing House, 1901.

Sugimoto Etsu Inagaki. *The Daughter of a Samurai*. New York: Doubleday, Page and Co., 1925.

Sumiya Mikio. *Kagawa Toyohiko*. Tokyo: Nihon Kirisuto Kyōdan Shuppambu, 1966.

——————. *Nihon Shakai to Kirisuto Kyō*. Tokyo: Daigaku Suppankai, 1956.

Suzuki Masahisa, "Letter of February 21, 1968," *Kyōdan* (Tokyo: The United Church of Christ in Japan), no. 23 (March 20, 1968), 1-3.

Swyngedouw, Jan, "The Catholic Church and Shrine Shintō," *The Japan Missionary Bulletin*, XXI/10-11 (November, December, 1967), 579-584, 659-663.

Takakura Tokutarō. *Fukuinteki Kirisuto Kyō*. Tokyo: Nagasaki Shoten, 1927.

Takasaki Takeshi, "The Function of Missionaries," *The Christian Century*, LXXXIII/1 (January 5, 1966), 19-22.

Takeda Kiyoko. *Dochaku to Haikyō*. Tokyo: Shinkyō Shuppansha, 1967.

Takenaka Masao. *Reconciliation and Renewal in Japan*. New York: Friendship Press, 1957.

Tejima Ikuo, "Genchi Fukuin Undō no Tokushitsu," *Inochi no Hikari*, IV/143 (July, 1962), 15.

Tenka Tōitsu (Nihon no Rekishi, vol. 7). Tokyo: Yomiuri Shimbunsha, 1961.

Thomas, Winburn T. *Protestant Beginnings in Japan*. Tokyo: Charles E. Tuttle, 1959.

Urakawa Wasaburō. *Tōhoku Kirishitanshi*. Tokyo: Nihon Gakujutsu Shinkōkai, 1957.

Van Hecken, Joseph L. *The Catholic Church in Japan since 1859*. Tokyo: Herder Agency, 1963.

Verbeck, Guido F. "History of Protestant Missions in Japan," in *Proceedings of the General Conference of Protestant Missionaries in Japan (1900)*. Tokyo: Methodist Publishing House, 1901.

Watanabe Shōkō. *Nihon no Bukkyō*. Tokyo: Iwanami Shoten, 1958.

Whitehead, Alfred North. *Science and the Modern World*. New York: The New American Library, 1958.

Wiedenmann, Ludwig. *Mission und Eschatologie*. Paderborn: Verlag Bonifacius-Druckerei, 1965.

Woodard, William P. *The Religious Juridical Persons Law*. Tokyo: The Foreign Affairs Association of Japan, 1960.

Yamaguchi Aijirō, "Shinto Hakken no Hyakushūnen," *The Japanese Missionary Bulletin*, XVIII/4 (May, 1964), 275-278.

Yamamoto Taijirō, *Uchimura Kanzō*. Tokyo: Shinkyō Shuppansha, 1949.
_____. *Uchimura Kanzō, Shinkō, Shōgai, Yūjō*. Tokyo: Tōkai Daigaku Shuppankai, 1966.
Yamamuro Gumpei. *Heimin no Fukuin*. Tokyo: Kyūseigun Shuppan Kyōkyūbu, 1954.
Yamamuro Tamiko, "Gumpei Yamamuro: an Officer of the Salvation Army," *The Japan Christian Quarterly*, XXIX/4 (October, 1962), 223-243.
Yanagita Tomonobu. *A Short History of Christianity in Japan*. Sendai: Seisho Tosho Kankōkai, 1957.
Yokoyama Shunichi. *Kagawa Toyohiko*. Tokyo: Kirisuto Shimbunsha, 1952.
Yoshida Shōgorō. *Kirishitan Daimyō*. Tokyo: Shibundō, 1954.

INDEX OF PLACES

INDEX OF PERSONS AND AUTHORS

INDEX OF SUBJECTS